D1623094

Leadership in American Politics

Leadership in American Politics

Edited by
Jeffery A. Jenkins
and
Craig Volden

 University Press of Kansas

Published by the University Press of Kansas (Lawrence, Kansas 66045), which was organized by the Kansas Board of Regents and is operated and funded by Emporia State University, Fort Hays State University, Kansas State University, Pittsburg State University, the University of Kansas, and Wichita State University

Library of Congress Cataloging-in-Publication Data

Names: Jenkins, Jeffery A., editor. | Volden, Craig, editor.
Title: Leadership in American politics / edited by Jeffery A. Jenkins and Craig Volden.
Description: Lawrence, Kansas : University Press of Kansas, [2017] | Includes bibliographical references and index.
Identifiers: LCCN 2017038276
ISBN 9780700625147 (cloth : alk. paper)
ISBN 9780700625154 (ebook)
Subjects: LCSH: Public administration—United States. | Political leadership—United States. | United States—Politics and government.
Classification: LCC JK421 .L38 2017 | DDC 352.23/60973—dc23
LC record available at https://lccn.loc.gov/2017038276.

British Library Cataloguing-in-Publication Data is available.

Printed in the United States of America

10 9 8 7 6 5 4 3 2 1

Contents

INTRODUCTION

Studying Leadership in American Politics

Jeffery A. Jenkins and Craig Volden

There is a leadership gap in American politics between the leadership needed to address the country's most pressing problems and that provided by the nation's elected and appointed leaders. If we turn to political scientists to shed light on such leadership issues, we find their work often lacking. As important as leadership is in explaining political choices and policy outcomes, studies of leadership are limited in many subfields of political science research and are missing altogether in others. Yet the tools and talents of political scientists have much to offer in shedding new light on leadership within and across American political institutions. We therefore urge a rebirth in the study of leadership within political science, and we put forth this volume in an attempt to draw renewed attention to the causes and consequences of the actions that public leaders take.

To help advance this broad research agenda, we assembled top scholars across many of the major subfields of American politics in a conference at the University of Virginia, jointly sponsored by the Miller Center of Public Affairs and the Batten School of Leadership and Public Policy. We asked these scholars to discuss the importance of leadership within their areas of expertise and to help set an agenda for future research. Their responses comprise the chapters of this volume, and they chart a fascinating course forward. In this introductory chapter, we briefly summarize the main arguments and insights from each chapter, then distill the commonalities down to a set of five lessons for how to study leadership in American politics.

Part One, Leadership from the Top, features five chapters exploring leadership across the three branches of the US federal government—legislative, executive, and judicial.

The first two chapters explore leadership in Congress, focusing separately on the House and the Senate. In "House Leadership and the Speakership of John Boehner," the late Barbara Sinclair (UCLA) and Gregory Koger (University of Miami) argue that Great Man narratives miss the broader context in which congressional leaders operate. To capture that context, scholars need a solid theoretical grounding. Sinclair and Koger offer such in discussing how to apply principal–agent models to congressional leadership. Such an approach highlights collective action problems and the difficulties of reaching agreement when party leaders and party members lack trust and a common vision. Contrasting Newt Gingrich and John Boehner, Sinclair and Koger review budget battles in different eras to make their case for the importance of context, common understandings, and significant resources at the disposal of party leaders.

On the other side of the Capitol, Steven S. Smith (Washington University in St. Louis) examines "Leaders and Partisanship in the Modern Senate." He argues that there is no single model of effective leadership, but that it is important for a leader's skills to fit the circumstances he or she faces. For example, Harry Reid and Mitch McConnell, the most recent Democratic and Republican majority leaders, do not exhibit many traditional leadership qualities, often lacking eloquence as the public persona of the party or being too quick-tempered as a negotiator. Yet in the context of a highly competitive and polarized era of congressional policy making, and in the rather open lawmaking institution of the Senate, they found ways to rely on committee leaders, adjust procedural strategies, and identify when and where compromises were possible. In short, Smith underscores that in the modern era, Senate leaders like Reid and McConnell must be flexible and innovative in order to be successful.

The next two chapters examine presidential leadership. In "A President's Decisions and the Presidential Difference," Matthew N. Beckmann (University of California, Irvine) makes an argument for why the study of leadership in American politics has receded in recent years, even by scholars focused on the presidency. Specifically, as political science research has become more quantitative, scholars have worked to detect leadership influence with a variety of measurable but ultimately overly blunt instruments. While such variables seem plausible on their face, they fail to capture the nuance and context-specific nature of leadership decisions. The exercise on the whole thus reveals little difference in outcomes across divergent leaders in American politics, including little influence of presidents over domestic and foreign policy. To escape this morass, Beckmann argues that scholars need greater specificity in developing context-guided theories and well-tailored measures.

Philip B. K. Potter (University of Virginia) likewise notes the constraints and opportunities available to leaders, specifically in the foreign policy realm. In "Presidential Leadership in American Foreign Policy," Potter argues that institution-based incentives and constraints better explain presidential policy choices than do presidential personalities. Such incentives can be broadly captured in terms of trade-offs. When foreign policy crises arise, the president has access to better information than do other actors in the American government. Presidential choices at that point can influence whether the policy becomes highly salient (such as with a military intervention) or not (as with diplomatic actions). On highly salient issues, the president becomes constrained by congressional and public reactions arising from increased information and scrutiny. On less salient issues, the lack of widespread concern with the issue means the president gains little credit and support. Taken together, these circumstances point to a president in American foreign policy who rarely exerts what might theoretically be thought of as effective leadership. Potter illustrates these considerations by comparing President Obama's intense interest in health care reform to his limited efforts on the Middle East peace process.

In contrast to studies of Congress and the president, Charles M. Cameron (Princeton University) and Mehdi Shadmehr (University of Calgary) tackle the question of how to conceive of leadership within an institution that lacks classical instruments of power such as the sword or the purse. In "Great Judges: Judicial Leadership in Theory and Practice," Cameron and Shadmehr argue that leaders in courts—or "great judges"—exercise power not through formal mechanisms but rather by persuasion. That is, great judges innovate, and other judges follow voluntarily. Cameron and Shadmehr offer a framework for understanding such leadership, based on a formal model grounded in game theory, in which a judicial leader uses an information-provision role to help followers coordinate on mutually beneficial outcomes. They then explore the plausibility of the theory by reviewing the actions of three commonly acknowledged great judges—Benjamin Cardozo, Roger Traynor, and Henry Friendly—and find general support for the theory's assumptions in the relevant case material. They conclude by noting the many avenues for further study, including analyzing why certain bids for leadership fail (or why certain judges are not perceived to be great) and more thoroughly examining the motivation of judicial followers.

Part Two, Leadership across Institutions, contains four chapters that show the challenges that leaders face in attempting to bridge institutional actors, including those located beyond the federal level in the American political system, as well as those outside of formal institutions of governance.

David Karol (University of Maryland) begins these examinations with his study "Parties and Leadership in American Politics." Parties often feature diverse coalitions of interests; discerning who leads at what point in time can be difficult. This is especially the case when those holding formal roles within the party actually lack true political power. Karol argues that politicians use a wide range of skills and techniques to manage partisan groups and individuals with intense demands. Context matters immensely, helping explain the different styles of Democrats and Republicans. Karol illustrates successes, failures, and complexities of party leadership with wide-ranging examples across levels of government, from the Daley machine in Chicago to gubernatorial nominating conventions in Virginia to party switching in the US Senate.

In "Leadership and Interest Groups," Timothy M. LaPira (James Madison University) explores leadership from outside of the institutions of government. He notes how scholars of interest groups have done an excellent job in studying both interests and groups while simultaneously neglecting the importance of the leaders of such groups. LaPira argues that effective interest group leaders must cultivate institutional access and issue expertise, making them valuable to policy makers. He then identifies and discusses four distinct theories of leadership along with four perspectives on interest groups, and articulates a framework for connecting them. At the heart of this framework is a way by which leadership scholars might envision interest groups as leaders in their theories.

John W. Patty (University of Chicago) then follows with his study "Leadership and the Bureaucracy." As in other areas of American politics, Patty notes how leaders within bureaucracies are understudied relative to their importance. Bureaucracies are often seen as broad organizations that react to political principals rather than as proactive participants in policy making headed by active and dynamic leaders. To change the direction of this scholarship, Patty argues that a three-part focus—on the information obtained by bureaucratic leaders, the decisions they make, and the implementation and management that follows on those decisions—will collectively help reorient the field of study toward the important actions available to leaders.

Finally, in "Leadership in the States," James Coleman Battista (University at Buffalo, SUNY) makes a strong case for studying leadership at the subnational level. There is significant variance across state legislatures in their constitutional and institutional structures as well as their policy problems and partisan considerations. This diversity of context helps researchers identify which factors blend well with different leadership abilities and styles to result in effective lawmaking. Defining leadership as the exploitation of institutional authority in pursuit of desired objectives, Battista highlights some of the lessons derived from previous scholarship on state legislative leaders. He ultimately concludes that for researchers to take the variance in institutional settings and the abundance of new data to their full potential, scholars need to develop some consistency in research designs, building on one another's strengths. Otherwise, the field will be littered with numerous inapplicable lessons that do not hold across cases.

The volume concludes with Part Three, Assessing Leadership in American Politics, which contains three chapters that are integrative, conceptual, and evaluative in nature. In "Leadership: A Definition," William G. Howell (University of Chicago) and Stephane Wolton (London School of Economics) assess the core elements needed to define leadership in general as well as in the context of American politics. They first survey existing leadership studies and find them lacking in a variety of ways. In contrast with prior approaches focused on the functions of leaders, the consequences of their actions, and the essence of their leadership styles,

Howell and Wolton develop a set of empirical and conceptual criteria that any working definition of leadership would need to meet. On the basis of these criteria, they offer the following provisional definition: "A leader publicly defines, extols, and eventually personifies high objectives, thereby orienting and coordinating the efforts of followers who seek to advance such objectives." The authors illustrate how this definition aptly fits a large number of leaders drawn from American and world history, as well as how this definition is open to such modifiers as "good," "authentic," or "effective." This definition therefore has the potential to guide future scholars in their endeavors.

Alan E. Wiseman (Vanderbilt University) then notes the importance of how American leaders are selected and of the contextual skills that they cultivate. Specifically, in his chapter "Filters and Pegs in Holes: How Selection Mechanisms and Institutional Positions Shape (Perceptions of) Political Leadership," Wiseman explores how the efficacy of leaders is profoundly related to the criteria that are used when they are being selected, as well as the political and institutional constraints that they face upon assuming positions of authority. He argues that normative claims about the quality of a particular leader are often influenced, at least in part, by the particular selection mechanism that was used to choose the leader, the institutional circumstances that she inherited with the leadership position, or both. As a result, Wiseman cautions that scholars of leadership need to be cognizant of these considerations when advancing arguments about ways to cultivate good leaders in a variety of political institutions and environments.

Finally, in his chapter "What Do Political Leaders Do?" Eric M. Patashnik (Brown University) reflects on the broad enterprise of studying leadership. He notes that leadership is an elusive topic to study, in part because it manifests itself in a number of ways. Thus, a deeper understanding of leadership requires an analysis of multiple questions about leadership: What does leadership mean? What do leaders in fact do? What are the constituent actions at the core of leadership? What contextual factors affect leadership? And what is the relationship between leaders and followers? While this complexity might seem daunting, Patashnik is more optimistic and sees a number of rich avenues for study. Moreover, he believes that a rigorous academic pursuit of such questions is vitally important because leadership lies at the heart of American democracy.

Taken together, this volume features top scholars of American politics wrestling with how to think about leadership within the contexts they know so well. These works are far from the last word on the subject. Rather, the authors here seek to start new debates and develop new literatures. Without a doubt, their essays examine how leaders struggle with the major policy issues of our time, including terrorism, foreign policy crises, health care, budget crises, and the fundamental values that Americans hold dear. It is in these many areas that we can truly understand the stakes involved in effective or poor leadership. It is in the coupling of theories and definitions with concrete applications that we develop new understandings of leadership in American politics.

Readers of this volume will undoubtedly come away with the view that studying leadership is a challenging endeavor. As Beckmann points out, leadership will seem irrelevant in empirical analyses that do not carefully and properly characterize the conditional roles of leaders. And, as Patty establishes, the constraints placed on leaders by other institutions and their own organizations make any assessment of the performance of specific leaders a difficult task. That said, for those scholars who wish to take up this important challenge, we believe that the authors in this volume offer at least five crucial lessons, which we summarize here.

Lesson 1: Build on a Coherent Definition and Common Terminology

Although many definitions of leaders and leadership have been offered across the years in numerous settings, it is beneficial for scholars of American politics to struggle themselves to develop a common definition and framework through which to study leadership. Howell and Wolton here offer one provisional definition that may serve the field well. It will undoubtedly be confronted and refined over time, but their approach sets one clear path forward. Battista's chapter shows some of the pitfalls from not developing common definitions, terminology, and scholarly approaches. When each researcher adopts a different research design, examines a new set of variables, and studies related phenomena from divergent angles, gaining a cumulative understanding that is more than the sum of its parts is difficult, despite the attractive opportunities for exciting research offered across state political institutions.

Lesson 2: There Is No Single Model of Effective Leadership

While commonality is attractive in the definition of terms, such commonalities should not be taken to imply that a single model of leadership exists or is effective in all circumstances. Smith, for example, raises a set of characteristics that are commonly associated with effective legislative leaders. He then goes on to establish that senators Harry Reid and Mitch McConnell have succeeded despite being limited in their skills across many of those classic dimensions. In other cases, it is hard to even identify leaders. For instance, LaPira offers examples of four lobbyists in order to illustrate some of the challenges involved in discerning who is an interest group leader. Finally, Karol demonstrates that those in seemingly key positions within political parties are often not the major brokers behind political and policy deals. For leaders who stretch across multiple institutions, identifying what actions they take to become successful may be more of an art than a science.

Lesson 3: Develop Fundamental Theories of Leadership

In part as a result of the lack of a single model of effective leadership, it is important for scholars to ground their research endeavors in sound theoretical frameworks. Just as there is no single best leadership style, so too is there no single best theoretical approach to studying leaders. Examples of useful approaches are found throughout this book. For example, Sinclair and Koger link principal–agent models to party leadership within the House of Representatives. Potter develops a theoretical framework of the demand for foreign policy action placed on presidents. Cameron and Shadmehr build a game theoretic model of the coordinating role of leaders within the US court system. Each theory helps researchers structure their thinking about the essence of leadership, and each offers predictions that can be explored and tested.

It is also likely the case that a true overarching theory of leadership is not possible, and that midlevel theories need to be developed within particular institutional contexts. Moreover, the temporal aspects of leadership might also deserve greater attention. Does our conception of what leadership entails and involves change at different points in history? A different way of thinking about this might be, how do leaders' choice sets differ based on historical context?

Lesson 4: Leaders in American Politics Operate within a Complex and Constraining Landscape rather than Mainly as Powerful Individuals

Many of the scholars in this volume express discomfort in characterizing the influence of leaders as powerful autonomous individuals, as visionaries or great men able to overcome challenges with the sheer force of will. Rather, they describe leaders in terms of their followers or in terms of the opportunities and constraints they face. Even considering the significant powers of the American president, both Beckmann and Potter note a variety of constraints on his ability to advance his policy objectives, as Presidents Eisenhower and Trump both took time to realize. Patty notes how bureaucratic leaders are hemmed in by their vast organizations and by political actors in the executive and legislative branches; he also describes challenges these leaders face in information acquisition and policy implementation. Sinclair and Koger argue that the Speaker of the House in Congress is limited by the powers that the party members are willing to give to their leaders.

Yet while agreeing that Great Man theories yield little utility, we also think that personal characteristics might be better incorporated into various theoretical accounts. One way to do this rigorously would be to establish types, such that general skills and abilities might be identified for effective (or ineffective) leaders. Thus, given contextual circumstances, certain types of leadership might be needed, and thus particular leaders might be chosen or avoided. Thinking in terms of congressional politics, when the majority party is divided, as the House Democrats were in the mid-twentieth century, an accommodating, conciliatory leader like Speaker Sam Rayburn was needed; however, when the majority party is quite homogeneous, as the House Republicans were in the 1990s, a bold, proactive leader like Speaker Newt Gingrich fit the bill.

Lesson 5: Context and Conditionality Are Crucial in Empirical Studies of Leadership

With the above four lessons in hand, the path forward in the study of leadership in American politics thus becomes one that demands careful attention to the conditions under which leaders matter and the contexts in which they exert the greatest influence. For instance, Beckmann notes how looking for broad impacts of presidents on policy outcomes may miss the nuanced but very real influence that presidents exert in specific settings. Wiseman highlights how the selection processes producing leaders and the institutional positions they inhabit together influence how they can and do lead and therefore how they should be evaluated. And Battista discusses how to use the variance found across institutions to uncover the circumstances under which leaders have the greatest effect. In combination, these five lessons offer the broad outlines of a research path forward while simultaneously setting a standard for assessing the value of new research contributions. In a variety of ways, the scholars contributing to this volume have offered examples of research that has been valuable to this overall endeavor, but they also note examples of where these research lines have not developed as fully as they might.

In sum, we believe that leadership in American politics is simultaneously woefully understudied and immensely important. We hope that the essays brought together in this volume serve to rejuvenate scholarship on leadership. At a minimum, they illustrate that scholars of American politics have the tools and capacity to significantly contribute to this endeavor. Indeed, they set a path forward that will fruitfully serve the scholarly community for years to come.

PART ONE

Leadership from the Top

CHAPTER ONE

House Leadership and the Speakership of John Boehner

Barbara Sinclair[†] and Gregory Koger

Pundits and the public tend to think of leadership as a talent inherent—or lacking—in individuals. You got it, or you don't. This is most obvious in discussions of the president. Brendan Nyhan (2009) identified the "Green Lantern theory" of presidential power, in which the person who wields the office possesses unlimited power as long as he or she is sufficiently creative and ruthless. The frame carries over to the media's take on congressional leadership, such as when House Speaker Newt Gingrich (R-GA) was portrayed in 1995 as an extraordinary leader who single-handedly created the surprising House Republican majority and transformed the position of Speaker into one of great power.

If success is the hallmark of leadership, then it is no surprise that the media labeled John Boehner's (R-OH) tenure as Speaker (2011–2015) a failure of leadership. Most analysts recognized that the character of Boehner's membership made his task difficult. That is, the political and institutional contexts affected the exercise of congressional leadership.

Political scientists have also grappled with the concept of leadership. Congressional scholars agree that the political and institutional contexts are crucial to understanding congressional leadership, and most subscribe to some form of principal–agent (P-A) theory: leaders use delegated power to serve the interests of party members. In this chapter, we examine Boehner's leadership through the lens of P-A theory, consider how adequate an understanding it yields, and determine what important questions are left unanswered. The first section lays out P-A theory as it has been applied in congressional studies and some critiques of the approach. It also presents a puzzle that the combination of Boehner's leader-

[†]Deceased.

ship problems and the current context poses. The next section—the heart of the article—empirically describes and analyzes Boehner's leadership. The last section considers how adequate the theory is, what questions remain unanswered, and how we might go about answering them.

P-A Theory and the Boehner Leadership Puzzle

P-A theory conceptualizes leadership in legislatures as having been instituted to ameliorate problems of collective action (Cox and McCubbins 1993; Koger and Lebo 2017; Rohde 1991; Sinclair 1995). By assumption, members of Congress want to change public policy, but they also look to party leaders to help them get reelected. These goals are interconnected; by enacting laws, legislators affect the reputation of the two political parties, help build electoral coalitions, and develop records of individual success they can highlight to their constituents.

Lawmaking is, however, a complex and time-consuming enterprise and one that, if successful, produces a collective good; consequently, it presents the legislature's members with collective action problems. Overcoming these collective action problems requires the delegation by members of powers and resources to agents. Delegation is, however, costly for members. Agents may use the powers granted them to pursue their own interests while neglecting those of their principal. The risks of delegation for a like-minded membership are relatively low; with intraparty agreement on policy goals high and policy decisions also likely to affect most members' reelection chances relatively uniformly, congressional party leaders who are elected biennially by their members and dependent on their members for reelection to their positions are highly likely to be faithful agents. Even so, delegation is intrinsically costly; the more power legislators cede to their leaders, the less direct their own role in the legislative process, so they become spectators rather their participants in their own jobs (Sinclair 1995; Koger and Lebo 2017). Finally—and critically for Boehner's leadership tenure—cooperating with party leaders means paying conformity costs. That is, legislators publicly support a strategically designed joint proposal rather than taking their own most-preferred position while rejecting everything else.

In addition to the similarity of party members' political interests and policy views, several variables may also influence legislators' willingness to delegate power to party leaders. First, legislators may delegate more power when legislating is more difficult, such as when the president is an aggressive opponent or as the size of a chamber increases. Second, the more eager legislators are to achieve policy change, the more likely they are to delegate power. This is likely when members perceive that they have an electoral mandate.

P-A theory contends that when the context changes in such a way as to alter member expectations, the level of delegated power and leadership influence will change in response. Furthermore, long-lasting change in preferences, context, or the behavior of the opposing party should lead to change in institutional arrangements (Koger and Lebo 2017; Rohde 1991; Sinclair 1983, 1995).

Some scholars object that P-A theory, with its emphasis on members' expectations as the prime determinant of leadership functioning, is too simple and leaves out the leader's own conception of leadership and his own goals. The objection became particularly prominent during the early days of Newt Gingrich's speakership, when he himself and many others were hailing him as a transformational leader. Taking issue with the P-A approach to explaining Gingrich's leadership, political scientist Ronald Peters argued that "it was not simply member expectations that enabled [Gingrich] to govern; it was that combined with or shaped by the culture of the Republican conference and his own attitude and approach to leadership" (1996, 24). Randall Strahan contended that

> Gingrich's role in the institutional changes that have occurred in the House in the 104th Congress illustrates the limits of the standard principal–agent theory and the need for a more complex model. . . . One such approach . . . is to place leadership in institutional time. Viewed from this perspective, Newt Gingrich has to be considered one of a number of extraordinary figures in the history of the House—not only for his success in establishing a new party government regime, but also for having helped create the critical moment in institutional time that made change on this scale a possibility. (1996, 22)

Boehner's speakership provides an interesting application of P-A theory to congressional leadership. On one hand, the high level of formal power delegated to Boehner corresponds to classic measures of preference homogeneity. And because the House Republicans were up against a Democratic president, a Democratic Senate majority, and a fairly cohesive House Democratic minority for most of Boehner's tenure, there were several reasons for the House Republicans to empower Boehner. Yet in practice Boehner's tenure was marked by persistent conflict within the House Republican Conference and revolt against Boehner's leadership.

Speaker Boehner's Leadership

To better understand Boehner's rocky speakership, we begin with his rise to power.

The Road to the Speakership

John Boehner was first elected to the House of Representatives in November 1990 from a solidly Republican southwest Ohio district. The House Republican Party he joined was in the midst of change. Minority Leader Bob Michel was a low-key leader, an institutional loyalist, and a conservative, but inclined to compromise with majority Democrats when he could. Minority Whip Newt Gingrich, in contrast, was aggressive and confrontational—and convinced that working with the Democratic majority only hindered the GOP's chances of becoming the majority party. Thus Gingrich sought to discredit the majority party and the institution it controlled. Gingrich's election as the party's second-ranking leader in 1989 over a candidate favored by Michel signaled how much the party's membership had changed since the late 1970s. New members, many from the South, were increasingly conservative and inclined to subscribe to Gingrich's slash-and-burn style.

Boehner made his mark early as a member of the Gang of Seven freshmen who highlighted the role of the Democratic majority and its leadership in the House bank scandal—members paid no penalties for overdrafting their checking accounts. The Gang of Seven's incessant and sometimes flamboyant floor attacks caught the media's attention. Propelled by these efforts, in the 103rd Congress, Boehner was elected head of the Conservative Opportunity Society, the organization Gingrich had set up in the 1980s to mount PR attacks on House Democrats, primarily using C-SPAN. After the Republicans unexpectedly won a House majority in the 1994 election, Boehner won the position of chair of the Republican Conference.

Boehner's first foray into party leadership was short-lived. After the government shutdown in the winter of 1995–1996, for which Republicans got the blame, discontent bloomed among the House Republican membership. Members blamed ineffective messaging, a task of the Conference and the leadership. Frustration with Gingrich's sometimes erratic leadership eventually led to a half-hearted coup attempt in which Boehner was implicated. When the 1998 elections proved a severe disappointment to House Republicans, reducing their numbers to 223 seats, Gingrich resigned, and in the subsequent leadership elections, Boehner lost his position.

Another leadership debacle gave Boehner a second chance. After leaving the party leadership, Boehner devoted himself to his committee duties. At the beginning of the George W. Bush administration, he became chair of the Education and the Workforce Committee and steered the No Child Left Behind education bill, a Bush priority, through to passage. He received high marks for his legislative acumen and ability to work with his liberal ranking member to produce a bill with bipartisan support. In early 2006, Tom DeLay stepped down as majority leader after he was indicted on state campaign-finance charges. House Republicans elected John Boehner as majority leader in his stead (Green and Harris 2007). The 2006 elections saw House Republicans lose their majority, Speaker Dennis Hastert resign from the leadership, and Boehner elected as the House Republicans' minority leader for the 110th Congress (2007–2008).

As minority leader, Boehner and the House Republicans faced off against a confident Democratic majority seeking to limit US involvement in Iraq, expand health care for low-income children, and make it easier for women to sue for equal pay. By the fall of 2008, sagging poll numbers for President Bush and a weak economy made Republican victory in the elections unlikely. But when the sagging real estate market sparked the collapse of the financial sector in September 2008, a full-scale economic crisis loomed. The Bush administration requested $700 billion from Congress to shore up the financial sector, setting up a difficult test of Republicans' commitment to free-market ideology and economic fairness just weeks before the election. The Troubled Asset Relief Program (TARP) failed an initial vote in the House, with Republicans opposing the Bush proposal by a vote of 65 to 133 (Hulse and Herszenhorn 2008). A revised version of the bill passed three days later with the Republicans breaking 91 to 108. Boehner voted "aye" both times.

TARP added fire to simmering conservative dissatisfaction with the Bush administration, and soon after the election, it would be a rallying cry for an emerging segment of frustrated conservatives: the Tea Party movement.

From the beginning of the 111th Congress, the House Republicans committed to a strategy of total opposition to the Democrats' agenda of economic stimulus, health care and financial reforms, and climate change legislation (Draper 2012). This was a political calculation as much as an ideological position: Republican collaboration would blur the lines between the two parties and make it more difficult to run against the Democratic agenda in the 2010 elections. This strategy succeeded: the 2010 elections were a Republican triumph. House Republicans gained a net of sixty-three seats, for a relatively comfortable majority of 242. Not surprisingly, the new Republican members, but most of the senior ones as well, read the election results as a repudiation of President Obama's agenda and of the erstwhile Democratic majority that had enacted it and a mandate for their shrink-the-government view.[1] And who would lead them? John Boehner.

The Institution of the Speakership

The Republican Conference nominated Boehner for Speaker on his birthday, November 17, 2010. He inherited two robust institutions: the speakership itself and the party nomination system for choosing a Speaker. By the late nineteenth century, strong norms had developed within each party to back its candidate when the House selects its Speaker on the first day of a new Congress (Jenkins and Stewart 2013). This ensures that the election will be quick and decisive—and determined by the majority party. It was neither surprising nor interesting when all 241 Republican voted for Boehner on the first day of the 112th Congress.[2]

Second, Boehner took over an office with a great deal of power. Since the late nineteenth century, Speakers have had discretion in recognition—they can choose who to call on. And since 1989, the Republican leader has directly appointed members of the House Rules Committee. Together, these powers give the Speaker great influence over the legislative agenda in the House.[3] The leadership commands a large staff and an elaborate whip system to gather information and persuade members. To sway members on specific issues, and even more to engender goodwill and store up credits, the leaders have available a variety of inducements: appointments to lesser leadership posts, help in passing minor but locally important legislation, campaign contributions, and aid raising money via appearances at members' fund-raisers in the district.

In practice, a Speaker's power depends on his members' consent, both in an immediate sense (special rules, the key to control of the floor, able to require majority approval) and in the longer run (to be reelected leader). To gain their consent, the leader must meet their expectations. And member expectations are shaped by the character of their districts, their own policy preferences, and the immediate political context.

The immediate political context was thus quite similar to the context in which the new Speaker, Newt Gingrich, operated during 1995 in the wake of the 1994 Republican electoral triumph, a context considered highly conducive to successful leadership. Like Gingrich, Boehner had a membership unified, at minimum, on their general policy thrust and determined to act decisively. And both Speakers faced a divided government. In Boehner's case, the Democrats retained a majority in the Senate and President Obama still had two more years in his first term. Furthermore, by 2011, party polarization was higher than it had been in the early 1990s, and Republicans had shown remarkable unity in opposition to majority Democrats in the 111th Congress.

Still, in one important respect, Boehner's resources were significantly less than Gingrich's had been. Gingrich was credited by his members, especially the junior ones, with having engineered the House Republican victory and consequently was hailed as a world-class political genius. No one attributed the Republicans' 2010 return to majority status to Boehner. Instead, a significant segment of the conservative Republican base considered Boehner part of the problem.

Early in 2009, Tea Party protests and groups formed around the country to express disapproval with the direction of the country (Bailey, Mummolo, and Noel 2012; Parker and Barreto 2013; Williamson, Skocpol, and Coggin 2013). While much of their disaffection was directed at Democrats and President Obama, many also blamed the Republican Party for ignoring the "limited government" elements of the conservative creed during the Bush administration, with TARP as a prominent example (Hirsh 2013). Several Tea Party–aligned candidates ran against establishment Republicans in congressional races, notably winning several Senate nominations and defeating incumbent senator Bob Bennett (R-UT) in a state party convention. The membership of a newly founded House Tea Party Caucus swelled from four members in July 2010 to forty-eight in early 2013, while the membership of the long-standing conservative group, the Republican Study Committee, expanded to over 170 members—about three-fourths of all House Republicans. From the outset, Boehner's speakership depended on the support of new members whose campaigns tapped into the restless and suspicious energy of Tea Party Republicans.

Boehner's Leadership: Strategy and Improvisation

Republican House members read the 2010 elections as a mandate dictating that they repeal Obamacare and drastically shrink government spending. After electing Boehner and approving the rules of the House, the members of the House spent their first day reading the Constitution aloud. Days later, they began acting as if they had never read it. The leadership provided members an immediate opportunity to demonstrate their bona fides on Obamacare; the first bill the leaders brought to the floor—designated H.R. 2 to indicate its high priority—repealed the health care legislation. Republicans voted unanimously to pass H.R. 2; all but three Democrats voted in opposition. Over the course of the 112th Congress, the leadership would provide their troops with multiple opportunities to vote to repeal the hated health care bill, satisfying member expectations in the short run. Each would fail because the House's proposals could not pass the Senate or gain President Obama's approval.

Government Spending and Debt Limits, 2011

Republican members' determination to make immediate cuts in government spending illustrated Boehner's challenging position. The 112th Congress's first order of must-do business was enacting appropriations legislation to fund the government's operations. The Democratic-controlled 111th Congress had failed to pass the regular appropriations bills by October 1, the beginning of fiscal year (FY) 2011, and had passed short-term stopgap legislation instead. After the 2010 elections in November, Senate Republicans blocked legislation appropriating funds through the remainder of FY2011; instead they agreed with the Democrats to pass a continuing resolution (CR) maintaining funding at current levels until March 4, 2011.

Many newly elected Republicans had specifically promised to cut at least $100 billion in nonsecurity discretionary spending in FY2011. Unlike symbolic votes to repeal the Affordable Care Act, however, appropriations bills are must-pass legislation. That is, there is a near consensus that failing to fund the government is too costly to bear, so the House, Senate, and White House had to find some way to agree. Legislation that satisfied the expectations of House Republicans for enormous cuts in domestic spending was unlikely to satisfy President Obama or a (super) majority of the Senate.[4]

Boehner sought to help members fulfill their campaign promises to cut federal funding by $100 billion, but only if this effort did not harm the overall reputation of the Republican Party. All Speakers who have been closely studied have seen it as their responsibility to go beyond attempting to satisfy their members' immediate wishes to anticipating the consequences of decisions for the party's reputation and thus for their members' future goal realization. Boehner believed that failing to enact must-pass legislation would severely harm the party's reputation.

Speaker Boehner and Republican appropriators unveiled their initial proposal in early February. Their contention was that because only seven months of the fiscal year remained, the $100 billion promise should be prorated to a $61 billion cut. The Obama administration and congressional Democrats condemned the severity of the cuts, while the hard-line conservatives of the Republican Study Committee objected that the party had promised to cut at least $100 billion in nonsecurity discretionary spending in FY2011, and anything less was a betrayal. Heritage Action, a far-right outside group, backed up the hard-liners by threatening to make opposition to a CR that did not cut enough a "key vote." In the face of this resistance, Boehner sent his appropriators back to find more cuts. The House passed the still more draconian H.R. 1 on February 19 with only Republican votes.

Neither Senate Democrats nor the While House would accept the House bill, but the hard-line House Republicans were unwilling to compromise. Senate Majority Leader Harry Reid attempted to draw Boehner into negotiations, and the White House signaled it was open to some cuts. Two short-term CRs were negotiated and passed, each on the eve of the drop-dead date. The true ideological chasm between the parties made reaching even these interim agreements difficult. It was clear to all participants that Boehner could not get the votes to pass any CR without spending cuts, and both short-term CRs included cuts—the first $4 billion and the second another $6 billion. But these were relatively easy cuts—ones that had been included in the president's budget, for example.

The conservative and Tea Party hard-liners were essentially playing a game of chicken with the Democrats. They wanted to make a take-it-or-leave-it proposal to the Democrats, backed up by a commitment to inflexibility—in this case, their earlier campaign pledges, backed up by statements indicating that they thought shutting down the government (by letting a CR lapse without a new spending plan) would not have deleterious policy or electoral effects. The hard-liners needed Boehner's cooperation for this strategy: he had to refuse to bring up any proposals other than theirs. Boehner, however, very much wanted to avoid a government shutdown. The government shutdown in late 1995–early 1996 had grievously wounded then-Speaker Newt Gingrich and congressional Republicans (Sinclair 1999).

Boehner soon disappointed the hard-liners by blinking. In early March, after the first short-term CR passed, negotiations on the long-term CR began in earnest. Talks behind closed doors culminated in an agreement two hours before the shutdown deadline. The deal made $39 billion in cuts, while most of the policy riders House Republicans had added were dropped. Although the omnibus appropriations bill passed handily in both chambers, fifty-nine House Republicans refused to vote for it, convinced that their leaders had compromised too much. And to get members to vote for a bill they disliked, Boehner promised that the party would hang tougher on the upcoming fight over raising the federal debt ceiling.

To forestall this fight, President Obama redoubled his efforts to strike a grand bargain to restrain the deficit, and Boehner too seemed willing. Obama worried that even a threat of default would hurt the economy; a bipartisan deal, on the other hand, would likely give the economy and his job approval ratings a boost. Boehner also had much to gain from striking a deal; he knew that Republicans could not refuse to raise the debt ceiling and consequently be seen as responsible for the US government defaulting on its debts and the financial turmoil that would follow.

Yet negotiations between Obama and Boehner in the summer of 2011 never reached fruition. Obama in 2011 had considerable leeway on the character of the deal he could agree to. Even though many Democrats would have detested cuts to entitlement programs by increasing the age for Medicare eligibility or switching to a less generous cost-of-living adjustment formula for Social Security, a majority of Democrats would have voted for such a deal had he struck one. The increasing role of partisan reputations in elections gives members of a party a huge investment in the reelection of a president of their own party; both their own electoral fortunes and their policy goals are at stake. Boehner, however, had much less leeway. His members believed the voters in the 2010 elections had given them a mandate for policies that Obama—and congressional Democrats—could never accept. And, it became increasingly evident, a considerable number believed not raising the debt ceiling was no big deal; they simply did not believe mainstream experts. When it became clear Boehner would not be able to persuade his members to vote for the deal that was taking shape, he pulled out of the negotiations.

Once again, on the eve of disaster, a perils of Pauline process yielded an agreement. The Budget Control Act passed on August 1, just before the August 2 deadline. It allowed the president to raise the debt limit by up to $2.5 trillion in two steps, and subject to disapproval by Congress by a two-thirds vote. The immediate increase in the debt ceiling was to be accompanied by $1 trillion in cuts in defense and domestic discretionary spending over ten years. A Joint Select Committee on Deficit Reduction was to be appointed by the four party leaders and charged with agreeing on another $1.5 trillion in cuts, with Congress required to vote for the committee's recommendations as a package. If the committee did not agree, or if Congress did not approve its package, automatic cuts (called sequestration) would take effect. The cuts would come half from defense and half from domestic spending, but Medicaid, Social Security, veterans' programs, and many programs targeted to low-income Americans would be largely exempt. Medicare was also mostly protected.

The final deal was struck only after stalemate appeared imminent. Many hardline Republicans were unhappy with the agreement, as were many progressive Democrats. Nevertheless the House passed the bill 269–161; Republicans split 174–66, Democrats 95–95. The next day, the Senate passed it 74–26, with six Democrats and nineteen Republicans voting against it.

The Fiscal Cliff

The 112th Congress's final must-do task was dealing with the so-called fiscal cliff. The Bush tax cuts were set to expire at the end of 2012, and after the Select Committee failed to reach an agreement, deep sequestration spending cuts were scheduled to go into effect on January 1, 2013. Economists argued that the double hit would wreck the economy and precipitate another recession. The Obama administration and most congressional Democrats were deeply concerned with the impact on the economy and also with the damage the across-the-board spending cuts would do to many government programs. Republicans strongly opposed letting any of the tax cuts lapse. Since the early 1990s, when President George H. W. Bush had reneged on his "no new taxes" pledge—and, Republicans believed, had thereby sealed his electoral defeat—any sort of tax increase was, for most Republicans, anathema.[5] Democrats, in contrast, insisted that a fair debt reduction deal should include higher taxes on wealthier Americans.

After the 2012 elections, Obama and Boehner again attempted to reach a grand bargain; immediately after the elections, Boehner had even intimated he was open to some increase in tax revenue, though not, he insisted, anything that could be considered a tax increase. Obama had been reelected, and Democrats had picked up two seats in the Senate and a handful in the House. The 2012 elections might well have been read as dissipating any mandate the 2010 elections had conferred. Yet the hard-liners did not pull back, as Boehner seemed initially inclined to do. Rather, they argued that because Republicans had maintained their House majority, they had as much of a mandate as Obama did, and they were no more inclined to compromise, especially in terms of raising taxes, whatever Boehner might call them.

On December 18, Boehner abruptly turned down the White House's latest offer. Again, he lacked enough support within his conference to make a deal with President Obama; even some of his broad leadership team were evidently opposed to the deal with Obama that had been taking shape (Khimm 2012). Instead, Boehner proposed a plan to the House Republicans that became known as Plan B. Plan B entailed making all the Bush tax cuts permanent for households with income below $1 million. Boehner hoped that the House Republicans would back the proposal and then stick behind it as a tempting take-it-or-leave-it proposal.

Once again, Boehner could not rally support from his own party. Although the leadership team attempted to sell the proposal as a means of giving Boehner bargaining leverage, Boehner's troops would not vote for anything that could be labeled a tax increase. Both Heritage Action and Club for Growth, another prominent far-right outside group, came out strongly against Plan B. Boehner pulled the bill, recessed the House until after Christmas, and issued a statement: "The House did not take up the tax measure today because it did not have sufficient support from our members to pass. . . . Now it is up to the president to work with Reid on legislation to avert the fiscal cliff" (Weisman 2012). The House Republicans had lost the initiative—and billions in tax cuts—because they could not bring themselves to vote for anything less than everything.

With that statement, Boehner withdrew and left it to Senate Minority Leader Mitch McConnell to work out an agreement with the White House. McConnell's members gave him more leeway than Boehner received from the House conference. The Senate Republican membership included fewer extreme hard-liners and more pragmatists, and their being in the minority took some of the pressure off satisfying the base. An agreement was reached on New Year's Eve and approved by both chambers the next day. It made permanent the Bush tax cuts for everyone with an income below $400,000; made some additional changes in tax law that increase taxes on the well-off; and extended benefits for the long-term unemployed. It also postponed the sequester until March 1. The Senate passed the bill by 89 to 8. The House vote was a comfortable 256 to 171, but, while Democrats supported the compromise by 172 to 16, Republicans opposed it 151 to 85. Majority Leader Eric Cantor and Majority Whip Kevin McCarthy voted no. Heritage Action and the Club for Growth had urged Republicans to vote no. To protect his party's reputation, Boehner had violated the so-called Hastert rule of bringing to the floor a bill that more than a majority of his membership opposed.

During the organizing caucuses for the 113th Congress, Boehner and his leadership team responded to the hard-liners' obstreperousness by stripping four of the most outspoken members of their best committee assignments. (The Speaker has multiple votes on the Republican Steering Committee, which serves as the party's committee on committees, but he does not command a majority.) If the purpose was to induce more teamwork, its impact was limited at best. On the speakership vote at the beginning of the 113th, twelve Republicans refused to vote for Boehner, nine voted for someone else, and three abstained. The rebels' aim was to prevent Boehner from receiving a majority of the votes cast, thus preventing a first ballot Boehner victory and so opening the door to another Republican to be chosen by the Republican Conference. Seventeen GOP votes for other candidates were required.

During the early days of the 113th Congress, Boehner brought two major bills to the House floor that did not command a majority of his membership. The Hurricane Sandy relief bill and the reauthorization of the Violence Against Women Act passed with Democratic votes. Boehner allowed the Senate to push him into bringing these measures to the floor without the support of a majority of House Republicans because he believed inaction would have severely damaged his party's reputation.

In the wake of the speakership vote and his violation of the Hastert rule on the fiscal cliff deal, Boehner worked to unify his party and assuage the hard-liners' anger and mistrust. At the House Republicans' annual retreat in January, he promised them a budget that balanced in ten years without any new tax revenue, no new taxes under any circumstances, and no compromise on sequestration (O'Keefe 2013). He had already promised he would not again negotiate with President Obama one on one. In return, he got his members to agree to suspend the debt ceiling for three months and pass a CR to fund the government without holding it hostage to cuts beyond those due to sequestration. This agreement soon became known as the Williamsburg Accord.

In the spring of 2013, the sequester cuts went into effect. Boehner, as he had promised his members, refused to negotiate over the sequester cuts. On March 21, the House passed a budget resolution that balanced the budget in ten years, shifted the defense sequester cuts to domestic programs, and decreased FY2014 spending approximately $50 billion below the sequester level. In response to member expectations, Budget Committee Chairman Paul Ryan had produced a budget plan even more austere than the year before. No Democrats voted for it, and ten Republicans defected as well; six of them argued that the budget Democrats considered beyond the pale still did not cut spending enough.

The CR funding the government until the end of the fiscal year and the suspension of the debt ceiling gave the Republican leadership some respite from those troublesome issues, but other problems emerged. In June, the farm bill was defeated on the House floor. Conservatives had insisted on bringing to the floor and passing amendments to add a work requirement for food stamps and to deregulate milk production. These amendments cut Democratic support, while the opposition of Heritage Action and Club for Growth led to sixty-two "nay" votes from House Republicans.

In late July, just before the August recess, House leaders pulled the transportation appropriations bill from the floor; although they gave other explanations, it was clear that they had not been able to muster enough votes to pass it. Suburban Republicans opposed the bill because of some of the draconian cuts that would impact their constituents, while the fiscal hard-liners refused to relent. "With this action, the House has declined to proceed on the implementation of the very budget it adopted just three months ago," a frustrated Hal Rogers (R-KY), chair of the Appropriations Committee, said (Rogers 2013). It seemed unlikely that House Republicans would be able to pass any of the domestic appropriations bills individually.

The new fiscal year begins October 1, requiring action—a new CR if not individual appropriations bills—to keep the government funded. The debt ceiling would also have to be raised sometime in the fall. In late March, the chair of the Republican Study Committee and a number of its members met with Boehner to inform him they would expect big concessions in return for another increase in the debt ceiling. By July, the Club for Growth and Heritage Action, two of the most aggressive far-right groups, were pressuring congressional Republicans to use the upcoming CR to defund Obamacare, and Senator Ted Cruz (R-TX) vociferously advocated that approach. Senators Mike Lee (R-UT), Ted Cruz, and ten of their party colleagues signed a letter pledging to vote against any CR that funded Obamacare. In the House, sixty Republicans soon followed suit, signing the so-called Meadows letter.

Boehner, a survivor of the 1995–1996 government shutdown, had all along opposed another, convinced that the Republican Party would be blamed. Now other, more pragmatic Republicans panned the idea. Representative Tom Cole (R-OK) told MSNBC that a shutdown over defunding the Affordable Care Act was a "suicidal political tactic." Senator Richard Burr (R-NC) called it the "dumbest idea I've ever heard of" (Pierce 2013). Boehner in closed party meetings and on conference calls worked at talking his members out of that course of action. In early August, the Republican leadership believed it had convinced its members of the folly of the shutdown strategy (Costa 2013).

During the August recess, however, GOP House members heard enthusiastic backing for the shutdown strategy from their activist constituents. And Heritage Action continued to press members to sign the Meadows letter in support. When the letter was unveiled on August 21, it had eighty signatures. By early September, Boehner and his leadership team had come up with a new approach; a separate bill defunding Obamacare would be considered and voted on as a package with the CR extending funding at the sequester level through December 15, 2013. The Senate could then separate the two bills and send the clean CR directly to the president for his signature. Far-right groups cried foul and pressed members to oppose the plan. Hard-line members quickly refused to go along, calling the proposal a gimmick and threatening to vote against the rule. Senators Cruz and Lee blasted the plan. The leaders postponed the vote.

On September 18, after a meeting of the full Republican House Conference, the leaders announced they would bring to the floor a CR that incorporated defunding of Obamacare. Boehner emphasized that it was not House Republicans' intention to shut down the government, and he apparently hoped that after forcing the Senate to go on the record on the defunding proposal, his hard-line members would be willing to pass a clean CR. On September 20, the House passed the CR with only two Democrats voting in favor and one Republican against.

On September 27, after stripping out the ACA defund provision, the Senate passed a clean CR and sent it back to the House, after enduring a twenty-one-hour pseudo-filibuster on the Senate floor by Ted Cruz that gained him much publicity but had no effect on the legislative process. Now the end of the fiscal year—and a shutdown—was only a few days away.

Boehner and his team spent the interim attempting to come up with a strategy that would unite their members and avoid a shutdown. Earlier in the process, they had tried to shift hard-liners' attention to the debt limit increase; now they proposed adding to a debt limit increase bill a GOP wish list extending from a one-year delay in Obamacare to approval of the Keystone XL pipeline to a broad rollback of environmental regulations. Hard-liners refused to go along. After the Senate passed the clean CR, Cruz and Lee came over to the House and lobbied hard-liners to hang tough. Boehner, evidently seeing no other road forward and unwilling to negotiate with Democrats, settled on adding a one-year delay of Obamacare and repeal of the tax on medical devices to the Senate-passed clean CR.

On September 30, the House passed its amended CR and sent it back to the Senate, which removed the House amendments and sent back the clean CR. The House then amended it again; the Senate quickly killed that as well and again sent back a clean CR. On October 1, the shutdown began.

As the House Republican leadership had feared, the public reacted negatively to the party's conduct. Polls showed that only 26 percent approved of how the GOP was handling negotiations over the budget (Pew 2013; Gallup 2013); still, 56 percent of Republicans approved, and these surely were the people the hard-liners were hearing from. The leaders undertook a series of moves aimed at shifting the blame. The House asked for a conference with the Senate on the CR, which Senate Democrats quickly rebuffed. The leaders then brought up and passed a series of micro-CRs funding individual popular programs—national parks, National Institutes of Health cancer trials, and veterans' programs. Although a few House Democrats voted for these bills, Senate Majority Leader Reid refused to consider them. The GOP leaders floated various proposals for negotiations; when Boehner suggested new talks on a grand bargain at a White House meeting, the Democratic leaders burst out laughing, convinced that Boehner was not serious—nor could he deliver even if he were.

Republicans argued that the shutdown was the fault of Obama and congressional Democrats because it was they who were unwilling to negotiate. Obama and Reid reiterated the position they had been articulating for months—they would not negotiate over the ACA, the signature achievement of Obama and the Democratic-dominated 111th Congress, which had been law for three years—and certainly not in return for Republicans simply funding the government. They made clear as well that there would be no negotiations over raising the debt ceiling, the deadline for which was quickly approaching. "If we get in the habit where a few folks, an extremist wing of one party, whether it's Democrat or Republican, are allowed to extort concessions based on a threat of undermining the full faith and credit of the United States, then any president who comes after me—not just me—will find themselves unable to govern effectively," Obama said (Calmes and Weisman 2013).

Dissent in House Republican ranks became more public. A number of pragmatic members stated publicly that they would be willing to vote for a clean CR.

Some began to threaten to defect, as hard-liners had often done, but when the time came, they did not follow through. The shutdown dragged on, and with the debt ceiling deadline of mid-October approaching, the House leadership realized its position was becoming increasingly untenable. Boehner had not wanted a government shutdown, but he especially knew he could not allow the US government to default on its debt.

White House meetings with congressional leaders led to some signs of progress late in the week of October 7. A deal centering on a temporary CR and debt ceiling increase coupled with talks on a longer-term budget deal seemed possible (Peters, Parker, and Baker 2013). Senate Majority Leader Reid and Minority Leader Mitch McConnell began serious negotiations on October 14. House hard-liners were very unhappy with the contours of the impending deal: "We've got a name for it in the House: it's called the Senate surrender caucus," said Tim Huelskamp (R-KS) (Shear and Peters 2013). Boehner decided to try again to salvage something from the debacle, and McConnell suspended his talks with Reid to give Boehner time to try.

On Tuesday, October 15, Boehner and his leadership team proposed attaching to the emerging Senate proposal a two-year suspension of the medical devices tax and a ban on health care subsidies for members of Congress, the president, and cabinet officials. Hard-liners shot it down. The House GOP leadership then proposed extending the subsidy ban to congressional and executive staff and shortening the length of the CR. This too was not enough for the hard-liners. Boehner gave up; time had run out.

On Wednesday evening, October 16, the Senate, 81–18, approved a deal that reopened the government and funded it until January 15, raised the debt ceiling through February 7, and convened a Budget Committee conference committee charged with hammering out a longer-term budget agreement by December 13. The House approved the bill a few hours later 285–144, with Republicans splitting 87 in favor to 144 against. Boehner again had to depend on Democrats to pass legislation he knew had to pass.

After the Shutdown

Boehner had hoped that the disastrous effects of a government shutdown on the Republican Party would curb the hard-liners' appetite for crisis bargaining. It did not. Instead, it marked a turning point in Boehner's willingness to indulge their beliefs that they could "win" by refusing to negotiate.

On December 10, Budget Committee Chairs Patty Murray and Paul Ryan announced they had reached a deal as the agreement called for. The package they unveiled partly undid the sequester and allowed greater discretionary spending for the next two years; this was paid for by various fees and by future spending cuts. The increased spending would be split between defense and domestic programs. In sum, it was a bipartisan compromise, designed to gain both Republican and Democratic votes. A number of hard-line House members reacted with dismay. Any move away from sequester-level spending was a betrayal of the Williamsburg Accords, those members argued. Others, however, reacted with resignation.

Heritage Action and some of the other hard-line outside groups denounced the deal even before it was made public. Speaker Boehner responded with sharp attacks on the groups who, he believed, were out to sabotage the deal. After denouncing them in public, Boehner, at a closed Republican conference meeting, charged, "They are not fighting for conservative policy. They are fighting to expand their lists, raise more money and grow their organizations, and they are using you to do it. It's ridiculous" (Hulse 2013). As the House prepared to vote on the deal, he told reporters at his weekly news briefing, "Frankly, I think they're misleading their followers. I think they're pushing our members in places where they don't want to be. And frankly, I just think that they've lost all credibility" (Milbank 2013). On the evening of December 12, the House passed the budget deal by a vote of 332 to 94; Republicans voted 169 in favor to 63 opposed. The Senate then approved the deal on a 64 to 36 vote, with Republicans splitting 9 to 36.

On January 13, 2014, Appropriations Committee Chairs Hal Rogers and Barbara Mikulski unveiled a $1.1 trillion spending bill to actually fund the government. The Murray–Ryan budget deal had set the top-level numbers; an appropriations bill was needed to fill in the outline. To avoid another shutdown, it had to be passed by midnight on January 15, when the CR that was part of the deal ending the shutdown ran out. Despite opposition from the same hard-line outside groups and some unhappiness on the part of members of all ideological stripes, the House passed the bill on a 359–67 vote, with sixty-four hard-line Republicans voting against it. The Senate approved the bill 72–26; Republicans split, 17 in favor to 26 opposed.

On January 30, Boehner unveiled the leadership's one-page "statement of principles" for immigration reform. Ever since Republican presidential candidate Mitt Romney received only 29 percent of the Latino vote in 2012, many Republicans had argued that passing immigration reform was essential if Republicans were to make headway with the fast-growing Latino vote. Boehner believed the time to respond had come. Even before the principles were released, far-right outside groups began a campaign against moving forward on broad immigration reform legislation, with Heritage Action calling the principles "a full embrace of amnesty." The Tea Party Patriots began a massive campaign to gin up phone calls to members from their districts, and FreedomWorks gathered signatures on a "fire the Speaker" petition (Weisman and Parker 2014a). When, on January 30, House Republicans discussed the principles at their annual retreat, the consensus among the membership was against acting on immigration reform. It would split the membership and offend their strongest supporters in an election year. A week later, Boehner retreated, saying he did not believe a bill could pass in 2014. His members were unwilling to follow his lead.

Passage of the omnibus appropriations bill in mid-January avoided another government shutdown. To avoid the even worse outcome of a government default on its debts, the debt ceiling needed to be raised by late February. Boehner had declared from the beginning that he would under no circumstances allow a default. This preemptive commitment strengthened his hand vis-à-vis the hardest of hard-liners but weakened it vis-à-vis Obama and the Democrats, who in any case had committed themselves to no negotiations on the debt ceiling. Yet Boehner knew that to get a majority of his members to vote for an increase, he would have to obtain something in return for raising the debt limit.

The Republican leadership spent early February seeking an add-on to the debt ceiling bill that would induce a Republican majority to vote for the bill and produce a majority of the House for passage. The leaders suggested a raft of different add-ons, major and minor, but found nothing that worked. On February 10, after yet another meeting with his membership where he became convinced his latest package could not garner a majority, Boehner gave up trying. The next morning, he announced he was bringing a clean debt ceiling bill to the floor, and that afternoon it passed the House 221 to 201. The majority was made up overwhelmingly of Democrats; only twenty-eight Republicans, including the top three leaders, voted for it (Weisman and Parker 2014b). Hard-liners were despondent and outside groups were livid, but the deed was done. As Boehner himself had said when he announced his intentions to his membership, he had gotten "this monkey off of our backs" (Newhauser 2014). Most of his members seemed to recognize that, but doing so came at a cost.

These episodes display a number of characteristics in common. Boehner was not very accurate at judging what his members would accept. Nor were House Republicans—at least the hard-liners—always willing to accept their leader's judgment about what was feasible and made political sense. Outside conservative groups featured prominently in this conversation by selecting which compromises were acceptable and which were selling out the conservative base. Nor was it feasible to craft proposals that attracted most House Republicans and enough Democrats to pass proposals without the hard-liners. Consequently, Boehner was frequently forced to rely on ad hoc proposals crafted on the fly after he learned that his preferred alternative would not pass. Furthermore, in order to get sufficient votes to pass must-pass measures at the last possible moment, Boehner resorted to a peculiar sort of kick-the-can-down-the-road tactic: he promised his members a tougher negotiation stance and a big victory on the next battle if they would vote with him on the current one. This made his task on each successive battle that much harder.

In several important instances, Boehner violated the Hastert rule by bringing to the floor legislation opposed by a majority of his membership and passing it with opposition party votes. He had been understandably reluctant to do so; after all, the Speaker is the leader of the majority party, chosen in reality by his party membership and dependent on those members for his continuation in office. As Speakers have in the past, he violated the Hastert rule when he considered it essential to protect his party's reputation. Yet the perils of Pauline processes, with their one-minute-to-deadline resolutions have, in and of themselves, damaged his party's reputation.

2015: Reelection and Resignation

The 113th Congress was widely panned as one of the worst, least productive sessions ever (e.g., Bolton 2014). At the beginning of the 114th Congress, Boehner again saw a revolt against his reelection as Speaker, with twenty-five Republicans voting for someone other than Boehner or Pelosi. Boehner's 216 votes for Speaker were less than a majority of the entire House, but twenty-five members did not cast a vote, so Boehner won with a majority of the votes cast.[6] The hard-liners had again failed to defeat Boehner by defecting on the floor vote, but they had not tired of trying.

Soon after Boehner's reelection as Speaker, the House Republicans gathered for a retreat in Hershey, Pennsylvania, to plan for the upcoming session. Nine of Boehner's opponents met and decided to organize an uber-conservative subgroup of the Republican conference, which they dubbed the Freedom Caucus (Gehrke 2015; Lizza 2015). Its explicit goal was to organize against and negotiate with Boehner: "The group had two rules for new members: they had to be willing to vote against Boehner legislation, but they also had to be willing to support him when the legislation met some, if not all, of the Freedom Caucus's goals" (Lizza 2015).

The conflict between Boehner and the hard-liners escalated. In February 2015, Freedom Caucus members voted against a special rule to bring up a bill granting President Obama trade promotion authority. Breaking with one's party on these agenda-setting votes is considered a grave act of disloyalty, and the hard-liners did it in part to show how committed they were (Lizza 2015). Boehner retaliated by removing Mark Meadows (R-NC) from a subcommittee chairmanship, while other hard-liners were denied the support of the House Republicans' campaign organization, the National Republican Congressional Committee (Lizza 2015).

The conflict came to a head when Meadows filed a motion to vacate the chair on July 28, 2015. Essentially this meant that Meadows wanted a public vote on whether the House should fire Boehner. Meadows hoped that the anti-Boehner faction could finally cast enough votes against Boehner to deprive him of the simple majority he needed to remain as Speaker. This would force the Republicans to meet and pick a new Speaker, or would force Boehner to rely on Democratic votes to remain in the chair. While it was not clear that this strategy would succeed, some

Boehner loyalists privately feared that another vote for Boehner would lead to a primary challenge in 2016. Boehner spared his allies this choice by tendering his resignation on Friday, September 25, and leaving office on October 29.

Like good nihilists, the Freedom Caucus members had no plan to replace Boehner. The next person on the leadership ladder was Kevin McCarthy (R-CA), but McCarthy withdrew from the race when it was clear he would not have Freedom Caucus support, and he did not want to be in the same no-win situation as Boehner. After several days, a genuinely reluctant Paul Ryan (R-WI) was drafted from his position as chair of the Ways and Means Committee to be the next Speaker (Lizza 2015). Ryan was elected Speaker on October 29 with ten Freedom Caucus votes against him.

Boehner essentially traded his resignation—long desired by hard-liners—for one last budget deal to avert a crisis. The House quickly passed a CR to continue funding the government through December 11, 2015, with Democrats providing most of the votes and the Republicans opposing the CR 91 to 151. This gave Boehner time to negotiate a deal to get the House through the 2016 election. In late October, Boehner and other congressional leaders reached an agreement with President Obama. Their agreement raised the debt limit, increased spending over the next two years, and averted a Medicare crisis (Herszenhorn 2015). Congress quickly ratified the deal, albeit with another violation of the Hastert rule: House Republicans opposed the deal with 79 ayes to 167 nays.

Overall, Boehner certainly saw himself as his members' agent, and he tried to meet his members' expectations. One can argue about whether Boehner could have been a more effective leader if he used different leadership strategies, but there is general agreement that the character of the Republican membership made effective leadership uncommonly difficult in the 112th and 113th Congresses. The congressional Republican Party, many analysts claim, was split between far-right Tea Party adherents and mainstream Republicans; Tea Party members elected in 2010 (and 2012), the argument goes, differed significantly from their more senior colleagues and were at the root of Boehner's problems. The next section evaluates these explanations for Boehner's struggles.

The House Republican Majority: What Sort of Split?

Was the House Republican membership during Boehner's speakership split along ideological lines?[7] Using the DW-NOMINATE first dimension score as the measure of ideology, one finds that the House GOP moved even further right in the 112th Congress but did not become appreciably more diverse (based on the standard deviation) (Figure 1.1). The members of the large 112th freshman class, often considered Tea Partiers and the source of Boehner's problem, were on average no further right (.68) than their more senior colleagues (.67). And the two groupings were equally diverse.

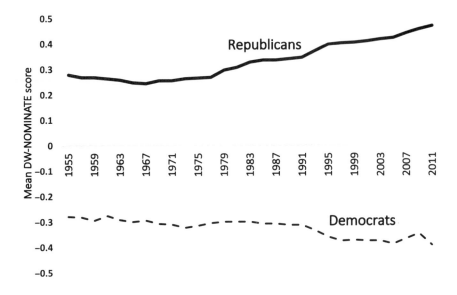

Figure 1.1. The House Parties Polarize. *Note:* DW-NOMINATE means, 84th–112th Congresses, 1955–2012.

Figure 1.2 suggests why Boehner may have been reluctant to try to form right-center majorities: there isn't much of a center. The gap between the rightmost Democrats and the leftmost Republicans (other than GOP maverick Walter Jones) is substantial, and the gap between the bulk of Republicans and enough Democrats to make a difference is vast. The price in terms of policy concessions was consequently likely to be greater than most of his members would be willing to tolerate—at least unless and until they were convinced there was no other course.

The DW-NOMINATE scores are based on all nonunanimous roll calls; specific major legislative battles have been at the heart of Boehner's troubles. The hard-liners as we have implicitly defined them are characterized by their unwillingness to go along on those battles. Are the hard-liners in fact a distinct group? Are they primarily members first elected in 2010 (and perhaps 2012) and so reasonably considered Tea Partiers?

To answer those questions, we examined GOP voting behavior on a set of roll calls on those major battles that split the Republican membership. They are, for the 112th Congress, the passage vote on the FY2011 omnibus appropriations bill, the passage vote on the debt limit bill, and the motion to concur in the Senate amendment on the bill incorporating the fiscal cliff deal. For the 113th, they are the Hurricane Sandy aid bill, the Violence Against Women Act, the motion to concur

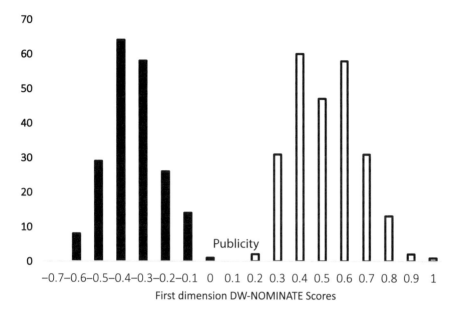

Figure 1.2. Distribution of First-Dimension DW-NOMINATE Scores, 112th Congress. *Note:* Democrats in black; Republicans in white.

in the Senate amendment on the bill ending the government shutdown and raising the debt ceiling, and the vote to approve the bipartisan budget deal in December 2013. In addition, the Meadows letter demanding defunding of Obamacare as the price of funding the government is included, with the eighty signers considered hard-liners.

We create two variables, each of which counts the number of times a GOP member voted pro–Tea Party on the selected roll calls in the Congress. The count variables are moderately correlated with the 112th DW-NOMINATE scores; the correlation for the 112th pro–Tea Party score is .53; for the 113th the score (for members who served in both the 112th and 113th Congresses) is .57. The count variables thus get at the same underlying predisposition measured by the DW-NOMINATE scores, but what it measured is not identical. If we believe the DW-NOMINATE first-dimension score captures ideology, then pro–Tea Party voting behavior is driven in part by ideology, but also by other factors. The 112th and 113th count variables are also moderately correlated ($r = .47$); almost no Republicans switched from high Tea Party support in the 112th to low support in the 113th; many continuing members did switch from low to high.

As Table 1.1 shows, the 2010 freshmen are indeed more likely to have cast two or three pro–Tea Party votes than their more senior colleagues in the 112th Congress;

Table 1.1. Holdover versus Freshmen Voting on Tea Party Issues, 112th Congress (2011–2012)

No. of Tea Party Votes	Holdovers	Freshmen
0	40.0%	26.4%
1	32.9%	32.2%
2	14.2%	19.5%
3	12.9%	21.8%
Total no. of cases	155	87

Tables 1.2 and 1.3 indicate the same pattern holds in the 113th Congress with the 2012 freshmen surpassing those first elected in 2010, who again surpass more senior members.[8] In none of the comparisons, however, are the differences huge or clear-cut. Senior members are less likely than more junior members to cast pro–Tea Party (or anti-Boehner) votes, but many of them nevertheless do so, and, given their greater numbers, they account for a larger number of anti-Boehner votes than their more junior colleagues do.

Southern Republicans are also more likely to cast pro–Tea Party votes than those from other regions; the relationship is a bit stronger for region than for seniority. This is not unexpected, as region is a crude proxy for the character of the district. Again, however, the relationship is fairly weak, and many Republicans from regions outside the South cast pro–Tea Party votes.[9]

A further indication of the importance of the district is the relationship between pro–Tea Party voting and the district's partisan character. Those most likely to cast numerous pro–Tea Party votes in the 113th Congress are likely to come from heavily Republican districts; the correlation between the 113th vote count variable and the partisan vote index is .42.[10]

Table 1.2. Holdover versus 112th versus 113th Freshmen Voting on Tea Party Issues, 113th Congress (2012–2013)

No. of Tea Party Votes	Holdovers	112th Freshmen	113th Freshmen
0	18.1%	12.7%	5.6%
1	19.7%	9.9%	11.1%
2	14.2%	16.9%	8.3%
3	22.8%	29.6%	33.3%
4	11.0%	18.3%	16.7%
5	14.2%	12.7%	25.0%
No. of cases	127	71	36

Table 1.3. Tea Party Votes

Issue	Bill No.	Date	Motion	GOP Vote (Yes–No)
FY2011 continuing appropriation	H.R. 1473	4/14/2011	Passage	179–59
Debt limit	S. 365	8/1/2011	Passage	174–66
Fiscal cliff	H.R. 8	1/1/2013	Motion to concur	85–151
Hurricane Sandy aid	H.R. 152	1/15/2013	Passage	49–179
Violence Against Women Act reauthorization	S. 47	2/28/2013	Passage	87–138
Meadows letter		8/21/2013		80–152
CR and debt limit extension	H.R. 2775	10/16/2013	Motion to concur	87–144
FY2014 budget agreement	H.J. Res. 59	12/12/2013	Motion to recede and concur	169–62

Note: FY = fiscal year.

Clearly, then, Republicans first elected to the House after the Tea Party move-ment emerged in 2009 do not make up most of those casting pro–Tea Party votes. And those casting pro–Tea Party votes more frequently are not a great deal more conservative as measured by DW-NOMINATE scores than those casting them less frequently. Republicans were moving right long before the Tea Party came on the scene. Congressional Republicans had decided on a strategy of all-out opposition to Obama's and congressional Democrats' agenda before President Obama's inau-guration (Draper 2012, 26; Sinclair 2011).

If Boehner's problems are not explained by a large group of new members who are much further to the right than holdover members, then what explains his diffi-culties? Certainly the 2010 election victory and the Tea Party activism that preceded it invigorated the antigovernment, antitax, anti-Obama forces in Congress. Far-right outside groups, many of which had seen an opportunity in the Tea Party pro-tests and had established ties of various sorts, often financial, with local Tea Party groups, saw an even bigger opportunity in the new House Republican majority and became highly active in pressuring members to take hard-line stances. But because we would expect a perception of mandate to make leadership easier, not harder, and because we expect pressure from outside groups to be filtered through members' perceptions of what they needed to do to attain their goals, these changes in con-text, as enormous as they were, do not by themselves explain Boehner's difficulties.

The Root of Boehner's Leadership Dilemma

Why, then, was effective party leadership so difficult for Boehner? Contrary to jour-nalists' assertions, the House Republican membership was ideologically homoge-neous; the Republican Party's median policy preferences had migrated far to the right before the 2010 elections. In the wake of elections perceived as carrying man-dates, we expect members to willingly follow their leaders as long as the leaders are leading them in the direction they want to go. Gingrich in the 104th Congress and Pelosi in the 110th and 111th Congresses are archetypal cases. But what if members' expectations are highly unrealistic and members do not have much trust in their leader?

An election victory sweeping enough to be perceived as carrying a mandate often does engender unrealistic expectations in those elected. Continuing members of Congress whose policy goals have been frustrated are almost as susceptible as new members brought in by the wave election. Normally, however, events and their desire for reelection force members to come to terms with reality and lower their ex-pectations. Yet the post-2010 House Republicans were extremely slow to do so, and even after the government shutdown, not all of them did. Many of these members, the evidence suggests, simply saw the world differently from what had formerly been the consensus view; they were suspicious of mainstream expertise and took their cues from different sources. Many really did not believe that going over the various cliffs was as catastrophic as the mainstream consensus posited. In January 2014, well after the government shutdown, the House leadership still felt it necessary to have Republican economist Douglas Holtz-Eakin explain to members why the debt ceiling really had to be raised. In essence, the split within the House Republican Party was primarily one over strategy and tactics, not over ideology, but because its roots lay in different understandings of reality, it proved even more difficult for leaders to manage.

Boehner was badly positioned to influence these members' views. With credit for the big victory attributed to the Tea Party and other grassroots activists, members did not consider Boehner a political genius. Instead, he was seen as a pragmatic politician and part of the Washington establishment—everything that GOP activists distrusted and disliked. The hard-liners did not agree with Boehner's judgment that their strategy would damage the party's reputation. They lacked confidence in Boehner's negotiation skills and in his commitment to pursuing the party's policy goals.

From the beginning of his speakership, Boehner truly faced a quandary. A critical segment of his conference had unrealistic expectations that they would not revise when experience proved them wrong. Boehner believed that going along with the hard-liners' strategy was likely to cause harm to the other members and to the party's reputation, putting him in a no-win situation. This was exacerbated by the fact that the enormous ideological distance between the parties made right-center coalitions unattractive to most Republicans and so empowered the hardest of the hard-liners. Boehner was slow to recognize his dilemma and tended to respond in a disjointed, ad hoc fashion. But, to be fair, no easy or obvious course was open to him.

P-A Theory and Congressional Leadership—Future Directions

P-A theory, we contend, helps us to understand Boehner's situation; applying it to Boehner's leadership also points us in directions that require rethinking and extensions.[11] Our account makes clear that congressional leadership must be understood as a relationship between members and leaders and that member expectations are more important than leaders' traits. Certainly leaders may play the hand they are dealt badly or well, but the hand—the character of their membership and contextual factors that shape their members' expectations—constrain, often severely, leaders' strategy choices.

The problem of agent faithfulness has played a central role in P-A theory but does not deserve that place in its application to congressional party leadership. Given the frequency with which congressional party leaders must stand for reelection and the high rate of interaction between leaders and members, leaders are seldom intentionally faithless agents pursuing their own goals at the expense of those of their members.

The issue that has received most attention in congressional studies is the multiple principals problem. The Speaker as leader of his or her party is the agent of 218-plus members. Even when those members are ideologically homogeneous by American standards, they are far from monolithic in their policy preferences or their reelection needs. Cox and McCubbins (1993) posit that leaders handle this problem by keeping issues that divide the party off the agenda. That implies a sparse agenda when the majority party is ideologically heterogeneous. Others have argued that as members become more ideologically homogeneous, they become more willing to give their leaders powers and resources, and allow them to use them aggressively because they can be confident that the leaders will use them to facilitate passage of legislation the members' favor (Aldrich and Rohde 2000; Sinclair 1995).

Congressional party leaders, even when relatively low in powers and resources, have available some side payments they can use to smooth intraparty friction. When ideological homogeneity generates strong party leadership and increases the internal rewards for acting as team members, the behavioral effects of externally based ideological homogeneity are amplified. Leaders now have considerable capacity to structure choices through procedure in a way that eases some of the problems for members that might otherwise arise. Thus we know a good deal about the effects of ideological homogeneity or heterogeneity on party leadership: on leaders' powers, on their freedom to use them aggressively, on the problems they confront in determining strategy and agenda. Still, there is much to do in this area.

An issue that requires more attention and more careful analysis can be labeled the multiple goal problem. Members have multiple goals: policy, reelection, influence, maintenance of their chamber majority. They expect their leaders to help them attain all these goals—or certainly to do nothing that makes achieving any of them less likely. Yet the best course for achieving one goal may be detrimental to the attainment of another. Enacting or attempting to enact bold policy departures may satisfy members' policy goals but may hurt at the ballot box. (Obamacare and the government shutdown over Obamacare are examples.) Conversely, passing voter-pleasing legislation may come at the cost of members having to vote for policies they abhor (for example, Republicans and Medicare Part D). Leaders have to weigh their members' multiple goals and the effects of various strategies on them, then attempt to persuade their members that they have made the correct choices. The political context determines how easy or difficult figuring out strategies acceptable to most members is, but of course the context is complex and the issue deserves more analysis. We need to think about what form intragoal conflicts are likely to take and when they are likely to arise, and examine leaders' and members' reactions to them.

Another issue that the Boehner leadership case raises is that of members with unrealistic expectations. The most similar instance occurred in 1995–1996 when House Republicans shut down the government. By late 1995, Speaker Newt Gingrich had decided that some flexibility and compromise were necessary; yet he was not able to persuade the bulk of his membership, especially the big junior classes, of that. Ideologically fervent and believing themselves mandated, junior Republicans especially remained staunchly committed to the strategy of attempting to bludgeon the president into agreeing to their policy positions by shutting the government down long after its disastrous impact on the Republican Party's popularity became clear (Drew 1996, 205–275; Sinclair 1999). The Republican membership's tendency to dump its leaders in the 1950s and 1960s might also be instances of the problem; the leaders had not delivered movement toward a Republican majority. In any case, these various instances make clear that the context may make satisfying members' expectations impossible.

Making progress toward a better understanding of congressional leadership requires theoretical development, but it also requires careful empirical analysis. Given the importance of member expectations, some return to interviews as an important data-gathering technique seems essential. Interviewing members of Congress and senior staff is difficult, time-consuming, and expensive but is a source of data not obtainable in any other way.

The P-A approach, we argue in conclusion, is the most useful theoretical framework currently available and can be made more so by elaboration in the directions suggested above. It is not, however, likely to ever become a truly testable theory when applied to congressional party leadership; the number of cases is too few and the number of significant context variables too many.

Acknowledgments

Barbara Sinclair prepared and presented the initial draft of this chapter for the conference on Leadership in American Politics, University of Virginia, June 2–3, 2013. Barbara Sinclair passed away on March 12, 2016, and Gregory Koger helped to finalize the text.

References

Aldrich, John, and David Rohde. 2000. "The Consequences of Party Organization in the House: Theory and Evidence on Conditional Party Government." In *Polarized Politics: Congress and the President in a Partisan Era*, edited by Jon Bond and Richard Fleisher, 31–72. Washington, DC: CQ Press.

Bailey, Michael A., Jonathan Mummolo, and Hans Noel. 2012. "Tea Party Influence: A Story of Activists and Elites." *American Politics Research* 40:769–804.

Bolton, Alexander. 2014. "Worst Congress Ever?" *The Hill*, March 10. http://thehill.com/.

Calmes, Jackie, and Jonathan Weisman. 2013. "Obama Sets Conditions for Talks: Pass Funding and Raise Debt Ceiling." *New York Times*, October 2. http://www.nytimes.com/.

Costa, Robert. 2013. "Shutting Down a Shutdown: Inside How House GOP Leaders Are Trying to Avoid One." *National Review*, August 13. http://www.nationalreview.com/.

Cox, Gary, and Mathew McCubbins. 1993. *Legislative Leviathan: Party Government in the House*. Berkeley: University of California Press.

Draper, Robert. 2012. *Do Not Ask What Good We Do: Inside the US House of Representatives.* Free Press.

Drew, Elizabeth. 1996. *Showdown: The Struggle between the Gingrich Congress and the Clinton White House*. New York: Simon & Schuster.

Gallup. 2013. *Gallup*, October 9. "Republican Party Favorability Sinks to Record Low." http://www.gallup.com/.

Gehrke, Joel. 2015. "Meet the Freedom Caucus." *National Review*, January 26. http://www.nationalreview.com/.

Green, Matthew N., and Douglas B. Harris. 2007. "Goal Salience and the 2006 Race for House Majority Leader." *Political Research Quarterly* 60:618–630.

Herszenhorn, David M. 2015. "House Approves Budget, Providing 'Clean' Exit that John Boehner Sought." *New York Times*, October 28. https://www.nytimes.com/.

Hirsh, Michael. 2013. "George W. Bush: He Gave Rise to the Tea Party." *National Journal*, October 3. https://www.nationaljournal.com/.

Hulse, Carl. 2013. "Boehner's Jabs at Activist Right Show GOP Shift." *New York Times*, December 13. http://www.nytimes.com/.

Hulse, Carl, and David M. Herszenhorn. 2008. "House Rejects Bailout Package, 228–205; Stocks Plunge." *New York Times*, September 30. https://www.nytimes.com/.

Jenkins, Jeffery A., and Charles Stewart III. 2013. *Fighting for the Speakership: The House and the Rise of Party Government*. Princeton, NJ: Princeton University Press.

Khimm, Suzy. 2012. "Boehner's Plan B, Explained." *Washington Post Wonkblog*, December 18. https://www.washingtonpost.com/.

Koger, Gregory. 2010. *Filibustering: A Political History of Obstruction in the House and Senate*. Chicago: University of Chicago Press.

Koger, Gregory, and Matthew J. Lebo. 2012. "Strategic Party Government and the 2010 Elections." *American Politics Research* 40:927–945.

———. 2017. *Strategic Party Government: Why Winning Trumps Ideology*. Chicago: University of Chicago Press.

Lizza, Ryan. 2015. "A House Divided." *New Yorker*, December 14. http://www.newyorker.com/.

Milbank, Dana. 2013. "Washington Is Selfie City." *Washington Post*, December 13. https://www.washingtonpost.com/.

Newhauser, Daniel. 2014. "The End of Debt Limit Brinkmanship? (Video)." *Roll Call*, February 11. http://www.rollcall.com/.

Nyhan, Brendan. 2009. "The Green Lantern Theory of the Presidency." *Brendan Nyhan*, December 14. http://www.brendan-nyhan.com/.

Nyhan, Brendan, Eric McGhee, John Sides, Seth Masket, and Steven Greene. 2012. "One Vote Out of Step? The Effects of Salient Roll Call Votes in the 2010 Election." *American Politics Research* 40:844–879.

O'Keefe, Ed. 2013. "Boehner: 'New tactical plan' on sequestration worked." *Washington Post,* March 28. http://www.washingtonpost.com/.

Parker, Christopher S., and Matt A. Barreto. 2013. *Change They Can't Believe In.* Princeton, NJ: Princeton University Press.

Peters, Jeremy, Ashley Parker, and Peter Baker. 2013. "Divide Narrows as Talks to Resolve Fiscal Crisis Go On." *New York Times,* October 11. http://www.nytimes.com/.

Peters, Ronald. 1996. "The Republican Speakership." Paper presented at annual meeting of the American Political Science Association, San Francisco, August 29–September 1.

Pew. 2013. "Pew Research Center for the People & the Press Poll, Oct. 2013: Do you approve or disapprove of the way . . . Republican leaders in Congress are handling negotiations over the government shutdown? [Q.05B]." *Pew Research Center,* October 6, http://www.people-press.org/.

Pierce, Emily. 2013. "Burr: 'Dumbest Idea' to Shut Down Government Over Obamacare." *Roll Call,* July 25. http://www.rollcall.com/.

Rogers, Hal. 2013. "Chairman Rogers Statement on the THUD Bill." Press release, *US House of Representatives Committee on Appropriations,* July 31. http://appropriations.house.gov/.

Rohde, David. 1991. *Parties and Leaders in the Postreform House.* Chicago: University of Chicago Press.

Shear, Michael D., and Jeremy W. Peters. 2013. "Senators Near Fiscal Deal, but the House Is Uncertain." *New York Times,* October 14. http://www.nytimes.com/.

Sinclair, Barbara. 1983. *Majority Leadership in the US House.* Baltimore, MD: Johns Hopkins University Press.

——. 1995. *Legislators, Leaders and Lawmaking.* Baltimore, MD: Johns Hopkins University Press.

——. 1999. "Transformational Leader or Faithful Agent? Principal Agent Theory and House Majority Party Leadership in the 104th and 105th Congresses." *Legislative Studies Quarterly* 24:421–449.

——. 2002. "The 60-Vote Senate." In *US Senate Exceptionalism,* edited by Bruce I. Oppenheimer, 241–261. Columbus: Ohio State University Press.

——. 2011. "Doing Big Things: Obama and the 111th Congress." *The Barack Obama Presidency: Appraisals and Prospects,* edited by Bert Rockman and Andrew Rudalevige. Washington, DC: CQ Press.

Strahan, Randall. 1996. "Leadership in Institutional and Political Time: The Case of Newt Gingrich and the 104th Congress." Paper presented at annual meeting of the American Political Science Association, San Francisco, August 29–September 1.

Weisman, Jonathan. 2012. "Boehner Cancels Tax Vote in Face of GOP Revolt." *New York Times,* December 20. http://www.nytimes.com/.

Weisman, Jonathan, and Ashley Parker. 2014a. "Boehner Is Hit from the Right on Overhaul for Immigration." *New York Times,* February 7. https://www.nytimes.com/.

———. 2014b. "House Approves Higher Debt Limit Without Condition." *New York Times*, February 11. https://www.nytimes.com/.

Williamson, Vanessa, Theda Skocpol, and John Coggin. 2013. "The Tea Party and the Remaking of Republican Conservatism." *Perspectives on Politics* 9:25–43.

Notes

1. In this election, House Democrats paid an electoral price for their overall level of partisanship (Koger and Lebo 2012) and especially for their support of the Affordable Care Act (Nyhan et al. 2012).

2. Indeed, the news of the day was the nineteen protest votes against Nancy Pelosi (D-CA) among the House Democrats (http://clerk.house.gov/evs/2011/roll002.xml).

3. Speakers also have influence over other committees. As Speaker, Boehner can influence assignments to most standing committees as a members of the Republican Steering Committee. Speakers also have nominal authority to assign bills to committees and to nominate conference committee members, although both these powers are constrained by rules and norms.

4. Like most bills, appropriations bills are vulnerable to a filibuster in the Senate. In practice, this means that supporters of a bill need a coalition of sixty or more senators to invoke cloture or end debate on a bill (Koger 2010; Sinclair 2002).

5. The fact that these tax cuts were scheduled to expire led to a confusing but fascinating debate over the meaning of the status quo in tax policy. Are tax cuts and tax hikes measured relative to the rates in place when the bills are written, or are they the rates that will take effect in the near future?

6. There were also four Democrats who voted against Pelosi. Twenty of the twenty-five nonvoters were Democrats.

7. This section was drafted by Barbara Sinclair.

8. Measures of association are significant but weak. Tau c for 112th = .18; for 113th, tau c = .17.

9. South includes border South as well as Deep South.

10. The Cook partisan voter index measures how the presidential vote in a congressional district in the previous two elections deviated on average from the nation as a whole (Cook Political Report, http://cookpolitical.com/).

11. This section is left as drafted by Barbara Sinclair.

CHAPTER TWO

Leaders and Partisanship in the Modern Senate

Steven S. Smith

Senate Democratic leader Harry Reid (D-NV) and Republican leader Mitch McConnell (R-KY) appeared together on *60 Minutes,* the CBS News magazine program, in late 2012. The theme of the segment was the broken Senate, and Reid and McConnell seemed to have been designated as the primary evidence. Steve Kroft, who interviewed the two senators together, reported, "It was very chilly. They did not look at each other once during the course of the interview. They kept saying 'my good friend, Harry' or 'my good friend, Mitch,' but it didn't seem very genuine" (Kroft 2012). No one who watched the two leaders on the Senate floor would be surprised. Their floor comments about the other party have been filled with acrimony and often bitterness.

These sometimes grim men reflect their long experience in a sometimes grim institution. The animosity between Reid and McConnell was often attributed to their exceptional personal partisan bias or limited professionalism. Personal factors always figure prominently in explaining the behavior of individuals, but I choose to focus on the political context in which Reid and McConnell operated. Political science has something to say about the effects of that context, and a close look at Reid and McConnell actually exposes the effects of that context to public view. In fact, the evidence suggests that Reid and McConnell have personal tendencies that would not lead us to predict that they would have been the distinctively partisan Senate leaders that they became. Instead, the political competition between the parties, the ideological polarization of the parties, and the institutional context of the Senate—its rules and practices—shaped their colleagues' expectations and the strategic challenges faced as party leaders.

The Political Personalities

Reid retired from the Senate at the end of 2016. By that time, he had served fourteen years as the Senate Democrats' leader, and McConnell was continuing to serve as the Republicans' floor leader after twelve years in the post. They seemed like hyperpartisan leaders who fit their parties well. That would be a surprise to observers of their early Senate careers. Each of them has a political history that is at least somewhat inconsistent with the roles they came to play.

Reid was an ambitious team player when he became leader in 2005, but he was not a senator expected to personify Senate liberalism. On the contrary, the senator from Searchlight, Nevada, is a surprise. First elected to the Senate in 1988, he was known as a probusiness social conservative who was somewhat out of step with most of his Senate Democratic colleagues. His predecessor as Democratic leader, Tom Daschle of South Dakota, was a charismatic, good-looking, and articulate floor leader who also was known at first as a quite moderate Democrat. After Reid supported Daschle for floor leader in 1994, Daschle appointed Reid to be cochair of the party's policy committee. Reid served as policy committee cochair from 1995 through 1998 and then as whip from 1999 through 2004. He was promoted to floor leader in 2005 after Daschle lost his bid for reelection in South Dakota by 4,508 votes. Reid became majority leader after his party gained a majority in the 2006 elections, which they held through 2014, and then served again as minority leader until he retired.

While his ambition and determination have been evident throughout his Senate career, Reid did not talk or look much like a national leader. Reid was always somewhat reserved and sometimes dour, tended to speak softly and even seemed to mumble, and smiled infrequently, at least in public settings. He seemed to be quite parochial. As whip, Reid acquired a reputation for an effective style—a reputation that carried over into his early years as floor leader. However, before becoming floor leader, he was not much of a spokesman for the party. He became appreciated for being a good listener; for carefully observing, recording, and accounting for his colleagues' interests and requests; and for being ideologically flexible.

At the time he was elected leader, Reid was a Senate insider but not a widely recognized liberal leader. Liberals had doubts about him. He adapted successfully. While he was never considered a deep thinker, Reid became known for his skill in identifying issues, compromises, and trades that won the support of his colleagues and kept his party unified. His colleagues reported that he recognized his own limitations and drafted into leadership roles colleagues whose talents complemented his own. He showed considerable deference to committee leaders, avoided the use of task forces to shape party policies and strategies, and preferred to let others take the lead in writing legislation.

The same can be said of Mitch McConnell as a conservative leader—a state-oriented senator with a strong ambition to be party leader. He became his party's whip in 2003, and after the retirement of Tennessee's Bill Frist in 2006, he became minority leader in 2007. After his party gained a Senate majority in 2014, he became majority leader.

Perhaps not as much of a surprise as Reid, McConnell nevertheless was known as a Washington insider, behind-the-scenes operator, and parliamentary expert. He gained this reputation through years of service on the Agriculture, Appropriations, and Rules and Administration Committees, later as chairman of the Rules and Administration Committee, and four years as Republican whip. Always conservative and more or less in line with his party, McConnell was known for championing opposition to restrictions on campaign fund-raising, a subject under the jurisdiction of the Rules and Administration Committee, for which he always received positive reviews among movement conservatives.

Nevertheless, McConnell was known as a deal maker and a guardian of Kentucky interests on his committees rather than as a leading conservative. He took pride in being a coauthor of bipartisan legislation on election reform and of controversial legislation that allowed the Food and Drug Administration to regulate tobacco products in exchange for federal buyouts of tobacco farmers. He also has been a Senate insider. Throughout his Senate career, McConnell has referred to Kentucky's Henry Clay, the Great Compromiser, as his model senator (C-SPAN 2012). In fact, some conservatives were dubious about McConnell's proclivity to deal making and compromise when he was elevated from whip to leader at the end of 2006.

In many respects, then, Reid and McConnell were cut from the same cloth but found themselves in different parties. Both were Senate insiders who lacked national visibility, and neither had presidential ambitions or prospects. Yet during most of the Obama presidency, McConnell was the face of minority obstructionism while Reid was the architect of majority procedural abuse. When party control of the Senate switched after the 2014 elections, it took only a few months for their roles to reverse. They are not the same people. They are team players whose paths moved in parallel, but neither of them was a leading ideologue as he took office as floor leader for his Senate party.

Their trajectory as partisan leaders did not take long to be conspicuous. In just a few years, their clashes on the Senate floor became routine and nearly legendary. In 2011, *The Onion*, the satirical newspaper, lampooned the pair with the headline, "Sources: Harry Reid Sleeping with Mitch McConnell's Wife in 1986 at Core of Senate Gridlock." The piece quoted an unnamed Republican staff member as saying, "I mean, what do you expect? Frankly, Mitch should have known better than to let Sherrill out of his sight in the first place. Harry was a real wolf back then."

In fact, news accounts about the two leaders indicate that their relationship was once good but soured over time. In 2011, they referred to each other as friends even during a period in which it looked to outsiders like their "relationship is one of unremitting hostility" (Bloomberg 2011). Their professionalism and pragmatism, many of their colleagues noted, kept the Senate operating and kept them from campaigning against each other's reelection efforts. In contrast, just after McConnell and Reid fashioned a compromise to avert a government shutdown that year, Reid observed that "the Republican leader's cooperation was essential to reach an accord," but then Reid added, "I've worked with McConnell for many years. That last bit has not been . . . [long pause] good." By the time they did a 60 *Minutes* interview in 2012, as Steve Kroft noted, the relationship was cool at best. In 2013, Reid went nuclear by forcing a change in the Senate's cloture threshold for presidential nominations. By that time, the two legislators regularly blamed each other for the partisanship and gridlock in the Senate, a blame game that went beyond the usual rhetorical flourishes one always can expect from congressional leaders (Alpert 2014; Easley 2014; Carney 2015). As the fall elections of 2014 approached, the *Las Vegas Sun* described their relationship as "a full-scale war." The article was entitled, "Keeping Score in the Senate Blame Game" (Philips 2014).

The Political Context

As their relationship deteriorated, it was natural for outside observers to blame Reid and McConnell personally for the political atmosphere in the Senate. Perhaps their personal limitations—their personalities, their skills, their intense partisanship—were the root cause of the sharply polarized parties and stalemate that came to characterize the Senate of the last two decades. The extreme version of this account was that all that Congress needed to reduce partisanship and get the legislative process back on track was better leaders. In the view of most scholars of congressional politics, this is an incorrect interpretation of events over the past few decades. Instead, there are important features of party politics that have changed that drive the strategies of Senate floor leaders and important features of the Senate that exacerbate partisanship even further.

Understanding the Reid–McConnell relationship requires a broader perspective. Congressional parties want to win legislative battles and gain or maintain majority status. The pursuit of these policy and electoral goals involves collective action and coordination problems that are addressed with organization and leadership. In fact, elections for leadership posts are largely about how those goals will be pursued. Complaints about leaders usually concern how a party should define and balance strategies to secure legislative goals and a Senate majority.

Three features of today's politics influence how leaders devise party strategy and deserve special attention (Smith and Gamm 2016).[1] Interparty competition for party control of the Senate drives much party strategy and at times motivates innovation in party organization and its leadership functions, which evolve to improve the capacity of a party to achieve collective goals. The distribution of policy preferences, especially factional politics within the majority party, complicates how legislative and electoral goals are defined and greatly influences how parties organize and operate. The Senate's rules limit the degree of majority party success and incentives for centralized leadership, intense interparty competition motivates organizational innovation that has a cumulative effect on a party's capacity, and the distribution of policy preferences shapes the aggressiveness of leaders in crafting the party's agenda and influencing senators. The institutional context (the Senate's rules and practices) sets rules of the game that rarely change, but when they do, they sometimes change in ways with important consequences.

Uncertain Majority Control

Interparty competition for control of the Senate is motivated by the partisan and individual advantages that come with majority party status. When control is in doubt, each party has a particularly strong incentive to improve its reputation and undermine the competition's reputation with voters. A congressional party can do this in a variety of ways: conspicuously supporting popular legislation and opposing unpopular legislation, forcing the other party to cast votes for unpopular legislation, intensifying messaging and other public relations efforts, and expanding fundraising and campaign operations. As electoral goals gain urgency, taking credit and attributing blame become higher priority activities.

Since 1980, party control of the Senate has almost always been in doubt, as Figure 2.1 suggests. Between 1959, when the Senate reached 100 seats for the first time, and 1980, the Democrats held the majority with an average of sixty-one seats. They fell to fifty-five only once. They lost their majority in the 1980 elections that brought Ronald Reagan to the White House and since then, largely because of seat losses in the South, remained a much smaller majority party when they were lucky enough to have a majority at all. In fact, since 1980, party control has changed seven or nine times, depending how we count the three changes associated with the 107th Congress (2001–2003), and the majority party conference has averaged just under fifty-four members, with a range of fifty to fifty-nine. This is an exceptionally long period of intense interparty competition for control of the Senate.

Polarized Parties

The effect of the distribution of policy preferences is characterized by the conditional party government thesis (Aldrich and Rohde 2001). The thesis is that legislators are elected on the basis of their policy or ideological outlooks. Polarized electoral parties—voters, party-oriented interest groups, party activists—will produce polarized parties in Congress. In turn, polarized congressional parties—internally cohesive parties with very different policy outlooks—centralize power in the hands

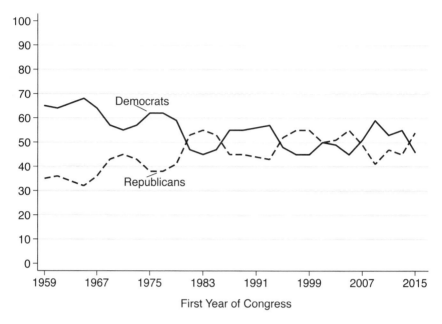

Figure 2.1. Percentage of Democrats and Republicans, US Senate, 1959–2016.

of party leaders. Great policy distance between the parties motivates a more concerted effort to win legislative battles, while like-minded partisans license party
leaders to aggressively pursue common policy goals. In contrast, intraparty factionalism on important issues can severely limit the majority party's strategic options,
produce opposition to strengthening central party offices, and create power-sharing
rather than power-concentrating organizational arrangements. Factionalism and
party polarization wax and wane with time, so the ability to sustain aggressive party
leadership will vary over time.

Senate parties, like House parties, are now more polarized than they were in the
1960s and 1970s. The record of roll-call voting is the most convenient way to show
this, but we must keep in mind that what comes to a vote and how legislators cast
their votes are subject to party strategies and influence. In Figure 2.2, I report how
the distribution of liberal–conservative scale scores has changed for Democrats and
Republicans for the period since the early 1970s. The considerable overlap of the
parties disappeared, the parties moved outward, and both parties are more cohesive. Republicans have moved considerably farther to the conservative side than
Democrats have to the liberal side, a pattern that can be found in several measures
of the overall voting record.[2]

Polarized parties do not emerge in a vacuum, of course. The partisan alignment
inside Congress primarily reflects the polarization of the organized interests, party

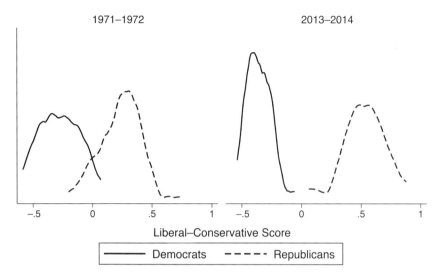

Figure 2.2. Liberal–Conservative Distribution of Senate Democrats and Republicans, 92nd and 113th Congresses. *Note:* DW-NOMINATE scores, by kernel density distributions (http://voteview.com/).

activists, and voter coalitions that put legislators in office. Those interests, activists, and many voters do not sit idle when a campaign ends on election. In fact, those political forces immediately mobilize to influence legislative activity more directly, dangling their future support and opposition. Both the campaign and legislative processes reflect the highly charged atmosphere that sharply polarized political coalitions generate.

Intense interparty competition for control of the Senate and deepened polarization between the parties have compounding effects. The desire to score political points against the opposing party can breed more party-line voting in both the attack and the response, making the parties appear even more polarized. When widening differences between the parties reduce the opportunities for compromise and make successful legislating unlikely, Senate parties will shift their emphasis to message politics and intensify their efforts to win elections. In both cases, a conspicuous consequence is more concerted party activity by the leaders, and their central role in setting collective strategy for their parties makes them appear more influential—and at times even the source of the interparty conflict.

Inherited Rules

There is a third factor, the institutional context of Senate policy making, that conditions the partisanship that we observe. The modern Senate has inherited rules and practices that give a large minority the ability to block most bills and success-fully oppose changes in the rules that the majority may want to impose in order to facilitate action on its legislative program. Most legislation can be blocked by filibusters, which forces the majority to find a three-fifths majority (sixty votes) to invoke cloture and get a vote on a bill. As Figure 2.1 shows, only one Senate major-ity since 1980, the Democratic majority for six months in 2009, had sixty members. The long-term condition of the Senate—now over thirty-five years—has been that a cohesive minority could block most legislation. This has encouraged the minority to obstruct majority action and has pushed the majority leader to pursue various parliamentary strategies by the majority. The move and countermove put the floor leaders in the middle of the action and intensify partisan frustration that leaders are expected to articulate.

Senate majority parties have considered changing the rules. While there are im-portant exceptions, changes in the rules can be filibustered by the minority, which means that efforts to enhance the majority leader's powers are seldom adopted. The majority party might give its leader more power over internal party matters, but majority party senators know that most cohesive minority parties can block their legislative proposals anyway.

Institutional rules do not change frequently, but when the rules do change, it can make a significant difference. The 1974 Budget Act set up important proce-dures that allow a simple majority to pass budget measures in both houses. The process encourages House and Senate majority parties to incorporate favored leg-islation in budget measures. In 2013, Senate Democrats forced a change in the interpretation of the cloture rule that allowed a simple majority of senators to close debate and get a vote on presidential nominations, with the exception of Supreme Court nominations. In 2017, Republicans extended simple majority cloture to Su-preme Court nominations. Nevertheless, the Senate minority remains in a position to block nonbudget legislation.

The Political Consequences

Over the long run, evenly matched, polarized parties, operating under the Senate's rules, can be expected to conduct the all-out war that the *Las Vegas Sun* described. Under those conditions, the Senate parties cannot be expected to act on major legisla-tion in the absence of a national consensus, but they can be expected to give winning more seats a higher priority than passing legislation. The relative emphasis shifts to symbolic moves—pushing legislation that has no chance of being enacted—to message politics—shaping public perceptions of one's own party and the other party—and to scoring political points—forcing embarrassing votes to be cast by the other side.

In this context, it is easy to see why Reid and McConnell seemed to be powerful forces behind the intense partisanship of Senate politics. As Reid and McConnell emphasized policy less and elections more, their behavior became more political, partisan, and visible and less compromising and cordial. Repeated over months and years, this can take a toll on personal relationships among senators, even between the two floor leaders who generally take professional pride in maintaining good relations with each other. Moreover, there is good reason to doubt that they could have retained their top leadership posts if they had not gone to battle with each other on behalf of their parties. This seems particularly true for McConnell, whose party moved to the right in the last two decades and whose party colleagues showed a willingness to obstruct the majority Democrats without his leadership.

Since the early twentieth century, modern leaders have managed their party organizations, devised floor strategy, built floor coalitions to win votes, served as intermediaries with the president, and acted as the leading spokespersons for their parties (Gamm and Smith, forthcoming). After the New Deal Congresses of the 1930s, and until the 1980s, Senate floor leaders took a backseat to committee chairs as the designers of major legislation and builders of majority coalitions (Davidson and Oleszek 1977). Known as the "era of committee chairman" and as the "textbook Congress," most policy initiative and responsibility for finding votes rested with committee chairs who managed nearly all important legislation. Party leaders served those chairs by arranging floor consideration for their bills and assisting chairs when requested, but leaders took the lead on only a few issues, usually those most important to a party's reputation, and had tiny whip organizations that often went unused. There have always been important exceptions, however, such as when Henry Cabot Lodge led the League of Nations fight in 1919–1920, but generally committee chairs and ranking minority members managed the legislation generated by their committees.

It is different today. Floor leaders are the chief strategists and agenda setters for the Senate. More than at any time since floor leadership in the early New Deal Congresses of the 1930s, party strategy drives the floor agenda and the minority response, floor leaders devise the legislative strategy and implement it, and those top leaders assume responsibility to sell the party's policy positions and parliamentary moves to the general public. Committee chairs take a backseat to the floor leaders.

In fact, by the time Reid and then McConnell became majority leaders, leaders were drawn into planning and executing annual plans for Senate action on nearly all major legislation. As party-oriented competition became more regular and intense and created more frequent parliamentary challenges on the floor leaders, their predecessors—Howard Baker (R-TN), George Mitchell (D-ME), Tom Daschle (D-SD), Bob Dole (R-KS), Trent Lott (R-MS), and Bill Frist (R-TN)—became more involved in negotiating unanimous consent agreements to gain action on bills and amendments, arranging deals about the substance of legislation, offering critical motions, and orchestrating negotiations with the president and House of Representatives. The details of legislation are still written by committee staff and the legislative counsel's office, but fewer outcomes on major bills are determined without significant involvement in shaping the policy and politics associated with the bills by the majority leader and often the minority leader.

The floor leaders do their jobs in an intense environment. The stakes are high, so their party colleagues develop strong views about party strategy and frequently find themselves at odds with each other about how to best balance the party's electoral and policy objectives. Leaders must manage these conflicts, which makes them even more central to the process. They are not always successful; their colleagues can insist on amendments, filibusters, and other moves on their own. In fact, for McConnell more than Reid, it appeared that the leader was drawn into more partisan tactics to stay in the lead as colleagues chose to challenge the other party on policy substance or procedure.

With these general considerations in mind, I turn to important features of Senate leaders' behavior. I focus on leaders' roles as policy leaders and floor strategists, as they interact with the president and represent their parties to the media and public. In each case, we find evidence of the influence of intense interparty competition, deep polarization, and Senate rules on the strategies that leaders pursue.

Service as Policy Leaders

As a general rule, leaders could not function if their own policy positions did not fit the central tendencies of their parties. This was labeled the "middleman thesis" following David B. Truman's contention, based on his observation of Senate leadership in the mid-twentieth century, that "location far from the center of the structure apparently is almost a disqualifying handicap to an incumbent or aspiring leader" (1959, 116). As Truman noted, there were exceptions to the rule, and, when that happened, it undermined the effectiveness of the leader.

In recent decades, during which the Senate parties have been competitive and polarized, a floor leader would be expected to assume responsibility for devising party strategy and advocating public policies that are in line with the preferences of most of his party colleagues. With the floor leader taking the initiative to use roll-call votes to score political points, the leader would naturally accumulate a voting record much like the rest of his party. An articulated policy outlook similar to most of his party colleagues would be the only way to maintain their confidence in the leader's strategic judgment and avoid challenges to his own election as leader.

For McConnell, the fit to his party was never a problem. The rightward shift of his party has made him appear more conservative than his predecessors as Republican senators from Kentucky, John Sherman Cooper and Marlow Cook. This was more of an issue for Reid, who started his Senate career on the more moderate side of the Democratic party, and he adjusted his voting behavior to fit his leader-

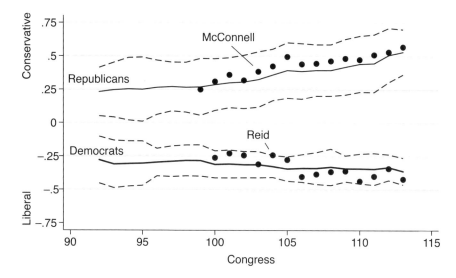

Figure 2.3. Liberal–Conservative Scores for McConnell, Reid, and the Parties, 1971–2016. *Note:* Means—solid lines; one standard deviation from mean—dashed lines; leaders—circles.

ship ambitions. The evidence in Figure 2.3 shows that the parties became more polarized as the Republicans, more than the Democrats, moved to a more extreme location. McConnell stayed near the average Republican as the party moved to the right. Reid, in contrast, moved from the conservative side to the liberal side of his party mean, with the break taking place in the 106th Congress (1999–2000), his first Congress as party whip. He stayed to the liberal side as floor leader. Like McConnell, he always was well within a standard deviation of his party's mean.

The same voting record underlies the party unity scores reported in Figure 2.4. Party unity scores capture the percentage of times a senator voted with his party on the subset of votes on which a majority of Democrats opposed a majority of Republicans. Both parties became more cohesive over the period since the early 1970s, although Republicans show some recent decline as a result of dissension on the most conservative side of their party. McConnell has always been supportive of his party, while Reid moved from being considerably less supportive of his party than the typical Democrat to being more supportive than average as he became whip in 1999.

As leaders, both McConnell and Reid were typical members of their conferences. We cannot explain their mutual antagonism as being out of line with their parties. They may have been leading or encouraging those differences, but it is probably most accurate to say that—however the agenda of floor amendments, bills, and procedural motions was constructed—the two leaders were nearly typical members of their parties in how they voted and have exhibited policy commitments that met the expectations of their colleagues.

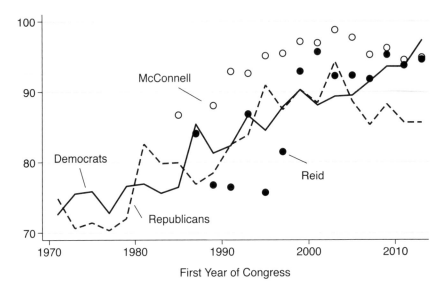

Figure 2.4. Party Unity Scores for McConnell, Reid, and the Parties, 1971–2014. *Note:* Means—solid lines; one standard deviation from mean—dashed lines; leaders—circles.

Service as Floor Generals

In the last two decades, the party leaders have played leading roles in the emergence of a syndrome of minority obstruction and majority-imposed limitations on debate and amendments that has changed the character of the Senate. The most conspicuous, and certainly important, development in the Senate is the deliberate, expansive obstructionism conducted by Senate minority parties and the responses of the majority party. This is a central theme of *The Senate Syndrome* (Smith 2014), in which I provide an extended discussion of the subject. I labeled this phenomenon a syndrome because it is a group of mutually reinforcing developments in Senate decision-making processes. Most senators and outside observers see this as an abnormal condition, a complex malady that involves the full exploitation of Senate rules and the deterioration of relations between senators of the two parties.

The rise of obstructionism as a minority strategy is well documented, but counting filibusters—or, more broadly, obstructionism—is not easy. It often takes the form of a hold or an objection to a unanimous consent request. It may or may not generate a cloture petition to close debate on a motion or measure. Nevertheless, the number of cloture petitions filed, usually by the majority leader, gives a general idea of the volume of obstructive tactics that the majority leader confronts in a Congress. A count of the number of cloture petitions filed for bills and for nominations and treaties is provided in Figure 2.5.

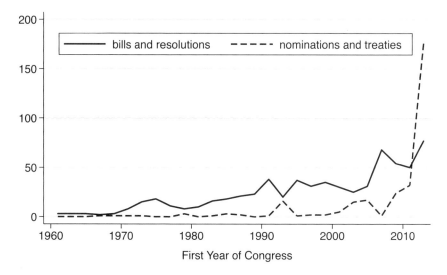

Figure 2.5. Number of Cloture Petitions Filed, 1961–2014. *Source:* US Senate (https://www .senate.gov/).

As the Senate moved from a few filibusters per Congress before the 1970s to several filibusters per Congress in the 1970s and 1980s, senators complained about the trivialization of the filibuster as obstructive tactics expanded to a larger range of issues. Over the course of the 1980s and 1990s, more obstruction occurred, but more often than not, the obstruction was initiated by minority party members other than the minority leader. In fact, there were times when the minority leader did not approve of the obstructive moves and other times when the minority leader seemed to join the filibuster only after it was initiated by colleagues who were not willing to let the leader take the lead. As I show in Figure 2.6, obstructive tactics became more common in the 1990s and early 2000s. Between 1995 and 2006, a period in which the Democrats were in the minority most of the time, a cloture petition related to legislation (as opposed to nominations) occurred about once every ten days of session. During this period, the majority leader, who had been the chief floor leader for his party for decades, became more intensely and proactively involved in managing the floor.

The frequency of minority obstructive efforts and formal majority responses reached even higher levels in recent Congresses. The number of days in sessions between cloture motions averaged five or six in the 2007–2014 period, when the Republicans were in the minority (Figure 2.6). During this period, the rhetoric of obstruction from the minority fully blossomed with use of the phrase "the sixty-vote Senate," which reflected the view, articulated frequently by McConnell, that reaching the cloture threshold was the normal standard for passing important leg-

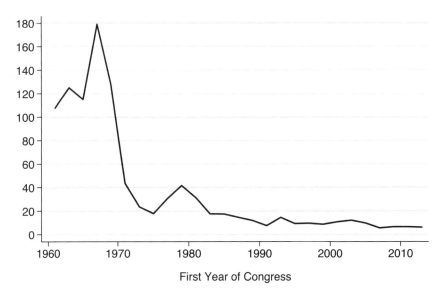

Figure 2.6. Number of Days in Session per Cloture Petition on Bills, 1961–2014. *Source:* US Senate and "Resume of Congressional Activities" (https://www.senate.gov/).

islation in the Senate. In 2007, for example, McConnell insisted that a Democratic senator's amendment to a defense authorization bill be allowed only if Democrats agreed that sixty votes would be required to pass it:

> What we have frequently done is simply negotiated an agreement to have the 60 votes we know we are going to have anyway, and the reason for that is—well, there are several reasons. No. 1, if a cloture vote were invoked, it would further delay consideration of the bill because potentially 30 more hours could be used post cloture on an amendment. So what we have done, in a rational response to the nature of the Senate in this era, is to negotiate 60-vote votes. . . . We are perfectly happy to enter into an agreement, as I suggested yesterday, for a vote on the Webb amendment and the alternative that we would have, the Graham amendment, by consent, two 60-vote requirements. That is not unusual in the Senate; it is just common practice in the Senate, certainly for as long as I have been here. (*Congressional Record* 2007)

McConnell was exaggerating how customary 60-vote thresholds had become in unanimous consent agreements by that time, as Reid was quick to observe: "It appears to me we are arriving at a point where, even on the Defense authorization bill, amendments leading up to a final vote on the Defense authorization bill, which is so important, are going to be filibustered. It is really wrong. It is too bad. We don't have to have this 60-vote margin on everything we do. That is some recent rule that has just come up in the minds of the minority" (*Congressional Record* 2007). Genuine debate was not McConnell's objective, of course, as the Republicans were quite willing to accept limited debate along with the sixty-vote threshold. In fact, McConnell was suggesting that the sixty-vote threshold be easy to apply, which would allow the minority to block the amendment without any responsibility for delaying other Senate business.

Deepening frustration with McConnell, who openly sought to slow down or block action on the Democrats' legislative agenda and President Obama's nominations, built over Obama's first term in office. In late 2013, Reid moved in a direction that he had refused to take for several years. If Reid had become a policy liberal, he remained a procedural conservative as leader, preferring to struggle under the inherited rules and practices of the Senate than to take drastic action to change them. This still was his view in early 2013, but broken promises of restraint on the Republican side and rising frustration on the Democratic side pushed him over the edge in the fall of 2013. He acquired enough support from his fellow Democrats to support his point of order that a simple majority may invoke cloture to overcome a filibuster on a presidential nomination to executive and judicial branch posts, with the important exception of nominations to the Supreme Court. This reform by parliamentary ruling violated at least the spirit of Rule 21, which requires a two-thirds majority to force a vote on a resolution to change the rules, but it was seen by Reid and nearly all Democrats as necessary to overcome continuing obstruction.

Reid's move rocked the Senate. For the first time, simple majority cloture became the effective rule for the Senate for an important class of business. Republicans complained loudly and forced Democrats to invoke cloture on nearly all nominations for the remainder of the 113th Congress (2013–2014), as Figure 2.5 shows. Nevertheless, after they gained a Senate majority in 2015, Republicans did not overturn the "Reid rule" and, after struggling with Democratic filibusters on key legislation in 2015, even created a task force to consider extending simple majority cloture to legislative business. At this writing, they have not moved on procedural reform, but there is considerable pressure on them from conservative groups and some House Republicans to do so.

Long before Reid's move in 2013, the majority leader had taken steps to respond to the obstructive strategy of the minority. For years, the primary response of the majority leader to minority obstruction was to work harder to acquire unanimous consent to limit debate and acquire votes on amendments and bills. Over the years, the majority leader, sometimes a Republican and sometimes a Democrat, occasionally responded by "filling the amendment tree." The term refers to offering a set of first- and second-degree amendments so that no other amendments may be offered until the Senate disposes of one or more of those amendments. The majority leader's right to be recognized to make a motion before other senators are recog-

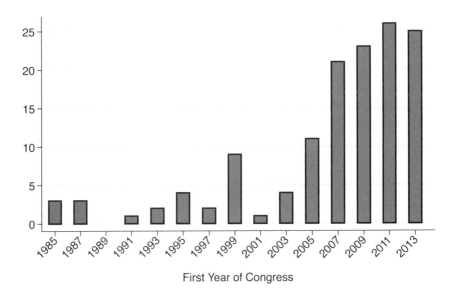

Figure 2.7. Number of Instances of Filling the Amendment Tree by Majority Leader or His Designee, 1985–2014. *Source:* Congressional Research Service, September 28, 2015. See note 2.

nized creates an opportunity for the leader to fill the tree, thereby preventing other amendments from being offered.

Like the filibuster, filling the tree was rare until recent decades. It is done by the majority leader, or sometimes by a bill manager, to freeze action on amendments. At a minimum, filling the tree temporarily prevents the consideration of amendments, which often includes minority senators' amendments that the majority party wants to avoid. In some circumstances, it gives the majority leader time to seek unanimous consent to limit the amendments that are considered and to limit debate so that final action of the bill can be acquired. If cloture has been invoked on a bill, filling the tree prevents the consideration of amendments while time for debate and amendments is exhausted, thereby blocking minority amendments.

Counting the number of instances of filling the amendment tree is prone to error because it is not a formally recognized action. Analysts at the Congressional Research Service do their best to respond to Senate requests for a count and have done a good job of searching for instances in which the majority leader, or his designee, offers a series of amendments in quick succession to fill the tree. Their count, summarized in Figure 2.7, was provided in a memo in September 2015 that was reported to have been distributed by Reid's office (Congressional Research Service 2015).

In response to the Democratic minority of the late 1990s and early 2000s, Republican leaders Lott and Frist filled the tree with some frequency, setting records for the time for the use of the tactic. Frist, most notably, turned to the tactic more often after the Gang of Fourteen, a group of seven Democrats and seven Republicans, blocked his threatened move to force simple majority cloture on judicial nominees in 2005. When the Republican minority ratcheted up obstructive action in the early Obama years, Reid doubled the use of the tactic. Many senators and other observers saw this as fighting fire with fire—the majority blocking minority proposals to gain some leverage when the minority exploits the rules to block majority bills. At times it looks like the majority party simply wants to avoid votes on controversial issues. It is all true. It also is true that the tactic contributes to gridlock, which is broken only with long delays, if at all.

When the syndrome of minority obstruction and majority response surfaces repeatedly, as it has in the last decade, it creates a backlog of legislation awaiting floor consideration. The majority party often is blamed for its inability to govern; it certainly is prevented from gaining much credit with the public for passing legislation to address the nation's problems. The minority party is sometimes noted for its obstructionism, but more often than not, the media has become so accustomed to the sixty-vote requirement that it notes the majority's failure more than the minority's obstructionism.

The result is that we get two parties that both behave like minority parties that have the primary objective of winning elections—deeply frustrated majority and minority parties that become fatalistic about accomplishing their legislative goals and turn to scoring political points against the other side as a primary short-term objective. This makes Senate politics look more purely partisan, as it is, and encourages senators to feed the public's cynicism with even more severe criticism of the other party and Washington.

Reid and McConnell are easy to blame for some of this. The full story is that they have tried to establish a truce and failed each time under pressure from Senate Republicans to oppose the Obama agenda. As majority leader, Reid negotiated two truces with McConnell that involved commitments to pull back from so much obstructionism by the minority and tree filling by the majority (Smith 2014, 242–254). Both efforts failed, and Reid retreated to protect Democratic political interests as best he could, but the pattern of obstruction and restriction continued.

At the beginning of the 114th Congress (2015–2016), McConnell, then majority leader, promised a return to "regular order," and for a time the Senate had fewer cloture votes and fewer instance of filling the amendment tree than in other recent Congresses. By the time the second session started in 2016, the Senate fell back to its old patterns. By August 2016, 118 cloture motions on legislation had been filed, and cloture had been successfully invoked over fifty times, on par with other recent Congresses. Through September 2015, the amendment tree was filled eleven times, on pace to be at least as frequent as the previous few Congresses.[3] Throughout the Congress, demands from rank-and-file partisans for the partisan moves were conspicuous.

Service as Intermediaries with the President

In this era, the out-party leader is highly constrained in working with the president to overlook legislative obstacles on major legislation. The House and the president are ever-present elements of political calculations in the Senate. Elected floor leaders serve as the primary liaison for their parties with leaders of the other chamber and with the president. In the case of the president, the most visible political actor in America and the chief lightning rod for partisan politics, relations with the president become a particularly sensitive matter for the out-party congressional leaders. In a hyperpartisan era, this relationship becomes even more delicate. A leader with close ties to an opposite-party president might be held in suspicion. Relations between a Senate leader and a president of the same party always are important and generally are cordial and supportive of each other. Relations between a Senate leader and a president of the other party are far more varied. This has been true for Reid and McConnell, whose relationships with a president of the opposite party ranged from toxic to nonexistent.

Reid became floor leader while President George W. Bush was starting his fifth year in office. It did not take long for the *New York Times* to report that the relationship between Reid and Bush was in the "deep freeze." The *Times* reporters averred that "not since 1919, when Henry Cabot Lodge called Woodrow Wilson 'the most sinister figure that ever crossed the country's path,' has a Senate majority leader appeared to harbor such deep and utter disdain, even loathing, for a president, as Mr. Reid does for Mr. Bush" (Herszenhorn 2007). That seems about right.

McConnell's relationship with President Obama was only slightly better. Many Republicans blame Obama for failing to put much effort into reaching out to them. In 2010, Senator Lamar Alexander (R-TN) observed that "the lack of the most elemental relationship between the president and the Minority Leader plays out day after day after day" (Pierce 2010). Private meetings were relatively uncommon, but given the obstructionist legislative strategies that the Senate Republicans pursued, it is not clear what purpose would have been served by more meetings called by the president. McConnell, after all, was frequently and openly masterminding Senate Republican strategy against most major administration proposals. By the time the Republicans won a Senate majority in 2014, six years into the Obama presidency, McConnell appears to have met alone at the White House with the president only once (Horowitz 2014).

Still, details matter. During the Obama years, the spear point of Republican strategy was often driven by House Republicans and their right wing. While senators like Jim DeMint (R-SC) and Ted Cruz (R-TX) sometimes set the agenda for conservatives, the Tea Party Republicans of the House pushed their conference to use the leverage of the House to (attempt) to force Senate Democrats and the president to accept conservative policies in exchange for passing spending bills or debt limit increases. McConnell found a formula that worked for him: he did not openly challenge fellow partisans in the House, holding back from committing to a course of action in the early stages of these episodes. Then, at the eleventh hour, he stepped in to construct a compromise solution, sometimes with the help of discussions with Vice President Joe Biden, that would pass the Senate and the House under emergency conditions. This was the pattern for a 2010 agreement to extend the Bush-era tax cuts, a 2011 pact to raise the debt ceiling, a New Year's Eve bargain in 2012 that averted the so-called fiscal cliff, the 2013 appropriations crisis over killing Obamacare, and the 2015 appropriations crisis over funding for Planned Parenthood. McConnell's strategy allowed him to avoid direct conflict with Tea Party forces while, at least on the Senate side of the Capitol, reducing the harm to the party's reputation. His strategy was not the product of good relations with the president.

While the Reid–Bush relationship was less civil than the McConnell–Obama relationship, the outcome was about the same. Personal limitations and eventually interpersonal animosities surely had something to do with these unproductive relationships. Nevertheless, it seems likely that these relationships were heavily influenced by the political fundamentals that I have emphasized. Party competition for control of the institutions of government and the polarized policy stances of presidents and the Senate parties sharply limited the opportunities for cooperation and encouraged both parties to engage in blame attribution as a basic strategy.

Majority Leader McConnell's response to the death of Supreme Court Justice Antonin Scalia in February 2016 seems to prove the point about how a leader relates to a president and addresses policy and electoral goals in a supercharged, partisan environment. About an hour after the justice's death was confirmed, McConnell announced that the Republican Senate would not consider any Obama nominee for the post. Two factors may have been at play. First, just a few months earlier, Speaker of the House John Boehner was pushed by Tea Party Republicans to resign from his office, and many of them considered McConnell a liability too. Taking a lead on the Scalia replacement issue assured Republicans that McConnell would not be facilitating the confirmation of Obama's nominee. Second, it seems likely that most Senate Republicans would eventually vote against an Obama nominee, which might not be popular by the time it happened, so killing the confirmation process early would end the matter early. For the eventual nominee, McConnell gave no additional advice to the president, and consent to the nomination was withheld.

Service as Party Spokesman

Public relations and salesmanship have long been considered a component of the floor leader's job. Formal statements to the press were issued in the 1910s, conversations with the small Capitol press corps were common, and by the mid-twentieth century, floor leaders' press conferences, usually held on the Senate floor before daily sessions began, were regularized. These developments were important, but not until more recent decades did leaders have staff dedicated to press or media relations (Gamm and Smith, forthcoming).

In recent decades, leaders and their parties have greatly expanded the staff and technology dedicated to public relations. These efforts have become intense. The Democratic leader's public relations effort is called the "war room," and that effort has been replicated by the Republicans. The label captures the flavor of today's Senate messaging politics. Created in late 2004 as a rapid response team of senators and staff, the effort was another step in a longer-term process of expanding party public relations staffs and their technology. This time, however, it reflected a transition of some importance: Reid's rise to minority leader and his effort to meld the legislative and messaging operations to strengthen the minority party's ability to compete with the Republican majority and president. When Reid wanted to reward Chuck Schumer (D-NY) for chairing the campaign committee for the 2006 cycle, which brought a new Democratic majority, he put Schumer in charge of the war room (Dewar 2004; Toner 2005). Republicans soon followed. The Republican effort was initiated in 2006 by Jim DeMint, who believed that his background in marketing made him a good leader for the effort. DeMint's efforts were expanded when McConnell took over for Frist at the end of 2006 (Bolton 2006, 2007; Billings 2007).

The war room efforts were designed to bring the techniques of modern election campaigns into the legislative process. In fact, the term "war room" was borrowed from the label given to the Clinton Little Rock headquarters during the 1992 presidential campaign. The designed effect of the Reid and McConnell initiatives was to serve the legislative and electoral goals of each party by getting an early start on public relations efforts, increasing the pace of messaging, and improving the coordination of party messaging, all intended to more fully integrate the messaging effort with legislative activity. The less intended effect was to sharpen partisan attacks and deepen the partisan divide.

The parties have funded their expanded operations with public dollars provided in the annual legislative appropriations bills. It is not easy to separate staff among the multiple staff functions of scheduling and clerical assistance, policy and political advising, and public relations, but the categories provided in the appropriations bills give some idea about where the money goes. Figure 2.8 shows the growth in major categories of Senate party spending. The parties split the funding evenly.

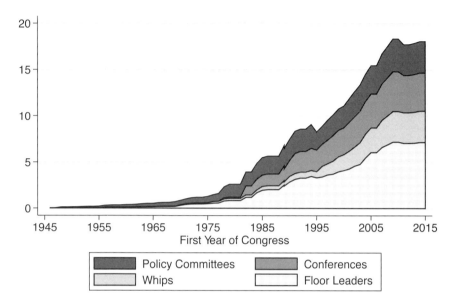

Figure 2.8. Spending on Senate Parties, 1945–2015 (in millions of dollars).

Senate parties were slow to acquire staff, but there has been a surge in spending on party operations since the 1980s. The first party staff were the floor assistants of the 1920s and 1930s. In 1944, the Republican policy committee under Robert Taft added a professional staff member. Not until the 1970s did the parties have more than minimal staff. Since that time, party funding and staffs have grown under both Democratic and Republican majorities. Spending caps have limited growth in the most recent Congresses.

Concluding Observations

In practice, the process of intensifying interparty competition and party polarization is usually not symmetric. In recent decades, Republicans moved farther to the right than Democrats moved to the left, led the way in making obstruction an everyday tactic in the early 1990s, responded to Democratic filibusters by filling the amendment tree more often before McConnell became leader, and took filibustering to a new level after losing their majority in the 2006 elections. Rank-and-file Republicans, many coming from the House, insisted on aggressive parliamentary strategies, and McConnell, sometimes struggling to stay in the lead of his party colleagues, became closely associated with the no-compromise strategy.

Reid took up the challenge, to be sure. Democrats were not bashful about filibustering Bush-era legislation and some nominations, but Republican took proce-

---

dural warfare to a new level in the Obama years. As majority leader during the first six years of Obama's presidency, Reid's were counterpunches. After his party lost its majority in the 2014 elections, he proved quite willing to force supermajority cloture on most important measures.

If Republicans led the move to more obstructive parliamentary strategies, Democrats tended to lead in organizational innovations as the minority party and then the out-party during much of the 1990s and early 2000s. Reid was central to the process. Daschle appointed Reid cochair of the party's Policy Committee in 1995, and Reid expanded the party's staff and technical capabilities. As leader, he oversaw the expansion of the campaign committee staff and later facilitated the creation of the war room operation. He created a new leadership post for Senator Chuck Schumer, who took the lead in the war room effort.

The forces behind the behavior of Reid and McConnell extend well beyond the Senate, but the competition between the parties and their diverging ideological outlooks drives the day-to-day developments that I have described here. In response to interparty competition, the parties have expanded their organizational capacity in ways that are unlikely to be reversed. Neither party has incentive to unilaterally disarm, even if it should be lucky enough to experience firm majority control of the Senate over many Congresses. The result is that the staff and technological machinery of the party tend to increase monotonically over time.

In contrast, political scientists have observed that reliance on strong party leaders tends to wax and wane with the polarization of the parties. In today's Senate, however, intense, long-term interparty competition for control of the Senate occurs simultaneously with polarized parties to produce exceptionally partisan politics that are an obstacle to legislating and a stimulant to a permanent campaign. Reid and McConnell are more than bit players, but their contributions have come primarily in the form of innovations and strategies that serve the interests of their parties. Those interests, which have become stronger and more homogenous in the last two or three decades, drive leaders' strategies far more than those strategies generate stronger and more homogeneous parties.

References

Aldrich, John H., and David W. Rohde. 2001. "The Logic of Conditional Party Government: Revisiting the Electoral Connection." In *Congress Reconsidered*, 7th ed., edited by Lawrence C. Dodd and Bruce I. Oppenheimer. Washington, DC: CQ Press.

Alpert, Bruce. 2014. "Senate Continues Blame Game on Stalled Keystone Pipeline Bill." *Nola*, June 25. http://www.nola.com/.

Baker, Richard A., and Roger H. Davidson. 1991. *First Among Equals: Outstanding Senate Leaders of the Twentieth Century*. Washington, DC: Congressional Quarterly.

Billings, Erin. 2007. "Parties Step Up Floor Messages." *Roll Call*, April 24.

Bloomberg. 2011. "Reid Friendship with McConnell Helps Bridge Gap between Parties." *Bloomberg*, January 19. http://www.bloomberg.com/.

Bolton, Alexander. 2006. "DeMint Starts Hitting Back." *The Hill*, March 22.

———. 2007. "Senate GOP Begins Repair of Messaging." *The Hill*, January 17.

Carney, Jordain. 2015. "Reid Blames McConnell for 'Manufactured' NSA Crisis." *The Hill*, May 31. http://thehill.com/.

Congressional Record. 2007. "Daily Digest, Page S8918." *Congressional Record*, July 10. https://www.congress.gov/.

Congressional Research Service. 2015. "Annual Breakdown of Instances in Which Opportunities for Floor Amendment Were Limited by the Senate Majority Leader or His Designee Filling or Partially Filling the Amendment Tree, 1985–2015." *Scribd*, September 28. https://www.scribd.com/.

C-SPAN. 2012. "US Senator Mitch McConnell on Henry Clay" (video). *C-SPAN*, September 6. https://www.c-span.org/.

Davidson, Roger H., and Walter J. Oleszek. 1977. *Congress Against Itself*. Bloomington: Indiana University Press.

Dewar, Helen. 2004. "Democrats Planning Watchdog Role." *Washington Post*, December 14.

Easley, Jason. 2014. "Mitch McConnell Blames Democrats for His Years of Senate Obstruction." *Politicus USA*, December 23. http://www.politicususa.com/.

Gamm, Gerald, and Steven S. Smith. Forthcoming. *Steering the Senate*. New York: Cambridge University Press.

Herszenhorn, David M. 2007. "Reid's Chilly Relationship with Bush Enters a Deep Freeze." *New York Times*, December 19. http://www.nytimes.com/.

Horowitz, Jason. 2014. "GOP Leader's New Role Could Take Strained White House Ties to Next Level." *New York Times*, November 6. http://www.nytimes.com/.

Jones, Charles O. 1976. "Senate Party Leadership in Public Policy." In *Policymaking Role of Leadership in the Senate*. Compilation of papers prepared for the Commission on the Operation of the Senate, 94th Cong., 2d Sess. Washington, DC: Government Printing Office.

Kroft, Steve. 2012. "An Exasperating Interview with Senate Leaders" (video). *CBS News, 60 Minutes Overtime*, November 4. http://www.cbsnews.com/.

Munk, Margaret. 1974. "Origin and Development of the Party Floor Leadership in the United States Senate." *Capitol Studies* 2:23–41.

Oleszek, Walter J. 1971. "Party Whips in the United States Senate." *Journal of Politics* 33:955–979.

Onion. 2011. "Sources: Harry Reid Sleeping with Mitch McConnell's Wife in 1986 at Core of Senate Gridlock." *The Onion*, January 5.

Philips, Amber. 2014. "Keeping Score in the Senate Blame Game." *Las Vegas Sun*, June 8. https://lasvegassun.com/.

Pierce, Emily. 2010. "McConnell's Relationship with Obama to be Tested." *Roll Call*, November 15. http://www.rollcall.com/.

Riddick, Floyd M. 1971. "Majority and Minority Leaders of the Senate: History and Development of the Offices of the Floor Leaders." 92nd Cong., 1st sess. S. Doc. 92-42.

Ripley, Randall B. 1969a. *Majority Party Leadership in Congress.* Boston: Little, Brown.

———. 1969b. *Power in the Senate.* New York: St. Martin's Press.

Rothman, David J. 1966. *Politics and Power: The United States Senate, 1869–1901.* Cambridge, MA: Harvard University Press.

Smith, Steven S. 1993. "Forces of Change in Senate Party Leadership and Organization." In *Congress Reconsidered*, 5th ed., edited by Lawrence C. Dodd and Bruce I. Oppenheimer. Washington, DC: Congressional Quarterly.

———. 2014. *The Senate Syndrome: The Evolution of Procedural Warfare in the Modern US Senate.* Norman: University of Oklahoma Press.

Smith, Steven S., and Gerald Gamm. 2016. "The Dynamics of Party Government in Congress." In *Congress Reconsidered*, 11th ed., edited by Lawrence C. Dodd and Bruce I. Oppenheimer. Washington, DC: CQ Press.

Thompson, Charles Willis. 1906. *Party Leaders of the Time.* New York: G. W. Dillingham.

Toner, Robin. 2005. "Demands of Partisanship Bring Change to the Senate." *New York Times*, May 20. http://www.nytimes.com/.

Truman, David B. 1959. *The Congressional Party: A Case Study.* New York: Wiley.

Notes

1. For background on the history of Senate party leadership, see Baker and Davidson (1991), Munk (1974), Oleszek (1971), Riddick (1971), Ripley (1969a, 1969b), Rothman (1966), Smith (1993), and Thompson (1906).

2. The figure is based on DW-NOMINATE scores calculated separately for each Congress (that is, without a linear trend built in for individual legislators as in normal DW-NOMINATE scores). Similar patterns for the parties are found using normal DW-NOMINATE or common space scores (http://voteview.com/).

3. By March 2016, cloture had been filed on presidential nominations only twice. The Democratic minority, of course, supported action of President Obama's nominees; the Republican majority did not have to filibuster to delay action on nominations.

CHAPTER THREE

A President's Decisions and the Presidential Difference

Matthew N. Beckmann

Entering office in the depths of the Great Recession, Barack Obama launched a multifaceted policy offensive aimed at reviving the economy. This initial legislative blitz included a major stimulus package, bailing out domestic automakers, and revamping financial and banking industry regulations, which also reformed student loan programs, credit card rules, and statutes for litigating gendered wage discrimination. None of these bills sailed to passage effortlessly, but buoyed by large Democratic majorities on Capitol Hill, President Obama signed each into law during his first year. The key planks of his economic agenda set, President Obama pivoted to his top priority: health care. His campaign promise was an ambitious one: "to finally keep the promise of affordable, accessible health care for every single American" (Obama 2008).

While the policy stakes were obvious for all to see, so too were the political risks. In fact, chastened by his predecessors' (many) failed attempts to enact universal health care in America, President Obama adopted a compliant approach to Congress, eagerly negotiating with Republican senators Charles Grassley (R-IA), the ranking member on the Senate Finance Committee, and Olympia Snowe (R-ME), one of the Senate's few remaining centrists. This bipartisan outreach continued for months but showed little to no progress. Then, in September 2009, Senator Grassley withdrew altogether: "I don't think it's going to be possible to work it out with the administration" (Benen 2009). Senator Snowe eventually did the same.[1]

As prospects for building a bipartisan coalition withered, the White House focused on corralling Democrats. This proved a comparatively easy assignment in the House, which adopted a rule limiting debate and amendments before passing its version of the Affordable Care Act, 220–215. All eyes then turned to the more imposing congressional hurdle, the Senate (filibuster). After considerable arm-twisting and some horse trading, all sixty Democratic-affiliated senators overcame a Republican filibuster on December 23, 2009, before formally passing their bill the next day. Although important work reconciling the House and Senate editions remained, the sense on both ends of Pennsylvania Avenue was that the biggest obstacles were conquered. Obamacare, it seemed, was headed to its namesake's desk.

Then, on the eve of Barack Obama's one-year anniversary as president, a special election to fill late senator Ted Kennedy's long-held seat flipped the script. Republican Scott Brown won—a Republican . . . in Massachusetts . . . comfortably. The next day's *New York Times* headline captured the reaction: "GOP Senate Victory Stuns Democrats." Actually, worse for Democrats than the shock of the election was the reality that their filibuster-proof Senate coalition was gone; Brown promised to oppose Obamacare at every turn.

After the Massachusetts election, President Obama reevaluated his options. In one ear was Rahm Emmanuel, the White House chief of staff, who argued that the president should pare back his demands to help ensure passage; in the other ear was Nancy Pelosi, Speaker of the House, who argued President Obama should recommit to far-reaching reform. The president eventually sided with the Speaker, a decision that was vindicated when Democratic leaders used parliamentary rules to circumvent another filibuster and pass the bill.

At the White House signing ceremony, Vice President Joseph Biden welcomed the audience and introduced the president. When President Obama reached the podium, Biden leaned over and whispered a personal message: "Mr. President, this is a big [expletive] deal" (Adams 2010). For those closest to the process, flagging President Obama's leadership as integral to enacting Obamacare was to state the obvious. After all, Barack Obama's involvement made the issue highly visible, his proposal structured the debate, his lobbying facilitated congressional passage, and his signature ultimately ushered the results into federal law.

Yet political scientists who study Washington politics are quick to question expansive claims of President Obama's influence. These scholarly critiques stem from basic empirical limitations: we cannot compare the world we observed with a counterfactual world in which things played out differently. There is no control group. As such, we cannot say definitively whether another president would have made different decisions, and even if he or she did, we cannot say definitively whether it would have made much difference.[2]

Because notions of leadership presume influence, a necessary precursor to appraising the former is to understand the latter. In this chapter, I revisit the nature of presidential influence using President Obama as an illustrative case. My basic thesis is the move from small-*n* qualitative to large-*N* quantitative analyses led researchers to underestimate what Fred Greenstein (2009) called "the presidential difference." This happens partly because quantitative tests typically combine blunt measures aggregated over some time frame on the models' left-hand side (i.e., dependent variables) with far better indicators of political context than presidential action on the right-hand side (i.e., independent variables). Thus tests of president-centered effects get operationalized as a version of the Great Man thesis, an implausible alternative that is readily rejected, $p < .05$.

In what follows, then, I first review the practical realities of presidential decision making, particularly its substantive breadth, programmatic ambiguity, and operational uncertainty. Focusing on presidential–congressional relations during President Obama's time in office, I then critique some of the widely utilized evidence (including mine) and analyses political scientists (including me) have used to infer that postwar presidents' individual impact is marginal at best. I conclude by envisioning how presidency research might better investigate the tenets of presidential leadership.

A President's Decisions

In the admittedly simplified legislative history above, we nonetheless observe President Obama make important decisions while pushing the Affordable Care Act—decisions on sequencing, on strategy, and on substance. Plainly, they are but a few of the many, varied important judgments Barack Obama has made to date:

- Facing ambiguous intelligence reports, a range of policy options, and a mix of advice, President Obama sent Seal Team Six to Abbottabad, Pakistan, on a secret mission to capture or kill Osama bin Laden. They did the latter.
- Since the Clinton presidency, military leaders adhered to the "don't ask, don't tell" policy, which barred openly gay, lesbian, or bisexual people from serving in the armed forces. With President Obama's encouragement, Congress enacted legislation repealing this prohibition, subject to the president certifying that the change would not harm military readiness. In July 2010, he issued that certification, and the ban was lifted.
- During his first term, President Obama nominated Sonia Sotomayor and Elena Kagan to fill vacancies on the Supreme Court. Both were confirmed. During his second term, President Obama nominated Merrick Garland, who was never confirmed.
- As commander in chief, President Obama managed the end of American combat operations in Iraq and Afghanistan while launching a military offensive in Libya and unprecedented unmanned drone strikes across Pakistan, Yemen, and Somalia.
- Overturning national policy toward Cuba since 1961, President Obama began easing travel restrictions, expanding international commerce, and formalizing diplomatic relations. The US embassy in Havana is now open, and travel to and from Cuba has surged.

Outside the White House, few people will make even one choice of such consequence, much less scores of them. For a president, however, rendering these sorts of high-stakes verdicts is standard fare. After hanging around President Obama for six months, what struck Michael Lewis most was the range and complexity of issues reaching the president's desk—which demand his decision, right away, so they could be publicly announced to the impatient reporters waiting outside. Lewis (2012) described the situation:

> But if you happen to be president just now, what you are faced with, mainly, is not a public-relations problem but an endless string of decisions. Putting it the way George W. Bush did sounded silly but he was right: the president is a decider. Many if not most of his decisions are thrust upon the president, out of the blue, by events beyond his control: oil spills, financial panics, pandemics, earthquakes, fires, coups, invasions, underwear bombers, movie-theater shooters, and on and on and on. They don't order themselves neatly for his consideration but come in waves, jumbled on top of each other.

Issues obviously vary in terms of their complexity, controversy, and consequence, and occasionally matters reaching the Oval Office are simple, consensual, or trivial. But those are exceptions. Former secretary of state Henry Kissinger noted that the president's inbox is filled with hard decisions, cases he dubbed "51/49 judgments." In an interview with Jake Tapper, President Obama described the job similarly: "The only things that land on my desk are tough decisions because if they were easy decisions, somebody down the food chain's already made them" (CNN 2013).

Implicit in such emphases on presidential decision making is the presumption that, first, different presidents would make different decisions, and second, different decisions would have important consequences. In other words, astute observers suppose presidents' decisions *cause* changes in the political process and/or policy outcomes. But are these presumptions about presidents' difference and impact justified?

The Presidential Difference

Establishing causal relationships is an onerous assignment, so it is understandable that social scientists get persnickety about causal claims. After all, the foremost obstacle to demonstrating cause and effect is not showing that two variables are correlated; rather, it is doing the painstaking work needed to winnow the myriad reasons they could be. The evidence required to expunge rival hypotheses is always difficult to obtain, and it can prove more or less impossible when the causal agent is not randomly assigned.[3]

As presidency researchers know all too well, little about their subject matter approximates random assignment. Whether it is decision making or coalition build-ing, public appeals or legislative vetoes, presidents' actions are carefully studied, highly strategic, and quickly updated. What's more, White House advisers do not merely seek to maximize the president's actual effectiveness; they also work hard to maximize the perception of his effectiveness (Howell 2013; Kumar 2010). This blurred line between sincere and revealed preferences further complicates research-ers' ability to estimate if (or when) presidents get what they *really* want.

Still, the fact that presidency researchers cannot attain laboratory-like con-trol does not mean we cannot achieve greater understanding through systematic research.[4] If anything, the inherent empirical challenges mean political scientists who study the presidency must be especially vigilant about the research designs we deploy, clear about the evidence we analyze, and cautious about the inferences we draw. In *The Presidential Difference* (2009), Fred Greenstein offers a noteworthy exemplar. What makes elements in Greenstein's analysis so gripping is not his anal-ysis of what postwar presidents have done; instead, it is his analysis of what other plausible presidents would have done facing the same decisions, under the same circumstances, and given the same information. Put differently, Greenstein offers several thought experiments that take the experimental metaphor seriously.

For example, Greenstein reviews the policy options presented to Lyndon John-son as communist forces advanced against the US-backed South Vietnamese gov-ernment. National security advisers posited the primary alternatives were to "salvage what little can be preserved with no major addition to our present military risks" or "use our military power in the Far East to force a change of communist pol-icy" (2009, 2). Knowing President Johnson chose the latter, Greenstein examines a critical counterfactual: What if Hubert Humphrey had been president instead of Lyndon Johnson? What Greenstein shows is that Humphrey not only preferred diplomacy to military deployment but also that he had forcefully expressed those views in a contemporaneous memo to President Johnson. Greenstein thus con-cluded, "Would a President Humphrey have taken a different course of action than Johnson? The answer is unknowable, but it is probable that he would have" (2).

A comparable thought experiment comes with the 2000 presidential election. Although George W. Bush ultimately prevailed over Al Gore, the election was decided by a few hundred (contested) votes in which minor changes to arbitrary factors would have reversed the outcome (Wand et al. 2001). In short, the 2000 election outcome was effectively decided by random chance. Yet after his inaugura-tion, President Bush explicitly shunned calls to seek consensus and instead forged ahead with his agenda. He began by pushing large tax cuts; then, after the terrorist attacks on September 11, 2001, led a national response that included a war in Iraq, permitting torture overseas, and greatly expanding surveillance operations inside the United States. At each turn and in real time, Al Gore opposed President Bush's policy decisions. Parroting Greenstein's verbiage, we wonder: Would a President

Gore have taken a different course of action than Bush 43? The answer is unknowable, but it is probable that he would have.

What makes these sorts of in-depth case studies so compelling is that they offer credible counterfactuals in which comparable politicians, facing the same decision at the same time, reached divergent conclusions. Per Greenstein's meticulous look at the evidence available, it seems unambiguous that a President McGovern would have differed from President Johnson on Vietnam, with dramatic effect, just as it seems clear a President Gore would have differed from President Bush 43 on Iraq with obvious and important consequences. It is not hard to imagine scores of equivalent comparisons would produce scores of similar conclusions.[5]

However, when it comes to saying definitively whether a particular president mattered even in seemingly clear-cut cases, Greenstein aptly acknowledges, "the answer is unknowable." In reality, there is only one president at a time, which is why even careful conjectures cannot satisfy the demanding experimental standard: holding all other things equal. What is more, utilizing fine-grained case studies like those Greenstein uses, just as thorny as the questions of internal validity (establishing causation) are those related to external validity—that is, saying whether inferences in specific cases generalize to other presidents, decisions, contexts, domains, and so on.

Seeking to assuage the inferential drawbacks small-n case studies present, presidency scholars purposefully migrated toward large-N research designs that utilized systematic sampling strategies, explicit coding rules, and precise statistical tests (Edwards and Wayne 1983; Edwards, Kessel, and Rockman 1993; Ragsdale 2008). Whether it was presidents' impact on public opinion (Edwards 2003; Waterman, Silva, and Jenkins-Smith 2014), the media (Edwards and Wood 1999), federal lawmaking (Bond and Fleisher 1990; Edwards 1989), or executive actions (Howell 2003), the results of these quantitative analyses dramatically reshaped the scholarly consensus. For instead of highlighting the president's will and skill as decisive, this subsequent scholarship supported Richard Neustadt's reflections in the last edition of his canonical study: "Presidential weakness was the underlying theme of *Presidential Power*. That remains my theme. . . . Weakness is still what I see: weakness in the sense of a great gap between what is expected of a man (or someday a woman) and assured capacity to carry through" (1960, ix).

Clarifying that presidents cannot meet citizens' heroic expectations or pundits' unrelenting demands has become standard grist for political scientists operating in the public sphere. In a *Monkey Cage* entry entitled "What Difference Will President Obama's Speech Make?" John Sides (2009) answered bluntly: "If history is any guide, not much." Likewise, Brendan Nyhan coined the "Green Lantern theory of the presidency" to scold analysts who presume the only thing restraining presidents' influence is willpower (or lack thereof).[6] Happily, these scholarly lessons are now percolating outside the academy; more and more journalists now invoke academic research to tamp down overhyped, overpersonalized depictions of presidential power.

Yet even as correcting Great Man theories of a president's influence is an important public service, rejecting an unrealistic null hypothesis teaches us only so much. More valuable still is discovering the mechanisms that animate an individual president's action and influence. To that end, the case against the president-centered thesis is less conclusive than often portrayed. The reason is previous insights have frequently been reduced to little more than metaphorical straw men, which are then tested against amorphous standards in the context of an imprecise statistical model: Is a dummy variable for Lyndon Johnson's legislative success positive and statistically significant? Is a dummy variable for Ronald Reagan's approval rating positive and statistically significant?

As a first step to reconsidering individual-level factors' significance on presidential decision making and influence, let me first focus attention on a venue where president-centered theories have been especially degraded: presidential influence in Congress.

Testing the Presidential Difference in Lawmaking

Among the presidency subfield's most researched topics is presidents' influence in Congress. This richness partly indicates the importance of national lawmaking, but it also reflects the fact that Capitol Hill offers fertile turf for abstract theories and statistical analyses. The legislative process' high stakes, savvy players, and clearly defined rules make abstract presidency-centered theories especially applicable; the array of votes and laws facilitate systematic quantitative comparisons president to president, Congress to Congress, year to year.

Of course, the very features that make presidential–congressional relations especially suitable to parsimonious theories and statistical tests also mean presidents' individual traits and interpersonal relationships are unlikely to provide much explanatory power. In his wonderful study of presidential vetoes, Charles Cameron (2000; see also Canes-Wrone 2009) argued that the context of presidential–congressional bargaining means institutional designs and political incentives leave less room for presidents' individual discretion and impact.[7] I paraphrased Cameron's point and then went further: "One question relevant here is how much of reputed skill is really a post-hoc construction?" (Beckmann 2010, 147). We are hardly the first academics to question whether skill is a significant factor in predicting presidential success on Capitol Hill (Bond and Fleisher 1990; Edwards 1989).

Considering the relative unimportance of president-centered variables for explaining presidential–congressional relations, studying postwar presidents' legislative records offers a nice window to look at the evidence underlying the inference. Let me now briefly review two of the most popular measures: presidential success on key roll-call votes and new laws.

Key Votes

Since 1953, CQ *Weekly* staffers have combed through congressional goings-on to identify those roll-call votes that comprise "a matter of major controversy, a test of presidential or political power, and a decision of potentially great impact on the nation and on lives of Americans" (CQ *Weekly* 2007, 60). The resulting assemblage yields each chamber's key votes for that year, which present nice properties for systematic research. In particular, these key votes offer standardized data on important issues in a format that permits statistical comparisons over time. Perhaps it is no surprise, then, that many political scientists appraised key vote indices as a good, albeit imperfect, indicator of presidents' legislative success (Shull and Vanderleeuw 1987).

Figures 3.1 and 3.2 display the percentage of time the president's stated position—yea or nay—prevailed on each year's sample of key votes for 1953 to 2013. Even at this elementary level, refutations to the simple president-centered theories become readily apparent. Neither the variations across presidencies (e.g., Johnson versus Carter), nor the ups and downs within each (e.g., Bush 2001 versus Bush 2007), nor the differences across chambers (e.g., 1986 House versus Senate) suggest that individual presidents' will and skill offer much explanatory power—on the contrary, familiar impressions of president-led lawmaking simply did not hold up to even the most rudimentary analyses.

On the other hand, each chamber's partisan composition is unambiguously related to presidents' success on key votes. Figure 3.3 plots the percentage of the president's fellow partisans in the House and Senate along with his corresponding annual key vote success rate. The bivariate trend in both chambers is clear: more

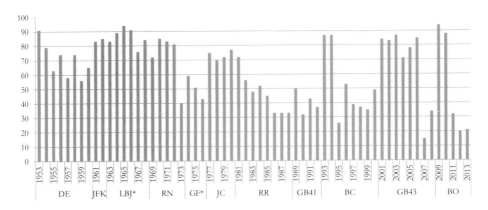

Figure 3.1. Presidential Success on Key Votes in the House of Representatives. *Source:* CQ *Weekly.* *Note:* Dependent variable: among House roll-call votes that CQ identified as "key" and the president's position was known, the percentage where the president's position prevailed. *LBJ and GF served only parts of the first year for which they are scored

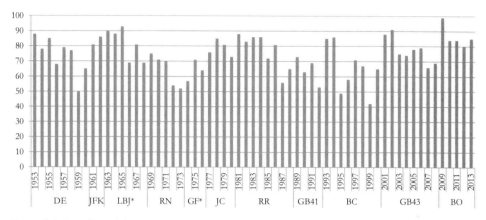

Figure 3.2. Presidential Success on Key Votes in the US Senate. *Source: CQ Weekly. Note:* Dependent variable: among House roll-call votes CQ identified as "key" and the president's position was known, the percentage where the president's position prevailed.
*LBJ and GF served only parts of the first year for which they are scored

presidential partisans equate to more presidential victories on key votes. Not surprisingly, this result is robust to adding additional covariates (e.g., years in office, approval rating, presidential skill) across a myriad of specifications. Jon Bond and Richard Fleisher thus conclude, "Only the Congress-centered variables have strong, statistically significant effects in both chambers" (1990, 225; see also Cooper and Brady 1981; Edwards 1980).

These analyses of roll-call voting pioneered systematic research on the presidency, and they led to much more accurate depictions about the nature of presidential influence—particularly its limits. George Edwards concludes, "Often outcomes that are popularly attributed to presidential leadership (positively or negatively) are actually products of other, more powerful forces structuring the environment of executive–legislative relations" (1989, 213). It is a lesson borne out time and again, even as new presidents come and go, and even as scores of additional votes extend the time series.

New Laws

Richard Neustadt famously proclaimed that a president's "impact on the outcome is the measure of the man" (1960, 4). As insightful as key vote analyses proved, ultimately outcomes matter most, and inasmuch as legislators' votes differ from legislative outcomes, the essential question of presidents' success in Congress remained unanswered. It is for this reason numerous political scientists have identified new laws as the crucial dependent variable.

Among those studying presidents' impact on legislative outcomes, the best

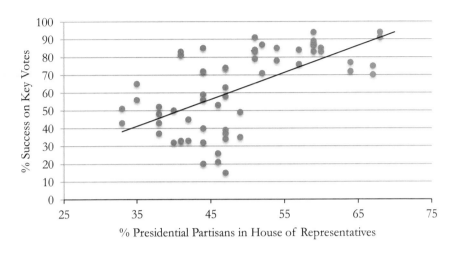

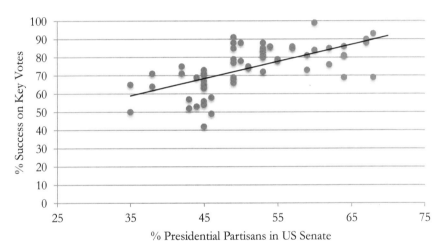

Figure 3.3. Presidential Success on Key Votes in the House and Senate, by President's Percentage of Fellow Partisans in the Chamber.

known is David Mayhew's influential research, introduced in *Divided We Govern* (2005) and developed further in *Partisan Balance* (2011). In the latter, Mayhew coded presidents' major proposals during the first two years of each term, along with an accounting of whether that proposal became law or not. Figure 3.4 relays Mayhew's score, "wins" and "losses," for major presidential proposals from Eisenhower to Bush 43.

Overall, Mayhew finds most major presidential proposals from the Eisenhower to Bush 43 administrations ended in a new law. However, as with the key vote studies,

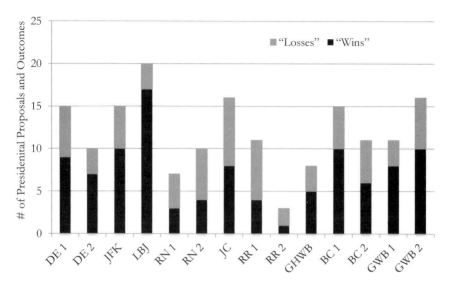

Figure 3.4. Number of Major Presidential Proposals Resulting in Legislative Wins and Losses, by President. *Source:* Mayhew (2011). *Note:* Dependent variable: presidents' major proposals (during the first half of each term) that resulted in a new law ("wins") or did not ("losses") during that term.

the outcome data refuted simple president-centered explanations of presidential–congressional relations. Actually, Mayhew's foremost takeaway about postwar lawmaking is that it plods along without much regard to the particular people, their partisan allegiances, or their policy agendas, even under divided government, and even amid extreme polarization. In this way, Mayhew's analysis supported Mark Peterson's: "During the presidencies of Eisenhower to Reagan, neither cooperation nor conflict has been the norm. Rather, both have characterized the institutional relationship, with instances of cooperation actually more common than instances of conflict" (1990, 99).

Although significant laws can (and do) pass during all presidencies, with a range of congressional combinations, across assorted political contexts, the match between a president's and lawmakers' partisanship and preferences produces the crucial explanatory variables. In fact, subsequent research has detailed how lawmakers' distribution of preferences (Brady and Volden 1998; Krehbiel 1998), leaders' control of the legislative calendar (Cox and McCubbins 1993, 2005), and partisans' electoral impulses (Groseclose and McCarty 2001; Lee 2009; Sinclair 2006) can expand or inhibit presidents' opportunities for passing legislation. So although laws may pass under a myriad of circumstances, Congress's composition predicts the degree of bargaining and compromises that will be required along the way. All of this suggests that Charles Jones's depiction of presidential–congressional relations remains apt: "When it comes to making laws in Washington . . . it is normally done with a substantial amount of cross-institutional and cross-partisan interaction through elaborate sequences featuring varying degrees of iteration" (1994, 273).

Presidency-Centered Influence

When it comes to presidents' legislative success on key votes and new laws, congressional variables have proven critical (albeit not dispositive). But the key question here is not whether congressional composition and political circumstance constrain presidents; they do. Rather, it is exploring the nature of presidents' influence given their particular congressional and political constraints. On this score, research shows presidents can leverage their institutional resources across Pennsylvania Avenue. They do so by setting agendas and drafting legislation, lobbying lawmakers and rallying citizens.

The first and most important mechanism behind presidents' legislative influence comes from their unique capacity to push preferred bills onto the congressional agenda. Studying presidential initiatives' congressional fate, George Edwards III and Andrew Barrett concluded, "The results are clear: the president can almost always place potentially significant legislation on the agenda of Congress" (2000, 120). Bond and Fleisher asserted: "The president's greatest influence over policy comes from the agenda he pursues and the way it is packaged" (1990, 220); Mark Peterson agreed, "nothing an individual president can do breeds success like clear priorities" (1990, 267). Constructing and credibly signaling the president's legislative "must list" thus comprises one of his most important enterprises (Light 1998).[8]

Beyond prioritizing certain legislative issues and drafting specific legislative language, presidents can also help build winning coalitions by lobbying for their legislative agenda. Archival research showed Lyndon Johnson's whipping operation united his fellow partisans (Sullivan 1990a), including legislators who were initially (perhaps strategically) hesitant (Sullivan 1990b). Also drawing on Johnson's example, Cary Covington's research revealed that Johnson (like Kennedy) mobilized congressional supporters to show up for key votes (1987a) and cross-pressured members whose support was important (1988), often by working quietly behind the scenes (rather than going public) when doing so facilitated deal making (1987b). My 2010 study clarified the general early-game and endgame strategies animating presidential lobbying, and it offered powerful evidence of their effectiveness.

The final bargaining strategy that today's presidents routinely deploy is grassroots lobbying. After Sam Kernell (1993) documented the rise of presidents' "going public" efforts, Brandice Canes-Wrone (2005) explicated the underlying logic: by selectively increasing the salience of popular initiatives, presidents sharpen the link between legislators' actions and voters' preferences, thereby leveraging public support outside Washington to ply lawmakers inside the capital. On the other hand, George Edwards (2003) gives reasons to be skeptical that presidential rhetoric will have much effect on the public one way or the other, and Frances Lee (2009) shows that presidential publicity may now do more to polarize lawmakers by party than persuade them to support the president.

President-Centered Influence

Given the presidency's persuasive options outlined above, it is intuitive to cast presidents' individual-level impact as merely a question of how well each president wields his office's arsenal. Because gathering data on the particulars of presidential coalition building—across issues, by legislator, over time—is difficult, if not impossible, scholars have instead utilized an indirect test of president-centered influence: do some presidents fare better or worse than expected, given their particular congressional and political backdrop? Richard Fleisher, Jon Bond, and B. Dan Wood explained the logic nicely: "If presidential activity exerts a general and systematic influence on success in Congress, then when compared to a baseline that accounts for political conditions, we should observe some presidents who are 'uncommonly' successful and unsuccessful" (2007, 192).

Applying this "uncommon" standard to presidential success on nonconsensual roll-call votes, Fleisher, Bond, and Wood found the residuals around the baseline models were more or less randomly distributed, leading them to conclude that "none of the ten presidents analyzed here were uncommonly successful or unsuccessful relative to the conditions they faced" (2007, 210). Similar analyses have led to similar conclusions. In earlier work, Bond and Fleisher found that "we must note how little hard evidence for the skills theory there is, especially when the importance of other variables is much clearer" (1990, 219), and George Edwards asserted that "presidential legislative skills are not closely related to presidential support in Congress" (1989, 211).

Utilizing comparable empirical strategies but different dependent variables—new laws rather than key votes—generated estimates that were comparable, albeit more equivocal. Although the differences were not statistically different, I found Lyndon Johnson fared better than expected, while Jimmy Carter fared worse than expected, which "may leave open some avenues for studying presidential 'skill' and legislation success" (Beckmann 2010, 147). This echoes Mark Peterson's point that although heroic claims of presidential skill can be readily dismissed, closer inspection leaves open the possibility that less heroic individual-level factors still matter: "But an essential measure of leadership ultimately has to be the capacity to prevail against the odds, and to know how to craft one's ambitions to fit the opportunities of the day" (1990, 267). Similarly, David Mayhew has suggested that a president's "agenda, will, and skill" may prove decisive at a particular moment but that it "performs on its own schedule" (2005, 118), making it hard to isolate without more detailed study.

Revisiting the Presidential Difference

When it comes to understanding presidential success on Capitol Hill, on key votes or in new laws, it is clear that congressional composition and political circumstances are critically important. Likewise, preliminary tests of president-centered theories suggest that inasmuch as presidents' individual-level factors matter, they likely do so "at the margins," as George Edwards (1989) put it. The obvious implication is one Fleisher, Bond, and Wood state baldly: "If presidential skill is to provide a theoretical understanding of presidential success on par with that provided by political conditions, then we should be able to observe more than idiosyncratic effects on a small number of issues. The burden of providing such systematic evidence rests on proponents of the skill part of the explanation" (2007, 210). At one level, the point is fair enough, and in fact fundamentally correct. Like all scientific theories, those citing president-centered factors as important to understanding presidential–congressional relations must identify the mechanism by which they do, deduce hypotheses that could be proven wrong, and then offer empirical tests that would reveal if they are (Figure 3.5).

On the other hand, just as we guard vigilantly against Type I errors (inferring presidents' individual-level influence when there is none), we should be equally

Reality of
President's Influence

		Yes Influence	No Influence
Tests of President's Influence	Yes Influence	True Positive	False Positive (Type I Error)
	No Influence	False Negative (Type II Error)	True Negative

Figure 3.5. Reality versus Tests of Presidential Influence.

wary about falling prey to Type II errors (rejecting presidents' individual-level influence when there is some). And by the second standard, research to date (including mine!) is far less definitive than its conclusions suggest. While all significance tests rely on something of an arbitrary standard, it is worth recalling that failing to reject a null hypothesis does not mean we should accept it.

President-Centered Testing

As noted, the typical approach to testing president-centered factors in federal lawmaking has been to ask the model's error term whether reputedly skilled presidents like Lyndon Johnson (et al.) scored significantly better than reputedly unskilled presidents like Jimmy Carter (et al.) on key votes and/or new laws. By design, the resulting answer presumes president-centered factors (e.g., the degree of legislative skill) are uncorrelated with presidency-centered ones (e.g., the volume of legislative lobbying), as well as a model's other independent variables (e.g., congressional composition or political context). Just looking at Johnson's case—the most skilled presidential lobbyist who also happened to enjoy the most favorable circumstances—suggests that this assumption is dubious at best, and more likely it is untenable. So even setting aside the particulars, the typical approaches used to test president-centered influence have tended to be biased against finding its "significance."

That leads to a second point about empirical tests of president-centered theories: the dependent variables typically deployed to test individual presidents' effectiveness are probably not well suited for the job. As Paul Light explains, "What has been missing from the debate between those who favor leadership-based versus institution-based explanations has been a strong dependent variable against which to measure impact" (1993, 162). Light argues that dependent variable should be a fine-grained measure of policy outcomes. He is right. Presidents tend to focus their efforts on particular provisions, meaning the core question is not whether one president wins "significantly" more key votes or passes "significantly" more laws than other presidents in similar circumstances; rather, it is whether the outcome is substantively different than it would have been absent the president's involvement, all else being equal.[9] To better test presidents' legislative success, then, scholars should calibrate to the legislative, not just the success.[10]

President-Centered Theorizing

Having critiqued prevailing research on presidents' individual-level influence, it is important to note that a basic problem for properly testing president-centered theories is, well, theoretical. The presidency literature has not yet disentangled presidency-centered influence from president-centered influence. Do individual-level factors work to offer an added contribution, above and beyond the office's impact?

Do individual-level factors condition, for better or for worse, the relationship between presidency-centered inputs and congressional outputs? More to the point, what are these individual-level factors? And what observable evidence would reveal their effects (or lack thereof)?

Let me admit up front that I do not have any compelling answers to these questions. However, earlier presidency scholarship offers some useful concepts, and examining it more closely illustrates how we might revitalize this research area (see Dickinson 2009 for a similar call to action). Take Richard Neustadt's exposition in *Presidential Power*. Neustadt cites each president's "professional reputation" as an important resource to maintain and leverage. He says: "A President who values power need not be concerned with every flaw in his day-by-day performance, but he has every reason for concern with the residual impression of tenacity and skill accumulating in the minds of Washingtonians-at-large. His bargaining advantages in seeking what he wants are heightened or diminished by what others think of him" (1960, 54).

Neustadt's conception of "professional reputation" is instructive as far as it goes, but it does not go very far. Neustadt does not unpack the dimensions of a president's professional reputation, explicate how it forms (or evolves), or examine what makes it credible. There is no portable theory that reveals the mechanisms that translate the president's reputation into influence. So although Neustadt offers an important insight about an individual-level factor that he believes affects presidents' influence, it was not developed in the manner of a rigorous scientific theory, which limited its impact on the field going forward.[11]

That being said, it is easy to imagine how researchers might extend Neustadt's conceptual foundation to gain some analytical leverage. For example, game theoretic conceptions of how, when, and why reputations matter (Gibbons 1992; Kreps et al. 1982) map onto Neustadt's original discussion rather nicely. Per this logic, a president's professional reputation is not just an omnibus assessment of the president's performance, nor is it a popular appraisal of the president's skill. Instead, the essential dimension is whether Washington's other key players expect that cooperating with the president now will pay off in the future, and that defecting against him will prove costly.[12] Put differently, does the president credibly signal he will reward other players' cooperation and punish their defection as his tenure unfolds?

Within this framework, we can envision how this specific president-centered variable—a president's professional reputation—could affect legislators, cabinet secretaries, lobbyists, reporters, White House staffers, and beyond. A president who establishes a reputation for playing hardball politics effectively should enjoy greater cooperation than one deemed indifferent, inconsistent, or irrelevant. Again, this does not mean a strong reputation can fundamentally alter congressional priors or political context; instead, it operates in a more nuanced fashion: a president with a reputation for playing tit for tat should attract (marginally) greater support (but not necessarily more votes) on his high-priority agenda items.

This leads us back to a key take-home point: the nature of presidents' individual influence operates in an intracontextual manner. However much structural and contextual forces explain variations from president to president or Congress to Congress at any given moment, such considerations receive little attention inside the Oval Office. Indeed, factors like congressional composition are seen as a basic reality to navigate, not change, which means individual-level factors like professional reputations likely work in more specific ways—issue to issue, person to person, day to day.

In order to understand individual-level factors' influence on presidential decision making and influence, then, presidency scholars must build from theoretical frameworks pitched at the operational level. We cannot just look for omnibus variations from president to president; we must also investigate policy variations within each presidency. This may not facilitate parsimonious theories and/or large-N data sets, but it will clarify each president's individual-level difference and influence during his or her particular moment.

Discussion

In the wake of Franklin Roosevelt's remarkable tenure in the White House, a myriad of presidency scholars corroborated Woodrow Wilson's famous aphorism: the presidency "will be as big as and as influential as the man who occupies it" ([1885] 1981). Study after study envisioned the presidency as not just the nation's most powerful policy-making office but rather as its singularly powerful policy-making office.[13] Inasmuch as a president's influence proved underwhelming, it was interpreted less as a reflection on the office than its tenant. James MacGregor Burns's *Presidential Government* exemplifies the idea: "Better than any other human instrumentality [a president] can order the relations of his ends and means, alter existing institutions and procedures or create new ones, calculate the consequences of different policies, experiment with various methods, control the timing of action, anticipate the reactions of affected interests, and conciliate them or at least mediate among them" (1965, 339).

Such appraisals of presidential power drew on in-depth analyses of specific presidents in specific cases. Comparisons between presidents were sometimes invoked, but in an ad hoc fashion. Selecting an equivalent sample of cases, isolating a specific set of behaviors, and measuring their effects while controlling for other variables were not so much eschewed as they were overlooked.

Since the 1980s, a burgeoning literature carefully subjected grand claims of presidential power to systematic empirical scrutiny. The resulting literature greatly sharpened our understanding of presidential power—both the mechanisms by which it operates and the structural forces that constrain its effects. We now know that although popular appraisals tend to vastly overestimate presidents' influence, it nonetheless remains true that a president's decisions about his or her agenda and lobbying can affect legislative processes and outcomes in important ways. Yet vital questions remain. Among these, the most basic are the essential elements of presidential leadership—namely, each president's individual-level difference and impact.

My aims in this chapter have been modest. I have not endeavored to evaluate notions of presidential leadership or develop my own. Instead, I critique prevailing research on presidential leadership's logical antecedent: president-centered influence. My foremost lesson is that research routinely cited to discount president-centered theories is not as definitive as frequently portrayed. Popular measures have been imprecise, and prominent tests have been indirect. Indeed, beyond disproving heroic personal conceptions of presidential power, we still know little, theoretically or empirically, about the presidential difference.

My hope, therefore, is to help breathe new life into scholarship that takes president-centered influence seriously. That means identifying specific individual-level factors that animate presidents' decisions and impact, tracking the mechanisms by which they do, and then gathering the fine-grained data that would reveal if they do not. Meeting these objectives will require innovative research designs and original data. Indeed, the phenomena where president-centered differences are most likely to matter—on 51/49 judgments, behind the scenes, or inside the White House—are the very domains that are hardest to monitor, much less measure. Elite interviews thus offer an especially promising avenue for obtaining new and important discoveries about the modern presidency—including its occupant's significance.

References

Adams, Richard. 2010. "Joe Biden: 'This Is a Big Fucking Deal'" (video). *Guardian*, March 23. https://www.theguardian.com/.

Beckmann, Matthew N. 2010. *Pushing the Agenda: Presidential Leadership in US Lawmaking, 1953–2004*. Cambridge: Cambridge University Press.

Beckmann, Matthew N., and Richard L. Hall. 2013. "Elite Interviewing in Washington, DC." In *Interview Research in Political Science*, edited by Layna Mosley, 196–208. Ithaca, NY: Cornell University Press.

Benen, Steve. 2009. "Grassley Giving Up on White House Talks?" *Washington Monthly*, August 25. http://washingtonmonthly.com/.

Bernstein, Jonathan. 2014. "Is Obama Weak or Is the Presidency?" *Bloomberg View*, May 20. https://www.bloomberg.com/.

Bond, Jon R., and Richard Fleisher. 1990. *The President in the Legislative Arena*. Chicago: University of Chicago Press.

Brady, David W., and Craig Volden. 1998. *Revolving Gridlock: Politics and Policy from Carter to Clinton.* Boulder, CO: Westview.

Burns, James MacGregor. 1965. *Presidential Government: the Crucible of Leadership.* Boston: Houghton Mifflin.

Cameron, Charles M. 2000. *Veto Bargaining: Presidents and the Politics of Negative Power.* Cambridge: Cambridge University Press.

Cameron, Charles M., and Jee-Kwang Park. 2008. "A Primer on the President's Legislative Program." In *Presidential Leadership: The Vortex of Power,* edited by Bert A. Rockman and Richard W. Waterman, 45–80. Oxford: Oxford University Press.

Canes-Wrone, Brandice. 2005. *Who Leads Whom? Presidents, Policy, and the Public.* Chicago: University of Chicago Press.

——. 2009. "Game Theory and the Studying of the American Presidency." In *The Oxford Handbook of the American Presidency,* edited by William G. Howell and George C. Edwards III, 30–50. Oxford: Oxford University Press.

CNN. 2013. "Did Obama Administration Lack in Preparedness to Deal with Syrian Chemical Attack?; Former Obama Aide Now One of Fiercest Critics of Administration's Stance on Syria; Is Obama's Influence Waning in Middle East?; Nyad Finally Makes History" (transcript, *The Lead* with Jake Tapper). *CNN,* September 2. http://www.cnn.com/.

Cooper, Joseph, and David W. Brady. 1981. "Institutional Context and Leadership Style: The House from Cannon to Rayburn." *American Political Science Review* 74 (2): 411–425.

Covington, Cary R. 1987a. "Mobilizing Congressional Support for the President: Insights from the 1960s." *Legislative Studies Quarterly* 12 (February): 77–96.

——. 1987b. "Staying Private: Gaining Congressional Support for Unpublicized Presidential Preferences on Roll Call Votes." *Journal of Politics* 49 (August): 737–755.

——. 1988. "Building Presidential Coalitions among Cross-Pressured Members of Congress." *Western Political Quarterly* 41 (March): 47–62.

Cox, Gary W., and Mathew D. McCubbins. 1993. *Legislative Leviathan: Party Government in the House.* Berkeley: University of California Press.

CQ Weekly. 2007. "GOP Leaders Scheduled Votes to Further Party Strategy." *CQ Weekly.* January 1, 60.

Dickinson, Matthew J. 2009. "We All Want a Revolution: Neustadt, New Institutionalism, and the Future of Presidency Research." *Presidential Studies Quarterly* 39:736–770.

Edwards, George C., III. 1980. *Presidential Influence in Congress.* New York: W. H. Freeman.

——. 1989. *At the Margins: Presidential Leadership of Congress.* New Haven, CT: Yale University Press.

——. 2003. *On Deaf Ears: The Limits of the Bully Pulpit.* New Haven, CT: Yale University Press.

Edwards, George C., III, and Andrew Barrett. 2000. "Presidential Agenda Setting in Congress." In *Polarized Politics,* edited by Jon R. Bond and Richard Fleisher. Washington DC: CQ Press.

Edwards, George C., III, John H. Kessel, and Bert A. Rockman, eds. 1993. *Researching the Presidency: Vital Questions, New Approaches.* Pittsburgh, PA: University of Pittsburgh Press.

Edwards, George C., III, and Stephen J. Wayne, eds. 1983. *Studying the Presidency.* Knoxville: University of Tennessee Press.

Edwards, George C., III, and B. Dan Wood. 1999. "Who Influences Whom? The President and the Public Agenda." *American Political Science Review* 93 (2): 327–344.

Fleisher, Richard, Jon Bond, and B. Dan Wood. 2007. "Which Presidents Are Uncommonly Successful in Congress?" In *Presidential Leadership: The Vortex of Power*, edited by Bert A. Rockman and Richard W. Waterman, 191–214. Oxford: Oxford University Press.

Gibbons, R. 1992. *Game Theory for Applied Economists.* Princeton, NJ: Princeton University Press.

Gleiber, Dennis W., Steven A. Shull, and Colleen A. Waligora. 1998. "Measuring a President's Professional Reputation." *American Politics Quarterly* 26:366–385.

Greenstein, Fred I. 2009. *The Presidential Difference: Leadership Style from FDR to Barack Obama.* 3rd ed. Princeton, NJ: Princeton University Press.

Groseclose, Timothy, and Nolan McCarty. 2001. "The Politics of Blame: Bargaining Before an Audience." *American Journal of Political Science* 45 (1): 100–119.

Hall, Richard L. 1992. "Measuring Legislative Influence." *Legislative Studies Quarterly* 17 (2): 205–231.

Howell, William G. 2003. *Power without Persuasion: The Politics of Direct Presidential Action.* Princeton, NJ: Princeton University Press.

———. 2009. "Quantitative Approaches to Studying the Presidency." In *The Oxford Handbook of the American Presidency*, edited by William G. Howell and George C. Edwards III, 9–29. Oxford: Oxford University Press.

———. 2013. *Thinking about the Presidency: The Primacy of Power.* Princeton, NJ: Princeton University Press.

———. 2014. "Presidential Prescriptions for State Policy: Obama's Race to the Top Initiative." Working paper, University of Chicago.

Jones, Charles O. 1994. *The Presidency in a Separated System.* Washington, DC: Brookings Institution.

Kernell, Samuel. 1993. *Going Public: New Strategies of Presidential Leadership.* Washington, DC: CQ Press.

Klein, Ezra. 2014. "The Green Lantern Theory of the Presidency, Explained." *Vox*, May 20. https://www.vox.com/.

Krehbiel, Keith. 1998. *Pivotal Politics: A Theory of US Lawmaking.* Chicago: University of Chicago Press.

Kreps, David M., Paul Milgrom, John Roberts, and Robert Wilson. 1982. "Rational Cooperation in the Finitely Repeated Prisoners' Dilemma." *Journal of Economic Theory* 27:245–252.

Kreps, David M., and Robert Wilson. 1982. "Reputation and Imperfect Information." *Journal of Economic Theory* 27:253–279.

Kumar, Martha Joynt. 2010. *Managing the President's Message: The White House Communications Operation.* Baltimore, MD: Johns Hopkins University Press.

Lee, Frances E. 2009. *Beyond Ideology: Politics, Principles, and Partisanship in the US Senate.* Chicago: University of Chicago Press.

Lewis, Michael. 2012. "Obama's Way." *Vanity Fair,* October. http://www.vanityfair.com/.

Light, Paul C. 1993. "Presidential Policy Making." In *Researching the Presidency: Vital Questions, New Approaches,* edited by George C. Edwards III, John H. Kessel, and Bert A. Rockman, 161–202. Pittsburgh, PA: University of Pittsburgh Press.

——. 1998. *The President's Agenda: Domestic Policy Choice from Kennedy to Clinton.* Baltimore, MD: Johns Hopkins University Press.

Mayhew, David R. 2005. *Divided We Govern: Party Control, Lawmaking, and Investigations, 1946–2002.* New Haven, CT: Yale University Press.

——. 2011. *Partisan Balance: Why Political Parties Don't Kill the US Constitutional System.* Princeton, NJ: Princeton University Press.

McIntyre, Adrianna. 2014. "21 Things Obamacare Does That You Didn't Know About." *Vox,* May 23. https://www.vox.com/.

Milgrom, Paul, and John Roberts. 1982. "Predation, Reputation, and Entry Deterrence." *Journal of Economic Theory* 27:280–334.

Neustadt, Richard E. 1960. *Presidential Power: the Politics of Leadership from FDR to Carter.* New York: Wiley.

Nyhan, Brendan. 2009. "The Green Lantern Theory of the Presidency." *Brendan Nyhan,* December 14. http://www.brendan-nyhan.com/.

Obama, Barack. 2008. "Transcript: Barack Obama's Acceptance Speech." *NPR,* August 28. http://www.npr.org/.

Peterson, Mark A. 1990. *Legislating Together: The White House and Capitol Hill from Eisenhower to Reagan.* Cambridge, MA: Harvard University Press.

Ragsdale, Lyn. 2008. *Vital Statistics on the Presidency.* 3rd ed. Washington, DC: CQ Press.

Rudalevige, Andrew. 2002. *Managing the President's Program: Presidential Leadership and Legislative Policy Formation.* Princeton, NJ: Princeton University Press.

Shull, Steven A., and James M. Vanderleeuw. 1987. "What Do Key Votes Measure?" *Legislative Studies Quarterly* 12 (4): 573–582.

Sides, John. 2009. "What Difference Will President Obama's Speech Make?" *Monkey Cage,* September 8. http://themonkeycage.org/.

Sinclair, Barbara. 2006. *Party Wars: Polarization and the Politics of National Policymaking.* Norman, OK: University of Oklahoma Press.

Snowe, Olympia. 2013. *Fighting for Common Ground: How We Can Fix the Stalemate in Congress.* New York: Weinstein Books.

Sullivan, Terry. 1990a. "Bargaining with the President: A Simple Game and New Evidence." *American Political Science Review* 84 (4): 1167–1196.

——. 1990b. "Explaining Why Presidents Count: Signaling and Information." *Journal of Politics* 52 (3): 939–962.

Wand, Jonathan N., Kenneth W. Shotts, Jasjeet S. Sekhon, Walter R. Mebane Jr., Michael C. Herron, and Henry E. Brady. 2001. "The Butterfly Did It: The Aberrant Vote for Buchanan in Palm Beach County, Florida." *American Political Science Review* 95 (4): 793–810.

Waterman, Richard, Carol L. Silva, and Hank Jenkins-Smith. 2014. *The Presidential Expecta-*

tions Gap: Public Attitudes Concerning the Presidency. Ann Arbor: University of Michigan Press.

Wilson, Woodrow. (1885) 1981. *Congressional Government: A Study in American Politics.* Baltimore, MD: Johns Hopkins University Press.

Notes

1. Olympia Snowe (2013) recounted one phone call where President Obama suggested, "You could be a modern day Joan of Arc." Senator Snowe then reminded the president how that story ended: "Yes, but she was burned at the stake!"

2. One interpretation of the preceding fact pattern is that President Obama optimized, getting a myriad of economic-related initiatives enacted before passing health care with a minimum winning coalition, at the last minute. An alternative interpretation holds that President Obama's cautious and conciliatory beginning wasted time, which ultimately kept the Democrats from passing even more legislation, such as immigration reform. Because we cannot observe the counterfactual case, we cannot say definitively which interpretation is correct.

3. Separating study subjects by random assignment helps create equivalent groups at the beginning of the study, which means that any differences we see between the beginning and the end of the study are likely the result of the different treatments each group received. Absent random assignment, it is hard to know whether any differences observed at the end of a study were there all along.

4. On the contrary, researchers utilizing innovative theories, creative evidence, and rigorous analyses have taught us a great deal about the conditions and strategies that conspire to forge presidents' influence (see Howell 2009 for a nice review).

5. For example, former vice president Henry Wallace urged accommodation with the Soviets at the beginning of the Cold War; Vice President Spiro Agnew (and Governor Ronald Reagan) questioned President Nixon's outreach to China; Vice President Dick Cheney urged President Bush 43 to launch a military strike against Iran before leaving office.

6. Brendan Nyhan (2009) introduced the Green Lantern metaphor; Ezra Klein (2014) then explicated the idea; and Jonathan Bernstein (2014) argued that the Green Lantern warning applied beyond the confines of presidential influence in lawmaking to say it also fit presidents' relations with the executive branch and even their own national party.

7. In contrast, Cameron argues "confusing, one-shot, trivial decisions made by relatively atomistic actors" will allow "a larger role for cognitive effect" (2000, 78). As noted, while few matters in the presidential inbox are trivial, many involve situations that are novel, conflicted, and/or complex—and that demand the president's decision arrive quickly, to be announced publicly. What is more, such cases often occur in domains where the president has considerably more discretion: executive

actions, foreign policy, military operations, statutory interpretations, budgetary machinations.

8. Part and parcel of presidents' agenda-setting advantage is the modern presidency's vast resources for drafting complex legislation. As Andrew Rudalevige explains, "Congress may not always be inclined to dispose, but presidents are now very much expected to propose" (2002, 2). One reason why, as Charles Cameron and Jee-Kwang Park have shown, is because the president's legislative allies benefit from letting him do the onerous work of drafting legislation, while the president benefits because he "can use proffered bills not simply to stimulate congressional action, but to shape the content of legislation" (2008, 48).

9. Adrianna McIntyre (2014) helps makes the point. In major legislation, such bundles are hardly uncommon. Will Howell's (2014) study of President Obama's Race to the Top initiative, including in the stimulus bill, has had substantial consequences for American education, even though it was but a comparatively minor provision in a major (health care) bill.

10. Richard Hall's (1992) interview-based measure offers an exemplary model. See also Beckmann and Hall (2013).

11. An exception helps make the point. In an effort to operationalize presidents' professional reputations, Gleiber, Shull, and Waligora suggest, "Professional reputation is elites' perception of the president, just as popular prestige is the mass public's perception of the president" (1998, 325). This is not an unreasonable definition, nor is it one that offers much analytic traction.

12. Recall that each president can "invest in his reputation" by demonstrating that he will reward cooperation (Kreps and Wilson 1982; Milgrom and Roberts 1982).

13. Richard Neustadt's seminal *Presidential Power*, first published in 1960, offers an important, albeit partial, exception. Neustadt's focus was on the president's personal actions and influence; close examination led him to believe the presidency's formal powers were weak, but a president's informal powers might not be.

CHAPTER FOUR

Presidential Leadership in American Foreign Policy

Philip B. K. Potter

Americans expect foreign policy leadership from their presidents. Even a cursory survey of the news bears this out with plentiful examples of journalists, pundits, and political opponents opining on the perceived successes and failures of presidential leadership.[1] These popular perceptions of leadership—regardless of whether they are doling out praise or criticism—share a common thread. In the public's mind, foreign policy leadership means presidential initiatives that are assertive, decisive, and successful.

In 2014 the editorial board of the *New York Times* surveyed the high and low points of Obama's foreign policy, and their comments shed light on how foreign policy leadership is popularly understood in the United States: "American presidents who stood as strong global leaders did so by setting high expectations in clear, if sometimes overly simplistic, ways. Mr. Obama's comments last week fanned the anger of people on the left and the right who find him unfocused, weak and passive . . . the perception—of weakness, dithering, inaction, there are many names for it— has indisputably had a negative effect on Mr. Obama's global standing."

This demand that presidents provide clear and assertive foreign policy leadership stands in notable contrast to what is expected (and typically possible) domestically. Here presidents are much more constrained and opportunities for leadership correspondingly less available. The distinction arises from the nature of presidential power and the division of labor within the American political system. As Wildavsky (1966, 162) puts it, "The United States has one president, but it has two presidencies: one presidency is for domestic affairs and the other is concerned with defense and foreign policy." The argument, subsequently honed by others who followed, is that presidents have mostly unfettered foreign policy powers but are much more constrained in their domestic preferences (Peterson 1994; Canes-Wrone, Howell, and Lewis 2008).[2]

Presidents and those who advise them instinctively understand that opportunities for leadership tend to diverge along these dimensions. As Brent Scowcroft, national security adviser to Gerald Ford and George H. W. Bush, notes, "Presidents always have more leeway in foreign policy than they do on the domestic agenda" (quoted in LaFranchi 2010). Driving the distinction home, when presidents want to show leadership and initiative on a domestic policy priority, they often resort to foreign policy terminology and frames—the "wars" on poverty and drugs, for example.

While decisiveness and success may be hallmarks of foreign policy leadership for political observers and the public, their presence or absence tends to be in the eye of the beholder. These criteria also leave little room for prudence; fixation on outcomes obscures half the picture by excluding situations in which presidents exhibit wise leadership by declining damaging engagements. Decisiveness and success are therefore weak foundations for a definition of foreign policy leadership. They are no better as a starting point for social scientists seeking to study the subject systematically. This is particularly so because, in the popular mind, they arise from personality and demeanor. Critics, for example, assert that American foreign policy floundered because Obama as an individual is equivocating, unimpassioned, and inclined toward small ball (O'Connell 2013).

How, then, can we productively assess leadership in US foreign policy? Certainly disposition and outcomes have their place in conversations about the quality of presidents and their policies, but this side of leadership must be set aside if the concept is to be analytically useful. This means treating leadership expansively—simply as engagement and activity in the foreign policy process. In the US context, this means presidential activity, given the executive's leading role in the foreign policy process. This is particularly true since leadership is more closely associated with the initiation of policy rather than reaction.[3] The preeminence of the president in the US foreign policy process also makes the resort to activity as a proxy for leadership more valid—when presidents are engaged, active, and setting the agenda, US foreign policy tends to move forward in a relatively coherent way. When presidents are personally disengaged, the nature of the system is such that foreign policy tends to stall and lose focus because no other actor is institutionally positioned to fill the void.

I argue here that if the goal is systematic knowledge of foreign policy leadership, then it will be more effective to understand the institutional factors that enable or impede leadership rather than the personalities of past presidents. Specifically, institutions shape when opportunities for leadership arise by mediating the ebb and flow of political constraint from the public and other political actors like Congress. At the same time, institutional factors deeply influence the incentives of presidents to seize these opportunities or allow them to pass by. Opportunities and incentives are much more stable things to predict and understand, and in this regard, they stand in contrast to actual success in foreign policy, which is far more subject to chance and the complexities of strategic interaction.

In this chapter I will focus narrowly on two institutional features of the American system that shape the opportunities and incentives for presidential foreign policy leadership. On the opportunity side, the executive branch has tremendous informational advantages that allow for certain types of leadership but can close the door to others. Because this informational advantage fades with time and issue salience, presidents have the greatest opportunity to lead decisively when the action is going to largely fly under the public's radar as a result of its low salience or when the action can be concluded quickly before the informational advantage erodes. On the incentive side, electoral institutions push the politically strongest presidents away from foreign policy altogether (and toward domestic policy). When they do opt for foreign policy, the incentives of strong presidents are biased toward otherwise constrained options, such as the use of major force at the expense of less constrained options like diplomacy.

These institutional pressures on opportunities and incentives are two sides of the same coin, but they push in opposite directions. Presidents with the greatest opportunity to provide meaningful foreign policy leadership (because they are relatively unconstrained by other political actors) have the least incentive to actually do it (because they would rather be doing something else with their accumulated political capital). This distinction goes a long way toward explaining why presidents seem to systematically underinvest in foreign policy, particularly early in their time in office, despite the leeway provided by the "two presidencies."

The failure of Obama's final push for resolution to the dispute between the Israelis and Palestinians sadly fits perfectly into this long-standing pattern. Presidents tend to attempt major foreign policy initiatives at the end of administrations, when opportunities for domestic action are off the table. Success would have been far from assured, but Obama certainly would have brought more to the table if he had pushed for a peace agreement when he was at the height of his powers early in his first term. Of course, the incentives for powerful presidents favor major domestic initiatives (e.g., health care), and that is precisely what Obama pursued.

The remainder of the chapter proceeds as follows. I begin by discussing the personality- and institution-based strands of the existing literature on foreign policy leadership. I then outline examples of how institutions shape presidential opportunities and incentives for leadership. These examples are in no way exhaustive but are simply meant to illustrate a potentially productive approach to systematically thinking about the nature of foreign policy leadership in the United States. I conclude with a discussion of avenues for future research.

Foreign Policy Leadership

The distinction between personality- and institution-based arguments about the origins of American foreign policy leadership is a long-standing one in the literature. The former approach has generally studied the individual-level components of leadership and is broadly president centered. Research in this tradition focuses on the idiosyncratic elements of psychology, management, and style (Renshon 1998; Mitchell 2010). In contrast, the institutional, presidency-centered literature revolves around the way that leadership is constrained by interbranch relations and enumerated powers (Moe and Howell 1999; Morey et al. 2012).

Neustadt's (1960) work on the personal aspects of presidential leadership remains among the most prominent on the president-centered side of the divide. He argues that the crux of presidential power and leadership is the personal ability to persuade. Because power at the federal level is separated but shared, persuasive power allows presidents to lead in both hierarchical and nonsubordinate situations. That said, Neustadt's arguments maintain an important institutional component. His view is that the institutional constraints on enumerated presidential powers create an environment that encourages the exercise of leadership through persuasive (personal) powers.[4] In this way, Neustadt presages work that followed that combines the personal aspects of leadership and the institutional constraints placed upon them.[5]

The institutional perspective on foreign policy leadership focuses more exclusively on these enumerated powers, and institutionally driven adaptations to them, rather than on personality, experience, or attributes. Much of this research focuses on the ability of the president to act unilaterally (Moe and Howell 1999) and how the office of the president controls a large and specifically purposed bureaucracy that can be brought to bear on foreign policy issues. Another significant theme in this type of presidency-focused work is the general deference that Congress pays the executive branch in matters of foreign affairs (Kellerman and Barilleaux 1991).

More recent work has considered the evolution of these powers over time, as well as the interplay between the branches. Howell, Jackman, and Rogowski (2013), for example, show that Congress is more likely to defer to presidential foreign policy leadership when the debates surrounding a conflict transcend local considerations to become national. The result is that wars such as World War II and the 2003 Iraq war significantly upgraded presidential power, while those that failed to invoke national themes, such as Vietnam, did not.

There is, of course, work on foreign policy leadership outside of American politics. In the international relations literature, arguments cast at the level of the leader, while once prominent, have generally fallen out of favor (but see Goldgeier 1994; Jervis 1976). There are several reasons for this. Foremost, system-level theorizing as well as the general tendency in political science to attempt to distance research from Great Man arguments pushed considerations of leadership and individuals into the background. More recently, the rationalist basis of most work on international conflict as well as the corresponding absence of systematic data on leader-level attributes that might be associated with risk have left leadership almost entirely absent from most discussions.

There has, however, been a recent resurgence in interest in foreign policy leadership among international relations scholars. Most of this work on foreign policy leadership focuses on the observable attributes of leaders as well as their experiences before taking office rather than on the institutional features of the countries that they govern. For example, research by Horowitz and Stam (2014), Saunders (2011), Colgan (2013), and others suggests that prior experiences play a critical role in shaping the beliefs and behavior of leaders once they enter office.

As I indicated in the introduction, my view is that when it comes to understanding the systematic aspects of American foreign policy leadership, an institutionally based approach is likely to be the more productive avenue. Recent trends in international relations are interesting because they open the door to the systematic study of individual-level attributes as contributors or impediments to national-level leadership. For the most part, this body of work is accomplishing this by assessing readily observable attributes (e.g., gender and age) or experiences (e.g., military service) over large numbers of countries and many years. This approach, however, is simply not on the table as a way of generating systematic knowledge about the specifics of foreign policy leadership within a single country that has had just forty-five presidents spread over two centuries.

Opportunities for Foreign Policy Leadership

Openings for presidential leadership often arise from the office's substantial informational advantages when it comes to foreign policy, particularly in the short term (Baum and Potter 2008). This advantage derives from the relative disinterest of other political actors and the public, but it also has an institutional basis. The presidency has important constitutional advantages in the foreign policy arena that are particularly felt in crisis situations, and they have been bolstered over time by the acquiescence of the legislative and judicial branches.

The National Security Act of 1947, for example, increased presidential influence over foreign policy by handing over the levers of bureaucratic control. The courts have further supported presidential preeminence in the foreign policy arena (Marra, Ostrom, and Simon 1990). It has been widely noted that while specific constitutionally enumerated foreign policy powers—including declaring war (with the consent of the Senate) and making treaties (again, with the consent of the Senate)—are actually quite limited, these limits have been widely ignored. In contrast, the more ambiguous power of the commander in chief has been embraced and interpreted expansively, often fueled by the informational advantages generated by control of the foreign policy bureaucracy. The result is that Congress and the public are typically playing catch-up, particularly in the shortened time frames that accompany crisis situations.

Informational advantages undercut potential constraints on unilateral executive action and thereby, for better or worse, create opportunities for leadership. The relationship between a democratic public (and Congress, to the extent that it should serve as a check on unilateral executive foreign policy action) and their elected leaders closely adheres to what Miller (2005) calls Weber's asymmetry, which describes the difference in power and information between principal and agent: the principal holds authority, but the agent—that is, the actor to whom the principal delegates the power necessary to implement the principal's preferences—has the informational advantage. As such, representative government creates a classic principal–agent problem, with presidents as the often unruly agents of citizens and congressional overseers. Downs and Rocke (1994), for example, develop this logic in the context of the decision to go to war. The chief executive is likely to possess far more information than typical citizens, who can only use the war's outcome as a basis for evaluating the chief's competence after the fact via elections (Baum and Potter 2015).

More generally, the principal–agent dilemma between representative government and citizens is one of accountability. Elected officials must be held accountable for their actions and those of their government, and citizens must use their voting power to keep good governments in place and to dismiss those that perform poorly. The asymmetry in information, however, creates an inefficiency in which citizens cannot easily differentiate between those officials who act with good strategy and intentions but achieve unlucky results, and those whose intentions may be contrary to best interests of the citizenry or focused on personal gain but whose policies nonetheless produce fortuitous positive outcomes (Downs and Rocke 1994).

Information helps alleviate this problem, but when it comes to American foreign policy, it can be hard to come by. Typical individuals do not know or care very much about foreign policy (Delli-Carpini and Keeter 1996; Holsti 1992). An uninformed public cannot independently evaluate a president's foreign policy. Moreover, when the public is disengaged and uninformed, it applies little pressure on other political actors such as Congress to put the brakes on presidential foreign policy leadership.

Citizens can mitigate their informational disadvantage through reliance on informational shortcuts (Sniderman et al. 1991; Popkin 1993), most notably the opinions of trusted political elites (Krosnick and Kinder 1990; Iyengar and Kinder 1987; Larson 2000). McCubbins and Schwartz (1984) refer to this process as fire alarm oversight, in which principals rely on third parties to notify them (that is, pull the fire alarm) when a problem emerges.

Information can also enter the equation in the form of output. Put differently, the results of a president's foreign policy leadership can enable citizens to judge his performance, even in the absence of complete information about the process. This simple retrospection means that while citizens may not have access to the range of information available to elected officials, they can punish presidents who fail to deliver on expectations.

The essential insight is that as the size of the information gap recedes, responsiveness increases, and the public can constrain the executive's foreign policy preferences over the longer term (Sobel 2001; Baum 2004; Canes-Wrone 2006). Constraint and responsiveness are virtually nonexistent when the information gap is largest, and these are the moments with the greatest potential for presidential foreign policy leadership. As the gap narrows, responsiveness rises until, when the gap is at its lowest level, responsiveness is essentially perfect and opportunities for leadership are significantly diminished.

What closes the information gap? First, most scholars draw a clear distinction between public attentiveness to foreign policy in general (which is extremely low) and attentiveness in relation to high-salience foreign policy issues such as conflicts or crises (which is somewhat higher). While the public is typically not closely attuned to the details of international politics, crises and casualties often attract meaningful public scrutiny and a demand for information. Second, time matters. When crises, conflicts, or other foreign policy engagements drag on, they tend to generate elite discord, public attention, and diminished informational advantages for the executive. It is unsurprising, then, that leadership autonomy tends to be particularly pronounced when the issue area is of such low salience that it fails to attract public attention, or early on in higher-salience engagements (Baum and Potter 2008).

To illustrate, consider the foreign policy informational advantage enjoyed by leaders relative to the public (that is, the information gap) over time. Typically, public attention to foreign policy (and as a direct corollary, demand for foreign policy information) is very low, resulting in equilibrium favorable to leaders. This is especially true in the early stages of a conflict. However, several factors—including casualties, elite discord, and evidence that leaders have spun the facts beyond credulity (Baum and Potter 2008)—can prompt the public to increase its demand for information, thereby narrowing the gap. This becomes more likely as a conflict drags on.

In many regards, if one is looking for public constraint on presidential foreign policy leadership, conflict is a best-case scenario; at least the gap closes over time, even if it is large at the beginning. In diplomatic, economic, or other lower-salience domains, public attention may never be activated, and meaningful constraint therefore never emerges. However, with a lack of attention comes a shortage of political rewards. It is to this question of incentives that I turn next.

Incentives for Foreign Policy Leadership

Given the substantial opportunities for leadership offered by presidential power, the limits on foreign policy leadership are as much about what presidents want to do as what they can. Scholars tend to think about foreign policy in a vacuum rather than in competition with domestic policy priorities, but the reality is that because presidential resources and capacity are finite, policies are constantly in competition for priority.[6]

Because presidents are less constrained by other political actors when it comes to foreign policy, opportunity for assertive foreign policy leadership is almost always available. But foreign policy is in general not where American presidents would prefer to spend their time, and their time is limited. As I have noted, most American citizens are not attuned to the details of international affairs, and most new presidents have very little experience with or interest in foreign policy (Potter 2007). As a result, electoral incentives and expertise tend to conspire to place domestic policy at the head of the list of presidential priorities.

Even among the minority of leaders who enter office with a strong interest and expertise in foreign policy, there are powerful pressures pushing them toward domestic affairs. It is a truism that Americans vote with their pocketbooks. Even when foreign policy plays a prominent role in elections, many more people vote on the basis of domestic political issues such as the economy. Furthermore, the rallies in public support that come from success in foreign policy are unpredictable and short. The implication is that foreign policy presents relatively more downside risk and fewer rewards.

It would seem, then, that presidents would always turn to domestic policy and do just the minimum with regard to foreign policy. The problem is, they often lack the political strength. Domestic policy, when compared to foreign policy, is more constrained by Congress and interest groups. Moreover, the ability of presidents to overcome these constraints and implement their agendas is highly subject to power in terms of popularity and the partisan composition of government (Potter 2013). The implication is that much of the time, foreign policy leadership is an afterthought. It is when opportunities for domestic achievements are shut down that presidents tend to shift to foreign policy, particularly in the lame-duck period at the end of an administration (Potter 2016).

In addition, there is important variation within the broader category of foreign policy in terms of the extent to which executive preferences are constrained. Work has demonstrated that presidents do not have equal autonomy in all areas of foreign policy (Brule 2006; Baum 2004). Two examples suffice to illustrate: diplomacy and the use of force.

Diplomacy

Presidential diplomacy is relatively unconstrained for a variety of reasons. First, Congress has few functional institutional levers with which to influence the diplomatic agenda, aside from the Senate's role in confirming State Department officials and ratifying treaties. Moreover, presidents have a variety of tools with which to circumvent the congressional role in the treaty process, most notably the use of executive agreements. While Congress decisively influences the content of diplomatic relationships in a few key instances—Taiwan and Cuba, for example—this is the exception rather than the rule. Congress exercises especially little influence on the president's personal diplomatic agenda in the form of summits and state visits.

Presidential diplomatic autonomy also arises from congressional disinterest stemming in turn from the public's disinterest. Congress has little incentive to expend effort to influence diplomatic relations because congressional constituencies are local rather than national, leading members to focus disproportionately on domestic politics and the relatively few aspects of foreign policy that garner public attention or directly impact their constituency. In the vast majority of cases, diplomacy operates well beneath the public's radar (Ostrom and Simon 1985). The result is that nonconflict foreign policy rarely contributes to congressional reelection prospects and is therefore less subject to fierce political rivalry. In reaction to these incentives, members of Congress tend to invest less in foreign policy expertise in general and diplomacy in particular (Gailmard and Patty 2012).[7]

This primacy is long-standing and has consistently been upheld by the courts. The case *Zivotofsky v. Kerry* (2015) nicely illustrates the trend. In it, the Supreme Court held that the president alone has the power of diplomatic recognition, and specifically that Congress had no power to require the State Department to issue passports indicating that Jerusalem is part of Israel when executive diplomatic policy considered that issue unsettled. The broader implication is that diplomacy remains an exclusively presidential domain.

When it comes to formal agreements with the United States, Congress has more tools with which to constrain than they do with regard to personal diplomacy or recognition, but presidents remain at a significant advantage. The Senate maintains a constitutional role in treaty ratification, but presidents now routinely circumvent this power through executive agreements. As a result, true treaties have become relatively rare while executive agreements have proliferated. While in theory not as binding as treaties, executive agreements are durable in practice and can yield substantial changes in trade and diplomatic relations.

While relatively uncontested, diplomacy and executive agreements remain attractive for politically weak presidents because, unlike Congress, they do have a national constituency and can turn to diplomatic engagement as a residual productive outlet for achieving their foreign policy objectives. As Simon and Ostrom (1989) note, under some circumstances, direct presidential diplomacy can lead to small increases in popular support. Although the political benefits of diplomacy can be transitory, weak presidents can therefore exhibit diplomatic leadership abroad to create windows of opportunity for improving their political standing (Mackuen 1983).

Use of Force

Other foreign policy domains, particularly the use of force, operate quite differently. Howell and Pevehouse (2005) demonstrate that, contrary to popular belief, Congress maintains a limited but meaningful ability to constrain the president's ability to resort to major use of force. They find that when the president's party holds more seats in Congress, the use of major force is more common precisely because partisan control allows the president to avoid or overcome constraint.

Given the arguments I have laid out, this is unsurprising. Presidents need some political power to lead with substantial military force because it is more politically salient than diplomacy. As I have noted, scholars draw a clear distinction between public opinion on foreign policy in general on the one hand, and public opinion in relation to conflict on the other. For example, Powlick and Katz (1998) argue that public opinion is typically latent and inactive, leaving presidents a free hand in most circumstances to conduct policy as they see fit. However, they suggest that under limited circumstances, particularly those surrounding the commitment of military forces, foreign policy issues may activate public attention. Thus, while the public is typically not closely attuned to the details of international politics, the commitment of significant US forces typically attracts attention. With public attention comes increased political salience and interference from political actors outside the executive branch.

Conflict also has more substantial potential benefits for presidents. Scholars have long noted that the public often responds positively in the short term to military engagements abroad, and a voluminous literature has investigated the validity and magnitude of the "rally" phenomenon. For example, Lee has noted, "The average man's reaction [to engagement abroad] will include a feeling of patriotism in supporting presidential actions" (1977, 253). Most empirical updates and tests confirm the existence of a short-term rally effect under at least some circumstances (James and Oneal 1991; Oneal and Bryan 1995). However, even if presidents are not banking on a durable rally in their approval ratings, military engagements provide presidents with an opportunity to change the political discourse and invoke their role as commander in chief.

The use of force, however, carries potential costs as well. Sizable military engagements typically last longer and attract more scrutiny than less forceful foreign policies. The result is a partial erosion of the president's informational advantage vis-à-vis both Congress and the public (Baum and Potter 2008). Moreover, lengthy engagements rapidly become costly ones. Even if Congress is poorly positioned to cut off funding to troops in the field, the power of the purse contributes to still more scrutiny. Several scholars have also argued that the casualties that may accompany the major use of force have the potential to turn public opinion against the engagement and the president who initiated it (Mueller 1973; Gartner and Segura 1998; Slantchev 2004). Kriner's (2010) finding that Congress is less likely to contest the president's conduct of major military actions when presidential approval is high suggests that these risks are potentially higher for presidents with low approval ratings to begin with. Finally, the returns on the use of force are unpredictable, particularly because rallies in opinion are not necessarily consistent or durable (Lian and Oneal 1993). Taken together, this suggests that while significant potential benefits accompany the use of substantial force, there are substantial risks as well. The implication is that while rally effects are real, the diversionary use of force as a leadership tactic is generally ill-advised.

These linkages between policy options, power, and incentives suggest that presidents are making trade-offs in their leadership decisions. In general, an increase in political strength will lead to an increase in otherwise constrained policies, but such an increase will also be associated with a decline in the incidence of less constrained policies. Such trade-offs can occur between domestic and foreign policy priorities, but also within foreign policy in terms of the decision to use diplomatic or military tools. This conception of the trade-offs that presidents face is congruent with the well-established literature on foreign policy substitutability (Most and Starr 1989), which, among other things, holds that leaders have a variety of foreign policy options that may achieve their goals (Bennett and Nordstrom 2000).

The point is that the most powerful presidents are going to disproportionately shy away from foreign policy in general (in favor of domestic policy) and away from diplomatic engagement in particular. This is, of course, very much in keeping with the story of presidential foreign policy leadership in the Palestinian/Israeli conflict that I pointed to in the introduction to this chapter.

Conclusion

I have argued here for an institutionally based understanding of leadership that clarifies the opportunities and incentives for presidential foreign policy action. This stands in contrast to an approach more oriented toward the specifics of past presidential behavior.

There are, however, a number of other issues in foreign policy leadership that warrant additional attention. To begin with, while I have largely bracketed them in this discussion, there are foreign policy leaders in the American system beyond the president. Admittedly, when other political actors in the American system wish to assert themselves in the foreign policy domain, they rarely rival the president. John McCain, for example, makes a lot of noise and headlines whenever prominent foreign policy issues arise, but when McCain's name is linked to foreign policy leadership, it tends to be to criticize presidential fecklessness (Wing 2012; Nakamura 2014). The point is that even leading opposition figures assume that presidents will be the preeminent foreign policy leaders in the United States.[8] That said, McCain often does propose independent foreign policy options, and, more generally, political actors aside from the president can and do matter under some circumstances and therefore need to be considered in any discussion of the study of American foreign policy leadership.

It is often lamented that Congress does not exercise the full extent of its foreign policy powers, but the larger puzzle actually is why members invest in foreign policy at all. The starting point for most studies of congressional legislative behavior is the notion that members are, at their core, single-minded seekers of reelection (Mayhew 1974). At the same time, it is well established that most voters know little about and care little for foreign policy. Taken together, these orthodoxies present a significant puzzle. Why do some members of Congress invest substantially in foreign policy expertise?

Those who see a role for Congress in foreign policy tend to view it as largely limited questions of military conflict. Howell and Pevehouse (2005, 2007), for example, argue that Congress constrains presidential preferences regarding the substantial use of the armed forces, and therefore that such substantial military interventions occur more often when the president's party has a majority in the legislature. They note, "Through legislation, appropriations, hearings, and public appeals, members of Congress can substantially increase the political costs of military action—sometimes forcing presidents to withdraw sooner than they would like or even preventing any kind of military action whatsoever" (2007, 103). There is, however, much more to foreign policy than military force, and congressional foreign policy powers are often substantial in these domains. The power of the purse allows Congress to at least occasionally push foreign policy initiatives onto the public agenda. This sort of nonmilitary leadership is where Congress is likely to be least informationally disadvantaged vis-à-vis the president and therefore is where the most meaningful opportunities for foreign policy leadership are likely to arise. Unpacking these incentives for congressional foreign policy leadership is a ripe area for research.

References

Baum, Matthew A. 2004. "How Public Opinion Constrains the Use of Force: The Case of Operation Restore Hope." *Presidential Studies Quarterly* 34 (2): 187–226.

Baum, Matthew A., and Philip B. K. Potter. 2008. "The Relationships between Mass Media,

Public Opinion, and Foreign Policy: Toward a Theoretical Synthesis." *Annual Review of Political Science* 11:39-65.

———. 2015. *War and Democratic Constraint: How the Public Influences Foreign Policy.* Princeton, NJ: Princeton University Press.

Beckmann, Matthew N. 2010. *Pushing the Agenda: Presidential Leadership in US Lawmaking, 1953-2004.* New York: Cambridge University Press.

Bennett, D. Scott, and Timothy Nordstrom. 2000. "Foreign Policy Substitutability and Internal Economic Problems in Enduring Rivalries." *Journal of Conflict Resolution* 44 (1): 33-61.

Brule, David. 2006. "Congressional Opposition, the Economy, and US Dispute Initiation, 1946-2000." *Journal of Conflict Resolution* 50 (4): 463.

Canes-Wrone, Brandice. 2006. *Who Leads Whom? Presidents, Policy, and the Public.* Chicago: University of Chicago Press.

Canes-Wrone, Brandice, William G. Howell, and David E. Lewis. 2008. "Toward a Broader Understanding of Presidential Power: A Reevaluation of the Two Presidencies Thesis." *Journal of Politics* 70 (1): 1-16.

Colgan, Jeff D. 2013. "Domestic Revolutionary Leaders and International Conflict." *World Politics* 65 (4): 656-690.

Delli Carpini, Michael X., and Scott Keeter, 1996. *What Americans Know about Politics and Why it Matters.* New Haven, CT: Yale University Press.

Downs, George W., and David M. Rocke. 1994. "Conflict, Agency, and Gambling for Resurrection—the Principal-Agent Problem Goes to War." *American Journal of Political Science* 38 (2): 362-380.

Editorial Board. 2014. "President Obama and the World." *New York Times*, May 3. https://www.nytimes.com/.

Fisher, Louis. 2004. "Presidential Wars." In *The Domestic Sources of American Foreign Policy: Insights and Evidence,* edited by Eugene R. Wittkopf and James M. McCormick, 155-170. Lanham, MD: Rowman & Littlefield.

Gailmard, Sean, and John W. Patty. 2012. *Learning While Governing: Expertise and Accountability in the Executive Branch.* Chicago: University of Chicago Press.

Gartner, Scott, and Gary M. Segura. 1998. "War, Casualties and Public Opinion." *Journal of Conflict Resolution* 42 (3): 278-300.

Goldgeier, James M. 1994. *Leadership Style and Soviet Foreign Policy: Stalin, Khrushchev, Brezhnev, Gorbachev.* Baltimore, MD: Johns Hopkins University Press.

Haass, Richard N. 2014. "A Foreign Policy Flirting with Chaos." *Wall Street Journal*, April 29. https://www.wsj.com/.

Holsti, Ole R. 1992. "Public Opinion and Foreign Policy: Challenges to the Almond-Lippmann Consensus." *International Studies Quarterly* 36 (4): 439-466.

Horowitz, Michael C., and Allan C. Stam. 2014. "How Prior Military Experience Influences the Future Militarized Behavior of Leaders." *International Organization* 68:527-559.

Howell, William G., Saul P. Jackman, and Jon C. Rogowski. 2013. *The Wartime President: Executive Influence and the Nationalizing Politics of Threat.* Chicago: University of Chicago Press.

Howell, William G., and Jon C. Pevehouse. 2005. "Presidents, Congress, and the Use of Force." *International Organization* 59 (1): 209-232.

——. 2007. *While Dangers Gather*. Princeton, NJ: Princeton University Press.

Iyengar, Shanto, and Donald R. Kinder. 1987. *News that Matters: Television and American Opinion*. Chicago: University of Chicago Press.

James, Patrick, and John R. Oneal. 1991. "The Influence of Domestic and International Politics on the President's Use of Force." *Journal of Conflict Resolution* 35 (2): 307-332.

Jervis, Robert. 1976. *Perception and Misperception in International Politics*. Princeton, NJ: Princeton University Press.

Kellerman, Barbara, and Ryan J. Barilleaux. 1991. *The President as World Leader*. New York: St. Martin's Press.

Kriner, Douglas L. 2010. *After the Rubicon: Congress, Presidents, and the Politics of Waging War*. Chicago: University of Chicago Press.

Krosnick, Jon A., and Donald R. Kinder. 1990. "Altering the Foundations of Support for the President through Priming." *American Political Science Review* 84 (2): 497-512.

LaFranchi, Howard. 2010. "After 'Shellacking,' Can Foreign Policy Be a Bright Spot for Obama?" *Christian Science Monitor*, November 4. https://www.csmonitor.com/.

Larson, Eric V. 2000. "Putting Theory to Work: Diagnosing Public Opinion on the US Intervention in Bosnia." In *Being Useful: Policy Relevance and International Relations Theory*, edited by M. Nincic and J. Lepgold. Ann Arbor: University of Michigan Press, 174-233.

Lee, Jong-Ryool. 1977. "Rally 'round the Flag: Foreign Policy Events and Presidential Popularity." *Presidential Studies Quarterly* 7:252-255.

Lian, Bradley, and John R. Oneal. 1993. "Presidents, the Use of Military Force, and Public Opinion." *Journal of Conflict Resolution* 37 (2): 277.

Mackuen, Michael B. 1983. "Political Drama, Economic Conditions, and the Dynamics of Presidential Popularity." *American Journal of Political Science* 27 (2): 165-192.

Marra, Robin F., Charles W. Ostrom Jr., and Dennis M. Simon. 1990. "Foreign Policy and Presidential Popularity: Creating Windows of Opportunity in the Perpetual Election." *Journal of Conflict Resolution* 34:588-623.

Mayhew, David R. 1974. *Congress: The Electoral Connection*. New Haven, CT: Yale University Press.

McCubbins, Matthew D., and Thomas Schwartz. 1984. "Congressional Oversight Overlooked—Police Patrols versus Fire Alarms." *American Journal of Political Science* 28 (1): 165-179.

Miller, Gary J. 2005. "The Political Evolution of Principal–Agent Models." *Annual Review of Political Science* 8:203-225.

Mitchell, David. 2010. "Does Context Matter? Advisory Systems and the Management of the Foreign Policy Decision-Making Process." *Presidential Studies Quarterly* 4 (4): 631-659.

Moe, Terry M., and William G. Howell. 1999. "The Presidential Power of Unilateral Action." *JLEO* 15 (1): 132-179.

Morey, Daniel S., Clayton L. Thyne, Sarah L. Hayden, and Michael B. Senters. 2012. "Leader,

Follower, or Spectator? The Role of President Obama in the Arab Spring Uprisings." *Social Science Quarterly* 93 (5): 1185–1201.

Most, Benjamin A., and Harvey Starr. 1989. *Inquiry, Logic, and International Politics.* Columbia: University of South Carolina Press.

Mueller, John E. 1973. *War Presidents and Public Opinion.* New York: Wiley.

Nakamura, David. 2014. "At AIPAC, John McCain Blames Obama's 'Feckless' Foreign Policy for Ukraine Crisis." *Washington Post*, March 3. https://www.washingtonpost.com/.

Neustadt, Richard. E. 1960. *Presidential Power: The Politics of Leadership.* New York: Wiley.

O'Connell, Ford. 2013. "Hope and Change? More like Indecisive and Ineffective." *US News & World Report*, September 13. https://www.usnews.com/.

Olson, William C. 1991. "The US Congress: An Independent Force in World Politics?" *International Affairs* 67 (3): 547–563.

Oneal, John R., and Anna L. Bryan. 1995. "The Rally 'round the Flag Effect in US Foreign Policy Crises, 1950–1985." *Political Behavior* 17 (4): 379–401.

Ostrom, Charles W., and Dennis M. Simon. 1985. "Promise and Performance—a Dynamic Model of Presidential Popularity." *American Political Science Review* 79 (2): 334–358.

Peterson, Paul. 1994. "The President's Dominance in Foreign Policy Making." *Political Science Quarterly* 109 (2): 215–234.

Popkin, Sam L. 1993. "Information Shortcuts and the Reasoning Voter." In *Information, Participation, and Choice: An Economic Theory of Democracy in Perspective,* edited by B. Grofman. Ann Arbor: University of Michigan Press, 17–36.

Potter, Philip B. K. 2007. "Does Experience Matter? American Presidential Experience, Age, and International Conflict." *Journal of Conflict Resolution* 51 (3): 351–378.

——. 2013. "Electoral Margins and American Foreign Policy." *International Studies Quarterly* 57 (3): 505–518.

——. 2016. "Lame Duck Foreign Policy." *Presidential Studies Quarterly* 46:849–867.

Powlick, Philip J., and Andrew Z. Katz. 1998. "Defining the American Public Opinion Foreign Policy Nexus." *International Studies Quarterly* 42:29–61.

Preston, Thomas. 2001. *The President and His Inner Circle: Leadership Style and the Advisery Process in Foreign Affairs.* New York: Columbia University Press.

Renshon, Stanley A. 1998. "Analyzing the Psychology and Performance of Presidential Candidates at a Distance: Bob Dole and the 1996 Presidential Campaign." *Leadership Quarterly* 9 (3): 377–395.

Saunders, Elizabeth N. 2011. *Leaders at War.* Ithaca, NY: Cornell University Press.

Simon, Dennis M., and Charles W. Ostrom. 1989. "The Impact of Televised Speeches and Foreign Travel on Presidential Approval." *Public Opinion Quarterly* 53:58–82.

Slantchev, Branislav. L. 2004. "How Initiators End Their Wars: The Duration of Warfare and the Terms of Peace." *American Journal of Political Science* 48 (4): 813–829.

Sniderman, P. M., R. A. Brody, and P. E. Tetlock. 1991. *Reasoning and Choice.* Cambridge: Cambridge University Press.

Sobel, Richard. 2001. *The Impact of Public Opinion of US Foreign Policy since Vietnam.* New York: Oxford University Press.

Wildavsky, Aaron. 1966. "The Two Presidencies." *Trans-Action* 4:7–14.
Wing, Nick. 2012. "John McCain Attacks Obama's 'Failed Leadership' on Foreign Policy" (video). *Huffington Post,* October 22. http://www.huffingtonpost.com/.

Notes

1. See, e.g., Hass (2014), who argues that Obama's failed leadership in Syria and elsewhere has undermined the potential for success in Asia.

2. Some work, however, has added a wrinkle to this orthodoxy by demonstrating that presidents do not have equal autonomy in all areas of foreign policy (Brule 2006; Baum 2004). For example, Howell and Pevehouse (2005, 2007) find that Congress constrains the use of substantial military force, but that presidents have more discretion over less politically salient actions such as minor uses of force. Potter (2013) shows a similar distinction in the constraints on diplomacy and the use of force.

3. For example, Congress might react to an engagement with its power of the purse, but it is presidents who set the process in motion by initiating a conflict to begin with.

4. Thus, for Neustadt, formal powers remain part of the three-legged stool that make up presidential power (along with reputation and prestige).

5. Beckmann (2010) and Preston (2001) are notable examples of this trend in the literature.

6. This tendency is in part the result of the way the American politics and international relations communities are siloed in political science. Even in political circles and administrations there tends to a distinction between those charged with the politics of campaigning and winning elections and those engaged in foreign affairs. In general, the foreign policy elite often fancies itself to be somewhat removed from the political process.

7. Gailmard and Patty (2012) speak to the deeper historical origins of the variation in presidential autonomy over diplomacy, crisis intervention, and the use of force. In their view, presidential claims of autonomy are important in part because they can be self-reinforcing. Thus, because the executive claim of diplomatic authority is older it is also more entrenched, reinforced, and unquestioned in American politics. Presidents wasted no time asserting diplomatic autonomy. While George Washington initially took the first part of the constitutional requirement for the Senate's "advice and consent" on treaties at face value and sought input on ongoing treaty negotiations and diplomatic missions, he quickly grew disenchanted with legislative involvement. Consultation gave way to updates, and by the beginning of the nineteenth century, presidents routinely presented completed treaties to the Senate for ratification but sought no input on their negotiation. Lower level diplomacy was the prerogative of the executive from the very start. In contrast, presidents began to assert themselves forcefully in matters of armed conflict in the twentieth century (Fisher 2004).

8. William Olson (1991, 548), for example, remarks that "while Congress certainly sometimes behaves independently from the administration, it is unlikely to develop a coherent independent policy of its own."

CHAPTER FIVE

Great Judges

Judicial Leadership in Theory and Practice

Charles M. Cameron and Mehdi Shadmehr

Common-law systems of law revere great judges. The great judges are hailed for their "comprehensive scholarship, sense of the 'right' result, craftsmanship, and versatility" (Judge Friendly on Justice Traynor), for their "analytic power, memory, and application" (Judge Posner on Judge Friendly), and above all for their "innovativeness," "generativeness," persuasiveness, and impact on the path of the law.[1] Citation analysis has become a cottage industry in the legal academy, undertaken not for the purpose of mapping networks of competing doctrinal schools as in White and McCann (1988), or uncovering the progression of doctrinal innovations across time and space—with some notable exceptions, discussed below—but instead for the explicit purpose of scoring individual judges on their impact and prominence within the judiciary (Landes, Lessig, and Solmine 1998). Compiling and comparing lists of "judicial saints"—Holmes, Brandeis, Cardozo, Hand, and so on—is a source of never-ending effort and untiring pleasure for adherents to the cult of the robe (Schwartz 1997). Judicial biographies abound, a peculiar literary genre celebrating individuals who, almost by definition and certainly by choice, lead lives of probity, free from scandal, drama, rebellion, color, or (one must say) much human interest. Top-notch judicial biographies include Mason (1968), Gunther (1994), and Dorsen (2012).

In contrast, the phenomenon of acknowledged great judges is virtually unknown in civil law systems. John Henry Merryman, in his famous book on civil law systems, makes the contrast explicit:

We in the common law world know what a judge is. He is a culture hero, even something of a father figure. Many of the great names of the common law are those of judges: Coke, Mansfield, Marshall, Story, Holmes, Brandeis, Cardozo. We know that our legal tradition was originally created and has grown and developed in the hands of judges. . . . But in the civil law world, a judge is something entirely different. He is a civil servant, a functionary. . . . [Civil law] judges of the high courts receive, and deserve, public respect but it is the kind of public respect earned and received by persons in high places elsewhere in the civil service. . . . The great names of the civil law are not those of judges (who knows the name of a civil law judge?) but those of legislators (Justinian, Napoleon) and scholars. . . . The civil law judge is not a culture hero or a father figure, as he often is with us. His image is that of a civil servant who performs important but essentially uncreative functions. (1969, 34–36)

As Merryman explains, in civil law systems, the official conception of law is a definitive statutory code produced by a democratically accountable legislature. Typically, civil law judges do not write long elaborate opinions. Instead, they merely announce case dispositions that supposedly follow from straightforward application of the legislature's clear-cut code. So in practice and often in literal fact, a civil law judge is a midlevel bureaucrat, essentially an expert clerk, and hence no more likely to achieve greatness than, say, the administrator of the local motor vehicles department or a GS-10 working at the IRS.

In common-law systems, though, much law has been and continues to be created by judges, not legislators. This is particularly true in critical areas of private law such as torts, contracts, and property. Much more judge-made law is derived from creative—in some cases wildly creative—judicial interpretation of cryptic ambiguous or contradictory statutes, as well as through interpretation of the gnomic US Constitution. In such a system, there is a real opportunity for individual judges to innovate new doctrine and then serve as judicial leaders—individuals whose innovations are cited, imitated, and adopted by other judges.

But this fact raises many questions. What allows one judge to lead, and—equally critically—what compels other judges to follow? What are the consequences of judicial leadership for the performance of a legal system? This essay begins to address these questions. To do so, we advance a novel theory of judicial leadership. Indeed, though there are many studies of judges who were leaders, we are aware of no other theory of judicial leadership.[2] We distinguish our theory—a theory of coordinative judicial leadership—from theories of authority in judicial hierarchies. We also focus attention on a fundamental trade-off or tension in judicial leadership, between (on the one hand) creating new doctrine that reflects what Holmes ([1881] 2009, 1) calls "the felt necessities of the times" and (on the other) maintaining settled law that allows a population of judges to administer justice consistently and predictably. The tension between innovation and consistency is a key element of our theory of coordinative judicial leadership. Flowing from this tension, the theory also highlights the perils of judicial leadership: because the leader can be so influential, her actions risk coordinating the followers on an incorrect doctrine. Recognizing this danger, the leader will not actually exercise leadership unless she herself is sufficiently confident of the soundness of the doctrine she advocates. Finally, the theory suggests several empirical regularities. Though we do not submit these to tests with systematic data, we do offer a plausibility check by reviewing the actions of several acknowledged great judges, including what they themselves say they were trying to do. We focus on three acknowledged great judges: Benjamin Cardozo, Roger Traynor, and Henry Friendly. The case materials are arguably broadly consistent with the theory, but they suggest some valuable extensions to it. The theory also points to important gaps in the empirical study of judicial leadership.

What Is Judicial Leadership?

The Two Faces of Judicial Power: Hierarchical Authority and Persuasive Argument

We begin with the classic definition of power: Power is a causal relationship between preferences and outcomes (Nagel 1975). Although there remain some conceptual issues with this definition, it has become the standard approach in political science. Let's apply it to the judicial setting. There, we may say Judge A has power over Judge B's choice of doctrine, if A desired B to opt for or enforce doctrine X rather than doctrine Y, and A's preference for this outcome caused B to choose or enforce doctrine X.

In fact, power relationships like this are the subject of a substantial theoretical and empirical literature in the study of judicial politics. There, an apex court like the US Supreme Court is conceived of as a principal and the lower courts as agents (Songer, Segal, and Cameron 1994). So in terms of judicial power, Judge A = the US Supreme Court, and Judge B = a lower court judge. The judicial principal–agent literature then analyzes the institutional devices that give bite to the power relationship. For example, the US Supreme Court uses the certiorari process for selecting cases. It appears to use cert as a form of strategic auditing to target errant decisions by lower court judges (Cameron, Segal, and Songer 2000; Spitzer and Talley 2000; Carrubba and Clark 2012). The rather strange rule of four used during the cert process empowers passionate minorities on the Supreme Court, but this has the effect of boosting the doctrinal power of the majority because deviations by lower court judges are likely to trigger a review that moderate majorities favor but might not themselves invoke (Lax 2003). On the intermediate court of appeals, dissents allow minority factions allied with the majority on the Supreme Court to blow a whistle, attracting higher-level review. En banc reviews on the US courts of appeal allow the majority faction in the circuit to control ideologically outlying three-judge

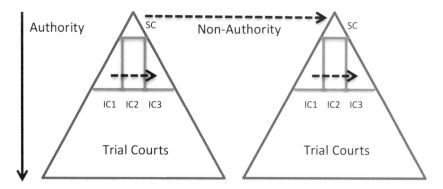

Figure 5.1. Authority Relations versus Leadership Relations in a Judicial Hierarchy. Each triangle denotes a judiciary composed of an apex court (SC = supreme court), intermediate courts of appeal (IC1–IC3), and lower-level trial courts. The authority relationship of the supreme court over lower courts in its hierarchy is denoted by the black solid line. A nonauthority influence is denoted by a dashed line.

panels, especially when that majority is aligned with the Supreme Court (Beim, Hirsch, and Kastellec 2014, 2015). And so on; many features of the federal judiciary give impetus to the authority vested in the US Supreme Court to enforce doctrinal uniformity throughout the judicial hierarchy.

As insightful as the principal–agent literature has been about power within a judicial hierarchy, it is crashingly silent about influence across judicial hierarchies, and it is likewise silent about influence within a hierarchy across equivalent levels absent vertical direction. To grasp these distinctions, consider Figure 5.1. Shown are two judicial hierarchies—for example, two state judicial systems, or the federal judiciary and a state judiciary. As is typical in judicial systems, each consists of three layers (Cameron and Kornhauser 2006). The lowest layer is composed of single-judge trial courts. Above them are multimember intermediate courts of appeal (denoted ICs in Figure 5.1). Above the intermediate courts is the apex court, a supreme court (denoted SC in Figure 5.1). The power relations studied in the principal–agent judicial literature are authority-based relations, which are denoted by the solid line in the left of the figure (helpfully labeled "Authority"). As Figure 5.1 indicates, these authority relations are top down. But top-down authority relations are not the only avenue of influence at work in judicial hierarchies. Two other pathways are readily apparent, shown by the dark dashed lines in Figure 5.1.

The first pathway is apex-to-apex influence. For example, Judge A on the supreme court of a state writes an opinion that creates a doctrinal innovation, and then this judge's innovation is adopted by Judge B on the supreme court of another state. Obviously judges in completely different state judicial systems are under no obligation to conform to one another's doctrinal choices. Yet this phenomenon frequently occurs, as several empirical studies have clearly demonstrated (Caldeira 1985; Graham 2015). Famous examples include cases authored by Benjamin Cardozo while a member of the New York Court of Appeals (that state's apex court) and by Justice Roger Traynor while a member of the California Supreme Court.

The second pathway concerns a judge on the intermediate court of appeals who creates a doctrinal innovation that is then adopted by other intermediate courts of appeal within the hierarchy. A critical feature of this pathway is that it does not lead through the apex court; in other words, the supreme court does not review the intermediate court's opinion, accept its doctrine, and then impose it on all the intermediate courts of appeal. (This process is studied in Clark and Kastellec 2013 and Beim 2016.) Rather, the first judge's innovation is adopted voluntarily by other judges at the same level in the hierarchy. Again, in the American system of jurisprudence, the latter judges are under no obligation to respect the first opinion—but they do, at least on occasion. Famous examples include opinions by Judge Learned Hand while a member of the Second Circuit and by Judge Henry Friendly while a member of that same circuit.

What occurs in apex-to-apex influence and intermediate court-to-intermediate court influence? Here we follow economist Benjamin Hermalin, who, reviewing studies of firms and corporate cultures, distinguishes the exercise of power through authority and the exercise of power through leadership: "Leadership should be seen as a phenomenon distinct from authority or the exercise of some office or title. The defining feature of leadership is that a leader is someone with voluntary followers. A central question is, therefore, why do they follow? What is it that leaders do that makes followers want to follow?" (2013, 435).

We return shortly to the vital issue of follower motivation but focus first on Hermalin's initial point: leadership is defined by voluntary followership. In the apex-to-apex pathway, the second state supreme court need not follow the first judge's lead—but it does, voluntarily. In the intermediate court-to-intermediate court pathway, the second intermediate court of appeals need not follow the first judge's lead—but it does, voluntarily. Thus, these two non-authority-based pathways of influence involve judicial leadership. Obviously judicial leadership is a type of power. But it is a type of power distinct from the authority-based power studied in the judicial principal–agent literature.

The Big Trade-Off: Innovation versus Consistency

The reader may readily admit that judicial leadership exists and is distinct from the authority-based power studied in the principal–agent approach to judicial hierarchies. But is there anything actually to explain? Weren't the famous opinions of Cardozo, Hand, Traynor, and Friendly simply excellent opinions that should have been followed by other judges virtually automatically? The answer is no, or at least not obviously. The issue turns on what we call the great trade-off in doctrinal adjustment—a trade-off between the benefits of modifying doctrine and the benefits from not doing so, the tension between innovation and consistency.

This tension is well captured in two of the most famous maxims about law, both formulated by great judges. The first maxim, attributable to Oliver Wendell Holmes Jr. ([1881] 2009, 1), addresses innovation: "The life of the law has not been logic; it has been experience." Holmes goes on to explain, "The felt necessities of the time, the prevalent moral and political theories, intuitions of public policy, avowed or unconscious, even the prejudices which judges share with their fellow-men, have had a good deal more to do than the syllogism in determining the rules by which men should be governed." Thus, Holmes asserts as a factual matter that law adapts to a changing society. However, he seems to go beyond a purely positive point. He appears to make a normative one as well: Law adapts to a changing society, and it is a good thing that it does. The benefit of periodic adjustments of legal doctrine is obvious. Law acts as the scaffolding of commerce, industry, government, and many personal relations. As society changes, that scaffolding must change too, lest it become an impediment rather than an assistance to desired social relations.

Holmes is silent on why judges might want to improve doctrine. In other words, how do doctrinal innovations enter the utility function of the innovative judge? Perhaps new doctrine allows the innovator to correctly decide the cases before him, affording the satisfaction of a job well done. In other words, the judge's utility function includes a term "correct dispositions that I personally produce." Here a doctrinal innovation is almost a private good for the innovator. Another possibility is that an innovative appellate judge receives satisfaction not only from deciding cases using good doctrine but also when subordinate judges under his jurisdiction do so as well. So the judge's utility function includes a term "correct dispositions under my responsibility." A final possibility is that an innovative judge receives satisfaction when his good innovation is adopted by others even if they are not his subordinates. In that case, the innovation (if adopted) resembles a public good created by the innovator, a public good—"good policy"—entering the utility function of the judge.[3] It would be hard to untangle these motivations simply by observing the behavior of judges. But as we shall see, great judges, when reflecting on their actions in their nonjudicial writings, often seem sensitive to the third motivation.

The second maxim, attributable to Justice Louis D. Brandeis (1932, 285), addresses the virtues of continuity: "Stare decisis is usually the wise policy, because in most matters it is more important that the applicable rule of law be settled than that it be settled right." Stare decisis—literally, "to stand by what has been decided"—is the legal principle that calls for adherence to precedent, to maintaining the doctrinal status quo. Brandeis's adage has such a ring of truth about it to the legal mind that it is frequently quoted without much reflection on the obvious rejoinder: why? Why is it better to be definitely wrong than only probably right? Or even definitely right? On this question Brandeis was silent. In other words, Brandeis's maxim should read, "It is more important that the applicable rule of law be settled than that it be settled right *because of Factor* X." Unfortunately, Brandeis offers us no Factor X.

But other judicial analysts have not been so reticent. In fact, two formal models supply explicit rationales for Brandeis's adage. In Cooter, Kornhauser, and Lane (1979), a single immortal judge considers whether to alter existing doctrine in order to improve it (that is, to bring it more into alignment with social needs). Implicit in the model are many private actors who enter into agreements "in the shadow of the law" (Mnookin and Kornhauser 1979). The structure of those agreements assumes current doctrine. If the judge alters existing doctrine, thousands of firms and individuals will need to renegotiate their existing contracts, alter their business practices, or change their private conduct. Doing so would be quite costly, perhaps immensely so. In the model, the court is sensitive to these social adjustment costs. If the adjustment costs are too high, the court maintains the status quo rather than adjust. Thus, social adjustment costs act as a brake on doctrinal change.

The answer offered in the second essay is rather different. In Bueno de Mesquita and Stephenson (2002), an appellate court—a principal—considers a new policy that will be implemented by a single mechanically faithful but possibly somewhat inept subordinate court, the agent. This creates the possibility of flat-out error by the subordinate; it simply misunderstands what the higher court wants. This chance for error by the agent in the principal–agent relationship induces the principal to proceed cautiously. If the subordinate is likely too ham-handed and the improvement from innovation modest, the principal may not adjust doctrine at all.[4]

These models surely capture some of the motivation behind doctrinal conservatism. However, neither the adjustment cost model nor the subordinate error model address what many legal analysts would see as the real thrust of Brandeis's adage, namely, the desirability of on-the-ground consistency in the administration of law. Consistency in implementation is central to the very idea of rule of law, one of the great desiderata of any legal system. Rule of law requires that the same case, if presented to any judge, results in the same disposition. Rule of law assures that judicial rulings depend only on the facts and the law, not on the luck of the draw of a judge. This consistency is important for simple fairness, which is essential if a legal system is to maintain the respect and allegiance of the citizenry. Consistency is also important if private agents are to make efficient arrangements in the shadow of the law.[5] Unfortunately, achieving consistency across a large number of trial judges isn't easy. Although clever institutional design can help, high levels of consistency may require trial judges to value consistency itself. Even if they do, high consistency demands implementers understand and agree on what doctrine is and what it demands each to do. However, achieving common agreement on doctrine among a plethora of implementers is no easy task, particularly when doctrine becomes a moving target. Hence we may complete Brandeis's adage: "It is more important that the applicable rule of law be settled than that it be settled right *because settled law conduces to consistent administration of justice by a multitude of implementers, and the value of consistency even with less-than-perfect doctrine often trumps the value of a better rule with less consistent implementation.*" In this account, Factor X = consistent administration by many judges. In other words, coordination by many judges on common doctrine.

Just to be clear, neither the adjustment cost model nor the subordinate error model address this Factor X, nor can they. In the adjustment cost model, the court itself implements policy so law on the ground is completely consistent and perfectly responsive to the innovator's wishes. In the subordinate error model, law on the ground is administered by a single agent, and consequently implementation is completely consistent, though perhaps somewhat discordant with the high court's preferred doctrine. Only if one takes seriously a world of many implementers can one pursue the logic of coordination as Factor X, then explore the big trade-off between doctrinal innovation and doctrinal consistency.

Just Judicial Activism?

If judges face a trade-off between innovation and consistency, are leading judges just judicial activists who highly value some pet innovations over consistency? Are their followers just judges who share their ideological bias? In fact, in their writings, many great judges do seem to value doctrinal innovation. However, that does not make them "judicial activists" as that phrase is commonly used. Judicial activism is usually taken to mean a court riding roughshod over perfectly adequate precedent or constitutionally valid legislation in pursuit of an ideological or partisan objective (Cross and Lindquist 2006). Of the great judges we consider, only one—Roger Traynor—at all resembles a judicial activist in this sense. Instead, the fields of leadership commanded by the great judges often lack a pronounced ideological or partisan bent. The motivation for leadership often seems less ideological than a desire, as Karl Llewellyn (1960) notes, to tidy up the law so that it is easier to understand, easier to implement, or easier to follow, or to just make it make more sense.

To provide a concrete example, consider Judge Friendly's preferred statutory targets as identified in his essay "The Gap in Lawmaking—Judges Who Can't and Legislators Who Won't" (in Friendly 1967). One might expect an essay with such a title to extol the judicial activism favored by the later Warren Courts, or Judge Traynor's California Supreme Court, or Rehnquist-era conservative activists like Justices Scalia or Thomas. But that is not Friendly's brief. Instead, he points to areas of the law where congressional action or inaction has created bizarre, contradictory, woefully incomplete, or manifestly idiotic laws leading to judicial inequities, miscarriages of justice, or economic inefficiency. (Judge Friendly is able to identify many such instances.) However, even in those areas, Friendly eschews a call for wide-ranging judicial innovation, though he himself was a famous innovator. Instead, he suggests ways Congress could do a better job. We will return to Friendly's jurisprudence shortly, but it's worth noting his criticism of one of the high-water marks of the Warren Court's judicial activism, the *Miranda* decision requiring police officers to warn suspects against self-incrimination. His essay "A Postscript on Miranda" (in Friendly 1967) argues the decision's constitutional justification was weak. But he does not blast the decision as unbridled activism, as one might expect from a committed conservative. Rather, his evaluation is conditional and pragmatic, essentially saying, "Let's see how this works out in practice."

Of course, some noted judicial activists take a temperate line in their official writings. But Friendly's jurisprudential writings do not come trailing the noxious odor of hypocrisy, unlike those of some notable Supreme Court activists. Though Friendly was an innovator and leader, in neither his actions nor his justifications does he resemble the stereotype of a liberal or conservative judicial activist. Something other than ideology was at play, both in his leadership and in the followership of other judges. But what?

Toward a Theory of Judicial Leadership

Return again to Hermalin's statement: "The defining feature of leadership is that a leader is someone with voluntary followers. A central question is, therefore, why do they follow? What is it that leaders do that makes followers want to follow?" Hermalin identifies a crucial element of any theory of leadership: it must also incorporate a theory of followership. Accordingly, we sketch a theory of judicial leadership with two distinct components: first, a theory of followership explaining why potential followers—judges who value correct adjudications but also uniformity of implementation—would be willing to follow the lead of a great judge; and second, a theory of the behavior of a great judge anticipating the responses of potential judicial followers. We draw on recent developments in the game-theoretic analysis of incomplete information coordination games. We argue that these models are particularly well suited for studying social situations like those facing judges—in other words, a situation in which the actors care about a social fundamental (such as, what is the best doctrine for a particular set of cases) but also care about the choices of the other players (hence, the doctrine that best maintains judicial consistency across judges).

The essential features of this class of game are the following. Within a coordination game setting, private signals about a social fundamental give rise to beliefs not just about the fundamental but also about the other players' beliefs about the fundamental. In turn, the beliefs about both entities—the fundamental and others' beliefs about the fundamental—affect individual choice. The remarkable findings are, first, incomplete information about the fundamental can break the standard multiplicity of equilibria in coordination games, leading to a unique equilibrium strategy for all players; and second, in an environment with both public and private signals about the social fundamental, individuals in some sense overweigh public signals because they provide information about what other players are likely to do.

Coordinate This! A Word about Judicial Rules

Before we sketch our theories of judicial followership and judicial leadership, we need to say a few words about the object of coordination: judicial rules.

Broadly speaking, the most basic job of a judge is to resolve a conflict between litigants by applying a rule to the facts in the case, thereby rendering judgment. As an example, consider a tort case involving injury from a defective product. There are two possible judgments: the defendant is liable, or the defendant is not liable. Under some tort rules, the relevant fact in the case is the degree of care exercised in manufacturing the product. So if the defendant exercised at least a certain level of care in manufacturing the product ("reasonable care"), the defendant should be held not liable. But if the defendant exercised less care, she should be (or at least could be) held liable. Thus, the legal rule has the following general form:

$$r(x,y) = \begin{cases} 1, & x \geq y \\ 0, & \text{otherwise} \end{cases} \tag{5.1}$$

where x denotes the facts in the case (e.g., level of care), y denotes a cut-point level of care (e.g., the level of care corresponding to "reasonable" care), 1 connotes one judgment (not liable), and 0 denotes the other judgment (liable). Another universally familiar example of a legal rule is a speed limit rule. In that context, x would denote the speed of the car and y the speed limit, and judgment 1 would be "guilty of speeding" and judgment 0 would be "not guilty of speeding."

The reasonable care tort rule and the speed limit rule are examples of a larger class of legal rules, so-called cut-point rules. In fact, many legal rules (though not all) have this general form. As in much of the formal literature on judicial politics, we focus on cut-point rules.[6] In many cases, the "official" cut point for a judge is set by statute or by a relevant apex court. However, often no cut point exists. In this instance, a court—often an appellate court—must create one in order to dispose of that case and similar ones. Given such a situation across a group of appellate courts (say, supreme courts in multiple states), coordination has a simple meaning: the courts use the same cut point y in rendering judgment in cases. In fact, the closer the two implemented cut points, the more closely the courts coordinate because they will decide almost all cases the same way. Conversely, the farther apart the two y's, the less coordinated the courts.

In addition, without being too specific, one can imagine a normative evaluation of different possible cut points. For example, one might imagine a cost–benefit analysis of different standards of care or different speed limits. Or one might imagine a convincing philosophical or jurisprudential evaluation of rights and obligations. But in either case, one can say on some grounds that one standard of care is better than another, or one speed limit is superior to another. In addition, one can speak of the best standard or cut point. Call the best cut point θ.

Judicial Followership: A "Beauty Contest" Approach

We can now consider a theory of followership. Our analysis is based on Shadmehr and Cameron (2017), which draws on Morris and Shin (2002) and Angeletos and Pavan (2007).

Consider two judges who make decisions in the absence of a definitive doctrinal cut point. Index the two judges by subscript $i \in \{1, 2\}$. Judge i will set doctrinal cut point $y_i \in \mathbf{R}$. In this action, he has two desiderata: set the cut point as close as possible to the best possible cut point $\theta \in \mathbf{R}$ (which one can regard as the state of the world) and set y_i as close as possible to the other judge's chosen cut point y_j. More specifically, judge i's payoff from choosing y_j is

$$u_i(y_i, y_j, \theta) = -(1 - r)(y_i - \theta)^2 - r(y_i - y_j)^2, \qquad i \neq j \qquad (5.2)$$

where $0 \leq r \leq 1$. In words, the judge wants her chosen rule to be as good as possible (close to θ) but also to match the rule chosen by the other judge. Overall utility is a weighted average of the two distinct components.[7] So if the judge cared only about setting doctrine correctly, $r = 0$ and utility reduces to $-(y_i - \theta)^2$. Conversely, if the judge cared only about coordination, then $r = 1$ and utility reduces to $-(y_i - y_j)^2$.

Critically, we assume the two judges do not know the best possible doctrinal cut point (the state of the world), θ. Rather, they have some initial beliefs about it, reflecting information acquired from hearing cases. Such information is purely private to a judge since only he hears testimony and the arguments of counsel. Then both judges read the opinion of a leading judge, an opinion that provides further information about θ. This information is a public signal, a public signal that opens the door to leadership by the prominent judge.

We first briefly consider two benchmark cases: known θ, then uncertain θ with private signals. We then consider the scenario of principal interest: a private signal and a public signal together.

Known Best Policy. As a benchmark, let's briefly consider what the two judges would do if they both knew the best cut point θ and this fact were common knowledge. Using Equation 5.2, It is easy to show that each judge's optimal choice is $y_i = ry_j + (1 - r)\theta$. So judge i's best action depends on the other judge's doctrinal choice (y_j) and on the value of the best possible cut point (θ).[8] Solving simultaneously for both cut points leads to $y_1{}^* = y_2{}^* = \theta$. In other words, the two judges would both choose the same doctrinal cut point: the best possible cut point θ.

As this benchmark indicates, the judges are in a strategic situation where coordination looms large. If there is a clear "best" coordination point, they will coordinate on that point.

Unknown Best Policy: Purely Private Signals. Now suppose, more realistically, that the two judges are unsure about the best judicial doctrine. To simplify, we'll assume that they are quite unsure: they initially believe that the best cut point could be any value at all, and that initially any one value is just as likely to be the best cut point as any other.[9] Then we imagine that the judges receive private, noisy information about the best doctrinal cut point. We imagine these private signals arise from information gleaned from hearing a case, listening to testimony, and studying the arguments of counsel. Thus, the information is purely private to judge i—no other judge sees judge i's information. However, any judge who hears a case receives her own private signal about good policy. We assume that signals have the form $s_i = \theta + \varepsilon_i$, where ε_i is a normally distributed random variable with mean 0 and variance σ_ε^2. In words, the signal is noisy but is at least somewhat informative about the best doctrine and is unbiased.

If a judge were just acting alone and received many such signals, her beliefs about the best doctrine would converge to the correct value as she learned more about the best doctrine. (For a model with this flavor, see Bueno de Mesquita and Stephenson 2002.) However, a judge sensitive to the actions of other judges has a more complex strategic problem: not only does she wish to set her doctrine to the best value, but she also wishes to set her doctrine to the same value as that chosen by other judges. So she has to ask herself, "Given the signal that I saw, what most likely did the other judges see, and what are they likely to do, given their signal?"

This added strategic component leads some analysts to call this type of game a beauty contest, after a British newspaper competition made famous in a passage in John Maynard Keynes's *General Theory of Employment, Interest, and Money* (1936). In the newspaper competition (according to Keynes), readers won a prize if they were able to select the most attractive person in photographs, as chosen by others. In other words, the point was not to pick the most attractive candidate but the candidate whom others found most attractive. Keynes claimed that the stock market is this kind of beauty contest because the value of a stock depends not only on its fundamentals but on the evaluations of those fundamentals by other investors. Stock picking is thus not just about which stocks are actually good businesses but which ones other investors will see as good businesses. Our claim is that judicial policy making across apex courts or across similar tiers in a judicial hierarchy has an element of a Keynesian beauty contest.

When private signals have the simple form $s_i = \theta + \varepsilon_i$ with $\varepsilon_i \sim N(0, \sigma_\varepsilon^2)$ judge i's best estimate of the true θ is just s_i. And given this belief about θ, she should believe that most likely the other judges saw a similar signal and will therefore have similar beliefs. Accordingly, following a logic similar to the known policy case, a judge who sees private signal s_i should set $y_i = s_i$. On average, a judge can do no better than this.

Unknown Best Policy: Private Signals and a Public Signal. Now consider the much more interesting case in which the judges hear cases and thus receive private signals about good doctrine, but also read the opinions of prominent judges like Cardozo or Traynor. The latter provide a public signal about good doctrine—a signal that many judges receive and know that other judges receive as well. When judges receive both types of signal, how should they evaluate or weigh them?

Let's call the public signal z and assume it has the same general form as the private signals, that is, $z = \theta + \eta$, where η is a normally distributed random variable with mean 0 and variance σ_ε^2. We'll assume that η is distributed independently of θ and the ε_is. It proves useful to rewrite the variance of η and the ε_is in terms of their precision, which is just the inverse of the variance. Call η's precision $a = 1/\sigma_\varepsilon^2$ and the ε_i's precision $b = 1/\sigma_\varepsilon^2$. Then from statistical decision theory, if judge i sees the pair of signals (z, s), she believes the expected value of θ is $(az + bs_i)/(a + b)$. Using the results in Morris and Shin (2002), one can derive that judge i's optimal choice of doctrine is

$$\frac{az + b\,(1-r)\,s_i}{a + b\,(1-r)} \tag{5.3}$$

This remarkable result has the following interpretation. First, suppose the judges had no concern with coordination but only wanted to set the best doctrine. Then $r = 0$ and Equation 5.3 says, "Set doctrine to your expected value of θ, given all the information you have received." Conversely, suppose the judges care only about coordination and are unconcerned about choosing the best doctrine per se. In that case, $r = 1$ and Equation 5.3 says, "Ignore your private signal and set doctrine strictly according to the information in the prominent judge's opinion." To the extent that judge i cares about both the quality of the doctrine and coordinating with other judges, she will use both pieces of information in setting doctrine—but in some sense will overweigh the public information from the prominent judge, relative to her actual belief about the best doctrine.

Why this overweighing of the public signal? The intuition is simple and clear: all the judges receive the common signal from the prominent judge, and they all know this. The common signal thus provides information not just about the best doctrine but also about the likely actions of the other judges. Because of the beauty contest aspect of the situation, this double whammy gives the prominent judge's opinion tremendous impact.

The Decision to Send Public Signals about Doctrinal Innovation

The potency of public signals raises interesting questions about the considered, deliberate diffusion of public information by aspiring leaders. When should a leading judge communicate her perception of the value of a doctrinal innovation, and when should she hold her peace?

We explore these points in some detail elsewhere (Shadmehr and Cameron 2017). We postulate a prominent judge who moves before the two follower judges, a judge who can send a public signal about doctrine. We do not assume the leading judge knows the best possible doctrine for sure. However, we assume he can reduce the variance of the signal he observes by working harder. More specifically, we allow the prominent judge to choose a, the precision of the public signal, by expending costly effort. Greater deliberation and care thus produce a more certain signal in the judge's opinion. Then we assume the other judges observe the public signal z, as well as their private signals s_i. In essence, the follower judges read the leading judge's opinion. We assume the leader judge, just like the follower judges, values both correct doctrine and coherent doctrine. But he may not value these objectives to the same extent as the follower judges. For example, he may be more or less concerned with establishing the best doctrine, and more or less concerned about doctrinal coherence. Further, we assume the leader judge is concerned about doctrine within the organization as a whole. Hence, we endow the leading judge with utility function $U_L = u_L(y_1, y_2, \theta) - C(a)$, where

$$u_L(y_1, y_2, \theta) = -(1 - R)[(y_1 - \theta)^2 + (y_2 - \theta)^2] - R[(y_1 - y_2)^2 + (y_2 - y_1)^2] \quad (5.4)$$

and $C(a)$ is the cost to the leader from setting the precision of his signal (the cost of judicial effort). Note that the leader's weight on coherence, R, need not be the same as the weight r on coherence used by the follower judges.

Consider the incentives facing the leading judge. Suppose the leading judge cared only about judicial coherence and not at all about the quality of doctrine (so in Equation 5.4, $R = 1$). In this case, the leader would just want the two followers to use the same doctrine. If the follower judges did not receive private signals, they would immediately coordinate on the leading judge's signal if it were at all informative. Of course, the follower judges do have private information, but the more precise the leading judge's signal, the greater impact it will have on their choice. Thus, if the leading judge cares greatly about coherence and not so much about correctness, he has strong incentives to send a precise, powerful signal.

Conversely, though, suppose the leading judge cares exclusively about finding the best doctrine and not at all about coherence among judges (so in Equation 5.4, $R = 0$). Then the situation is more complicated. To maximize the chance of finding the best doctrine, the following judges should utilize both their own information and that from the leader. Of course, more precise information from the leader is helpful in discerning the best doctrine. However, because the follower judges are concerned about coordinating, they tend to overweigh the leader's public signal. Greater precision in that signal actually makes the overweighing worse. So from the leader's perspective, greater precision in his own signal is a double-edged sword: on the one hand, it provides useful information to the followers; but on the other, it distorts their incentives and may lead them to coordinate on a worse policy than they would have if they had paid more attention to their own signals.

A full analysis of the model is somewhat involved because the leader must anticipate the response of the followers to any message he might send. But Figure 5.2 illustrates one of the insights. Figure 5.2 shows the leader's expected utility from increasing signal precision, neglecting the cost of action (the figure shows Equation 5.4, taking into account the followers' actions). Remarkably, the leader's expected utility initially decreases in signal precision. This occurs because the public signal encourages the followers to ignore their private information. As the precision of the public signal increases further, the leader's expected utility increases. This occurs both because a powerful public signal helps coordinate the followers and because a highly precise signal likely points the way to good doctrine. However, if the cost

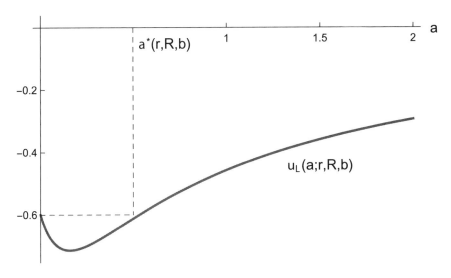

Figure 5.2. Signal Precision and the Leading Judge's Expected Utility. Shown is the judge's expected payoff as a function of the public signal's precision, ignoring the effort costs of producing that level of precision (see Equation 5.2). In the region indicated by the dashed line, no signal is better than sending a signal. The figure assumes $b = 2$, $r = 0.8$, $R = 0.2$.

of effort is sufficiently high for the leader, he may prefer to send no signal at all. As the picture demonstrates, even absent any direct costs of judicial effort, the great judge prefers sending no signal at all (zero precision) rather than sending a relatively inaccurate signal (precision less than about half). This is more likely to occur when the leading judge cares more intensely about getting the policy right than about coordination and when increasing precision (writing a more insightful opinion) is particularly costly for the leader.

Great Judges: What They Do, How They Think

We've elaborated a theory of judicial followership and judicial leadership but have yet to examine concrete examples of great judges in action. Let us do so! But first we need to clarify some ambiguous points.

How Do You Tell a Great Judge When You See One?

Immediately: How do you tell a great judge when you see one? Answer: A great judge successfully innovates great doctrine. Let's unpack this seemingly straightforward definition, examining the terms "doctrinal innovation," "success," and "great."

First, what constitutes a doctrinal innovation in the law? Graham (2015) offers a close study of the diffusion of twenty innovations in tort law, with briefer analysis of seven more innovations. Tort law, the law of harms and compensation for harms, is a natural area for studying judicial innovation because much of the law is judge created, typically by state court judges. Graham offers this definition of a doctrinal innovation: "An innovation is a change or complement to existing doctrine that is perceived as new by an individual or other unit of adoption" (97). This definition emphasizes the subjective perception of novelty by informed members of a community of practitioners. Graham notes the difficulty of definitively scoring innovations, particularly because some doctrinal changes may be so incremental as to defy the term. Still, experts in tort law would probably feel comfortable with most of his examples, ten of which are displayed for illustrative purposes in Table 5.1. These examples include perhaps the two most famous tort innovations, the *MacPherson* doctrine in product liability cases and strict products liability for defective products (the *Escola* doctrine). Some examples in Table 5.1 are consequential, but others are quotidian—for instance, the so-called Connecticut rule requiring that a premises owner exercise reasonable care when removing natural accumulations of snow and ice from his property.

Second, when might a doctrinal innovation be deemed a success? The key points are persuasiveness and voluntary adoption by other judges. Thus, in his study of diffusion of tort innovations across the states, Graham (2015) treats a doctrinal innovation by one state as successful if it is adopted by another state. He views

Table 5.1. Ten Doctrinal Innovations in Tort Law

No.	Doctrinal Innovation
1	Strict liability for product injuries due to defective products (the *Escola* doctrine).
2	Products liability not restricted just to contract holders (the *MacPherson* doctrine).
3	A right to privacy enforceable in tort.
4	A cause of action for wrongful discharge (firing) in violation of public policy.
5	Abolition of categories of invitee, licensee, and trespasser for liability of land occupiers.
6	A claim for "loss of a chance" (of survival or recovery) in medical malpractice suits.
7	Abrogation of parental immunity in motor vehicle accidents occasioned by negligence.
8	Privacy torts for putting a defamee in a false light.
9	Overturn of the rule barring recovery for injuries suffered in utero.
10	Connecticut rule for reasonable care when removing ice and snow from one's property.

"adoption" as meaning definitive endorsement of the doctrine by the adopting state's highest court or its legislature. He scores the adoption decisions himself. Bird and Smythe (2012), in their case study of the diffusion across the states of the strict liability rule for manufacturing defects, use a similar standard. Dear and Jessen (2007) use a somewhat looser measure, viewing one state's cases as influential if another state's cases follow the first state's cases. Here, "follow" has the specific meaning that a well-known legal service, Shepard's Citation Service, scores the second case as citing the first case and substantively adopting or relying on the first cases. Both of these definitions could be extended to innovations by federal circuit judges. Thus, an innovation by (say) a judge in the Second Circuit is successful if adopted by judges in other circuits, absent a vertical command by the Supreme Court. An innovation by a circuit judge is also successful if adopted by the Supreme Court. Graham also notes the value of an innovation being incorporated into the restatements of law issued by the American Law Institute, a prestigious organization of legal academics, judges, and practitioners. The restatements are treatises intended to summarize the law in various areas such as torts, contracts, property, securities, and trusts. Inclusion of the innovation gives a kind of imprimatur to it.

Third, when is a successful doctrinal innovation a "great" innovation? Distinctions here may seem impossibly subjective, but one can discern two separate lines of argument. The first—call it the legal significance criterion—purses the thought suggested by Posner (1994, 523) in his interesting review of Gunther's biography of Learned Hand: "I believe that the test of greatness for the substance of judicial decisions, therefore, should be, as in the case of science, the contribution that the decisions make to the development of legal rules and principles rather than whether the decision is a 'classic' having the permanence and perfection of a work of art."

This legal significance or impact criterion leads to empirical measures such as how many states follow a state's doctrinal innovation, the speed of adoption among potential followers, or the durability of a doctrinal innovation before its replacement with another. In general, the legal significance criterion can be addressed, at least in principle, using legal materials. The second line of thought—call it the social significance criterion—scores innovations by their social impact or consequence. So, for example, strict products liability is enormously more consequential socially than the Connecticut rule. Measuring social significance requires nonlegal materials and might be extremely difficult to quantify in practice, though cost–benefit studies across adopting and nonadopting states might be feasible.

Real Opinions, Judicial Rhetoric, and the Theory

Appellate court opinions play an important (perhaps disproportionately important) role in legal education, and their construction and interpretation have generated vast literatures by legal scholars. One strand addresses the rhetoric of judicial opinions, the art of constructing opinions in order to make them persuasive to practitioners in a common-law legal system (Llewellyn 1960). Not surprisingly, the secondary literature on specific notable opinions tends to track the academic literature. Much of it thus concerns the rhetoric of great opinions—the selective marshaling of facts, reweaving of existing doctrine and manipulation of precedents, and the artful unveiling of an innovation. In contrast, our theory focuses on the strategic character of the players' interactions. Thus, in our theory, a leading opinion is simply a truthful report on the value of new doctrine (θ) broadcast with a degree of precision and surely heard by a cohort of potential judicial implementers. An obvious question is, what is the relationship between actual opinions and this bare-bones abstraction?

Here it is helpful to know a little about the construction of judicial opinions.[10] In every case, the court must issue a disposition indicating which of the contending parties prevails. In addition, the court may issue an opinion explaining how the application of a legal rule to the facts in the instant case leads to the indicated disposition. Doctrinally innovative cases offer a new or modified rule for deciding the instant and similar cases. In our reading of cases and commentaries, the rhetoric supporting an innovative rule typically has two components: first an argument that the innovation actually has precedential roots in existing case law, and second an argument that the innovation is an improvement over present doctrine and helps solve a social problem. The first component is a doctrinal argument, and the second a policy argument. The appropriate balance between the two components is a matter of long-standing controversy in the legal academy and the bench, as are the standards for a "good" doctrinal argument and an "appropriate" policy argument. Roughly speaking, and ignoring various subtleties, the school labeled "formalism" or "legalism" (sometime pejoratively) and the "legal process" school of the 1950s and 1960s privilege rhetorical strategies that emphasize the doctrinal component and downplay the policy component. Conversely, the schools of "legal realism" and "judicial pragmatism" favor greater rhetorical scope for policy arguments and may in turn downplay the doctrinal component. However, we suggest an empirical regularity: great opinions usually include both components. They offer a precedential basis for the innovation (however tenuous or strained), and they also argue that it is a good idea (however airily). The first component, which is essentially hermeneutics, helps practitioners view the judicial innovation as lawful and hence acceptable. The second component, which is essentially policy analytic, helps practitioners view the innovation as socially beneficial and hence attractive.

The theory includes an explicit representation of the policy component in the form of θ. We included a representation of the precision of the signal, which one might view as embedding or at least partially reflecting the quality of the leading judge's hermeneutics. Again, one might imagine leading judges exerting costly effort in order to increase the hermeneutic acceptability of their signal. In sum, extension of the basic model can partly address recognizable aspects of judicial rhetoric.

In considering several great judges and their acts of judicial leadership, we won't dwell at length on the details of their judicial rhetoric or the actual doctrinal innovations—for one thing, acute readings of this form are available, which we cite. Instead, we'll review examples of leadership to look for signs of θ and precision, seek evidence of judicial motivation, and examine the reception of the innovation.

Benjamin Cardozo

Benjamin Cardozo (1870–1939) served for eighteen years on New York's highest court, the New York Court of Appeals, and then an additional eight years on the US Supreme Court. His famous opinions date primarily from his service on the state court and deal with common-law topics, notably tort and contracts. Posner notes, "His judicial opinions continue to be a staple of teaching and scholarly discussion in contracts, torts, and other fields; the passage of time has not dulled their luster" (1990, 21). Posner convincingly mounts a variety of citation-based empirics to back this claim.

Cardozo penned numerous landmark opinions, but two in particular stand out. They continue to play a prominent role in legal education and are studied by nearly all law students: *MacPherson v. Buick Motor Co.* and *Palsgraf v. Long Island Railroad.* Posner reports that these are Cardozo's most-cited cases. Both have generated extensive literatures, including book-length texts. Both opinions ventured doctrinal innovations in tort law. The first vastly expanded the liability of manufacturers of defective products; the second offered a way to restrict the liability of companies whose employees negligently injure people.

How should we think about Cardozo's report on θ in these cases? If one takes a literal approach to θ, then one simply doesn't find much that looks like conventional policy analysis in *MacPherson*, *Palsgraf*, or indeed in most of Cardozo's other famous opinions, like *Murphy v. Steeplechase Amusement Co.* For example, they offer no systematic empirical evidence of any kind, and one finds very little that leaps out as economic reasoning. In fact, in his treatise on Cardozo's reputation, Posner (1990) mildly criticizes Cardozo's opinions for being insufficiently policy analytic. But this is to somewhat misunderstand Cardozo's persuasive strategy.

To grasp Cardozo's public reports, one needs to understand a little about the logical structure of legal doctrine. As James Henderson notes in his study of *MacPherson*, "All rules of tort law call for liability to follow from delineated sets of facts, using an **If–Then** format: 'If A kicks B without sufficient reason, **then** A is liable in damages to B'" (2003, 53, emphasis in original). More generally, one can formalize this logical structure—to wit, a rule is a mapping from a fact space into a disposition space. (The formalism was created in Kornhauser 1992 and is explicated in a relatively nontechnical way in Cameron and Kornhauser 2016.) The formalism suggests two broad avenues for doctrinal innovation: broadening or restricting the fact space, and altering the treatment of cases (the mapping) in a fixed portion of the fact space. The former approach roughly corresponds to what William Riker (1986) dubbed heresthetics, the art of political manipulation. It is also closely related to distinguishing a case, a standard rhetorical maneuver taught in the first year of law school.

The heresthetical manipulation of the fact space is Cardozo's favored modus vivendi, a point that has not escaped close students of the cases. For example, Henderson (2003) shows that Cardozo's summation of the facts in *MacPherson* was quite selective or perhaps even misleading. Rabin and Sugarman (2003) make the same point about *Palsgraf*, an observation forcefully reiterated in Posner (1990). Then, having artfully reconstructed the fact space, Cardozo moves in for the kill. Simons (2003), in an analysis of Murphy, explains:

> His opinions typically begin with a cinematic narration of the injury. Doctrinal standards [that is, Cardozo's doctrinal innovation] often first appear more as background props than as primary actors. But the technique is a sly one: when he tells a compelling story, he also insinuates that the legal standard is as compelling as the tale. In the end, the reader (or viewer) comprehends the facts and the law as one. (204)

In other words, having manipulated the fact space, Cardozo then suggests a doctrinal mapping that appears so natural, logically compelling, administratively feasible, commonsensical, and obviously in the public interest that much more policy analysis would just be overegging the pudding. In essence, the typical Cardozo report is: "Given the fact pattern I just showed you, my doctrinal innovation obviously has a high θ." It is not logically necessary to show that the old doctrine yields absurd results in the new fact space, though Cardozo often offers some arguments along those lines too.

The heresthetical heavy lifting, which I am associating with a kind of report about θ, is analytically distinct from the hermeneutic component of the opinions. This component of the opinions typically tries to show that the actual innovation is not really an innovation at all but rather merely a minor tweak on existing law. Again, legal commentators have had a field day showing how Cardozo "twisted 19th century doctrine inside-out," "re-named and enlarged" existing categories, cited minority opinions as if they were controlling majority ones, and engaged in much other hermeneutical legerdemain.[11] This aspect of the cases has contributed to Cardozo's reputation as tricky, and indeed one cannot work through a careful doctrinal analysis of, say, *MacPherson*, actually reading the preceding key cases, and fail to come to a similar conclusion (Levi 1949, section 2, remains evergreen). Again, one can see this aspect of the cases as boosting the likelihood of a positive reception, though this is somewhat outside the model we sketched.

What of the likelihood other judges would read his opinions and be exposed to his arguments? An obvious point is the New York Court of Appeals was the leading state court of Cardozo's day. It heard a high volume of cases, and those cases reflected important changes in the economy and American society that were spreading elsewhere. In the phrase of Dear and Jessen (2007, 703), the New York court had "depth of inventory." In addition, the court's bench included a number of extremely able judges, as documented in Posner (1990). The western legal reporter for the Northeastern United States made the court's opinions readily available to other state judges in major population centers (Caldeira 1985). Finally, Cardozo was involved in creating the American Law Institute, whose restatements of tort law featured Cardozo innovations. In short, in the 1920s and 1930s, if you were a state judge interested in developments in tort law, you would naturally turn to the New York court's opinions, which you could obtain relatively easily. Thus, when Cardozo offered his innovations, he could be confident he was facing a high r.

Cardozo's writings embraced more than judicial opinions. Perhaps most notable is his book *The Nature of the Judicial Process* (1921), in which he elaborated his conception of the job of a leading appellate judge. The book is often taken to be an exemplar of legal realism or judicial pragmatism, and it is easy to see why:

> One of the most fundamental social interests is that law shall be uniform
> and impartial. There must be nothing in its action that savors of prejudice or
> favor or even arbitrary whim or fitfulness. Therefore in the main there shall be
> adherence to precedent. There shall be symmetrical development, consistently
> with history or custom when history or custom has been the motive force, or

the chief one, in giving shape to existing rules, and with logic or philosophy when the motive power has been theirs. But symmetrical development may be bought at too high a price. Uniformity ceases to be a good when it becomes uniformity of oppression. The social interest served by symmetry or certainty must then be balanced against the social interest served by equity and fairness or other elements of social welfare. These may enjoin upon the judge the duty of drawing the line at another angle, of staking the path along new courses, of marking a new point of departure from which others who come after him will set out upon their journey. If you ask how he is to know when one interest outweighs another, I can only answer that he must get his knowledge just as the legislator gets it, from experience and study and reflection; in brief, from life itself. (112–113)

One could hardly hope for a clearer statement about the value of good doctrine versus uniformity of administration, and about the need for leading judges to innovate good doctrine. In cases like *MacPherson* or *Palsgraf*, we see Cardozo practicing what he preached.

Last, what was the response to Cardozo's bids for leadership? Did other courts actually follow, particularly other courts that need not have done so? Two recent studies specifically examine state tort law and the impact of *MacPherson* and *Palsgraf*. Investigating the impact of *Palsgraf*, Cardi (2011) examines the contemporary negligence cause for action in all fifty states and the District of Columbia. His findings are complex, not least because subsequent analysts have identified several doctrinal bids in the case. Several of these fizzled. But Posner's reading of the case is somewhat blunter: "Cardozo's bottom line is that there is no liability to an unforeseeable plaintiff, however that status be defined in a particular case" (1990, 41). Cardi (2011, 1890) notes, "It is a more specific question whether courts condition the existence of a duty on the foreseeability of the plaintiff. On this score, Cardozo has clearly won the day. When faced with the issue, thirty-three (of fifty-one) courts hold with fair consistency that whether the plaintiff was a foreseeable victim is a question to be decided in the duty context." In the bulk of the remaining states, Cardi (2011) found the law unclear. To be fair, in most of the states unforeseeability—the key idea in *Palsgraf*—does not have pride of place but is merely one of multiple factors cited. Still, one would have to say that most states followed where Cardozo led, though not completely slavishly.

The reception of *MacPherson* is also somewhat more complex than one might imagine. Henderson notes, "Privity died a relatively slow death" (2003, 65). The diffusion rates calculated by Graham (2015) in his study of twenty successful judicial innovations provides some confirmation of Henderson's observation. For example, the average number of adopters after ten years averaged twenty-two among the innovations Graham studies. The equivalent figure for *MacPherson* was eighteen. However, the average number of adopters after twenty years was thirty-six, and this is exactly the number of adopters of the *MacPherson* doctrine. Similarly, *MacPherson*'s number of adopters after thirty years was at the average mark. So after a slightly slow start, *MacPherson*'s impact caught up with that of the other successful innovations studied by Graham.

Roger Traynor

Roger Traynor (1900–1983) earned his law degree as well as a PhD in political science from the University of California at Berkeley, where he subsequently became a law professor. In his ten years on the faculty of the law school, he became a prominent legal scholar, briefly serving as dean of the law school. In addition, he was active in tax reform and administration in California and served as state deputy attorney general. He was appointed to the California Supreme Court in 1940 and became its chief justice in 1964. He served in that capacity for six years, retiring in 1970.

Often regarded as the leading state judge of his day, Traynor authored over 900 opinions, many of which were landmarks of liberal jurisprudence. However, perhaps his most famous opinion was actually a concurrence, in the 1944 case *Escola v. Coca Cola Bottling Co.* In this opinion, Traynor created what is known as the strict products liability doctrine. Indeed, strict liability for defective products is often dubbed the *Escola* doctrine even though not a single other judge in the majority joined Traynor's concurrence. It was not until 1963, in the case *Greenman v. Yuba Power Products* that the California Supreme Court adopted strict liability, as expressed in Traynor's majority opinion. *Greenman* is usually regarded as the landmark case for strict product liability.

In contrast to Cardozo's somewhat coy depiction of his innovation's policy value, Traynor in his opinions in *Escola* and *Greenman* is extraordinarily forthright about θ: he argues that a switch in doctrine to strict liability would be an improvement in public policy. To be sure, he offers a doctrinal hermeneutic argument why his radical innovation is logically entailed by or at least consistent with earlier case law. Here his argument draws on *MacPherson* as well as some cases about contaminated foods. In essence, he breaks the link between implied warranties and contracts, instead reconceptualizing products liabilities as a field of torts (Geistfield 2003, 242). In retrospect, many legal scholars see this intellectual move as extremely clever. But asserting that this doctrinal innovation is arguably legal is not the same as showing that it is a good idea. For this, he relies on arguments about deterrence and risk spreading. In other words, his argument is a model of law-and-economics-style reasoning, and indeed modern law and economics scholars find the arguments both sound and prescient. Impressively, the risk-sharing arguments anticipate much later work in information economics. Combining the hermeneutics with the policy analysis, in *Escola* Traynor famously concludes, "If public policy demands that a manufacturer of goods be responsible for their quality regardless of negligence there is no reason not to fix that responsibility openly."[12]

However clever Traynor's *Escola* opinion was, it fell with a thud: Traynor failed to persuade anyone on his own court, much less on others. This fact raises serious issues about *r*. Evidently Traynor's *r* was tiny. But this should come as no surprise, for in 1944, Traynor was a relatively new arrival on the court—just a successful legal academic with limited judicial experience. Thus, the true audience for his opinion was not other courts but the other members of his own court. As a result, he need not have feared that his opinion would undermine the consistency of legal admin-istration because, after all, no other courts were listening to him.

In 1949, a case similar to *Escola* was again heard by the California Supreme Court. Traynor again made his argument for strict liability, and again not a single member of his own court found his opinion persuasive. In 1958, the court again heard a similar case, again Traynor made his argument, and again no one on the court joined him. But the sands began to shift. In 1960, the court again heard a related case and began to move somewhat in Traynor's direction without fully endorsing his argument. In 1961, the American Law Institute adopted a draft rule applying strict liability to sellers of food products. In 1962, it extended the rule somewhat. Then in 1963 came Traynor's breakthrough, the *Greenman* case. Here, in a dramatic shift, the entire court adopted Traynor's doctrinal innovation, making it the law of the land in California.[13]

By 1963, California had replaced New York as the leading state supreme court in the sense that its opinions were the most frequently cited of all state courts by other state supreme courts (Dear and Jessen 2007; Friedman et al. 1981). Already some of its cases were doctrinal landmarks, and over the next decade and half, many would become so (Rabin 2003b). Further, Traynor was no longer an obscure jurist with academic leanings but a national figure. The idea of strict products liability was no longer outlandish and outré but recognizable as an actual doctrinal option. Arguably, in 1963 Traynor's visibility was large; with his assent to the chief justice-ship the following year, it became enormous. The visibility of the case was further boosted in 1964 when Traynor's friend, William Prosser, wrote its doctrine into the American Law Association's *Restatement (Second) of Torts* (1965), adopting the *Escola* arguments lock, stock, and barrel and thus acting as a kind of megaphone for them.

As a successful academic and intellectually ambitious judge, Traynor laid out his philosophy of judging in many law review articles, and there is no reason to doubt their candor. Like Cardozo, he was a legal realist and saw good policy as an important consideration in judging. But he went much farther than Cardozo. "The real concern [is] not the remote possibility of too many creative opinions but their continuing scarcity" so that "the growth of the law, far from being unduly accelerated by judicial boldness, is unduly hampered by judicial lethargy that masks itself as judicial dignity with the tacit approval of an equally lethargic bar." Traynor thus concluded that true "judicial responsibility connotes . . . the recurring formulation of new rules to supplement or displace the old [and the] choice of one policy over another" (quoted in Ursin 2009, 1276). So not only did Traynor practice judicial activism with a distinctly liberal orientation, but he also defended it intellectually. More than that, he attacked judicial process scholars as essentially dishonest for their reliance on "magic words" (1961) rather than forthright and clearly articulated policy analysis. In our model of judicial leadership, the leading judge weighs good policy and consistency equally, but if we take his words at face value, Traynor seems to have placed much heavier weight on good policy than on consistency. Of course, such an evaluation would conduce to judicial activism.

Graham (2015) provides data on the diffusion of strict products liability across the states in the wake of *Greenman*. In contrast to the long, slow sell to the California Supreme Court, Traynor's innovation—once adopted in California—was clearly something of a thunderclap for other state courts. Of the twenty innovations studied by Graham, strict product liability spread the fastest, taking only eleven years to be adopted by thirty states. It has now been adopted by all but five states (Bird and Smythe 2012, 568).

Henry Friendly

Henry Friendly (1903–1986) is often regarded (with Learned Hand) as the greatest federal judge never to have served on the US Supreme Court. (The subtitle of a 2012 biography by Dorsen calls him "the greatest judge of his era.") His background was unusual, for a federal judgeship was Friendly's second career. In his first, he was a corporate lawyer, serving most notably as chief legal counsel for Pan American World Airways. In addition, he helped found a major international law firm, Cleary Gottlieb (originally Cleary, Gottlieb, Friendly, and Cox). Only after thirty-two years in private practice was he appointed to the federal bench, in 1959 by President Eisenhower. He then served almost twenty-seven years on the US Second Circuit, the New York–based circuit court that hears most federal cases involving corporations and business law. There he wrote more than 1,000 opinions. In addition to this flood of judicial opinions, he was a prolific author of law review articles, essays, lectures, and other writings, some of which were collected as books.

What are examples of Friendly's greatness? The answer is somewhat different from doctrinal innovations announced in distinctive and famous high court cases á la Cardozo or Traynor. There are three reasons why this avenue for greatness was constrained for Friendly. First, he was a judge on the federal intermediate courts of appeal. A great deal of the business of these courts lies in reviewing dispositions from trial courts, which the circuit courts are obliged to take. Only a relative hand-ful present provide plausible vehicles for doctrinal innovation. This is in notable contrast to the opportunities available to judges on apex courts like the New York Court of Appeals, the California Supreme Court, or the US Supreme Court. Sec-ond, Friendly's greatest area of expertise was administrative law. But the Second Circuit hears only a small number of these cases, which is the specialty of the DC Circuit. So in the area where he had the most creative and valuable ideas, Friendly heard few cases (though he made the most of them). Third, a primary (but hardly sole) audience for Friendly's doctrinal innovations was the US Supreme Court. But Friendly was a conservative in an era in which the Supreme Court was actively liberal, so he faced a frequently rather unsympathetic audience. More than that, many of Friendly's innovative impulses were naturally directed at limiting the War-ren Court's more adventuresome departures or addressing the unintended conse-quences and unanticipated shortcomings that resulted. Defying or contradicting the High Court is no easy job for a serving intermediate court judge; in fact, it is nearly impossible because "success" requires the Supreme Court to reverse course.

Friendly nonetheless found ways around these limits. First, many of his innova-tions lie in relatively technical and nonideological areas of the law. Dorsen (2012, 249) notes that he "helped rationalize, modernize, and promote fairness" in admi-ralty, antitrust, bankruptcy law, the law of punitive damages, and many other areas. These innovations are well known and appreciated by specialists but hardly have the revolutionary character of an *Escola* or *MacPherson*. Still, they remain influential. Second, in the area of administrative law, he substituted law review articles and books for the cases he did not have. Although his handful of administrative law cases made important points that the Supreme Court adopted, his biggest impact on the Supreme Court, on judges on the DC Circuit, and on the practices of federal agencies came from noncase writings (such as Friendly 1962). Many of the ideas in these writings made their way into law, just not from his cases. Third, his anti-Warren efforts addressed shortcomings that even the High Court could see. And again, his preferred vehicle was law reviews. Two examples are often noted. In "Is Innocence Irrelevant?" Friendly (1970) criticized a Supreme Court case that had opened a floodgate of meritless habeas corpus cases, straining the resources of federal courts for no good purpose. Friendly suggested remedial moves, which the Supreme Court quickly adopted. Similarly, in "Some Kind of Hearing," Friendly (1975) suggested how to prioritize among the uses of hearings, thereby bringing some order to an area of law thrown into chaos by a Supreme Court case. Again the Supreme Court quickly adopted Friendly's innovations, which continue to be cited and used in related cases today (Friendly 1975).

Both in his cases and in his influential articles, Friendly's use of policy-oriented arguments—what we called θ—is prominent. Though a master of case law, he put much less emphasis on hermeneutic gymnastics. Because of Friendly's tendency to be a nonformalist eclectic who was not tightly bound by the legal materials before him, Judge Richard Posner has called him "something of a judicial buccaneer" (Dorsen 2012, xiii). In the same vein, Friendly's biographer notes that his attitude to Supreme Court precedent was "sometimes cavalier" (Dorsen 2012, 349). This was not because Friendly had a hobbyhorse constitutional theory that he rode on all occasions. Rather, notes Dorsen, he creatively used precedent, holdings, and dicta to support his policy arguments, and in some cases, he simply disregarded or overruled Supreme Court precedent outright. For example, in *Hudson Valley Freedom Theater, Inc. v. Heimbach,* he not only overruled Supreme Court precedent but confidently predicted that, if given an opportunity to review his decision, the Court would follow him, not itself.[14]

However, his willingness to be an innovator and leader was scarcely absolute. He recognized the desirability of clear rules for others to follow, writing in one particular case, "We realize that, by deciding both phases of the case upon the particular facts here presented, we are not giving bankruptcy judges the guidance which they doubtlessly desire and it is our duty to provide if we properly can." But, he continues, "It is better to fail in this respect than to attempt to give guidance without having seen the variety of factual situations, having heard from the adversarial presentations, and having the benefit of the scholarly community which time will undoubtedly afford."[15] This expression offers an interesting alternative to our earlier stare decisis result: a highly influential judge may decline to strike off in a new doctrinal direction if he is not sufficiently certain the behavior of followers will be an improvement.

His opinions proved extremely influential on the Supreme Court, being cited more than 150 times by the High Court. Two studies have found him to be the second-most cited circuit court judge in law reviews, again behind Hand but far in the lead compared to his contemporaries (Dorsen 2012, 355, table 2; Posner 1990, 77, table 3). More relevant to us is his influence on coordinate judges before the adoption of his views by the Supreme Court and on state courts not directly answerable to the US Supreme Court. No study seems to have assessed his influence there quantitatively, but there is little doubt he was a force.

In sum, the actual exercise of judicial leadership by an intermediate-level federal judge is quite different from that of a high court state judge. However, one can still see the lineaments of the theory of coordinative leadership at work, at least arguably.

Lessons from the Cases

One should be cautious in drawing lessons from a handful of cases. At best they provide a helpful plausibility check and offer some food for thought. However, they are no substitute for systematic canvassing of appropriately gathered evidence. Moreover, our research design (to use a perhaps overambitious term) has an important limitation: we examined successful bids for leadership but did not (and could not with available materials) examine failed bids or bids that did not come but could have. The latter is a painful lacuna because the theory makes an interesting prediction about the circumstances when a potential leader will decline to lead. Nonetheless, several points stand out.

First, the leading cases we reviewed not only offer formalistic arguments why the proposed innovation was legal but also argue that the innovation is a good idea on policy grounds. This is less pronounced in Cardozo's landmark cases because he goes to great lengths to downplay the innovativeness of his innovations, working mostly through heresthetical manipulation of facts. But the policy arguments are pronounced in Traynor's and Friendly's leading opinions. On this reading, a clear and convincing statement about θ—the value of the innovation—is a recurring element.

Second, at the time of their big innovations, the leading judges commanded big audiences. They faced a high chance of being read. To some extent, this fact is baked into the cases by our selection of great judges. But Traynor's failure to gain much traction as a relatively obscure novice judge, compared to the big bang of his later efforts, is suggestive. In addition, the recurring importance of boosters or megaphones like the restatements of torts is striking.

Third, in their extrajudicial writings, these great judges emphasized the necessity of doctrinal innovations in order to improve the law. At the same time, they clearly recognized the importance of administrative consistency and the need to balance the two desiderata. A key assumption of the model thus finds some support in these materials. However, Traynor is a slight exception because he strongly emphasizes the value of innovation. Of the three great judges, he is clearly the only judicial activist.

Fourth, the materials do not allow us to see cases where the great judges declined to lead because of uncertainty about the value of the innovation or fear that a bid for leadership would severely disrupt administrative consistency. The sole exception is Friendly's explicit refusal to lead in bankruptcy law because he was unsure where the best innovation lay. That example is suggestive, however.

Fifth, the available materials do not speak much to the motivations of followers. Why did the states rush to adopt Traynor's strict liability innovation following its 1963 adoption in California? When Friendly urged administrative agencies to use more rule making and less adjudication, why did many of the agencies start to do just that? Was it merely the force of the arguments, or did the followers (as the theory suggests) desire conformity with their peers and thus tended to overreact to the public signal from a leading judge? This is a vital question that unfortunately the case materials can't address. However, it seems to us that the observed patterns of adoption are at least consistent with the global games approach.

In sum, the cases reveal complex elements not addressed by the theory—for instance, the value of legal hermeneutics for the acceptance of innovations, the role of noncase materials like law review articles and books, and the value of publicity boosters like the American Law Association's restatements of law. As the same time, we see the cases as relatively supportive of the basic fit between the theory and actual judicial leadership. In some sense, one value of the theory may be to highlight what is absent in the traditional literature—for example, leadership failures and demurrals to lead and much consideration of the motivations of voluntary followers.

Conclusion: Leadership—Judicial and Otherwise

The battlefield, the boardroom, the halls of Congress—these may seem the natural venues for the exercise of leadership, not the courtroom. Indeed, the very notion of stare decisis and the widely understood obligation of judges to follow precedent argue against judicial leadership. "Follow me" is the motto of the US Infantry; "Follow the law" is the equivalent for the judiciary.

It is thus perhaps not so surprising to find that, though there are many studies of great judges, there is no existing theory of judicial leadership. In fact, however, the great judges so revered in common-law systems do exercise leadership. They innovate, and other judges follow—and do so voluntarily. Great judges are perceived by other judges as leaders, and as we indicated, they see themselves that way too.

We argued that judicial leadership is an extreme or pure example of a special kind of leadership—leadership based on persuasion of followers whose obedience is entirely voluntary and based largely on a desire to undertake effective, coordinated action. Taking this to be the essential strategic setting, we essayed a simple theory of judicial leadership incorporating these elements. To do so, we drew on recent theoretical advances in the analysis of coordination games, the theory of global games. We also incorporated strategic public signals by a potential leading judge. This move follows similar cutting-edge efforts to model regime change, revolutionary action, and organizational leadership. As a simple plausibility check on the theory, we reviewed the actions of three acknowledged great judges, Benjamin Cardozo, Roger Traynor, and Henry Friendly. In our view, the case material is broadly consistent with the theory's assumptions about the motivations and behavior of judicial leaders. But the cases also suggest some worthwhile extensions in the theory—for example, allowing judges to exercise effort to gain larger and more receptive audiences. At the same time, the theory points to important gaps in current studies of great judges, in particular a need to examine failed bids for leadership or demurrals in exercising leadership. Finally, the theory suggests the need for a closer look at the motivations of voluntary followers, such as other state apex courts or legislatures.

References

Ahlquist, John S., and Margaret Levi. 2011. "Leadership: What It Means, What It Does, and What We Want to Know About It." *Annual Review of Political Science* 14:1–24.

Angeletos, George-Marios, and Alessandro Pavan. 2007. "Efficient Use of Information and Social Value of Information." *Econometrica* 75 (4): 1103–1142.

Beim, Deborah. 2016. "Learning in the Judicial Hierarchy." *Journal of Politics* 79:591–604.

Beim, Deborah, Alexander V. Hirsch, and Jonathan P. Kastellec. 2014. "Whistleblowing and Compliance in the Judicial Hierarchy." *American Journal of Political Science* 58 (4): 904–918.

——. 2015. "Signaling and Counter-Signaling in the Judicial Hierarchy: An Empirical Analysis of En Banc Review." *American Journal of Political Science* 60 (2): 490–508.

Berch, Michael, Rebecca White-Berch, Ralph Spritzer, and Jessica Berch. 2010. *Introduction to Legal Method and Process.* 5th ed. St. Paul, MN: West Academic Publishing.

Bird, Robert C., and Donald J. Smythe. 2012. "Social Network Analysis and the Diffusion of the Strict Liability Rule for Manufacturing Defects, 1963–87." *Law and Social Inquiry* 37 (3): 565–594.

Brandeis, Louis B. 1932. *Burnet v. Coronado Oil & Gas Co.,* 285 U.S. 393, 52 S. Ct. 443, 76 L. Ed. 815 [1932])

Bueno de Mesquita, Ethan, and Matthew Stephenson. 2002. "Informative Precedent and Intrajudicial Communication." *American Political Science Review* 96 (4): 755–766.

Caldeira, Gregory A. 1985. "The Transmission of Legal Precedent: A Study of State Supreme Courts." *American Political Science Review* 79 (1): 178–194.

Cameron, Charles M., and Lewis A. Kornhauser. 2006. "Appeals Mechanisms, Litigant Selection, and the Structure of Judicial Hierarchies." In *Institutional Games and the US Supreme Court,* edited by Roy B. Flemming, Jon R. Bond, and James R. Rogers, 173–204. Charlottesville: University of Virginia Press.

——. 2016. "Theorizing the Supreme Court." In *Oxford Research Encyclopedia of Politics,* edited by William R. Thompson. New York: Oxford University Press.

Cameron, Charles M., Jeffrey A. Segal, and Donald Songer. 2000. "Strategic Auditing in a Political Hierarchy: An Informational Model of the Supreme Court's Certiorari Decisions." *American Political Science Review* 94 (1): 101–116.

Cardi, W. Jonathan. 2011. "The Hidden Legacy of Palsgraf: Modern Duty Law in Microcosm." *Boston University Law Review* 91:1873–1913.

Cardozo, Benjamin. 1921. *The Nature of the Judicial Process.* New Haven, CT: Yale University Press.

Carrubba, Clifford J., and Tom S. Clark. 2012. "Rule Creation in a Political Hierarchy." *American Political Science Review* 106 (3): 622–643.

Clark, Tom S., and Jonathan P. Kastellec. 2013. "The Supreme Court and Percolation in the Lower Courts: An Optimal Stopping Model." *Journal of Politics* 75 (1): 150–168.

Cooter, Robert, Lewis Kornhauser, and David Lane. 1979. "Liability Rules, Limited Information, and the Role of Precedent." *Bell Journal of Economics* 10:366–373.

Cross, Frank B., and Stefanie A. Lindquist. 2006. "The Scientific Study of Judicial Activism." *Minnesota Law Review* 91:1752–1784.

Dear, Jake, and Edward W. Jessen. 2007. "'Followed Rates' and Leading State Cases, 1940–2005." *UC Davis Law Review* 41:683–711.

Dorsen, David M. 2012. *Henry Friendly: Greatest Judge of His Era.* Cambridge, MA: Belknap Press of Harvard University Press.

Friedman, Lawrence, Robert Kagin, Bliss Cartwright, and Stanton Wheeler. 1981. "State Supreme Courts: A Century of Style and Citation." *Stanford Law Review* 33 (5): 773–818.

Friendly, Henry. 1962. "The Federal Administrative Agencies: The Need for Better Definition of Standards." *Harvard Law Review* 75:863–903.

———. 1967. *Benchmarks.* Chicago: University of Chicago Press.

———. 1970. "Is Innocence Irrelevant? Collateral Attack on Criminal Judgments." *University of Chicago Law Review* 38:142–172.

———. 1975. "Some Kind of Hearing." *University of Pennsylvania Law Review* 123:1267–1317.

———. 1983. "Ablest Judge of His Generation." *California Law Review* 71:1039–1044.

Gambetta, Diego. 1996. *The Sicilian Mafia: The Business of Private Protection.* Cambridge, MA: Harvard University Press.

Geistfield, Mark. 2003. "*Escola v. Coca Cola Bottling Co.*: Strict Products Liability Unbound." In Rabin and Sugarman (2003a), 229–258.

Gilmore, Grant. 1977. *The Ages of American Law.* New Haven, CT: Yale University Press.

Graham, Kyle. 2015. "The Diffusion of Doctrinal Innovations in Tort Law." *Marquette Law Review* 99 (1): 74–177.

Gunther, Gerald. 1994. *Learned Hand: The Man and the Judge.* New York: Oxford University Press.

Henderson, James A., Jr. 2003. "*MacPherson v. Buick Motor Company:* Simplifying the Facts while Reshaping the Law." In Rabin and Sugarman (2003a), 41–71.

Hermalin, Benjamin E. 2013. "Leadership and Corporate Culture." *The Handbook of Organizational Economics,* edited by Robert Gibbons and John Roberts, 432–478. Princeton, NJ: Princeton University Press.

Holmes, Oliver Wendell Jr. (1881) 2009. *The Common Law.* Reprint, Cambridge, MA: Harvard University Press.

Kaufman, Andrew. 1998. *Cardozo.* Cambridge, MA: Harvard University Press.

Kornhauser, Lewis A. 1992. "Modeling Collegial Courts. II. Legal Doctrine." *Journal of Law, Economics, and Organization* 8 (3): 441–470.

Landes, William M., Lawrence Lessig, and Michael E. Solimine. 1998. "Judicial Influence: A Citation Analysis of Federal Courts of Appeals Judges." *Journal of Legal Studies* 27 (2): 271–332.

Lax, Jeffrey R. 2003. "Certiorari and Compliance in the Judicial Hierarchy Discretion, Reputation and the Rule of Four." *Journal of Theoretical Politics* 15 (1): 61–86.

Levi, Edward H. 1949. *An Introduction to Legal Reasoning.* Chicago: University of Chicago Press.

Llewellyn, Karl N. 1960. *The Common Law Tradition: Deciding Appeals.* Boston: Little, Brown.

Mason, Alpheus Thomas. 1968. *Harlan Fiske Stone: Pillar of the Law.* Hamden, CT: Archon Books.

Merryman, John Henry. 1969. *The Civil Law Tradition: An Introduction to the Legal Systems of Europe and Latin America.* Stanford, CA: Stanford University Press.

Mnookin, Robert H., and Lewis Kornhauser. "Bargaining in the shadow of the law: The case of divorce." *The Yale Law Journal* 88.5 (1979): 950–997.

Morris, Stephen, and Hyun Song Shin. 2002. "The Social Value of Public Information." *American Economic Review* 92:1521–1534.

Nagel, Jack. 1975. *The Descriptive Analysis of Power.* New Haven, CT: Yale University Press, 1975.

Posner, Eric A. 2016. "Presidential Leadership and the Separation of Powers." *Daedalus* 145 (3): 35–43.

Posner, Richard. 1986. "Henry J. Friendly: In Memoriam." *Harvard Law Review* 99 (8): 1724–1725.

———. 1990. *Cardozo: A Study in Reputation.* Chicago: University of Chicago Press.

———. 1994. "The Learned Hand Biography and the Question of Judicial Greatness." *Yale Law Journal* 104 (2): 511–540.

Rabin, Robert. 2003. "*Rowland v. Christian*: Hallmark of an Expansionary Era." In Rabin and Sugarman (2003a), 73–97 (see next entry).

Rabin, Robert, and Stephen D. Sugarman. 2003a. *Torts Stories.* New York: Foundation Press.

———. 2003b. Introduction to *Torts Stories.* In Rabin and Sugarman (2003a), 1–10.

Riker, William H. 1986. *The Art of Political Manipulation.* New Haven, CT: Yale University Press.

Schwartz, Bernard. 1997. *A Book of Legal Lists: The Best and Worst in American Law, with 100 Court and Judge Trivia Questions.* New York: Oxford University Press.

Shadmehr, Mehdi, and Dan Bernhardt. 2016. "Vanguards in Revolution." Working paper, Department of Economics, University of Miami and Department of Economics, University of Illinois.

Shadmehr, Mehdi, and Charles Cameron. 2017. "A Theory of Judicial Leadership." Working paper, Department of Politics, Princeton University, and Department of Economics, Calgary University.

Simons, Kenneth W. 2003. "*Murphy v. Steeplechase Amusement Co.*: While the Timorous Stay at Home, the Adventurous Ride the Flopper." In Rabin and Sugarman (2003a), 179–206.

Songer, Donald R., Jeffrey A. Segal, and Charles M. Cameron. 1994. "The Hierarchy of Justice: Testing a Principal–Agent Model of Supreme Court–Circuit Court Interactions." *American Journal of Political Science* 38:673–696.

Spitzer, Matthew, and Eric Talley. 2000. "Judicial Auditing." *Journal of Legal Studies* 29 (2): 649–683.

Traynor, Roger J. 1961. "No Magic Words Could Do It Justice." *California Law Review* 49:615–630. http://scholarship.law.berkeley.edu/californialawreview/vol49/iss4/2.

Ursin, Edwin. 2009. "How Great Judges Think: Judges Richard Posner, Henry Friendly, and Roger Traynor on Judicial Lawmaking." *Buffalo Law Review* 57:1267–1360.

White, Douglas R., and H. Gilman McCann. 1988. "Cites and Fights: Material Entailment Analysis of the Eighteenth-Century Chemical Revolution." In *Social Structures: A Network Approach*, edited by Barry Wellman and S. D. Berkowitz, 380–400. New York: Cambridge University Press.

Notes

1. The latter criteria for assessing judicial greatness are specified by Judge Posner, particularly in reference to Judge Learned Hand; see Posner (1994, 523–524). See also Friendly (1983, 1040) and Posner (1986, 1724).

2. Summarizing studies of presidential leadership in the legal academy, Eric Posner notes, "Legal scholars rarely discuss 'leadership'—of the president or anyone else" (2016, 35). This is a bit harsh, neglecting Richard Posner's (1990, 1994) conclusions. The latter in particular is extremely stimulating, but the focus is on measuring influence rather than formulating a theory of judicial leadership. In contrast, there are extensive literatures on leadership across the social sciences; Ahlquist and Levi (2011) provide an excellent overview. However, none of these considers leadership within judicial systems.

3. Cameron and Kornhauser (2016) provide further discussion of these motivations and how to incorporate them into formal models of courts.

4. This summary does not do full justice to the model, which provides some informational foundations. In particular, the initial policy is supported by a series of signals (rulings) from the principal, so the subordinate has tight beliefs about the proper doctrine. The shift in doctrine negates the value of this string of signals, which must begin all over again.

5. Private agents may be able to contract around inconsistent judges—for example, by setting up private orderings or relying on third-party mafias and the like (Gambetta 1996). However, the need to do so imposes considerable transaction costs on the agents. As a result, one would expect many profitable interactions to go unfulfilled when official justice becomes little better than a lottery.

6. For more on legal rules, see Cameron and Kornhauser (2016).

7. It is possible to microfound this utility function using a "dispositional" utility function and an expected distribution of cases; see Cameron and Kornhaser (2016). We omit these technical details here.

8. This is judge i's best response function. Both best response functions are increasing in the other judge's action, so this game involves strategic complements.

9. Technically, the two have improper uniform priors over the real line, and this is common knowledge.

10. A classic introduction is Levi (1949); a standard textbook is Berch et al. (2010).

11. "Re-named and enlarged" is from Levi (1949, 24). On the perception of Cardozo as "tricky," see Posner (1990, 15). The "twisted" doctrine is from Gilmore (1977, 75). Citing minority opinions as if they were controlling majority ones is from Kaufman (1998, 272).

12. *Escola v. Coca-Cola Bottling Co.*, 24 Cal.2d 453, 150 P.2d 436 (1944).

13. This paragraph draws on Geistfield (2003, 239–241).

14. *Hudson Valley Freedom Theater, Inc. v. Heimbach*, 672 F.2d 702, 707 (2nd Cir. 1982). For a discussion, see Dorsen (2012, 350).

15. *In re B. D. International Discount Corp.*, 701 F.2 1071, 1077 (2nd Cir 1983).

PART TWO

Leadership across Institutions

CHAPTER SIX

Parties and Leadership in American Politics

David Karol

Clear it with Sidney.
—President Franklin Roosevelt, in reported conversation with Democratic
National Committee chair Robert Hannegan, July 1944

The chairmanship of the party, as you know, is one thing, but after all you're the chairman of the party when the truth is known. You're the fella who will arrange these things politically in the different states or you'll arrange it in the Congress or you'll arrange it in the Senate or any other place because everyone looks to the president.
—Mayor Richard J. Daley of Chicago, in recorded conversation with
President Lyndon Johnson, November 21, 1964 (audio available at http://
millercenter.org/)

Studying party leadership in the United States is challenging because American parties are so amorphous and polycentric. As Joseph Schlesinger (1984, 379) noted, "The formal structure is obviously not the real organization." This is not something that a student of Congress or the presidency would write. Scholars of Congress may describe how a leadership role like the speakership (Jenkins and Stewart 2012) or the Senate majority leadership (Gamm and Smith 2002) has developed. Yet compared to parties Congress is a very well-bounded institution. Similarly, studies of the presidency may reveal important change in the extent to which the chief executive operates as a partisan leader (Rossiter 1960; Neustadt 1960; Lowi 1985; Milkis 1993; Galvin 2010; Skinner 2012), yet there is no doubt where the buck stops in the executive branch.

Parties, by contrast, are best understood as networks (Schwartz 1990; Bernstein and Dominguez 2003; Cohen et al. 2008a, 2008b). Networks have some actors who are more central than others but lack a centralized leadership. Hierarchy exists within institutions that make up the party network, but not in the party as a whole.

The two quotations opening this chapter suggest different answers to the question of where power lies in parties. The first highlights the role of interest groups, and the second foregrounds the influence of officeholders. Both capture part of the truth.

In the first case, Roosevelt was referring to Sidney Hillman, chair of the Political Action Committee of the Congress of Industrial Organizations (CIO). This alliance of industrial unions arose during the New Deal and rapidly became a force within the Democratic Party. Yet the party was a diverse coalition, and important factions, including Southerners and urban machines, did not want Vice President Henry Wallace, a CIO favorite, to be renominated. Liberal factions, including the CIO and African Americans, opposed Wallace's chief rival, James Byrnes of South Carolina. The fact that Roosevelt was seriously ill, which was known by elites if not voters, raised the stakes of this fight.

As wartime commander in chief, Roosevelt—then still the only president to have addressed a convention—preferred not to appear at a partisan gathering. So Roosevelt would not be present in Chicago for the selection of his running mate. The president claimed to have no problem with Wallace, but told Democratic National Committee (DNC) chair Robert Hannegan that he would happily run with Justice William O. Douglas or Senator Harry Truman, his probable true choice. Truman was a product of the Kansas City machine and a border state politician on good terms with his Southern colleagues. Yet the Missouri senator was also a New Dealer who had voted for labor and civil rights measures. He emerged as the compromise choice.[1]

News of Roosevelt's conversation with Hannegan leaked. The president's statement, rendered as the more ominous "Clear everything with Sidney" by Arthur Krock of the *New York Times* (Ferrell 1994), was seized on by Republicans as proof that Democrats were in the pockets of labor bosses (*Time* 1944). The fact that Hillman was a Jewish immigrant with radical ties made his prominence even more polarizing (Fraser 1991).

In the second case, President Johnson consulted with Mayor Daley about John Bailey, Kennedy's choice for DNC chair. Johnson was not close to Bailey and weighed replacing him with legislative liaison Larry O'Brien. Daley advised that dumping Bailey, a loyal functionary, was not worth the controversy it might provoke. Johnson acted as the mayor advised, although Daley's influence on this decision is unclear. He retained but marginalized Bailey and found another position for O'Brien the following year.

Beyond highlighting the roles of interest group leaders and elected officials in parties, these examples also illustrate the importance of informal processes in parties. Hillman held no post in the Democratic hierarchy and was a founder of New

York state's American Labor Party (which also nominated Roosevelt). While Daley was the chairman of the mighty Cook County Democratic Party, he was not a DNC member. Johnson likewise had no formal role at the DNC. Yet both men understood that Johnson, like presidents before and after him, would select the party chairman, and this choice would be rubber-stamped by the national committee members.

Also notable is the secondary role of the DNC chair in both cases. In 1944 Hannegan was a liaison between his party's president and a key interest group leader. In 1964 the chairmanship was discussed, but the chairman himself was not in the conversation and was not seen as a peer by either participant.

In this chapter I cover three main points: the limited importance of the formal leadership of national, state, and local party chairs; the central role of politicians in managing the groups of intense policy demanders that are the core of parties; and differences in leadership practices among Republicans in contrast to Democrats.

Beyond Party Committees: The Limited Role of the Formal Party Structure

A major obstacle to the understanding of political parties is a literal-minded focus on the formal structure of party committees. While elected officials are legislators or executives as well as partisans, party committees may appear to be the party phenomenon in its purest form. This is a mistake, especially if we are concerned with leadership. The services party committees provide candidates are real and have increased since the 1970s, along with the budgets and staffing of the Democratic and Republican national committees and the congressional campaign committees (Coleman 1996; Herrnson 2013). State-level organizations are better funded than they once were as well. It is only at the local level where the patronage-oriented traditional party organizations were based (Mayhew 1986) that there has been some decline, and even that only in the minority of counties where such organizations had been strong. Yet while leaders serve, "parties in service" (Aldrich 1995, 7) to candidates are not leading.

There is no truly paramount leader even of the formal party structure. The chairs of the parties' national committees do not pick the heads of the various congressional and other national campaign committees. The "Hill committees" are run by members of Congress (MCs) appointed by congressional leaders in the case of Democrats and elected by the party conference in the case of Republicans. Conflict between the chairs of the national committees and Hill committees is not unknown.

For example, DNC chair Howard Dean was elected chairman after pledging a fifty-state strategy of long-term party building, which would entail the national committee subsidizing parties in Republican states where Democrats had difficulty raising funds and where organization had atrophied. This plan was popular with such state parties, all of which had national committee members with votes in the election for chair. Dean followed through on this promise despite the angry insistence of Democratic Congressional Campaign Committee chair Rahm Emanuel and Democratic Senate Campaign Committee chair Chuck Schumer that funds would be more usefully directed to competitive congressional races (Galvin 2008). Dean's strategy was one of the more important independent initiatives of a national chair. He was able to pursue it, but he could not make the chairs of the Hill committees adopt his approach any more than they could compel him to desist.

There are also now separate campaign committees in both parties dedicated to raising funds for gubernatorial, state legislative, and subgubernatorial executive branch candidates.[2] These too are autonomous organizations. Nor do national chairs appoint state party chairs.

The chair of the party that does not occupy the White House is genuinely elected by the hundreds of committee members and is somewhat more visible and autonomous than his in-party counterpart. Yet Donald Trump's dismissive description of then RNC chair Reince Priebus—"we're not dealing with a five-star army general"—is not inaccurate about party chairs in general (Haberman 2015). Few have great authority or stature. Only one former chairman became a president (George Herbert Walker Bush), and the chairmanship was but one of his many stepping-stones.[3] On a handful of occasions the chairmanship was split into two positions: a general chairmanship filled by a prominent elected official who served as a spokesman and fund-raiser, and a national chairmanship occupied by a relatively obscure operative focused on nuts and bolts.

The president is the de facto leader and face of his or her party, but that is an informal status and a limited one. The president is the party "fundraiser in chief" (Doherty 2010), a task that has become increasingly time-consuming. By custom, the president chooses the chair of his or her party's national committee (who is then formally elected by committee members), but he or she does not select congressional leaders or control their campaign committees or state party organizations. Presidents cannot bestow nominations to elective office, even if they recruit candidates and try to shape the field. In any case, only one party at a time has a president, and there is no leader of the opposition in the United States.

To paraphrase Schattschneider (1942), parties are best understood as coalitions that seek to gain control of the government via elections. The key decisions are the choice of candidates, the choice of platforms, and, while in power, the choice of policies and priorities among them. The heads of formal party structures have only a modest influence over candidate selection and no direct influence over policy.

The formal structure of party committees can influence candidate selection by setting the rules by which nominations are determined. For example, the Virginia Republican Party's frequent resort to the convention nomination system favors conservative candidates, as does the California Republican Party's insistence on a closed primary. The national parties also regulate the timing and delegate selection methods used by state parties in presidential nominations. These choices are made by party committees, however, and are not typically the prerogative of committee chairs. Rule making by a large body is not generally counted as leadership.

The other important way in which the formal party structure can influence candidate selection is via recruitment, and here the chairs of various party units are prominent. A party committee may adopt a rule, but only an individual can have a private conversation with a potential candidate. Scholars have long found that party chairs play an important role in recruiting candidates for national, state, and local offices and discouraging other aspirants (Eldersveld 1982; Herrnson 1988; Kazee and Thornberry 1990; Sanbonmatsu 2006; Lawless 2011). These actions shape the field of candidates that voters encounter in primaries.

Yet even in recruitment, where their role is greatest, chairs of party committees are far from the only actors. Elected officials, interest group leaders, and party activists also participate in recruiting. Recruitment by chairs is also focused on competitive seats (Herrnson 1988; Maestas, Maisel, and Stone 2005) that elect a minority of MC and state legislators, while other policy-demanding interest groups and activist elites recruit in safe districts as well (Masket 2009; Bawn et al. 2014).

Party elites beyond the formal organization do more than shape the field. They can help the candidates of their choice and undermine others. My colleagues and I (Cohen et al. 2008) show that even in the postreform era of presidential nominations, party elites typically back a candidate who is later nominated and that elite endorsements are associated with success, even controlling for candidates' fund-raising success and early poll numbers. Dominguez (2011) and Hassell (2016) report similar findings for House and Senate nominations. Masket (2009) shows a similar pattern in state legislative contests.

Yet while the recruitment and endorsement activity of party elites is quite significant both in encouraging and discouraging candidates (Herrnson 1988; Hassell 2016), and in bolstering them once the primary field is set, voters have the last word. The remarkable nomination of Donald Trump in 2016 is the most dramatic illustration of this point. Voters picked Trump, as Republican elites were fragmented among other candidates or sat worriedly on the sidelines. This nomination caused some to doubt whether elites retained influence in the process. Yet it might be argued that Trump is anomalous and that GOP leaders did not manage to unify behind any alternative, so that his nomination—while an undoubted failure for party elites—does not disprove claims that a cohesive party elite can still prevail (Cohen et al. 2016).

Still, even a unified party elite can be rebuffed by voters. One case is illustrative. In 2009 longtime GOP senator Arlen Specter switched parties. Senate Democratic leader Harry Reid and Vice President Joe Biden wooed Specter, who had barely won renomination in 2004 and doubted he could do so in 2010 (Yoshinaka 2016).

Leading Democrats, including President Obama, Pennsylvania governor Ed Rendell, and Senator Bob Casey Jr., along with the state Democratic Central Committee and the American Federation of Labor–Congress of Industrial Organizations (AFL-CIO), backed Specter (Newton-Small 2009; *Politico* 2009; AP 2010; Isenstadt 2010). They had reason to do so. Specter was not only a crucial vote on the Affordable Care Act but also seemed to be the Democrats' best hope of holding the Pennsylvania Senate seat in 2010. Other potential switchers also might have been watching to see how Specter fared in his new party.

In many countries party leaders could have ensured Specter's renomination and even his reelection. In countries with proportional representation, party chiefs can often give defectors a safe position on the party's list of candidates. In district-based systems, they can place switchers in a safe seat, if necessary parachuting the defectors into new districts, even overriding the objections of local activists.[4] By contrast, American political norms made it impossible for Specter to run in another state. Democratic leaders backing him could not even convince US Representative Joe Sestak, who had become a candidate before Specter changed parties, to drop out of the primary, despite possibly offering him a political appointment (Bresnahan 2010). Moreover, despite all his support from party elites, Specter ultimately lost to Sestak, ending his long political career. Days before the primary, when polls signaled Specter's defeat, Obama refused to campaign for the senator, seemingly fearing to reveal the limits of his political pull among Democratic voters (Thrush and Martin 2010). As Democrats had feared, Sestak went on to lose the general election. Specter's experience was not unique. Yoshinaka (2016) shows that the path of party switchers is often not a smooth one because party leaders can influence nominations but not determine them. In other cases, party elites failed to secure the nomination for their favored candidate in open-seat races as well. To fully appreciate the phenomenon of party leadership, we need to look elsewhere.

Party Politicians and Interest Groups: Leadership as Coalition Management

In previous work exploring the question of how parties change positions on issues (Karol 2009), I found three processes distinguished by the connection between party politicians and interest groups: coalition maintenance, in which a group develops new policy preferences and the politicians of the party to which they aligned adapt in order to continue to represent the group; coalition group incorporation, in which politicians take new stands on issues in order to bring new groups into their party coalitions; and coalition expansion, in which politicians take stands on issues that are not marked by groups focused on the topic in hopes of winning support across the board. These behaviors are all examples of coalition management. Yet as coalition managers, party politicians do not only respond to party-aligned groups.

They lead them as well. There has been research about how politicians guide groups, but much discussion of such "reverse lobbying" has focused on interest groups and public policy (Weir 1995; Skocpol 1996; Shaiko 1998) and much less on parties.

An early exception was Schattschneider (1960, 43), who observed, "The political education of business is a function of the Republican Party." Similarly, Phillips-Fein (2011) reported that the support of Senate minority leader and GOP gubernatorial nominee William Knowland for a right-to-work initiative was key to its appearance on the California ballot in 1958. Knowland wrongly thought the issue could help his gubernatorial bid, which was intended to launch a presidential campaign in 1960. In 1956 the Eisenhower campaign had not wanted this divisive issue on the ballot. In both years conservative activists and business interests supported anti-union policies. The key difference between 1956 and 1958 was not a change in the preferences of business or conservative activists but a shift in the view coming from the top of the GOP ticket.[5]

There is also evidence of this phenomenon in the Democratic Party. Unions had worked closely with Senator Edward Kennedy (D-MA) in advocating a single-payer national health insurance plan in 1971–1972, at a time when President Nixon favored an employer-mandate approach. Kennedy and other Democrats aligned with unions rejected the Nixon plan as inadequate. After both plans failed, Kennedy worked with Ways and Means chair Wilbur Mills and negotiated with Nixon to advance a more modest plan. The AFL-CIO rejected this bill (Quadagno 2005), and the subsequent scandal-driven departures of both Nixon and Mills stalled momentum.

By 1978 Kennedy saw the employer-mandate approach Nixon had promoted, which he and unions had once rejected, as "the only politically viable road to universal coverage" (Hacker 1997, 85). Still committed to what had become his signature issue, the Massachusetts senator began promoting a mandate-based plan. Yet while Kennedy's next proposal was less ambitious than the one unions had rejected only a few years earlier, this time labor largely sided with him. Gottschalk (2000) contends that Kennedy's shift, along with President Carter's less supportive position, influenced labor leaders to modify their own stands. While this plan also failed, it helped reorient unions' and Democrats' positions on health insurance, contributing to the employer-mandate focus of the Clinton health care plan fifteen years later.

The politics surrounding the failed Clinton health care initiative of 1993–1994 furnish yet another example of party politicians guiding the activity of aligned interest groups. After Clinton's election, many observers believed that some sort of health care reform was inevitable as a result of both the Democrats' renewed control of Congress and the White House and of public discontent with the status quo. This assessment, along with concern about rising insurance costs, underlay the Chamber of Commerce's initial posture of seeking to influence the nature of reform rather than opposing it (Berke 1993). Yet in a dramatic reversal, the chamber turned against the Clinton health care reform efforts in late 1993 after intense criticism and lobbying by Republican MCs and activists. Conceivably the corporate lobby simply realized that GOP opposition meant that reform was no longer inevitable, and it was safe to stop supporting it. This view may have some merit because divisions existed within the chamber and the business community more broadly on health care policy.

Yet this interpretation gives too little credit to the sincere concerns of some of the Chamber of Commerce's constituency and understates the element of coercion by politicians involved. In a remarkable episode, US Representative John Boehner (R-OH), then a young leader of the Conservative Opportunity Society, wrote to members of the chamber advising them to resign from the lobby if it did not abandon its support for an employer mandate (Martin 1995). Party politicians also attempted to direct the activities of aligned interest groups in the G. W. Bush years. Sinclair (2006) describes how GOP leaders insisted to business lobbyists that the latter support the second round of income tax cuts the Bush administration promoted in 2003 before they would bring up the narrower tax measures that were actually of greater concern to corporations.

GOP Senate leader Mitch McConnell offers a more recent example of party politicians leading interest groups. In 2009 the Kentucky senator lobbied the National Rifle Association to come out against the nomination of Sonia Sotomayor to the US Supreme Court.[6] McConnell asked the gun rights group if they would "score" the vote on Sotomayor—that is, include it among the votes used to calculate ratings for senators. The gun rights group had never taken a position on a Supreme Court nominee and reportedly was wary of taking on a fight that was neither a priority nor likely to succeed. While elected officials must take a position on all bills and nominations that reach the floor, a lobby can choose its battles. Avoiding visible defeat may make a lobby seem more formidable. Yet the Senate GOP leader apparently felt the NRA could help him minimize defections among Republican senators. With this tactic, McConnell could also force Democrats from pro-gun states to choose between supporting a nominee who appealed to Democratic constituencies, including feminists and Latinos, and maintaining their NRA ratings. McConnell's tactic appears to have swung a handful of votes at most (*Huffington Post* 2009). It did not derail Sotomayor's nomination, and it is unclear whether any Democratic senators were defeated because of their votes for the jurist.[7] Yet the case is still interesting as a recent example of the phenomenon of party leaders and politicians guiding interest groups as well as being guided by them. Because the NRA was part of the Republican coalition, they were subject to influence by its leading politicians.

The previous examples of reverse lobbying are not meant to indicate that this is the dominant form of interaction between party politicians and interest groups. Nor are such attempts always fully successful, as two other cases illustrate. When he became chairman of the National Republican Congressional Committee in 1975,

US Representative Guy Vander Jagt traveled the country encouraging business interests to establish political action committees, hoping to establish a counterweight to labor PACs that would help the GOP gain seats (Jackson 1988). While there was an explosion of business PACs in the 1970s, many adopted an incumbent-oriented strategy that reinforced the dominance of House Democrats in that era, much to Vander Jagt's chagrin. A more recent example of failed pressure on interest groups was the so-called K Street Project, in which the House majority whip, Tom DeLay (R-TX), working with Grover Norquist, Senator Rick Santorum (R-PA), and others, leaned heavily on trade associations and lobbying firms to hire Republicans. While many former DeLay aides were hired (Mann and Ornstein 2006), this might have occurred anyway, given the proclivity of trade associations to hire well-connected former MCs and staffers. Meanwhile, the initiative became public and increased scrutiny on DeLay, who was admonished by the ethics committee and later departed Congress amid scandal.

What are we to make of these examples? In most cases party politicians did not convince interest groups aligned with their parties to abandon their basic preferences, and they certainly were not unresponsive to group concerns. Yet at times they led their interest group allies to take actions they would not have on their own. Politicians did not simply accept the demands of their parties' "intense policy demanders" (Bawn et al. 2012, 573) and attempt to sell them to the public. Instead, politicians managed these groups in the interest of the party as a whole.

This is leadership. Yet in evaluating this activity, we should note that the politicians guiding the groups were not necessarily moving the parties to the center. Kennedy convinced union leaders to back less ambitious health care policies. Yet when McConnell got the NRA to score the vote on Justice Sotomayor he was contributing to polarization. In pushing the corporate lobbies to support the 2003 Bush tax cuts, Republicans were emphasizing their more saleable issue but still moving policy rightward.

The relationship between a party's elected officials and its interest groups is one of mutual dependence. Interest groups need politicians to affect public policy. In turn, the groups provide important resources to politicians during campaigns (Skinner 2007; Karol 2015) and influence the nomination process (Cohen et al. 2008a, 2008b; Karol 2009; Bawn et al. 2012). Moreover, a party's elected officials and groups often share values. Yet the groups' influence is limited. In a two-party system, many groups are "captured" by one of the major parties and typically can only threaten to abstain, not to trade sides.[8] Groups retain some influence via the nomination process even then, however.

While coalition management is chiefly the province of elected officials, some interest group leaders play a role that transcends factional concerns. When they are sufficiently prominent in a party, a group's leaders may identify their interests with the party's and temper their demands. Looking at the role of labor in the Democratic Party, especially in states where it is strongest, like Michigan, both Greenstone (1969) and Galvin (2013) found evidence that far from hindering the party, union leaders recognized that it could not simply reflect their views and supported centrist candidates. They acted as party leaders as much as union ones.

Exploring Differences between the Parties

The similarities between Democrats and Republicans are great when viewed in comparative perspective. The constitutional framework and electoral laws create strong incentives for political actors to coalesce into two parties and for a federal structure isomorphic to the political institutions that the parties seek to control. State regulation of parties, dating back to the Progressive Era, also works to make the parties similar in many of their structures and practices. But occasionally scholars turn their attention to the differences between the parties (Freeman 1986; Klinkner 1994; Grossman and Hopkins 2016). Yet this is infrequent. A few concerns may contribute to this neglect. One factor may be a perceived need to seem nonpartisan (Ornstein and Mann 2012). While one may describe differences between party practices with no overt normative judgment, there is always a danger that description will be seen as pejorative. So where differences are noted, they are often not dwelt upon or explained satisfactorily. Still, such concerns have not stopped scholars of diverse views from noting the asymmetric nature of party polarization in Congress, to which changes among Republicans have contributed most (Hacker and Pierson 2005; McCarty, Poole, and Rosenthal 2007). Probably a more important factor is simply the desire to generalize. Students of comparative politics, accustomed to studying groups of countries, each with its own multiparty system, are happy to create typologies, including "catchall," "sectoral," and "protest" parties. Americanists, having only two significant cases at the national level, want to be able to talk about "party" behavior in general.

If one looks at behavior in the short and medium term, elites' perceptions of their parties' strategic situation loom large. Parties in office have more power but also more responsibility. Scholars have refined these distinctions beyond simply the ins and outs. Green (2013) explores the behavior of the deep minority—that is, the minority party in the House of Representatives when it does not have a copartisan in the White House. Unlike the Senate minority, which retains a measure of influence as a result of the supermajority rules governing that body, the minority in the House, when it cannot even sustain vetoes, has limited relevance in our polarized era. Thus their leaders and the caucus focus largely on messaging rather than attempting to influence policy outcomes.[9] Lee (2013) found that the MCs whose party controls the White House are more likely to vote to raise the debt ceiling, as are those in the majority. More generally, I argue that presidents are closer than Congress to elite opinion. As a result, their copartisans in Congress, having a stake in the president's success, will tend to favor policies elite opinion prescribes, including foreign aid and free trade (Karol 2013). Donald Trump is the sole exception since World War II.

Beyond the current status of the party, its leaders' and constituent elements' perception of their strategic situation is key. If party leaders feel that their current status in the majority or minority may change, they will behave differently than if they see it as inevitable. Jones (1970, 170) noted that congressional Republicans, who then had been in the majority for only four of the previous forty years, had a "minority party mentality." He found that "accepting minority status as a fact of life" was most prevalent among long-serving members. Seniority had brought many of these Republican MCs into ranking minority member (RMM) positions. Yet despite serving in leadership posts, they still focused on individualistic goals and tried to make deals with Democratic chairs, rather than adopting an oppositional posture that might increase the odds of a return to majority status. House minority leaders John Rhodes and Robert Michel became increasingly unpopular among Republicans, who felt that they were too defeatist and willing to settle for crumbs from Democrats rather than building an electorally useful record of clear partisan distinctions. Fenno (1997) contends that pressure from more militant younger Republicans led both Rhodes and Michel to retire. Scholars offer divergent assessments of the results of one-party dominance. Fenno argued, "When both parties expect to alternate in power, the party temporarily in the majority has an incentive to consult, cooperate and compromise with the party temporarily in the minority" (1997, 11). Yet Lee (2016) found that the fact that both parties have recently experienced and can readily imagine subsequent shifts of control results in stronger party leaders, more teamlike behavior, and more polarization, along with position taking and partisan gamesmanship as opposed to legislating.

What is true for MC is also true for presidents. Skowronek (1993) discusses "third way" presidents elected when their party is seen as the less popular one. Such presidents have tended to adopt less ambitious policy goals than those from the dominant party and to use governing strategies that allowed them to reach across party lines to win support in Congress. Galvin (2010) explains variation in the extent to which presidents worked as party builders based on their understanding of their party's position. Republican chief executives, even those who worked with congressional Democrats and ran far ahead of their party in elections, like Eisenhower and Nixon, were party builders. By contrast, Democratic presidents before Bill Clinton were party predators. The difference in behavior flowed from a shared view that Democrats were the natural majority. GOP presidents tried to strengthen their party's apparatus in order to compensate for Republicans' smaller numbers, while until recently Democratic presidents felt no such need.

Another set of explanations for party differences concerns the composition of the parties' coalitions. Congress scholars working with principal–agent theory (Aldrich and Rohde 1997; Sinclair 1998) have long seen the preferences of party members as the key factor determining the strength of leadership. A more homogenous legislative party will be more willing to delegate authority to leaders to advance collective goals.

Beyond the issue of diversity, scholars also find explanations in the nature of the groups that align with each party. Klinkner (1994) looks to differences in the nature of party coalitions to explain the divergence he finds in the behavior of the "out" parties' national committees. He argues that when Republicans lose the White House, the fact that they are the party associated with business leads them to focus on improvements in marketing and logistics. By contrast, Democrats, being a far more diverse coalition, seek to create structures to enhance the representation of various groups.

One place to look to explore differences in party leadership practices is in Congress. Although one can note differences in the parties' presidential nomination processes (Polsby 1983; Citrin and Karol 2009; Karol 2014), only one party controls the White House at any given time, so it is difficult to disentangle period effects from partisan ones when focusing on the presidency. By contrast, both parties are always represented in the Congress, even if one is necessarily in the minority.[10]

Looking at the departures from office of modern Democratic and Republican House leaders reveals a striking difference between the parties. The causes of Democratic leaders' departures were generally external, whereas Republicans left in a majority of cases because their position in their own party had become untenable. Among Republicans, Joseph Martin and Charles Halleck were unseated by vote of the GOP conference. Gingrich left because he saw the writing on the wall. The resignation of Rhodes and the retirement of Michel also stemmed from pressure from their conference (Fenno 1997). Most recently and dramatically, John Boehner resigned in the middle of the 114th Congress after a protracted conflict with the right wing of his party. Ford left to become vice president, and Hastert's retirement seems to have been a personal choice. Thus, only two of nine modern Republican leaders departed truly voluntarily.

Among Democrats, Sam Rayburn died in office, Tom Foley was defeated in a general election, and John MacCormack retired for reasons of age and scandal. By all accounts, Tip O'Neill's retirement at age seventy-four was a voluntary one. Jim Wright resigned in the wake of scandal. His case was very different from those of GOP leaders whose colleagues were simply dissatisfied with their performance. Gephardt faced little challenge despite several failures to regain the majority status the party had long enjoyed. He left the leadership to pursue a presidential bid. Nancy Pelosi retained the leadership despite losing the majority in 2010 and failing to regain it in the next three elections. The case on the Democratic side that most closely parallels the treatment several Republican leaders have received is that of Speaker Carl Albert. Albert was clearly unhappy in the postreform Congress and was criticized by the young Turks, but there is only modest evidence that he was pushed out (*Naples Daily News* 1976). The pressures on Rhodes and Michel from House Republicans seem to have been far greater.

Another way to distinguish the parties when looking at leadership transitions is to consider the path to the top of the party hierarchy. How often did the next in line get the leadership position, be it the speakership, the majority leadership, or the minority leadership?

Twelve men have served as Republican Senate leaders since the end of World War II. Of these, only five (Kenneth Wherry, Everett Dirksen, Hugh Scott, Trent Lott, and Mitch McConnell) had served as GOP whips before being elected as leaders. Of the other seven leaders (Wallace White, Styles Bridges, Robert Taft, William Knowland, Howard Baker, Robert Dole, and Bill Frist), none had served as chair of the Senate Republican Conference, and only two had served as chair of the Republican Policy Committee, seen as the fourth-ranking position (Taft and Knowland). Moreover, the Republican whips who were bypassed were not elderly or enmeshed in scandal. In three cases (Robert Griffin in 1977, Ted Stevens in 1985, and Don Nickles in 2002) they were simply defeated in the conference. Leverett Saltonstall was bypassed three times. He, unlike the others, may have been deemed too liberal.

Once again, the story is different for the Democrats. Only nine men have served as Senate Democratic leaders, and five were previously whips (Scott Lucas, Lyndon Johnson, Mike Mansfield, Robert Byrd, and Harry Reid). Ernest McFarland, George Mitchell, Tom Daschle, and Chuck Schumer did not serve as whip before becoming leader. The difference between five out of nine Democrats who rose from the whip's position, compared to only five out of twelve Republicans, suggests some difference in party styles, but these small numbers mean that we cannot be too confident on the basis of the comparisons alone.

However, close examination of the cases in which the Democratic whip did not succeed to the leadership are instructive. In 1950 both the Democratic majority leader Scott Lucas and his whip, Francis Myers, were defeated in elections. In 1989, when Alan Cranston was bypassed and George Mitchell was elected to replace Robert Byrd, Cranston was already seventy-five years old and enmeshed in the Keating Five scandal, which would lead him to retire at the end of his term. He was not a candidate for leader. When Mitchell was replaced in 1995, the Democratic whip, Wendell Ford, was seventy. He also did not run for the leadership. In 2017 Schumer became leader instead of the seventy-two-year-old whip, Dick Durbin. By contrast, none of the Republican whips who were skipped over were beyond their early sixties, and none were plagued by scandal. While the number of cases is not large, they suggest that Senate Republicans are less likely to elevate their whips and are less governed by the notion that the next in line should succeed to leadership posts.

On the House Republican side, things have been messier. When Halleck replaced Martin in 1959, the GOP deviated from the Democratic transition pattern in two respects: Halleck forced Martin out in an election, and he was not, formally speaking, the next in line. Halleck bypassed Representative Les Arends, the minority whip and the de jure second in command. Admittedly, Halleck had served as majority leader in the 80th and 83rd Congresses, so this point is arguable. Similarly, when Gerald Ford in turn ousted Halleck in 1965, he was Republican Conference chairman, the position immediately below Arends in the hierarchy.

Yet other examples are harder to dismiss. When Ford became vice president and vacated the minority leadership, Arends, by then nearly eighty years old yet still whip, was bypassed once again. But so was the third-ranking member of the leadership, GOP Conference chairman John Anderson. Anderson was only fifty-one but was apparently considered insufficiently conservative. Instead, Republicans turned to the fourth-ranking member of the leadership, longtime Policy Committee chairman John Rhodes, to replace Ford.

Bob Michel was the GOP whip when he replaced John Rhodes in 1981 yet was nearly defeated in the GOP Conference by National Republican Campaign Committee chairman Guy Vander Jagt. Gingrich was the whip when he succeeded Michel in 1995, but Dennis Hastert was elevated to the speakership from the relatively obscure position of chief deputy whip in 1999. Boehner was the GOP's No. 2, the House majority leader, in the Congress before he succeeded to the minority leadership. Yet he had reached the majority leadership only months earlier in the wake of Tom DeLay's resignation by narrowly defeating the GOP whip, Roy Blunt. So here too Republicans did not simply turn to the next in line.

In 2015, when Boehner resigned, it initially seemed that House majority leader Kevin McCarthy would be his successor. Yet there was a revolt against McCarthy in the wake of a politically maladroit admission on his part that the Benghazi investigation was being used as a political weapon against Hillary Clinton. When McCarthy fell out of favor, the next in line, House majority whip Steve Scalise and Republican Conference chair Cathy McMorris Rogers, were bypassed as Republicans turned to Paul Ryan, who was not, formally speaking, even a member of the leadership.

The seniority system was long seen as a hindrance to parties by reformers. The authors of the famous 1950 American Political Science Association report *Toward a More Responsible Two-Party System* complained, "It is not playing the game fairly for party members who oppose the commitments in their party's platform to rely on seniority to carry them into committee chairmanships. Party leaders have compelling reason to prevent such a member from becoming chairman" (9). While House Democrats were the first to challenge the seniority system in the mid-1970s, Republicans have moved much further away from the norm since the 1990s (Deering and Wahlbeck 2006; Pearson 2015). This is true both in that Republicans term limit their committee leaders (in both chambers), and it is also evident in the selection of House chairs and RMMs.

A key difference between the congressional parties is the Republicans' use of term limits since the 104th Congress, when they gained the majority in both chambers for the first time in forty years. A term-limit movement was then nationally prominent. It succeeded in states where the initiative process allowed it to bypass the legislators whose terms would be limited. The Contract with America included a pledge to bring a constitutional amendment limiting MC terms up for a vote. Different versions of that proposal failed, even in a Republican House. Yet in both chambers Republicans did impose six-year term limits. In the House, this was made a rule. Initially it included an eight-year limit for the Speaker, but this was later abandoned (Anderson 2003). The longer and then-unlimited term for the Speaker strengthened him vis-à-vis term-limited chairs.

In 2009 House Democrats repealed this rule before it had any consequences for their own allocation of leadership positions. In the Senate the rule was adopted in 1996 by the Republican Conference, not by the Senate as a body. In both chambers Republicans have counted service as chair and RMM against the limit. These rules have been followed in most cases. House Republicans have granted waivers to a handful of well-regarded legislators, allowing them to continue as chair or RMM. More common has been the scenario in which a termed-out chair leaves Congress, often to become a lobbyist, having little more to aspire to on Capitol Hill. In other cases a termed-out chair was able to move to the leadership of another committee or make do with a subcommittee chair.

The difference in party practices has evident consequences for tenure in committee leadership posts in recent Congresses. In the 113th Congress (2013–2014), while the median House Republican chair and Democratic RMM were both in their second terms as committee leaders, the party means were somewhat different as a result of a longer-serving minority among Democrats that has no parallel on the GOP side. The mean length of service on the part of House Democratic RMMs was 6.1 years, while that for Republican chairs was only 2.8. The analogous figures for the current 115th Congress are 3.8 years for Republicans and 7.5 for Democrats. In the Senate, where Democrats were in the majority in the 113th Congress, the median chair was serving in his second Congress in that post, while, remarkably, the median Republican RMM was new to his position. Party means also reveal clear, if not enormous, differences, with Democratic Senate chairs in place for 5.2 years and their GOP counterparts only 2.8 years. In the 115th Congress, however, Republican Senate leaders had been in place 3.8 years on average, while their Democratic counterparts had only been committee leaders for 3.4 years

In the House, a handful of Democratic MCs occupy committee leadership posts they have held for more than a decade. Yet while there is no counterpart to these on the Republican side of the aisle, the aggregate party differences in tenure, while real, are perhaps less dramatic than we might have expected. Other consequences, including retirements among senior House Republicans that probably would not have occurred otherwise, are more striking.

The difference between the parties was notable in 1995 when Newt Gingrich led the Republicans to the majority after forty years in the desert and unilaterally decided to deviate from seniority in selecting committee chairs (Aldrich and Rohde 1997). Gingrich's actions differed from the handful of Democratic violations of seniority in years past. Democrats deviated from seniority when legislators were ideological outliers, were enmeshed in scandal, or were too old to effectively perform the chair's duties. By contrast, Gingrich violated seniority simply because he preferred another choice. For example, Representative Carlos Moorhead of California, only in his early sixties and a solid conservative, was disinherited, losing two important chairmanships he would have once been able to choose between by dint of his seniority, because the Speaker felt that the Californian did "not project the right image" and was not "an activist" (Karmin 1994).

Nor was this Republican downgrading of seniority's importance limited to the Gingrich years. Deering and Wahlbech (2006) found that seniority played a limited role in Republicans' decisions regarding the replacements of termed-out chairs in 2001. These scholars found that seniority was a significant predictor of a representative becoming finalist for a chair—that is, being asked to speak before the Steering Committee and make one's case. Yet within the pool of finalists, differences in seniority did not predict the ultimate selection. By contrast, Democratic leader Nancy Pelosi has "continued to respect seniority in most instances" (Peters and Rosenthal 2010, 70).

The distribution of committee leadership posts in the House reported in Table 6.1 suggests that Republican practices have changed little since then and that Democrats remain somewhat more observant of the seniority norms, although less so than in years past. Looking at the eighteen standing committees in the 113th Congress (excluding the Budget Committee, where term limits have historically been the rule) reveals interparty differences regarding seniority that go beyond term limits and their consequences. Of the thirty-six chair and RMM positions, fourteen were occupied by representatives next in line according to seniority, junior only to a legislator who took a more desirable chair, or, in the case of Republicans, behind a representative who termed out of the chair. Another eleven leapfrogged one colleague to reach the chair or RMM position. GOP representatives who bypassed two colleagues held five committee chairs. Another six were occupied by MCs who bypassed four or more legislators.

These numbers indicate that seniority is still relevant in that a disproportionate share of GOP committee leadership posts are held by the most senior or second most senior eligible legislator. Yet most positions are no longer held by the senior representatives who once monopolized them. Almost a third went to an MC who was elevated over several colleagues, showing a great decay of the seniority norm. Importantly, the category of chairs elevated over four or more colleagues with greater committee seniority is entirely composed of Republicans. A closer look at these six cases reveals instances in which seniority was entirely disregarded. In the

Table 6.1. Committee Leadership and Seniority, US House of Representatives, 113th Congress (2013–2014)

Party	Was Next in Line	Jumped Over One Colleague	Jumped Over Two Colleagues	Jumped Over Three Colleagues	Jumped Over Four or More Colleagues	Total
Democrat	9	5	4	0	0	18
Republican	5	6	1	0	6	18
Total	14	11	5	0	6	36

113th Congress, Representative Candice Miller (R-MI) became chair of the Administration Committee despite having not served on it previously because GOP leaders wished to diversify an otherwise entirely white and male roster of chairs (Cahn 2012).

Similarly, in the 111th Congress, Representative Richard "Doc" Hastings (R-WA) was made RMM of the Resources Committee despite not having served on it previously. Reportedly, the ethical troubles of the previous RMM, Don Young of Alaska, made Hastings an attractive choice, given his background as chair of the Committee on Standards of Official Conduct, his closeness to leadership as evidenced by his service on the Rules and Republican steering committees, and his background in relevant issues resulting from his rural Western district (Bontrager and Straub 2008). Disregard for seniority in bestowing the Resources chair was not unprecedented among Republicans; in 2003 they had bypassed nine more senior representatives, including six who were not termed out and had no more attractive chair, to select Richard Pombo of California to lead this panel (Coile 2004). In other cases, a legislator had served on the committee before his elevation but was allowed to bypass several colleagues, some of whom were seemingly respectable candidates, as a result of his closeness to leadership or prominence in the GOP conference. In the 113th Congress, this was true of Education and the Workforce chair John Kline, Financial Services chair Jeb Hensarling, Oversight chair Darrell Issa, and Transportation and Infrastructure chair Bill Shuster.

In the 114th Congress, most House chairs and RMMs were holdovers from the previous Congress. However, a look at the new committee leaders again reveals Democrats to be far more respectful of seniority norms than Republicans. Of the five new Democratic RMMs, all were next in line according to seniority, except Raul Grijalva, who leapfrogged Grace Napolitano. The seventy-eight-year-old Napolitano did not run against Grijalva (Dumain 2014). On the Republican side, once again deviations from seniority were far more significant. Of the six new chairs, only two had been next in line. Two leapt over one MC, one skipped over three colleagues, and another bypassed four more senior representatives to sit in the chair (Fuller 2014).

In the 115th Congress, the picture is much the same. Among seven new House committee chairs, only two Republicans (Rodney Frelinghuysen of Appropriations and Greg Harper of House Administration) had been next in line, and only one (Virginia Foxx of Education and Workforce) leapfrogged only one colleague. The remaining five new chairs bypassed from two to six colleagues in ascending to their new positions. Of the three Democratic RMMs, one ascended according to seniority (John Yarmuth of Budget). Richard Neal became RMM of Ways and Means when eighty-five-year-old Sander Levin stepped down. Only Tim Walz, the new RMM of Veterans Affairs, bypassed more than one Democratic colleague who was not of very advanced age.

In sum, forty years after the liberal revolt against the committee chairs in the post-Watergate 94th Congress, it is House Republicans who have moved furthest away from the seniority norm, both in imposing term limits on chairs and in frequently bypassing the most senior representatives when picking chairs.

Comparison of Republican and Democratic practices regarding congressional leaders also reveals key differences. Republicans have been much tougher than Democrats on their leaders. Leadership succession on the GOP side has also been less likely to occur via routine elevation of the next in line. Republicans have shown less respect for the waning seniority norm than Democrats, not only term limiting committee chairs but also reaching far down the committee roster to find a chair or RMM, or even occasionally parachuting a representative who has not been on the panel into a leadership role.

How can we understand these differences? Some of the possible theories do not seem to fit the facts. Students of political psychology find that while conservatism is not the same as authoritarianism, the two phenomena are correlated, and Republican respondents score higher on authoritarianism (Hetherington and Weiler 2009). Yet if psychological dispositions were key to the behavioral differences related to leadership we observe, we would expect Republicans to be more deferential to their leaders and more respectful of seniority. In fact the opposite is the case. Similarly, Freeman's (1986) account of the Republican Party as a top-down organization that stigmatized dissent and values deference and order seems at odds with these findings.

While the diversity of the Democratic Party leads to more respect for seniority and tends to make leaders' positions more secure, there are also countervailing drives to which Democrats are subject more than Republicans as a result of their beliefs and the nature of their coalition. Diversity is a Democratic value and also characterizes the Democrats' coalition, both in Congress and the electorate. This commitment is evident in practices such as the extensive affirmative action requirements for convention delegates and the requirement that nomination contests allocate delegates proportionally.

As the Democrats moved into the minority in 2010, they anticipated that incoming chair Darrell Issa would use the Oversight Committee in an aggressive manner and wanted a strong RMM to counter him. The outgoing chair, Ed Towns of New York, was not seen as that person. The Democratic leadership signaled to Towns that he had lost their support, and he stepped down. However, Democrats did not turn to the next in line, Carolyn Maloney, but rather to the second in line, Elijah Cummings. There was nothing disqualifying about Maloney, but the Democrats, having pushed aside Towns, an African American, turned to Cummings, also an African American, to replace him (Beutler 2010; Brown 2010).

Conclusion

Assessing leadership in parties requires defining them. This is challenging in the case of American parties, which lack formal membership. The most useful definition of party is a group that unites to win elections and control the government. Party is the basis for the leaders who dominate the legislative and executive branches at the national and state levels. However, the heads of party committees who on paper occupy leadership roles are of limited importance. National- and state-level party committees control more resources and play more active roles in campaigns than they did a generation or two ago, but on their own, they are not "the party" in any meaningful sense. While there are structures of hierarchy within some party institutions, parties are best understood as networks including officials and candidates, interest groups and activists.

Party leadership is exercised, mostly informally, by elected officials interacting with aligned interest groups. The president is the closest thing to a national party leader that exists, but he has no counterpart in the party not controlling the White House. Acting as coalition managers, politicians balance the concerns of the groups within their party's coalitions while trying to attract new ones and win broad-based support. Sometimes they adopt new policies due to group demands, but they also can direct party-aligned groups, at least tactically, orienting them to support other party policies and sometimes even revisit positions.

While both of these points—the limited influence of formal party leaders and the central role of politicians and interest groups—hold true for both major parties, important differences between Republicans and Democrats are evident as well. Congressional Republicans are more likely to force out their leaders, less likely to replace them with the next in line, and much less respectful of seniority than Democrats. Republicans not only impose term limits but are also more likely to elevate relatively low-ranking committee members and occasionally those with no prior service on a panel to the position of chair or RMM. This behavior is not consistent with some accounts of Republicans as a hierarchical, deferential party or marked by authoritarian personality traits. The greater homogeneity of Republicans may make it is easier for consensus to form against leaders and lead GOP legislators to place less stock in norms that keep the peace, such as the seniority system.

The messiness of American political parties means that the study of leadership in them is challenging. Many elites interact, and organizational charts can be highly misleading guides to who wields power. Yet given the parties' importance in our political system, it is a worthwhile inquiry. Because parties are constantly changing, all answers will be provisional and new investigations are always justified.

References

Aldrich, John H. 1995. *Why Parties? The Origin and Transformation of Parties in America*. Chicago: University of Chicago Press.

Aldrich, John H., and David W. Rohde. 1997. "The Transition to Republican Rule in the House: Implications for Theories of Congressional Politics." *Political Science Quarterly* 112 (4): 541–567.

American Political Science Association. 1950. *Toward a More Responsible Two-Party System: A Report of the Committee on Political Parties*. Menasha, WI: American Political Science Association.

Anderson, Nick. 2003. "GOP-Led House Will Lift Term Limits for Speaker." *Los Angeles Times*, January 7.

AP. 2010. "Arlen Specter Endorsed by Pennsylvania Democratic State Committee." *Associated Press*, February 6.

Bawn, Kathleen, Knox Brown, Angela Ocampo, Shawn Patterson, John Ray, and John Zaller. 2014. "Parties on the Ground: A Preliminary Report on Open Seat House Nominations in 2014." Paper presented at the annual meeting of the American Political Science Association, Washington, DC.

Bawn, Kathleen, Martin Cohen, David Karol, Seth Masket, Hans Noel, and John Zaller. 2012. "A Theory of Political Parties: Groups, Policy Demands and Nominations in American Politics." *Perspectives on Politics* 10 (3): 571–597.

Berke, Richard L. 1993. "Clinton Finds a Friendlier Chamber of Commerce." *New York Times*, April 14. http://www.nytimes.com/.

Bernstein, Jonathan. 2012. "The NRA's Party Stories." *Washington Post*, December 27. https://www.washingtonpost.com/.

Bernstein, Jonathan, and Casey B. K. Dominguez. 2003. "Candidates and Candidacies in the Expanded Party" *PS: Political Science and Politics* 36 (2): 165–169.

Beutler, Brian. 2010. "Pelosi Power Play Doomed Towns on Oversight Committee." *TPM*, December 16. http://api.talkingpointsmemo.com/.

Bontrager, Eric, and Noelle Straub. 2008. *EE News*, December 10. "Young Out as Natural Resources Ranking Member–GOP Aides."

Bresnahan, John. 2010. "Sestak Confirms WH Job Offer to Get Out of Senate Race." *Politico*, May 23. http://www.politico.com/.

Brown, Matthew Hay. 2010. "Cummings Named Top Democrat on Oversight." *Baltimore Sun,* December 16. http://www.baltimoresun.com/.

Cahn, Emily. 2012. "Boehner Taps Candice Miller to Helm House Administration Committee." *Roll Call,* November 30. http://www.rollcall.com/.

CBS News. 2014. "NRA Withholds Endorsement in Alaska Senate Race." *CBS News,* September 25. http://www.cbsnews.com/.

Citrin, Jack, and David Karol, editors. 2009. *Nominating the President: Evolution and Revolution in 2008 and Beyond.* Lanham, MD: Rowman & Littlefield.

Cohen, Marty, David Karol, Hans Noel, and John Zaller. 2008a. "Political Parties in Rough Weather." *Forum* 5 (4): 3.

———. 2008b. *The Party Decides: Presidential Nominations Before and After Reform.* Chicago: University of Chicago Press.

———. 2016. "Party versus Faction in the Reformed System of Presidential Nominations." *PS: Political Science and Politics* 43 (4): 701–708.

Coile, Zachary. 2004. "Profile: Rep. Richard Pombo: Lawmaker's Agenda Just Part of His Nature." *San Francisco Chronicle,* May 3. http://www.sfgate.com/.

Coleman, John J. 1996. "Resurgent or Just Busy? Party Organizations in Contemporary America." In *The State of the Parties: The Changing Role of Contemporary American Parties,* edited by Daniel M. Shea and John C. Green, 312–326. 2nd ed. Lanham, MD: Rowman & Littlefield.

Deering, Christopher J., and Paul J. Wahlbeck. 2006. "Determinants of House Committee Chair Selection: Republicans Play Musical Chairs in the 107th Congress." *American Politics Research* 34 (2): 223–242.

Doherty, Brendan J. 2010. "Hail to the Fundraiser in Chief: The Evolution of Presidential Fundraising Travel, 1977–2004." *Presidential Studies Quarterly* 40 (1): 159–170.

Dominguez, Casey B. K. 2011. "Does the Party Matter? Endorsements in Congressional Primaries." *Political Research Quarterly* 64 (3): 534–544.

Dumain, Emma. 2014. "Grijalva Faces Clear Path to Natural Resources Ranking Member." *Roll Call,* November 12. http://www.rollcall.com/.

Eldersveld, Samuel J. 1982. *Political Parties in American Society.* New York: Basic Books.

Fenno, Richard F. 1997. *Learning to Govern: An Institutional View of the 104th Congress.* Washington DC: Brookings Institution.

Ferrell, Robert H. 1994. *Choosing Truman: The Democratic Convention of 1944.* Columbia: University of Missouri Press.

Fraser, Steven. 1991. *Labor Will Rule: Sidney Hillman and the Rise of American Labor.* New York: Free Press.

Freeman, Jo. 1986. "The Political Culture of the Democratic and Republican Parties." *Political Science Quarterly* 101 (3): 327–356.

Frymer, Paul. 1999. *Uneasy Alliances: Race and Party Competition in America.* Princeton, NJ: Princeton University Press.

Fuller, Matt. 2014. "Chaffetz Wins Four-Way Showdown for Oversight Gavel." *Roll Call,* November 14. http://www.rollcall.com/.

Galvin, Daniel J. 2008. "Changing Course: Reversing the Organizational Trajectory of the Democratic Party from Bill Clinton to Barack Obama." *Forum* 6 (2): article 3.

———. 2010. *Presidential Party Building: Dwight D. Eisenhower to George W. Bush.* Princeton, NJ: Princeton University Press.

———. 2013. "Resilience in the Rust Belt: Michigan Democrats and the UAW." IPR Working Paper, Northwestern University. http://www.ipr.northwestern.edu/publications/docs /workingpapers/2013/IPR-WP-13-04v2.pdf.

Gamm, Gerald, and Steven S. Smith. 2002. "Emergence of Senate Party Leadership." In *US Senate Exceptionalism*, edited by Bruce I. Oppenheimer, 212–238. Columbus: Ohio State University Press.

Gottschalk, Marie. 2000. *The Shadow Welfare State: Labor, Business and the Politics of Health Care in the US.* Ithaca, NY: Cornell University Press.

Green, Matthew N. 2013. *Underdog Politics: The Minority Party in the US House of Representatives.* New Haven, CT: Yale University Press.

Greenhouse, Linda. 2012. "The NRA at the Bench." *New York Times*, December 26. https:// opinionator.blogs.nytimes.com/.

Greenstone, J. David. 1969. *Labor in American Politics.* New York: Knopf.

Grossman, Matt, and David A. Hopkins. 2016. *Asymmetric Politics: Ideological Republicans and Group Interest Democrats.* New York: Oxford University Press.

Haberman, Maggie. 2015. "Donald Trump Says RNC Chairman Called to Congratulate Him." *New York Times*, July 9. https://www.nytimes.com/.

Hacker, Jacob. 1997. *The Road to Nowhere: The Genesis of President Clinton's Plan for Health Security.* Princeton, NJ: Princeton University Press.

Hacker, Jacob S., and Paul Pierson. 2005. *Off-Center: The Republican Revolution and the Erosion of American Democracy.* New Haven, CT: Yale University Press.

Hassell, Hans J. G. 2016. "Party Control of Party Primaries: Party Influence in Nominations for the US Senate." *Journal of Politics* 78 (1): 75–87.

Herrnson, Paul S. 1988. *Party Campaigning in the 1980s.* Cambridge, MA: Harvard University Press.

———. 2013. "National Parties in the Twenty-First Century." In *The Parties Respond: Changes in American Parties and Campaigns*, edited by Mark D. Brewer and L. Sandy Maisel, 133–160. Boulder, CO: Westview Press.

Hetherington, Marc J., and Jonathan D. Weiler. 2009. *Authoritarianism and Polarization in American Politics.* New York: Cambridge University Press.

Huffington Post. 2009. "NRA Threatens to Punish Lawmakers on Sotomayor . . . No One Listens." *Huffington Post*, August 9. http://www.huffingtonpost.com/.

Isenstadt, Alex. 2010. "Specter Wins the AFL-CIO." *Politico*, March 30. http://www.politico .com/.

Jenkins, Jeffrey A., and Charles Stewart II. 2012. *Fighting for the Speakership: The House and the Rise of Party Government.* Princeton, NJ: Princeton University Press.

Jones, Charles O. 1970. *The Minority Party in Congress.* Boston: Little, Brown.

Karmin, Craig. 1994. "Gingrich Ignores Seniority in Selecting Key Chairmen." *The Hill*, November 16.

Karol, David. 2009. *Party Position Change in American Politics: Coalition Management.* New York: Cambridge University Press.

——. 2013. "Congress, the President and Elite Opinion in Historical Perspective." Paper presented at the 12th Annual Meeting of the Congress and History Conference, Columbia University, New York, June 21, 2013.

——. 2014. "Parties Revised and Revived: Democrats and Republicans in the Age of Reagan, 1980-2000." In *CQ Press Guide to US Political Parties*, edited by Marjorie Randon Hershey, 129-142. Thousand Oaks, CA: CQ Press.

——. 2015. "Party Activists, Interest Groups and Polarization in American Politics." In *American Gridlock: Causes, Characteristics and Consequences of Polarization*, edited by James A. Thurber and Antoine Yoshinaka, 3-85. New York: Cambridge University Press.

Kazee, Thomas A., and Mary C. Thornberry. 1990. "Where's the Party? Congressional Candidate Recruitment and American Party Organizations." *Political Research Quarterly* 43 (1): 61-80.

Klinkner, Philip L. 1994. *The Losing Parties: Out Party National Committees, 1956-1993.* New Haven, CT: Yale University Press.

Lawless, Jennifer L. 2011. *Becoming a Candidate: Political Ambition and the Decision to Run for Office.* New York: Cambridge University Press.

Lee, Frances E. 2013. "Presidents and Party Teams: The Politics of Debt Limits and Executive Oversight, 2001-2013." *Presidential Studies Quarterly* 43 (4): 775-791.

——. 2016. *Insecure Majorities: Congress and the Perpetual Campaign.* Chicago: University of Chicago Press.

Lowi, Theodore J. 1985. *The Personal President: Power Invested, Promise Unfulfilled.* Ithaca, NY: Cornell University Press.

Maestas, Cherie L., Sandy Maisel, and Walter J. Stone. 2005. "National Party Efforts to Recruit State Legislators to Run for the US House." *Legislative Studies Quarterly* 30 (2): 277-300.

Mann, Thomas E., and Norman J. Ornstein. 2006. *The Broken Branch: How Congress Is Failing America and How to Get It Back on Track.* New York: Oxford University Press.

Martin, Cathie Jo. 1995. "Stuck in Neutral: Big Business and the Politics of National Health Reform." *Journal of Health Politics, Policy, and Law* 20 (2): 431-436.

Masket, Seth E. 2009. *No Middle Ground: How Informal Party Organizations Control Nominations and Polarize Legislatures.* Ann Arbor: University of Michigan Press.

Mayhew, David. 1986. *Placing Parties in American Politics.* Princeton, NJ: Princeton University Press.

McCarty, Nolan, Keith Poole, and Howard Rosenthal. 2007. *Polarized America: The Dance of Ideology and Unequal Riches.* Cambridge, MA: MIT Press.

Milkis, Sidney M. 1993. *The President and the Parties: The Transformation of the American Party System since the New Deal.* New York: Oxford University Press.

Naples Daily News. 1976. "Carl Albert Pondering Quitting?" *Naples Daily News* (UPI), January 12, 8A.

Nelson, Garrison. 1977. "Partisan Patterns of House Leadership Change, 1789–1877." *American Political Science Review* 71 (3): 918–939.

Neustadt, Richard. 1960. *Presidential Power.* New York: Wiley.

Newton-Small, Jay. 2009. "Some Thoughts on Specter." *Time,* April 29.

Ornstein, Norman, and Thomas E. Mann. 2012. *It's Even Worse Than It Looks.* New York: Basic Books.

Peabody, Robert. 1967. "Party Leadership Change in the United States House of Representatives." *American Political Science Review* 61 (3): 675–693.

Pearson, Kathryn L. 2015. *Party Discipline in the House of Representatives.* Ann Arbor: University of Michigan Press.

Peters, Ronald M., and Cindy Simon Rosenthal. 2010. *Speaker Nancy Pelosi and the New American Politics.* New York: Oxford University Press.

Phillips-Fein, Kim. 2011. "'As Great an Issue as Slavery or Abolition': Economic Populism, the Conservative Movement, and the Right-to-Work Campaigns of 1958." *Journal of Policy History* 23 (4): 491–512.

Politico. 2009. "Casey Endorses Specter." *Politico,* May 9. http://www.politico.com/.

Polsby, Nelson W. 1983 *Consequences of Party Reform.* New York: Oxford University Press.

Porter, Andrew. 2008. "Shaun Woodward Becomes Unlikely Confidant of Gordon Brown." *Telegraph,* July 27. http://www.telegraph.co.uk/.

Quadagno, Jill. 2005. *Uninsured: Why the US Has No National Health Insurance.* New York: Oxford University Press.

Reporter. 1958. "The Battle Bricker Didn't Want." *Reporter,* November 27, 19.

Rossiter, Clinton. 1960. *The American Presidency.* New York: Harcourt, Brace & World.

Sanbonmatsu, Kira. 2006. "The Legislative Party and Candidate Recruitment in the American States." *Party Politics* 12 (3): 233–256.

Schattschneider, E. E. 1942. *Party Government.* New York: Farrar & Rinehart.

———. 1960. *The Semi-Sovereign People: A Realist's View of Democracy in America.* New York: Holt, Rinehart & Winston.

Schlesinger, Joseph. 1984. "On the Theory of Party Organization." *Journal of Politics* 46 (2): 369–400.

Schwartz, Mildred. 1990. *The Party Network: The Robust Organization of Illinois Republicans.* Madison: University of Wisconsin Press.

Shaiko, Ronald G. 1998. "Reverse Lobbying: Interest Group Mobilization from the White House and the Hill." In *Interest Group Politics,* edited by Allan J. Cigler and Burdett A. Loomis, 259–267. 5th ed. Washington, DC: CQ Press.

Sinclair, Barbara. 1998. *Legislators, Leaders, and Lawmaking: The US House in the Postreform Era.* Baltimore, MD: Johns Hopkins University Press.

———. 2006. *Party Wars: Polarization and the Politics of National Policy Making.* Norman: University of Oklahoma Press.

Skinner, Richard M. 2007. *More Than Money: Interest Group Action in Congressional Elections.* Lanham, MD: Rowman & Littlefield.

——. 2012. "Barack Obama and the Partisan Presidency: Four More Years?" *Society* 49 (5): 423–429.

Skocpol, Theda. 1996. *Boomerang: Health Care Reform and the Turn against Government.* New York: Norton.

Skowronek, Stephen. 1993. *The Politics Presidents Make: Leadership from John Adams to Bill Clinton.* Cambridge, MA: Harvard University Press.

Thrush, Glenn, and Jonathan Martin. 2010 "President Obama Steers Clear of Shaky Specter." *Politico,* May 17. http://www.politico.com/.

Time. 1944. "Political Notes: Clear Everything with Sidney." *Time,* September 25.

Washington Times. 2009. "NRA Threats Fail to Sway Senators on Sotomayor." *Washington Times,* August 2.

Weir, Margaret. 1995. "Institutional and Political Obstacles to Reform." *Health Affairs* 14 (1): 102–104.

White, Michael. 2001. "Lord Prentice of Daventry" (obituary). *Guardian,* January 22. https://www.theguardian.com/.

Yoshinaka, Antoine. 2016. *Crossing the Aisle: Party-Switching by US Legislators in the Postwar Era.* New York: Cambridge University Press.

Notes

1. In more recent cycles, the presidential nominee has openly chosen the vice presidential candidate, even though formally this decision requires the delegates' approval.

2. The Democratic Legislative Campaign Committee, the Democratic Governors Association, the Republican Governors Association, and the Republican State Leadership Committee are all increasingly active in campaigns.

3. In a few other cases (William G. Miller, Bob Dole, and Tim Kaine), a politician who served as chair was nominated for vice president not long afterward, but even these men had other credentials that were more important.

4. Prominent examples in the United Kingdom include Shaun Woodward, who moved from the Conservative Party to Labour in 1999, and Reginald Prentice, who switched from Labour to the Conservatives in 1977. Both switchers were nominated in different constituencies and were rewarded with ministerial posts by their new parties. See White (2001) and Porter (2008).

5. While Schattschneider (1960) seems to suggest a similar dynamic in Ohio that year, where a popular vote on right to work also not only failed but also produced a backlash that sank GOP candidates, the journalistic account he cites actually suggests that the similarly conservative Senator John Bricker, unlike Knowland, tried to convince GOP funders of the folly of this plan and only reluctantly acceded to their insistent requests for support (*Reporter* 1958).

6. While McConnell denied trying to influence the NRA, independent conservative observers, including some present at the meeting in question, reject his denial (*Washington Times* 2009). See also Greenhouse (2012) and Bernstein (2012).

7. The NRA did cite the Sotomayor and Kagan nomination votes as a reason for staying neutral during the otherwise solidly pro-gun rights Senator Mark Begich's (D-AK) unsuccessful 2014 bid for reelection. See *CBS News* (2014).

8. Frymer (1999) suggests this fate is limited to African Americans and perhaps LGBT voters, but I believe it is far more widespread.

9. There were occasional exceptions to this rule, when Speaker Boehner needed Democratic support because Tea Party or Freedom Caucus Republicans would not support must-pass legislation.

10. Peabody (1967) found interparty differences and attributed them to parties becoming crankier the longer they were in the minority. Nelson (1977) rejected this explanation without presenting a compelling alternative.

CHAPTER SEVEN

Leadership and Interest Groups

Timothy M. LaPira

Former representative Vin Weber is the consummate Washington insider. Corporation CEOs, association presidents, union leaders, and grassroots organizers from across the political spectrum seek out his strategic political and policy advice, as do presidents, Speakers of the House, Senate majority leaders, and those who seek to occupy those leadership posts in government. He is regularly featured on Top 10 lists of movers and shakers, strategic consultants, and lobbyists in Washington, and has also been featured on virtually every national media outlet.

Weber began his political career as the Minnesota-based campaign manager and aide to Representative Tom Hagedorn and Senator Rudy Boschwitz before running for Congress in Minnesota's sixth and second congressional districts. In Congress, he quickly rose through the ranks to join the Republican leadership team, preceding none other than Representative Tom Delay as the Republican Conference secretary. He is considered to have been among then–minority leader Newt Gingrich's closest allies. He was a cofounder of the Conservative Opportunity Society, a chief architect of the Republican's Contract with America, and helped assure the 1994 Republican victory in the House.

Ironically, Weber did not run for office himself in 1994. Rather, he opted to go through the so-called revolving door, and—along with Democrat representative Tom Downey—opened the Washington office of Clark & Weinstock, a new breed of public affairs consulting that seamlessly blended political, policy, and public relations advice to a wide variety of clients. In 2011, the firm merged with a public relations firm specializing in grassroots mobilization to become Mercury/Clark & Weinstock. In his twenty years with the firm, Weber has represented companies from virtually every sector in the economy on issues as diverse as taxes, transportation, agriculture, health care, education, and veterans affairs.

Undoubtedly, Vin Weber can accurately be described as a leader in the vast, complex, and growing Washington interest group system. Yet so is Sandi Stuart. Most people have never heard of Sandi Stuart; nor should they have. Stuart never ran for office, has never been the object of PBS documentaries, and is not a household name to political junkies like Weber. Now a principal at her own lobbying firm, the Stuart Murray Group, she was a partner at Weber's Clark & Weinstock. After earning her JD from Monterey Law School, she joined the staff of California representative Vic Fazio, rising through the ranks to chief of staff of his Washington office. She also served a variety of positions on the Democratic staff of the House Budget Committee. In 1993, she was appointed assistant secretary for legislative affairs at the Department of Defense—the Pentagon's lobbyist on Capitol Hill—where she served all three of President Bill Clinton's defense secretaries. In 1999, she joined Clark & Weinstock, where Fazio and Weber were cochairmen. Upon her resignation, senators Trent Lott—the Republican party leader—and Carl Levin—the leading Democrat on the Armed Services Committee—took time out of their busy schedules to offer tributes to Stuart on the floor of the world's most deliberative body.

Most people may never have heard of her, but those who mattered inside the Beltway most certainly had. In her fifteen years as a policy strategist and lobbyist, she has represented many of the same clients as Weber, such as Freddie Mac, Oxfam International, and PhRMA. The issues she has lobbied the government on include, unsurprisingly, defense and homeland security, but also policies dealing with clean air and water, taxes, trade, banking, agriculture, telecommunications, food production, and consumer product and safety. As with Weber, the breadth of her policy expertise is extremely broad.

Stuart's and Weber's careers are very different, yet they ended up in very similar positions in Washington's influence industry. They now both command salaries that dwarf their federal paychecks. What's different between them is that Weber's story is well known—and extremely rare. Stuart's trajectory through the halls of power is not well recognized but is much more common. Contrast these two political and policy leaders in the interest group system with Allison McKay and Sarah Alexander. Much like Stuart, McKay and Alexander never held elective office. Unlike Stuart, Alexander and McKay have most likely never even met Levin and Lott, let alone been the subject of their public gratitude in the Senate. The honorific "the honorable" has never appeared before their names. They have never earned a paycheck from the federal government. And their names are on no Top 50 lists of Washington influence peddlers. They are, however, lobbyists just like Stuart and Weber.

Allison McKay was director of public and government affairs for Safran USA, the American affiliate of the French aerospace company, for fifteen years. McKay had previously held an entry-level position in marketing at B/E Aerospace that she landed immediately after graduating with a degree in business. She earned her new job at Safran after a series of complex mergers and acquisitions. She was periodically listed as one of three or four in-house lobbyists for Safran on federal disclosure reports from 2008 through 2013. She lobbied the government on defense and homeland security issues—and nothing else.

Sarah Alexander is deputy organizing director at Food & Water Watch, a Washington-based nonprofit organization that advocates for sustainable and environmentally friendly agriculture. Alexander has interned, volunteered, or worked professionally at a variety of local, national, and international nonprofit groups such as Green Corps, Ojibwe Wind and White Earth Land Recovery Project, and the American Community Gardener Association. Though her specialty at Food & Water Watch is strategic online organizing, fund-raising, and social media strategy, she was registered to lobby on the 2008 farm bill. She lobbied the government on food industry issues—and nothing else.

Like Stuart and Weber, Alexander's and McKay's careers are very different, yet they ended up in very similar positions. Though they represent markedly different kinds of interests in Washington, they both developed industry- and issue-specific expertise by working up through the ranks with their respective employers. McKay used her background in business to become a lobbyist for a major defense contractor; Alexander used her nonprofit experience to become a lobbyist for an environmental group. Both only ever represented a single interest group and were only ever active on a small set of very similar issues. Neither will ever earn the kind of money that Weber and Stuart do.

Though the concept of "political leadership" is highly contested and theoretically muddled, any credible, qualitative assessment of these four lobbyists would conclude that Weber and Stuart are leaders in the interest group system. Democrat Stuart and Republican Weber held senior appointed and elective office in the government; they also parlayed that experience into a career in the private sector representing a whole host of interests on a diverse set of policies. Their clients seek them out precisely because they are leading figures inside Washington's impenetrable circles of power. They know people. They know how decisions really get made.

McKay and Alexander—whose party affiliations are not public and, frankly, unimportant—respectively represent ideological caricature interests: a "conservative" defense contractor and a "liberal" environmental advocacy organization. Most observers would not consider them leaders in Washington's influence industry. Though they remain within their niches, we may not be surprised to hear colleagues who work most closely with them—even those colleagues who may regularly find themselves on opposite sides of key political issues—describe them as leaders. These highly specialized policy experts likely know more about aerospace contracting and environmental agriculture advocacy than anybody else, making them leading figures in their fields.

The problem for interest group scholarship is that we have no meaningful way to distinguish whether, or to what degree, these four lobbyists are leaders. In this essay, I explore how various perspectives on political leadership and competing schools of thought on interest group politics may guide political scientists into advancing our knowledge of who is and who is not an interest group leader.

First, I review how political science and public administration scholars have explored political leadership. I point out that scholars of political leadership tend to focus on the qualities of individual people—presidents, party leaders, military commanders, agency heads, and the like. More recently, studies have begun to take seriously the context in which individuals lead. The major contribution of leadership theory has been to isolate both the intrinsic personal characteristics and extrinsic institutions that compel or constrain political success.

Second, I make the case that interest group scholars have made great progress in our collective understanding of the extrinsic political context, but that they have largely ignored the intrinsic personal characteristics of those engaged in that context. By focusing exclusively on the "interest" or the "group" in interest group politics, we are missing an important part of the "politics": the people who represent those interests. Policy entrepreneurs, social movement leaders, lobbyists, political strategists, and the like are not interchangeable, though interest group scholars tend to assume they are. The people whose vocation is to represent organized interests vary in important and meaningful ways—ways that may be informed by integrating elements of political leadership theory to the study of interest representation.

Finally, I present an agenda for studying interest group leadership that promises to move the field forward. I make the case that interest group scholarship will benefit from shifting attention to individual agents who represent organized interest principals.

Four Perspectives on Political Leadership

In his classic text on pluralism that serves as a cornerstone study for interest group scholars, David Truman bluntly remarks, "Leadership is a subject, particularly as it deals with politics, that has long been mired in a morass of mysticism and superficiality" ([1951] 1971, 188). Perhaps because one of the founding thinkers of pluralism so easily dismissed the concept of leadership, interest group scholars have since avoided evoking the term for fear of accusations of amateurism.

Yet in his dismissal of the leadership concept, Truman was making a profound statement about the nature of politics that spanned disciplines and that remains central to our thinking today. Truman, Dahl, and their pluralist contemporaries were rejecting the Great Man theory of history and were instead rethinking how social, economic, and political forces drove the process of government from the ground up. Though critics pointed out how the pluralists ignored power structures (Mills 1956) and the nature of collective action (Olson 1965), they all predominantly accepted that seemingly fuzzy concepts like "leadership" granted people too much agency and failed to account for the world in which they sought power.

By outright rejecting or ignoring the concept ever since Truman declared it dispensable, interest group scholars—and much of political science more broadly—have not kept abreast of developments in leadership theory that may be useful. In contrast, scholars of the presidency, parties, courts, and especially public administration have made significant advances. The concept of leadership is no longer "a morass of mysticism and superficiality," yet interest group scholars continue to overlook the insights it may offer to understanding interest representation. Leadership theory has made significant advances, especially in its application to classic public management problems that suffer from inherent principal–agent problems. Rooted primarily in Burns's (1978) critique of existing leadership theory and original idea of the transformational leader, I briefly outline four broad perspectives on leadership that have advanced outside the interest group literature since Truman.

Great Man/Trait Perspective

Though the Great Man theory, rooted in nineteenth-century Enlightenment philosophy, may be easily dismissed because of its inherent biases, it did serve as a foundation for a more generalizable model of leadership. The Great Man approach assumed a select few—who were invariably white and male—possessed indefinable, innate qualities that inexorably led them to be leaders. Though contemporary social critics and historians criticized the Great Man approach, it at least succeeded in contributing to the idea that there was some master list of traits, qualities, and personal characteristics that all leaders possessed to some degree.

Thus, trait theories advanced the notion that some qualities were generalizable across different kinds and types of leaders. Unfortunately, what traction trait theories gained in generalizability they lost in parsimony. Virtually any positive connotation or personal attribute could be inserted into the sentence, "Leaders are x." Leaders are charismatic. Leaders are intelligent. Leaders are attractive. Leaders are visionary. No longer were leaders born with greatness as their destiny; now, anybody who had the ability to convince others of his or her positive qualities could achieve greatness.

Behavioral Qualities and Personal Style Perspective

Though listing traits gained leadership little traction per se, it laid the foundation for the behavioral revolution in the social sciences to empirically observe and systematically catalog the elements of successful (and unsuccessful) political leadership. The behavioral perspective focuses on what managers actually do in their role as organizational leaders. Borrowing from Freudian psychology, Adorno et al. (1950) interpreted leaders' personality traits on the F-scale that purported to measure their degree of fascism. That is, by deconstructing personality traits like aggression, superstition, and toughness, they claimed to identify an authoritarian syndrome that is capable of influencing others to engage in actions they otherwise would not. Although *The Authoritarian Personality* was criticized for attributing individual-level personality traits broadly to societies—especially as it applied to the German people under the Third Reich—it was still largely influential for introducing the idea that leadership potential could be observed in its constituent psychological parts. Perhaps the specific traits of the F-scale were misidentified, but the idea that measurable psychological characteristics predicts leadership behavior endures to this day.

Moreover, the authoritarian personality perspective could be generalized across contexts, including the highly polarized politics in the United States today (Hetherington and Weiler 2009). In one of the most ethically controversial psychological studies ever conducted, the Stanford prison experiments arbitrarily pitted hypothetical leader-guards against follower-prisoners to show that simply attributing leadership legitimacy itself induces authoritarian behavior (Zimbardo 1970; see also Zimbardo 2007). The behavioral approach, then, introduced the potential that individual-level behaviors—or personalities when aggregated—could be the key to transforming the typically normative discipline of political science into one that objectively and rigorously uncovered patterns in politics (Easton 1965). Whether we are concerned with how people choose elected leaders or how leaders make decisions on behalf of those they govern, the behavioral revolution offered a systematic way to understand politics through basic research.

Transactional/Transformational Perspective

Critics of the behavioral revolution moved away from psychology and toward economics to better understand leadership. That is, the rational choice state-of-the-world approach could offer insight into how rules, conditions, and institutions induce behaviors. As a corrective to the behavioral revolution in political science, rational choice theory offered an opportunity to explain behavior with the simple and straightforward assumption of human self-interest. It does not rely on unobservable, complex personality traits. In this vein, James MacGregor Burns (1978)—primarily a presidency historian—developed his theory of transformational leadership to differentiate it from transactional leadership.

Burns's theory of leadership is less known for its empirical analysis of presidents as leaders and more for its reconsideration of the assumptions about leadership more generally. He distinguished between transactional leaders and transformational leaders. Transactional leaders engaged in routine, managerial tasks for their own self-interest. They may lead organizations, governments, or political systems poorly or exceptionally, though they do little to positively impact the organization. The transaction is simple: the leader exchanges rewards or deals out punishments to followers on the basis of their commitment and loyalty. The outcome of the transaction is predictable: the organization meets the needs of the leader, not the followers.

Transformational leaders, on the other hand, motivate followers to change the nature, purpose, and influence of the organization itself. The rational self-interest is that of the organization, government, or political system, not the leader. As a result, both leaders and followers are better off because the collective pursues its rational self-interests, not the constituent individuals that belong to it. At center, Burns was trying to understand both the intrinsic characteristics and the external context—and the interaction between the two—that produced transformational leaders.

The most significant attribute of the transactional–transformational theory of leadership was its decidedly normative approach to leadership. In his reflection on the topic, Burns unapologetically makes the case that leadership and its study is not value neutral:

> Leadership is an expanding field of study that . . . remains in its growing stages; it has as yet no grand, unifying theory to provide common direction to thinkers and researchers. Even the meaning of the term itself remains controversial. Some will use it neutrally, dispassionately, to analyze qualities of both, say, a Gandhi and a Hitler. I believe leadership is not only a descriptive term but a prescriptive one, embracing a moral, even a passionate dimension. Consider our common usage. We don't call for good leadership—we expect, or at least hope, that it will be good. "Bad" leadership implies no leadership. (2003, 2)

That is, leadership to Burns is more than simply observable behaviors or personality attributes. It is instead a normative ideal that the self-interest of the whole ought to be sought, not the self-interests of the followers or leaders themselves. The normative implication is that political leaders in a democratic system who are merely transactional are failures. In a democracy, those who consent to be governed expect to be led by those who can improve the means by which they are governed. Transactional leaders therefore abuse the public trust in pursuit of their own personal gain.

Yet even though Burns's writings were deeply normative, the transactional–transformational leadership model gained traction mostly through its application to public management.

Situational/Contingency Perspective

In a line of research distinct from Burns's normative theories, public administration and organizational management scholars adopt the perspective that leadership mechanisms vary according to the context. The leadership contingency perspective is most consistent with the cognitive revolution in political science and public administration. This view assumes no single method of leadership but rather attempts to systematically explain how leaders adapt to organizational needs, challenges, and process (Simon 1947; Cyert and March 1963; Lindblom 1959; Cohen, March, and Olsen 1972). Rather than being strictly rational, organizational leaders are boundedly rational information processors who, to use Simon's (1947) term, satisfice.

More broadly in political science, the information processing approach to political decision making has introduced theories about social cognition and heuristics that explain how individuals evaluate people, objects, and events. The information processing perspective assumes that humans respond to stimuli in their environment but are only capable of processing a limited amount of information at any point in time (Simon 1996; Hastie 1986; Tversky and Kahneman 1974; Kahneman and Tversky 1984).

The most innovative application of this approach to leadership in political science is Graham Allison's *Essence of Decision* (1971; see also Allison and Zelikow 1999), a deep case study of the Kennedy White House—notably not just Kennedy alone but within the context of the institutionalized presidency. Kennedy made a series of decisions to avoid nuclear catastrophe. The insight from this case is how the Kennedy administration made many poor calculations because they were operating with incomplete information and were constrained by their own biases about what they (often incorrectly) assumed about Khrushchev's intent. Of course, in the end tragedy was averted, but the result was not because the administration made calculated decisions based on concrete information. The lesson is that to understand leaders' decision making, we must not only know what their rational motivations and self-interests are, but we must also account for the leaders' actual information environment and cognitive biases.

Following Allison, political scientists have applied the contingency-based information processing approach to institutional leaders like presidents (Canes-Wrone 2006), members of Congress (Miler 2010), and agency heads (Meier et al. 2007), but not leaders of nongovernmental organizations such as interest groups. Interest group scholars have not followed suit.

Four Perspectives on Interest Groups

Just as prevailing political science thinking about leadership has evolved over time, so too has the study of interest group politics. Broadly, scholars have approached the study of interest groups by asking two general questions: Where do groups come from? How much do they participate in the policy process? Interest group scholarship is concerned in the first instance with individual-level interest mobilization and system-level bias, and in the second with interest group influence and policy change (Baumgartner and Leech 1998). These questions are often difficult to distinguish in both theory and empirical observation, but this general categorization of the objectives of interest group scholarship helps us gain some purchase on how the subfield has evolved over time. Moreover, I point out that the evolution of interest group scholarship runs parallel to developments in the study of political leadership. I briefly discuss each school's orientation to both the mobilization and influence questions. Then I argue that interest group scholars can exploit these parallel developments by synthesizing political leadership insights about individual behavior, and vice versa.

Corruptionism

In *Federalist No. 10*, Madison (1787) articulates the presumption that factions—the Platonic ideal type we now think of as parties or interest groups—as being inherently corrupt, or "adverse to the rights of other citizens, or to the permanent and aggregate interests of the community." Madison assumed institutionalized constitutional protections would cancel out competing factions and minimize their harm to the greater good. Yet the underlying assumption that latent or organized groups of like-minded people are intrinsically corrupt remains the dominant normative view in the journalism and jurisprudence of special interests today (Briffault 2014). That is, the corruption school of thought on interest groups remains grounded in legal institutionalism. This theoretical approach relies almost exclusively on historical and qualitative interpretations of American constitutional law.

Typically argued in the context of the *Citizens United* and *McCutcheon v. FEC* Supreme Court decisions, the common jurisprudential assumption about interest mobilization is that resource-rich organizations and individuals exploit constitutional liberties of free speech and assembly—such as electoral institutions, campaign finance laws, lobbying regulations—to engage in de facto corruption. The corruption framework emphasizes that special interests do not violate de jure principles of bribery, fraud, or quid pro quo exchanges, though they engage in behavior that appears as if it is corrupt. In his 2011 polemic *Republic, Lost*, constitutional scholar Lawrence Lessig articulates this view: "Theorists of corruption don't typically talk much about decent souls. Their focus is upon criminals—the *venally corrupt*, who bribe to buy privilege, or *the systematically corrupt*, who make the people (or, better, the rich) dependent upon the government to ensure that the people (or, better, the rich) protect the government" (7–8). Instead, he prefers a definition of institutional corruption: "Not a corruption caused by a gaggle of evil souls. On the contrary, a corruption practiced by decent people, people we should respect, people working extremely hard to do what they believe is right, yet decent people working with a system that has evolved the most elaborate and costly bending of democratic government in our history. There are good people here, yet extraordinary bad gets done" (8).

Thus, the institutionalized corruption perspective argues that power is concentrated in a select few that compel government to act in its interests, and not that of the general welfare (Schweizer 2013; Teachout 2014). In the long run, the wealthy win because they systematically corrupt political institutions, all while keeping their hands clean in the eyes of the law. The implication is that current legal-constitutional institutions do not resolve the problems of faction that Madison feared most.

The perspective that interest groups are inherently and incorrigibly corrupt generates several implicit—not explicit—theoretical assumptions about interest mobilization and influence. As for the first mobilization question, institutionally corrupt groups consist exclusively of rich people. It remains unclear how these rich people join together, as simply having the means to do so is sufficient. To the second question of influence, well-organized rich people depend on the government to maintain their wealth, and they therefore use their expansive resources to keep the regime intact. The implied exchange is not direct but organized like a gift economy: a voluntary contribution today may be voluntarily rewarded, or (less likely) not, at another time (Lessig 2011). By simply infusing politics with money, the well-organized and well-off perpetuate a government that keeps them well-off and therefore well organized. The institutionally corrupt cycle perpetuates itself ad infinitum.

These claims are supported with selected anecdotes of corporate influence in politics and policy making. Despite evidence to the contrary that actually very little money enters into politics (Ansolabehere, Snyder, and de Figueiredo 2003) and that money alone rarely, if ever, simply buys political outcomes (Baumgartner et al. 2009), the "have money, will influence" logic of institutionalized corruption is so simple that its adherents do not question the absence of clear causal mechanisms. Rather, the debate is one of jurisprudential interpretation over the appropriate constitutional role of government to regulate the money-in-politics gift economy (Hasen 2012).

Pluralism (And Its Critics)

The discipline's classic pluralists, such as Truman, Dahl, and Lipset—as well as their plural-elitist critics, such as Schattschneider and Lindblom—were primarily concerned with how power and influence were distributed throughout the system of organized interests outside of government, and how that distribution afforded them influence inside it. Rather than simply asserting that selected, well-heeled groups simply generated public policies, the pluralists' project was to better understand the process by which otherwise disconnected individuals in society and the economy joined together, and once organized, how organized groups interacted with each other to ultimately achieve a natural balance, or democratic equilibrium of interest representation where power was distributed proportionally.

The foundation of pluralism is Truman's ([1951] 1971) disturbance theory. At any given time, there likely exists equilibrium of competing interests. Then some event in society or in the economy occurs that some previously disorganized group of people perceive as a threat. The group then organizes itself as a movement or organized interest that seeks a resolution from government. The disturbance motivates an otherwise acquiescent Madisonian faction—whether it consists of citizens, professionals, identity groups, or even businesses within an affected industry—to join together to resolve their common problem. The interest group then seeks greater government involvement in corresponding economic and social affairs, resulting in greater government's involvement in their interest. In Truman's formulation, the same mechanism that mobilized the latent group also influences policy outcomes; the government is merely a passive venue to which its influence is focused.

Critics responded that social and economic structures made group mobilization less seamless (Mills 1956; Domhoff 2006) and influence less proportionate to the distribution of actual disturbances or public problems (Schattschneider [1960] 1975; Schlozman and Tierney 1986). Dahl (1961) refuted this by pointing out that biased representation was disaggregated across a wide variety of loci, with no single faction or group controlling policy across multiple areas of government. Though this summary of one of the great debates in political theory is oversimplified, the controversy between pluralists and their critics was one of magnitude, not kind. All else being equal, groups of people mobilized in response to problems and influenced government by providing a means for citizens to hold public officials accountable. The degree to which all was equal is what divided pluralists and their critics.

Extractionism

The major theoretical critique that undermined the basic assumptions of pluralist mobilization and influence came from Olson's *Logic of Collective Action* (1965). Olson's theory refuted the mechanisms by which people mobilize for political action, thus implying that the pluralist mechanism for influence was irrational. Simply, only those with the resources to offer particularized benefits to potential members have the capability to organize for political action. Absent the particularized benefit, people free ride. When nobody contributes—even if they are faced with a threat—the latent group lacks the organizational resources to spontaneously seek a solution to their shared problems. Simply put, the free rider problem limits the ability of some groups to mobilize, resulting in a distribution of organized interests that disproportionately favors the economically advantaged (Schattschneider [1960] 1975; Schlozman and Tierney 1983, 1986). Thus, Olson's model has the advantage of better explaining the logic of why and when individuals contribute at the micro level, but it could also explain the maldistribution of interest representation at the macro level.

Olson's *Logic* was fundamentally a theory addressing the question of mobilization. The book frankly punted the question of influence, claiming that lobbying and any gains made were merely a by-product of successfully overcoming the free rider problem. Yet it laid the groundwork for the economic theory of rent seeking, which explicitly modeled the act of organized interests influencing government distribution of wealth (Buchanan and Tullock 1962; Tullock 1967; Krueger 1974). After resolving the collective action dilemma, companies, associations, unions, and nonmember institutions seek direct economic benefits from the government.

Salisbury (1969) pointed out that interest group entrepreneurs have an incentive to exploit the ability to extract particularized benefits by mobilizing groups from the top down. The exchange theory of interest group mobilization held that entrepreneurs would cover the transaction costs associated with overcoming the free rider problem in order to generate a demand for particularized benefits, such as government contracts, direct subsidies, sympathetic tax codes, or favorable regulation from government, with the consequence that the government will expand. This school of thought endures in current economics-oriented interest group scholarship that reveals returns on investment or benefits accrued as a function of lobbying expenditures (Alexander, Mazza, and Scholz 2009; Richter, Samphantharak, and Timmons 2009; Dahan, Hadani, and Schuler 2013).

The common thread in this school of thought is that groups have a clear and logical motivation to extract private goods from public sources, which distinguishes it from the corruptionist direct exchange, whether as quid pro quo bribes or gift economy. The exchange in the extractionist approach is between the interest group entrepreneur and the group member, where the member provides resources and the entrepreneur offers a greater than zero likelihood of success via an inflated return on investment.

Neopluralism

The problem with the extractionist school of thought is not that it is illogical or does not explain empirical outcomes, but that it is incomplete. That is, lobbying expenditures at t_1 may explain lower effective tax rates at t_2, which are measurable benefits. But the same cannot be said for lobbying expenditures at t_1 and the more ambiguous policy output, such as the watered-down Volker rule legislative language found in the Dodd–Frank Wall Street reform bill at t_2. Though certainly banks and investors wary about the costs of regulation favored the outcome, how exactly do we measure that particular rent? To some degree, could it not also be seen as a success for those favoring additional regulation of financial services institutions? That is, any theory of interest group mobilization that relies exclusively on the policy objective of extracting a precise, tangible, and exclusive benefit only applies in those settings where the policy process produces one. That scenario is not always the case, and in fact may rarely be, implying that interest group extraction depends on the political and economic context of the policy process.

The neopluralist school of thought purposely tries to account for the many varieties of group mobilization and influence that depend on the many contingencies and contexts of the political process (Baumgartner and Leech 1998; McFarland 2004; Lowery and Gray 2004; Lowery 2007). The neopluralist school's hallmark is its promotion of multiple paths of interest mobilization and influence. It is less a consensus view of a consistent set of hypotheses about how groups form and how they influence policy, and more a tacit acceptance among interest group scholars that many, often contradictory, hypotheses explain these phenomena under different conditions. What may appear to be a generalizable causal mechanism in one policy niche—say, a handful of defense contractors gaining a distinct advantage in weapons systems sales—may not be relevant in another—such as tariff rate quotas, which fluctuate across industries and time on the basis of a variety of global and local economic and political conditions.

The original work in this vein is Heinz, Laumann, Nelson, and Salisbury's *The Hollow Core* (1993), the wide-ranging, multimethod account of the structure, organization, and activities of those in Washington's legal and lobbying profession. Heinz and colleagues borrowed elements of both the extractionist and pluralist perspectives in an effort to understand when they might be consistent with observations in the real world of lobbying. They conclude, much like the pluralists, that there is no single source of unequal representation and influence in the group system. In line with the extractionists, they conclude that there are many opportunistic interest group entrepreneurs who appear to be more central and influential actors in their respective policy domains. The key to understanding the distribution, then, is to better understand the opportunity structures that give some interests greater influence than others.

A steady stream of interest group scholarship that intentionally factored in context and contingency followed. Gray and Lowery published *The Population Ecology of Interest Representation* (1996), which reconsidered mobilization and system-level bias as a function of internal organizational factors, but also a product of the complex system of competing and collaborating organizations and government objectives. Soon after, Baumgartner and Leech's (1998) extensive literature review and meta-analysis of years of published work revealed that the predominantly case-based methods led to inconsistent conclusions about group influence. Consequently, they called for advancing a more unified project that broadened the subfield's scope across many domains, issues, and institutions to generate more general theories that explicitly accounted for observations of political context. Hojnacki and colleagues (2012) revisited progress along these lines in a meta-analysis of interest group publications in the field's top general-interest journals between 1996 and 2011. They concluded that a great deal of progress in projects of large empirical scope—cross-sectionally across policy issues and venues, as well as geographically and longitudinally over time—had occurred, but less progress had been made in advancing a coherent, grand theoretical framework.

The advances in both theory and empirical research on interest group politics since the launch of the neopluralist approach in the 1990s can hardly be overstated. Prestigious award-winning projects include the multiyear study by Baumgartner et al. (2009) of a large sample of issues that found conditional mobilization bias and little evidence of outright rent-seeking success. Likewise, Schlozman, Verba, and Brady's (2012) multifaceted study yielded mixed results: "Most of the interest organizations in Washington politics do not conform to a stereotype of the well-heeled operation with resources to burn. . . . Although the weight of advocacy by organizations representing business interests varies across domains of organized interest activities, in no case is it outweighed by the activity of either organizations representing the less privileged, or public interest groups" (442).

The conclusions from these subfield-defining projects are testament to the neopluralist skepticism that group mobilization and influence can be simply described as the inherently dishonest rich always win (corruptionism), the many inevitably attain a representative equilibrium (pluralism), or the opportunistic entrepreneur innately succeeds in his or her pursuit of particularized benefits (extractionism). But that is not to deny that the few are better represented than the many (Strolovitch 2007; Bartels 2008; Grossmann 2012; Gilens and Page 2014). Thus, the neopluralist school has made great advances in improving our collective understanding of the complex, conditional, and context-dependent world that groups mobilize and influence policy.

Leadership Theories and Their Interest Group Analogs

Though their objective concerns are different, these loose categories of leadership and interest group theories parallel in several meaningful ways. Table 7.1 provides a framework that connects theories of leadership with their analog interest group schools of thought, suggesting how leadership theorists may perceive the role of interest group agents as leaders.

First, the Great Man/trait leadership theories share the corruptionist assumptions of uninhibited human agency and circular causal logic. Great leaders, or those with sufficiently positive attributes, simply achieve their goals because they are great and have positive attributes; corrupt rich special interests get what they want from government because they are corrupt and rich. The logical fallacies fit well when leadership theory is applied to interest group mobilization and influence theory.

I contend that it is not coincidental that the corruptionist approach to interest group politics is grounded in legal-institutional thought, which itself is primarily rooted in the Enlightenment promotion of contract-based market economies and

Table 7.1. The Leadership–Interest Group Matrix

Leadership Theory	Interest Group Analog	Interest Group Leadership	
		Group Mobilization and Maintenance	Advocacy Activities and Policy Influence
Great Man/trait theories	Corruptionism	Leaders have innate talent to command like-minded activists/patrons	Leaders inevitably succeed through bribes or gift economy exchanges
Behavioral qualities and personal styles	Pluralism	Leaders develop skills to recruit members to contribute to the collective goal, achieve pluralist equilibrium	Leaders with appropriate political styles will voice preferences in proportion to the interests' policy intensity
Transactional/transformational	Extractionism	Transactional leaders manage the organization to achieve their self-interests; transformational leaders inspire followers to improve the public interest	Transactional leaders engage in rent-seeking behavior; transformational leaders improve the quality of deliberation
Situational/contingency	Neopluralism	Leaders use information asymmetry to strategically mobilize interests based on political opportunity structure and context	Leaders create information asymmetries and exploit opportunities to provide useful and biased information to policy makers

their contingent self-governing republics. To corruptionists, interest group politics is a contractual exchange between the state and the many mischievous factions. Constitutions are intended to prevent interest group leaders from successfully bribing their way to the fruits of the lawmaking process.

Though there is certainly an ethical prerogative to minimize outright graft, the presumption that all interest group politics is corrupt is counterproductive to learning how organized interests and their leaders behave. Both the Great Man/trait leadership theories and the corruptionist school base their tenets on legal abstractions rather observations of human behavior. The fact is, most interest group leaders do not behave the way disgraced lobbyist Jack Abramoff did (Lowery and Marchetti 2012).

Second, personality-based leadership theory and pluralism are firmly grounded in the behavioral revolution of the mid-twentieth century. Despite Truman's dismissal of leadership theory in politics, interests will be sufficiently represented by those who follow the Washington adage, "If you're not at the table, you're on the menu." In Dahl's (1961) classic statement of pluralism, no one interest rules. He found that community leaders and "subleaders" in New Haven representing various stakeholders earned their seat at the table, whether it was schools, teachers, and parents in education or retailers, developers, and other notables in urban redevelopment policy.

These observations are consistent with the idea that leaders may not simply have intrinsic positive traits but can develop the domain-specific knowledge, communication skills, and professional networks needed to be influential in their respective spheres of influence. Interest group actors will lead those who would remain otherwise dormant to act collectively to pursue their shared interests. Leaders within the niche will have clout if they can cajole, persuade, or otherwise convince colleagues in and out of government that the interests they represent offer the best solutions to public problems.

I argue that these insights are at least partly true, but that they ignore the inherent collective action dilemma. That is, those people who ascend to leadership positions within interest organizations or more broadly in policy domains will possess the skills and qualities of all organizational leaders, just as in business, nonprofits, and other institutions. Those with superior skills and relevant political styles are more likely to be leaders than those without. But no amount of skill or style can resolve the free rider problem.

Third, the transactional–transformational dichotomy matches well with the extractionist school of thought. In short, the normal mode of interest group leadership will be a transactional leader seeking personal self-interest. Whether doing so benefits the interest organization is secondary, though we ought to expect most organizations to structure their governance to reward leaders who achieve its mission and objectives. That is, rent-seeking interest group leaders will succeed if they extract particularistic interests from public coffers on behalf of the organization's members, patrons, or shareholders. The interest group leader's self-interest advances as the organization's mission progresses.

Transformational leaders, rather, would "minimize rent-seeking, and maximize deliberation" (Mansbridge 1992, 47). Mansbridge's normative justification for interest groups is that they have the potential to represent those excluded from other institutional mechanisms, such as parties, and the potential to improve the policy debate. Transformational leaders inspire others to advance the common good, not just seek out the good of the special interest to which they belong. The democratic need for organized interests rests on their ability to improve the public debate. Better deliberation will advance the common good despite the interests of any one organization or leader. Just as Burns's formulation of leadership is inherently normative, so too is the deliberative democratic prescription for advancing the quality of the policy process.

Finally, situational/contingency leadership theories and neopluralism correspond nearly perfectly. The context-dependent group mobilization and multifaceted information provision influence models are nearly restatements of contingency-based models of organizational leadership. According to the neopluralist approach, interest group agents adopt context-appropriate strategies to mobilize interests, recruit members, and attract donors and patrons. These strategies will vary between corporate interests and nonprofit advocacy organizations. For example, consider the hypothetical case of a policy debate over cancer research funding. A pharmaceutical manufacturing interest may appeal to the industry's perceived need to reduce regulatory and tax burdens that hinder its ability to produce profitable drugs, whereas nonprofits seeking increased research funding for a rare disease may use heart-wrenching anecdotes of families battling childhood cancer. In each case, interest group leaders strategically use their information asymmetries about these complex government programs to craft a message to both mobilize support and influence the policy debate.

Synthesizing Leadership and Interest Group Theory

My overview of both leadership and interest group literatures reveals a number of parallels between them, but also one notable discrepancy. Social scientific models of political leadership and interest group politics differ mostly on their primary, and theoretically presumed, objects of analysis. Leadership scholars almost exclusively center on individual persons, usually those who hold some authoritative and legitimate political office or administrative appointment. Alternatively, interest group scholars are almost wholly concerned with policy domains and the interest group population at the macro level and with organizations at the micro level, not the individual people who are employed by, contribute to, or represent them.

I advocate that interest group research ought to borrow leadership theory's orientation and focus on key interest group personnel: organization managers, lobbyists, political consultants and strategists, and related professionals in the private sector whose mission is to influence events and decisions in the public sector. Models of interest group mobilization and influence have greatly improved over time, and the quality and availability of empirical data on organized interest entrepreneurship and lobbying behavior have become better and more abundant. Yet there remain many unresolved questions about how key interest group actors behave. These questions would benefit from reconsidering Truman's rejection of political leadership as a concept worthy of study.

The most promising avenue for scholars to understand interest group leadership is where situational leadership theory and neopluralism converge. The political world has changed dramatically since the peak of pluralism theory in the mid-twentieth century. Today, American politics faces unprecedented extreme polarization, information overload, and public policy complexity, as well as illiberal threats to democratic legitimacy and the rule of law (Foa and Mounck 2016). Scholars need to recognize these contextual changes and identify how individual people representing organized interests change with them. We may ask new questions like:

- How have organizational managers adapted to a seemingly dysfunctional and hopelessly gridlocked Congress? What political conditions cause them to adapt?
- Have lobbyists shifted their attention from Congress to the executive branch and the states? If so, why?
- Have policy strategists, lobbyists, and consultants adapted their strategies and tactics to influence the policy and campaign process?
- Are there certain types of organizational managers or lobbyists who are better than others at forging supportive coalitions in and out of government?

Like Allison's (1971) case study of the Cuban missile crisis and presidential leadership, interest group scholars ought to try to answer these and other questions by focusing on how key actors cognitively process information, and how doing so biases their efforts to represent social and economic interests.

To understand lobbyists and other actors as interest group leaders, scholars must recognize them as imperfect agents of the interest groups they represent. This position is not without precedent, but it has been largely secondary in interest group scholarship. Kersh points out how political scientists view lobbyists as mere vehicles for the interests they represent: "Individual lobbyists, it should be noted, are an afterthought in most accounts of interest groups and policy making" (2000, 239). Aside from some notable exceptions, most recent theoretical and empirical research on interest groups tends to take research on individual people for granted, even though it is relatively obvious that lobbyists are imperfect agents of the organized interest principals they represent. Stephenson and Jackson (2010) reconsider the lawyer–client principal–agent literature to that of lobbyist–client, and Lowery and Marchetti (2012) take stock in how interest group scholars may apply principal–agent theory to lobbying activities.

Generally, interest group theories assume that any variation in agency costs associated with individual organization managers and lobbyists is not systematic. The oversight is understandable because professional service providers like doctors and lawyers—and perhaps lobbyists—are typically governed by strict contractual arrangements (Williamson 1981). More importantly, lobbyists and interest organization managers are bound by their need to maintain reputations in a competitive information supply context (Rosenthal 2001; Hall and Deardorff 2006). Some lobbyists will perform well or poorly, but there's no reason to expect that poor- or well-performing lobbyists are distributed unequally across interest organizations, economic industries, policy domains, specific issues, or any other analytic unit of interest. Lobbyists are interchangeable. Organization managers are merely cogs in the larger influence industry.

A few formal theories have applied the principal–agent model to questions of interest group mobilization, organization, and influence. Salisbury (1969) and Moe (1980) explicitly model interest group entrepreneurs as the key to mobilizing interests, and Ainsworth and Sened (1993) extend the lobbyist as an agent of both the group and their policy-maker targets. Ainsworth and Sened model lobbyists as the link between interest group members and policy makers. In the Ainsworth–Sened signaling game, lobbyists are entrepreneurs that simultaneously resolve the classic Olsonian collective action dilemma to recruit potential members and prospective clients (Olson 1965; Moe 1980; Hansen 1991; Ainsworth and Sened 1993), as well as convince reelection-oriented policy makers that providing particularized benefits outweigh the costs to the government (Bauer, Poole, and Dexter 1963; Hall and Deardorff 2006). Lobbyists need to both sell the idea that their lobbying services will yield a policy success and the idea that providing the policy good will generate more support at the ballot box. The logic of the Ainsworth–Sened model that lobbyists serve as a critical link between two audiences is pretty straightforward.

However, the model's assumptions assume a static, one-shot game that cannot account for significant changes in the interest group system that has occurred since. That is, the population of interest groups in Washington has both expanded and become significantly more diverse. The 1970s and 1980s witnessed the so-called interest group explosion, in which postmaterial interests grew prolifically (Berry 1999). The 1990s and 2000s saw the pendulum swing back to business-oriented interests. The number of business firms with direct (in-house) and indirect (for-hire) representation in Washington and the number of intraindustry trade associations has increased dramatically in the past twenty-five years (Smith 2000; Waterhouse

2013; Drutman 2015). Moreover, the mobilization of interests depends at least as much on government agendas as it does on the wants and needs of individual groups (Gray and Lowery 1996; Leech et al. 2005). The empirical observation that different kinds of interests mobilized at different rates at different points in time for different policies indicate that the recruitment of interest group members depends on the political context at least as much as the Olson, Moe, Hansen, and Ainsworth–Sened models suggest.

As a result, this new world of interest representation—where mobilization and maintenance are significantly easier—has also affected how interest groups strategically deploy political leaders to influence policy. These changes have created a political context for new kinds of interest group managers and lobbyists to exploit: those who can communicate with policy makers across multiple and unrelated policy domains (LaPira and Thomas 2017).

If interest group agents have generalized political process knowledge outside a given policy domain, then we should see jack-of-all-trade revolving door lobbyists Vin Weber and Sandi Stuart—compared to the industry- or issue-specific lobbyists Allison McKay and Sarah Alexander—act as leaders in the interest group system. No doubt there are many more professional, behavioral, and other leadership qualities about individual interest organization managers and lobbyists not highlighted here. But it is precisely the absence of these leadership qualities that offers a potential for advancing our understanding of how interest group politics works.

References

Adorno, Theodore, Else Frenkel-Brunswik, Daniel J. Levinson, and R. Nevitt Sanford. 1950. *The Authoritarian Personality.* New York: Norton.

Ainsworth, Scott, and Itai Sened. 1993. "The Role of Lobbyists: Entrepreneurs with Two Audiences." *American Journal of Political Science* 37:834–866.

Alexander, Raquel Meyer, Stephen W. Mazza, and Susan Scholz. 2009. "Measuring Rates of Return for Lobbying Expenditures: An Empirical Case Study of Tax Breaks for Multinational Corporations." *Journal of Law and Politics* 25 (4): 401–457. http://dx.doi.org/10.2139/ssrn.1375082.

Allison, Graham. 1971. *Essence of Decision: Explaining the Cuban Missile Crisis.* Boston: Little, Brown.

Allison, Graham, and Philip Zelikow. 1999. *Essence of Decision: Explaining the Cuban Missile Crisis.* 2nd ed. New York: Pearson.

Ansolabehere, Stephen, John M. de Figueiredo, and James M. Snyder Jr. 2003. "Why Is There So Little Money in US Politics?" *Journal of Economic Perspectives* 17:105–130.

Bartels, Larry. 2008. *Unequal Democracy.* Princeton, NJ: Princeton University Press.

Bauer, Raymond A., Ithiel de Sola Pool, and Lewis A. Dexter. 1963. *American Business and Public Policy: The Politics of Foreign Trade.* New York: Atherton Press.

Baumgartner, Frank R., Jeffrey M. Berry, Marie Hojnacki, David C. Kimball, and Beth L. Leech. 2009. *Lobbying and Policy Change: Who Wins, Who Loses, and Why.* Chicago: University of Chicago Press.

Baumgartner, Frank R., and Beth L. Leech. 1998. *Basic Interests: The Importance of Groups in Politics and in Political Science.* Princeton, NJ: Princeton University Press.

Berry, Jeffrey M. 1999. *The New Liberalism: The Rising Power of Citizen Groups.* Washington, DC: Brookings Institution Press.

Briffault, Richard. 2014. "The Anxiety of Influence: The Evolving Regulation of Lobbying." Columbia Law School Public Law and Legal Theory Working Paper 14-367.

Buchanan, James M., and Gordon Tullock. 1962. *The Calculus of Consent: Logical Foundations of Constitutional Democracy.* Ann Arbor: Ann Arbor Paperbacks, University of Michigan Press.

Burns, James MacGregor. 1978. *Leadership.* New York: Harper.

———. 2003. *Transforming Leadership: The Pursuit of Happiness.* New York: Atlantic Monthly Press.

Canes-Wrone, Brandice. 2006. *Who Leads Whom? Presidents, Policy, and the Public.* Chicago: University of Chicago Press.

Cohen, Michael D., James G. March, and Johan P. Olsen. 1972. "A Garbage Can Model of Organizational Choice." *Administrative Science Quarterly* 17:1-25.

Cyert, Richard M., and James G. March. 1963. *A Behavioral Theory of the Firm.* Englewood Cliffs, NJ: Prentice-Hall.

Dahan, Nicolas M., Michael Hadani, and Douglas A. Schuler. 2013. "The Governance Challenges of Corporate Political Activity." *Business and Society* 52:365-387.

Dahl, Robert A. 1961. *Who Governs?* New Haven, CT: Yale University Press.

Domhoff, G. William. 2006. *Who Rules America? Power and Politics, and Social Change.* New York: McGraw-Hill.

Drutman, Lee. 2015. *The Business of America Is Lobbying: How Corporations Became Politicized and Politics Became More Corporate.* New York: Oxford University Press.

Easton, David. 1965. *A Framework for Political Analysis.* Englewood Cliffs, NJ: Prentice-Hall.

Foa, Roberto Stefan, and Yascha Mounck. 2016. "The Danger of Deconsolidation: The Democratic Disconnect." *Journal of Democracy* 27 (3): 5-17.

Gilens, Martin, and Benjamin I. Page. 2014. "Testing Theories of American Politics: Elites, Interest Groups, and Average Citizens." *Perspectives on Politics* 12:564-581.

Gray, Virginia, and David Lowery. 1996. *The Population Ecology of Interest Representation.* Ann Arbor: University of Michigan Press.

Grossmann, Matt. 2012. *The Not-So-Special Interests: Interest Groups, Public Representation, and American Governance.* Stanford, CA: Stanford University Press.

Hall, Richard L., and Alan V. Deardorff. 2006. "Lobbying as Legislative Subsidy." *American Political Science Review* 100 (1): 69-84.

Hansen, John Mark. 1991. *Gaining Access: Congress and the Farm Lobby, 1991-1981.* Chicago: University of Chicago Press.

Hasen, Richard L. 2012. "Lobbying, Rent-Seeking, and the Constitution." *Stanford Law Review* 64:191-254.

Heinz, John P., Edward O. Laumann, Robert L. Nelson, and Robert H. Salisbury. 1993. *The Hollow Core: Private Interests in National Policy Making.* Cambridge, MA: Harvard University Press.

Hetherington, Marc J., and Jonathon D. Weiler. 2009. *Authoritarianism and Polarization in American Politics.* New York: Cambridge University Press.

Hojnacki, Marie, David C. Kimball, Frank R. Baumgartner, Jeffrey M. Berry, and Beth L. Leech. 2012. "Studying Organizational Advocacy and Influence: Reexamining Interest Group Research." *Annual Review of Political Science* 15:379-399.

Kahneman, Daniel, and Amos Tversky. 1984. "Choices, Values, and Frames." *American Psychologist* 39:341-350.

Kersh, Rogan. 2000. "State Autonomy and Civil Society: The Lobbyist Connection." *Critical Review* 14:237-258.

Krueger, Anne O. 1974. "The Political Economy of the Rent-Seeking Society." *American Economic Review* 64:291-303.

LaPira, Timothy M., and Herschel F. Thomas. 2017. *Revolving Door Lobbying: Public Service, Private Influence, and the Unequal Representation of Interests.* Lawrence: University Press of Kansas.

Leech, Beth L. Frank R. Baumgartner, Timothy M. LaPira, and Nicholas A. Semanko. 2005. "Drawing Lobbyists to Washington: Government Activity and the Demand for Advocacy." *Political Research Quarterly* 58 (1): 19-30.

Lessig, Lawrence. 2011. *Republic, Lost: How Money Corrupts Congress—And a Plan to Stop It.* New York: Twelve Books. http://republic.lessig.org/.

Lindblom, Charles. 1959. "The Science of 'Muddling Through.'" *Public Administration Review* 19:79-88.

Lowery, David. 2007. "Why Do Organized Interests Lobby? A Multi-Goal, Multi-Context Theory of Lobbying." *Polity* 39:29-54.

Lowery, David, and Virginia Gray. 2004. "A Neopluralist Perspective on Research on Organized Interests." *Political Research Quarterly* 57 (1): 163-175.

Lowery, David, and Kathleen Marchetti. 2012. "You Don't Know Jack: Principals, Agents, and Lobbying." *Interest Groups and Advocacy* 1 (2): 139-170.

Madison, James. 1787. *Federalist No. 10. The Same Subject Continued: The Union as a Safeguard against Domestic Faction and Insurrection.* https://www.congress.gov/resources/display/content/The+Federalist+Papers#TheFederalistPapers-10.

Mansbridge, Jane. 1992. "A Deliberative Theory of Interest Representation." In *The Politics of Interests*, edited by Mark P. Petracca, 32-57. Boulder, CO: Westview Press.

McFarland, Andrew S. 2004. *Neopluralism: The Evolution of Political Process Theory.* Lawrence: University Press of Kansas.

Meier, Kenneth J., and Laurence J. O'Toole Jr. 2007. "Modeling Public Management: Empirical Analysis of the Management-Performance Nexus." *Public Management Review* 9:503-527.

Miler, Kristina C. 2010. *Constituency Representation in Congress: The View from Capitol Hill.* New York: Cambridge University Press.

Mills, C. Wright. 1956. *The Power Elite.* New York: Oxford University Press.

Moe, Terry M. 1980. *The Organization of Interests: Incentives and the Internal Dynamics of Political Interest Groups.* Chicago: University of Chicago Press.

Olson, Mancur, Jr. 1965. *The Logic of Collective Action.* Cambridge, MA: Harvard University Press.

Richter, Brian Kelleher, Krislert Samphantharak, and Jeffrey F. Timmons. 2009. "Lobbying and Taxes." *American Journal of Political Science* 53 (4): 893–909.

Rosenthal, Alan. 2001. *The Third House: Lobbyists and Lobbying in the States.* 2nd ed. Washington, DC: Congressional Quarterly.

Salisbury, Robert H. 1969. "An Exchange Theory of Interest Groups." *Midwest Journal of Political Science* 13:1–32.

Schattschneider, E. E. (1960) 1975. *The Semisovereign People.* New York: Wadsworth.

Schlozman, Kay Lehman, and John T. Tierney. 1983. "More of the Same: Washington Pressure Group Activity in a Decade of Change." *Journal of Politics* 45:351–377.

———. 1986. *Organized Interests and American Democracy.* New York: Harper & Row.

Schlozman, Kay, Sidney Verba, and Henry Brady. 2012. *The Unheavenly Chorus.* Princeton, NJ: Princeton University Press.

Schweizer, Peter. 2013. *Extortion: How Politicians Extract Your Money, Buy Votes, and Line Their Own Pockets.* New York: Houghton Mifflin Harcourt.

Simon, Herbert A. 1947. *Administrative Behavior: A Study of Decision Making Processes in Administrative Organizations.* New York: Macmillan.

———. 1996. *The Sciences of the Artificial.* 3rd ed. Cambridge, MA: MIT Press.

Smith, Mark A. 2000. *American Business and Political Power: Public Opinion, Elections, and Democracy.* Chicago: University of Chicago Press.

Stephenson, Matthew C., and Howell E. Jackson. 2010. "Lobbyists as Imperfect Agents: Implications for Public Policy in a Pluralist System." *Harvard Law Review* 47:1–20.

Strolovitch, Dara. 2007. *Affirmative Advocacy.* Chicago: University of Chicago Press.

Teachout, Zephyr. 2014. *Corruption in America: From Benjamin Franklin's Snuff Box to Citizens United.* Cambridge, MA: Harvard University Press.

Truman, David B. (1951) 1971. *The Governmental Process: Political Interests and Public Opinion.* Berkeley, CA: Institute of Governmental Studies.

Tullock, Gordon. 1967. "The Welfare Costs of Tariffs, Monopolies, and Theft." *Western Economic Journal* 5:224–232.

Tversky, Amos, and Daniel Kahnemann. 1973. "Judgment Under Uncertainty: Heuristics and Biases." *Science* 185 (4157): 1124–1131.

Waterhouse, Brendon. 2013. *Lobbying America.* Princeton, NJ: Princeton University Press.

Williamson, Oliver E. 1981. "The Economics of Organization: The Transaction Cost Approach." *American Journal of Sociology* 87 (3): 548–577.

Zimbardo, Philip G. 1970. "The Human Choice: Individuation, Reason, and Order versus Deindividuation, Impulse, and Chaos." In *1969 Nebraska Symposium on Motivation,* edited by William J. Arnold and David Levine, 237–307. Lincoln: University of Nebraska Press.

———. 2007. *The Lucifer Effect: Understanding How Good People Turn Evil.* New York: Random House.

CHAPTER EIGHT

Leadership and the Bureaucracy

John W. Patty

As a term, the "federal bureaucracy" refers to a large group of agencies, commissions, and—yes—bureaus that have widely varying missions, procedures, clienteles, and histories. While the importance of the bureaucracy in modern democratic governance is widely acknowledged, the concept of leadership within these organs of governance is vague—perhaps more so than in relation to the other branches of government.[1] While leadership within hierarchical organizations has been a topic of attention for many decades now (Simon 1947; Blau 1955; Weber 1968; Miller 1992; for a more general overview, see Ahlquist and Levi 2011), focusing on bureaucratic leadership entails acknowledging two defining characteristics of bureaucracy. First, bureaucratic agencies are public. They exist to implement, on a day-to-day basis, duly enacted statutes, and they are publicly acknowledged and sustained for this purpose alone. Bureaucratic authority is necessarily delegated authority. Second, as endogenously created organs of government, they serve multiple principals (voters, legislators, executives, judges, firms, interest groups, etc.) with potentially widely varying interests. To the degree that leadership is equated with independent authority (i.e., the ability to lead and direct at will), these characteristics necessarily hem in any attempt to conjure a robust and romantic notion of the ideal bureaucratic leader. However, before proceeding to offer a more precise definition of bureaucratic leadership, it is useful to briefly consider each of these characteristics in turn.

Leader or Delegate? For the most part, bureaucratic policy making within a democracy is considered legitimate only insofar as the decisions it is composed of are guided, or at the very least constrained, by the wishes of either the people, or again at the very least, their elected representatives (Hyneman 1950).[2] Furthermore, in the original tradition of organizational theorists such as Weber (1968) and Taylor (1947), the ideal-type notion of a bureaucracy is that of a setting in which proce-

dures and norms essentially eliminate individual discretion and unilateral authority. In a nutshell, a well-tuned bureaucracy is one in which individual decisions are
relegated to functional steps; a bureaucracy that requires leadership is in some sense
imperfectly designed.[3]

While this conception of the role of the bureaucracy might be seen as minimizing at least the normative desirability of bureaucratic leadership, this constraint
is helpful. In particular, the presumption that legitimate bureaucratic leadership
involves serving the interests of external actors implies that we can set aside what
are referred to as Great Man theories of leadership (Kirkpatick and Locke 1991).
While the discussion in this chapter does from time to time refer to idiosyncratic
features of individual behaviors of bureaucratic leaders, the focus throughout is
largely on leadership behaviors and styles, as opposed to personal characteristics
of leaders per se. In other words, there are more and less effective forms of bureaucratic leadership, and the relative effectiveness of these leadership styles varies
across management situations. I focus in this chapter on the activities that foster
effective management of bureaucratic decision making and, to a lesser degree, the
individual characteristics that tend to be correlated with strong performance in
these activities.

Leading in Front of Multiple Audiences. Most bureaucratic agencies are expected to
be responsive to an array of actors, and these actors' interests are not always well
aligned. Arguably the canonical example of such varied interests confronting an
agency is consumers and producers. For example, the Federal Aviation Administration is responsible for the advancement, safety, and regulation of the airline industry in the United States; the Consumer Product Safety Commission is charged with
ensuring the safety of thousands of consumer products; and the Federal Reserve
Board is directed to maintain both low inflation and low unemployment on behalf
of the American public while also (directly) representing the interests of private
banks. This is just a small sample of a long list of federal agencies simultaneously
charged with making policy decisions and answering to multiple audiences possess-
ing potentially conflicting goals.

Attempting to be responsive to a heterogeneous group of actors typically produces a number of pathologies that simultaneously stymie and heighten the value
of effective leadership. For example, many agencies have too much to do in the
sense that they are asked to pursue multiple goals (Wilson 2000; Biber 2009). In
addition, as public bureaucracies, agencies are expected to be at least somewhat
transparent and inclusive with respect to their decision making. For example, bureaucratic agencies are in many cases expected and often required to provide rationales for their decisions (Patty and Penn 2014b), a job that is made much harder
when the degree to which a rationale justifies the decision will be evaluated by

multiple actors with divergent interests (West 2004). Accordingly, a key role of a bureaucratic leader is to conserve the agency's autonomy and discretion in the face of competing interests among its multiple audiences (Terry 2003).

A Process Definition of Bureaucratic Leadership. The two distinctive characteristics of government agencies discussed above each highlight the heightened role of process in bureaucratic leadership, as opposed to leadership in other institutional environments. In the end, even the most potent bureaucratic leader is ultimately exercising delegated power on behalf of the public and must make decisions that are in accord with the public's desires.

Along these lines, a useful definition describes bureaucratic leadership as an active process that "entails the exercise of power, authority, and strategic discretion in pursuit of the public interest" (Terry 2003, 4). This description is mostly constructive, combining broadly described tools ("power, authority, and strategic discretion") with a unifying, if arguably chimerical, purpose ("pursuit of the public interest").[4] Moving closer to the subject at hand, Terry argues that the "primary function" of bureaucratic leadership should be the protection and maintenance of "administrative institutions in a manner that promotes or is consistent with constitutional processes, values, and beliefs" (24). Thus, in Terry's conception, bureaucratic leadership centers on conservation. The implications of adopting this conception are deceptively minimal, as protecting administrative institutions can require proactive action. In the end, the political actors residing just outside and above the organs of administration are generally directly interested in the decisions, and by implication in the processes of these institutions. Accordingly, protecting the autonomy and legitimacy of these institutions necessarily requires nimble direction of their decisions. Such direction is, in the end, the corpus of bureaucratic leadership.

Perceptions of Bureaucratic Leadership. While Terry (2003) offers an appealingly clear definition of bureaucratic leadership, it arguably does not comport well with popular perceptions of bureaucrats and/or bureaucracy. Returning to a point I touched on earlier, and speaking more directly to the American case, it is fair to describe the conventional portrait of bureaucratic legitimacy as being grounded on, and constrained by, the separation of powers doctrine of the US Constitution (Rosenbloom 1983, 2000; Strauss 1984, 1996; Patty and Penn 2014b). Within this portrait, the bureaucracy exercises delegated powers; in the best of situations, it does so faithfully guided by clear directions emanating from the elected branches. Accordingly, legitimate bureaucratic leadership is properly exercised by nonbureaucrats.

Perhaps because of the appeal of this portrait, there is remarkably little attention paid to the perception of bureaucratic leaders. Instead, popular opinion about bureaucratic leadership is often measured through the public's evaluation of "the bureaucracy." That is, as opposed to opinion polling that measures the public's evaluation of a given leader, such as President Barack Obama, or concerning the public's evaluation of the office or institution led by the leader (i.e., the executive branch), there is little attention paid to separating the evaluations of the bureaucracy from those of the men and women who lead it.

The closest thing to an exception to this is a body of work that examines public opinion about features of government that are directly tied to the personnel of the bureaucracy, such as civil service rules like collective bargaining provisions and tenure protections (Bouckaert, van de Walle, and Kampen 2005).[5] In my mind, this exception actually highlights the degree to which, at least among scholars, the notion of leadership within the bureaucracy is not viewed as an important measure of the quality of government.[6] That exception noted, my discussion of the empirical study of bureaucratic leadership leans heavily on the extant scholarly literature on leadership qua management of bureaucratic organizations.

Before considering this literature, I first consider the public perception of bureaucratic leadership.

How Is Bureaucratic Leadership Perceived?

Before considering the determinants of effective leadership in public bureaucracies, and with the caveats I mentioned about the measurement of bureaucratic leadership, it is useful to consider the perceived quality of bureaucratic policy making writ large. Over the past forty years, public evaluations of bureaucrats and bureaucracy have declined in many Western nations.[7] This dynamic has been accompanied by calls for reform, most notably embodied in the new public management.[8] The debates about the desirability, frequency, and performance of new public management reforms (Osborne 2006) illustrate the challenge of positing that the notion of effective leadership is the same in private bureaucracies as in public ones.

Stepping back from the distinction between different types of bureaucratic organizations, it should be noted that evaluating leadership in any organization requires at least some notion of how to measure or evaluate that organization's performance. A useful schematic for measuring organizational performance is provided in Figure 8.1. The basic idea of the scheme is to distinguish between three intuitive phases of bureaucratic policy making: inputs, outputs, and outcomes.[9] Inputs are things used by the agency,[10] outputs are things produced by the agency, and outcomes are things affected by the agency.[11]

The distinction between inputs, outputs, and outcomes illustrates a key difficulty facing the managers of public bureaucracies. In particular, each of the multiple audiences interested in the performance of a given agency might have preferences about any subset of these aspects of the agency's actions and processes. Even focusing only on the variety of ways one might measure the outcomes within the agen-

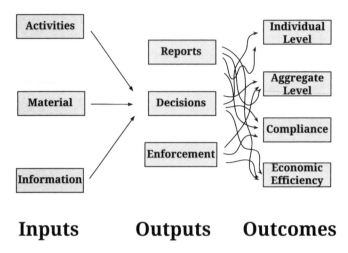

Figure 8.1. Evaluating Bureaucratic Performance: Inputs, Outputs, and Outcomes.

cy's policy domain, and even after setting aside concerns about causality, standard arguments from social choice theory indicate the inextricable possibility that it may be impossible to construct a well-ordered, unidimensional, and nonpathological measure of agency performance.[12]

Space precludes a more in-depth treatment of this issue, but I note it because I believe that the point is too often overlooked in studies of public bureaucracy. A general glossing over of the difficulty in constructing even a single performance measure (much less aggregating a variety of such measures constructed by various audiences of the agency) is of course understandable, given the nature of most policies that are directed by bureaucratic agencies, but it is important to at least recall this difficulty when considering the public perception of bureaucratic leadership: bureaucratic leaders may be faced with a truly (i.e., logically) impossible challenge.[13] Once one moves beyond considering "merely" outcomes, this challenge is amplified by the fact that, aside from agencies whose missions revolve around "simple" collection and disbursement tasks (e.g., the Internal Revenue Service and the Social Security Administration), most bureaucratic agencies' tasks are characterized by having inputs and/or outputs that are difficult to observe (Wilson 2000). The ongoing debate about value-added modeling in assessing the performance of teachers provides a good example of three common difficulties in this realm. I discuss them in a little detail because they each indicate some of the characteristic challenges for a bureaucratic leader.

Measuring Outputs versus Outcomes

It is important to distinguish between outputs—things that are actually produced by the agency (e.g., regulations, diplomas, adjudications, permits, test scores)—and outcomes, which are the things most citizens actually care about. Of course, these frequently overlap, but in many cases, the outcomes that are not outputs are typically difficult to measure.[14] While test performance is fairly easy to measure, it does not represent the end of interest; few citizens are interested in producing good test takers. Rather, they want schools to produce well-educated citizens, as indicated by the recurring worry that evaluation through standardized tests simply leads to teachers teaching to the test. It is important to note that education is in one sense a best case in terms of measuring bureaucratic outputs; the students are right there, after all.[15] Measurement is difficult in this case for two reasons: any feasible test is an imperfect measure of knowledge, and, more importantly, the value of instilled knowledge is temporally far-reaching. That is, ideally, we want to measure the impact of (say) kindergarten education on economic and social outcomes twenty years hence. This reality indicates a second problem with measuring performance: while we have broad agreement that education, broadly construed, produces social benefits, we understand too little about how education does this.

How Do Inputs Translate into Outcomes?

The production technology is itself poorly understood. It is fair to say that there is nothing approaching consensus on the best way to educate children. While this is common to some other policy areas, it is far from universally true. For example, it is known that burning fossil fuels produces carbon dioxide, that inhaling asbestos fibers causes mesothelioma, and that lead exposure can have seriously deleterious neurodevelopmental effects. In each of these cases, it is clear how one can limit carbon dioxide emissions, reduce mesothelioma, or promote healthy neurodevelopment. While the costs of each of these interventions and social value of their corresponding impacts are contestable, there is at least broad agreement about the conclusion that these interventions would work. There are frustratingly few analogies to this in social policies—clear and reliable relationships between simple interventions and measurable outcomes are few and far between—and education is arguably one of the most vivid examples of this. Indeed, this lack of understanding about which educational techniques work (not to mention how they work) is an argument in favor of well-designed performance evaluation. But the reality is that other issues more closely tied to the incentives of teachers (e.g., moral hazard), voters (e.g., efficiency), and legislators (e.g., appearing responsive to voters' interests) also suggest that evaluation might be beneficial. The difficulty is that these incentives are not uniform; they arise to different degrees in different places and at different times. This brings me to the next challenge for public bureaucrats.

Why Evaluate?

The development and use of value-added modeling itself is not independent of perceptions about performance. That is, tools such as value-added modeling are costly to use and controversial, and accordingly they are more likely to be adopted by school systems where performance is perceived to be a problem. As has been noted by many, particularly after the passage of the No Child Left Behind Act in 2001 (Ryan 2004), evaluation can create perverse incentives precisely when evaluation is the basis of putatively providing incentives for improvement. The importance of this for bureaucratic leadership is amplified by the fact that bureaucratic leaders are necessarily simultaneously subordinates. Particularly when organizational performance is perceived to be lackluster by a bureaucratic leader's superiors (legislators, voters, courts, etc.), evaluation techniques and concomitant incentive systems—often applied to both the bureaucratic leader and his or her subordinates—are imposed on the leader. When imposed, such systems generally constrain the set of leadership strategies available to the leader. In addition, to the degree that the evaluation systems alter the incentives of the leader's subordinates, these systems can also change the relative benefits and costs of the remaining leadership approaches. In other words, even optimally designed evaluation may create additional management problems for the leader.[16]

Summary: Perceptions, Evaluations, and Leadership

A distinctive characteristic of a public bureaucracy is that its potential audience is always large. Specifically, even citizens who aren't clients of an agency may have an interest in how the agency operates, even if only in terms of minimizing its costs. Notions such as due process impinge more strongly on public bureaucracies than private ones, and they imply concomitantly greater fiduciary responsibility for their leaders. Accordingly, the issues that I raised above regarding measurement and evaluation cannot be merely set aside by bureaucratic leaders. They are inherent to management and accordingly to leadership in bureaucracies. That noted, I now turn to theories of leadership per se.

Theories of Leadership

While leadership is frequently recognized as an important topic in both practical and scholarly terms, there is remarkably little known about what constitutes good leadership, even in theory. For example, in a summary of the literature on public sector leadership penned a decade ago, Montgomery van Wart (2003, 225) concluded that "there is a striking need for a comprehensive leadership model that integrates transactional and transformational elements." Similarly, while there is sustained interest in how leaders ought to behave (Adams and Balfour 2009; Denhardt and Denhardt 2011), much of this debate is guided by normative concerns about the subordinates and/or clients of the administrators. These normative concerns represent the clearest division between the consideration of leadership in private bureaucracies (e.g., corporate and business leadership) and public ones (e.g., bureaucratic and political leadership).

Trait Theories of Leadership

Much of the research on organizational leadership has fallen into a camp broadly describable as being based on the traits of individual leaders, and to a lesser degree based on the match between the leader's traits and the characteristics of the job or jobs being performed by the group he or she leads.[17] For example, early research carried out at Ohio State University identified two main dimensions of leadership, consideration and initiating structure (Fleishman 1953; Fleishman and Peters 1962). Consideration refers to traits that are associated with interpersonal relationships (e.g., is the leader perceived as approachable and/or open to suggestions), whereas initiating structure refers to behaviors associated with organization, such as setting clear standards, objectively evaluating performance, and clarifying individuals' responsibilities.

Contingency Theories of Leadership

Following on the trait theories of leadership, a class of theories that I refer to here as contingency theories emerged. These theories are linked by their consideration of both the leader's specific characteristics and the organization he or she leads. For example, Fiedler (1967) explicitly considered the match between leader traits and organizational purposes and cultures. Fielder's contingency theory places leaders on a unidimensional scale, ranging from strongly valuing interpersonal relationships to strongly valuing task completion/performance. It also situates leadership situations ("contingencies") within a three-dimensional space representing (1) the quality of the leader's interpersonal relationship with his or her subordinates, (2) the degree of formal authority possessed by the leader, and (3) the clarity and complexity of the jobs to be performed by the organization (Fiedler 1964). In the same vein, Blake and Mouton (1984) extended the Ohio State leadership research through the development of a managerial grid approach to leadership, which distinguishes between organizations on the basis of how the organization values interpersonal relations and comity relative to production and outcomes.

Leadership Styles

As some became disillusioned with the ability of trait theories to adequately explain leadership effectiveness, attention turned to more classically behavioral measures of leadership. Prominent among such approaches is the path-goal theory of leadership (House 1971, 1996; see also House and Mitchell 1974; Filley, House, and Kerr 1976). Path-goal theory introduced the idea of leadership styles into the measurement of effective leadership, conditioned on the characteristics of both the organization and the job it carries out. The four leadership styles laid out in the path-goal theory are essentially distinguished on two dimensions: first, the degree to which the leader gives clear directions to his or her subordinates, and second, the degree to which the leader emphasizes performance and subordinates' individual responsibilities for achievement. This theory has been extended in several directions, including explicitly considering the proper degree to which subordinates are and should be involved in different decisions (Vroom and Yetton 1973; Vroom and Jago 1974, 1978), and the role of the maturity (education, experience, capability) of the subordinates (Hersey and Blanchard 1969; Blanchard, Zigarmi, and Nelson 1993; Graeff 1997).

This research also led to what is known as transformational leadership theory, which distinguishes between leadership styles that focus on providing rewards in line with subordinates' existing desires and goals (transactional leadership) and styles that instead motivate subordinates to focus on new goals, in effect seeing a bigger picture (transformational leadership) (Burns 1978, 2003; Bass 1985; Bass and Riggio 2012). This literature focuses on the ability of leaders to be focal in altering the motivations of the subordinates. This is an interesting topic to tackle from a strategic standpoint, but unfortunately space and time constraints require me to omit further discussion of this literature. Instead, I turn to a complementary notion: in addition to thinking about leaders, theorists and empiricists alike have thought a lot about the tasks that leaders must carry out.

Typologies of Leadership Situations

As the contingency and situational theories of leadership matured, attention became more focused on the different types of situations that leaders encounter.[18] Mintzberg (1973) distinguished between three types of roles that leaders must play from time to time: interpersonal, informational, and decisional. These categories actually map neatly into the ternary structure of bureaucratic leadership I present below.

Mintzberg's (1973) conception of leadership focused on the roles played by the leader. Stepping up to a more macro understanding of leadership, and in line with the discussion of evaluation above, Wilson (2000) follows Mintzberg and divides agencies into four types of organizations: production, procedural, craft, and cop- ing.[19] Using the terminology of this chapter, Wilson's typology is based on the ob- servability of the inputs and outputs. Production agencies are those in which inputs and outputs are each observable. Procedural agencies are those in which only inputs are observable, while craft agencies are those in which only outputs are observable. Finally, neither the inputs nor the outputs of coping agencies are observable.

This distinction between agencies is important to keep in mind when consider- ing how measurement and evaluation affect the incentives of managers and lead- ers in various bureaucratic settings. Leadership is necessarily measured differently across these agency types: the effectiveness of leadership is most easily measured in production agencies and most difficult to gauge in coping agencies. While proce- dural and craft agencies fall somewhere in between these two extremes, they present their own unique challenges (Bueno de Mesquita and Stephenson 2007).

Policy Making: Information, Decisions, and Management

While real-world policy making comes in a dizzying variety of forms when viewed in detail, all policy decisions can be described as fitting within a three-step, sequen- tial process: first, information is obtained, after which a decision is made, leading finally to the management of how the decision is implemented. Of course, rarely is life so tidy that the three steps are clearly distinguishable, and indeed it is com- mon for one or both of the first two to be repeated multiple times before, as well as during, the prosecution of the third. Furthermore, effective leadership involves recognizing that the realities of management might alter any or all relevant actors' incentives when making decisions, and similarly that the realities of both manage- ment and making decisions are relevant in determining the most effective strategies for collecting information.[20] That said, it is useful to describe the steps in turn as a foundation for subsequently providing a ternary structure of leadership.

Information

Policy-relevant information comes in many forms, but it can be usefully divided into two (nonexclusive) categories, depending on the types of decisions for which it is valuable: information about what to do, and information about how to do it. The two forms are complementary, and accordingly much policy-relevant information potentially carries both types of implications. For example, detailed data regarding the solvency of large financial institutions can provide information not only about which financial institutions might require government intervention but also how important each such intervention is.

To exemplify the distinction and links between these two types of information, consider the current regulation of air pollution by the Environmental Protection Agency (EPA). From 1980 until 2007, the EPA interpreted its regulatory authority as extending to only those specific pollutants that the EPA had designated as what is known as criteria air pollutants.[21] After the Supreme Court ruled in *Massachusetts v. EPA* (2007) that the EPA was required by the Clean Air Act to include greenhouse gases as pollutants, the EPA was faced with two types of decisions. The EPA had to decide which pollutants had to be added (i.e., which tasks to undertake) as well as how to regulate each included pollutant (i.e., how to undertake each task).

Picking Which Tasks to Undertake. The ubiquity of transaction costs implies that information about what to do is universally important. It is difficult to imagine a bureaucratic leadership position that did not entail at least some responsibility for overseeing subordinates and/or other third parties (e.g., even a unitary regulator is concerned with the actions and information held by other actors). Regardless of whether the information is about the behavior of strategic actors (e.g., subordinates or regulated firms) or exogenous states of affairs (e.g., disease prevalence or flood levels), it is useful to link information about what to do with oversight.

Along these lines, the seminal distinction drawn by McCubbins and Schwartz (1984) between "fire alarm" and "police patrol" oversight describes two archetypical leadership styles. Fire alarm oversight is a passive information collection strategy on the part of the leader: he or she waits until some third party alerts the leader that circumstances might warrant a change in current policy. Taken to the extreme, the approach minimizes information collection costs at the risk of incurring policy costs from policy being too infrequently recalibrated—if it is recalibrated at all. Police patrol oversight, on the other hand, involves active and continuous monitoring of the relevant facts by the leader. In the extreme, such information collection is expensive in terms of direct costs, but it can maximize the match between decisions and the relevant facts.[22]

Choosing How to Perform the Undertaken Tasks. A foundational aspect of (legitimate) bureaucratic governance is that it is an exercise of delegated authority in pursuit of goals dictated with varying degrees of precision by elected representatives of the citizens.[23] The clean air example mentioned above provides a useful reference point. In 2007, the Supreme Court effectively directed the EPA to pursue regulation of greenhouse gases. After this (and setting the issue of compliance to the side), the EPA still retained significant discretion. In addition to having to decide which pollutants to regulate, the EPA also recognized that it faced an enforcement (or management) problem. Specifically, the Clean Air Act establishes a hard cap on allowable emissions: any source that exceeds these limits[24] would be required to obtain a permit from the EPA. For the greenhouse gas pollutants, using these caps would require millions of new permits to be issued. Accordingly, in June 2010, the EPA issued a finalized tailoring rule that raised these caps for greenhouse gases (*Federal Register* 2010). The EPA's justification for this action was in part that "implementing these requirements . . . would have brought so many sources into those programs so as to overwhelm the capabilities of . . . permitting authorities to issue permits, and as a result, would have impeded the ability of sources to construct, modify or operate their facilities" (*Federal Register* 2012, 41051). This fact led the EPA to cite the *Chevron* decision[25] as justification for establishing limits other than those prescribed by Congress in the Clean Air Act.

Even though the EPA was acting at the behest of the Supreme Court, its actions were clearly taking the lead on clean air policy. Much information it gathered during the process of finalizing the rule dealt with the practical challenges of enforcement. Especially given the fact that the EPA does not directly issue permits in most cases—most permitting is handled by state and local authorities—the policy effects of any decision the EPA ultimately made would be mediated by the management task after the promulgation of the new rule. I consider the issue of management within the context of bureaucratic policy making below, but I first turn to the second stage of bureaucratic leadership.

Decisions

From a theoretical perspective, it is almost nonsensical to think long about a bureaucrat who isn't from time to time required to make some policy-relevant decision. However, speaking empirically, the act of making decisions is perhaps the least visible of the three components of bureaucratic policy making. At least part of the information step, described above, is quite visible in the form of "notice and comment" rule making processes and agencies' quasi-judicial adjudicatory hearings. Many instances of the management step are also visible in the form of published agency procedures, civil service requirements, licensing/permitting processes, and audits by organs such as the Government Accountability Office and the Office of Management and Budget.

Bureaucratic decisions, on the other hand, are typically made behind closed doors. While due process and the rule of law lead to bureaucrats' decisions ultimately being made public in most cases, the details of how a decision was made are generally only selectively available to the public. This opacity partly follows from simple transaction costs arguments: it is rare that the point in time at which an important policy decision is unambiguous, displaying how the sausage is made requires effort, and it is uncommon for the deciders to have an incentive to invest any time in providing such transparency. Instead, policy decisions often evolve over time, with alternatives being thrown into and excluded from the mix until one remains for final ratification as "the decision." In other words, compared to legislatures voting on final passage or executives signing legislation into law, it is rare for there to be a singular observable moment that can clearly be described as the bureaucracy choosing policy.

Accordingly, the most active aspect of bureaucratic leadership is the maintenance and shepherding of the decision process. Bureaucratic decisions are, almost by definition, dependent on the menu of options available when the decisions are made. Setting aside the useful fiction of a unitary actor considering the array of all possible choices and choosing from among them, the reality is that the link between bureaucratic decision making and bureaucratic leadership is tautological until one recognizes that most, if not all, bureaucratic decisions are the product of many bureaucrats' individual inputs. Bureaucratic leadership is the stitch that ties all of these potentially discordant individual choices into a cohesive policy decision.

Management

Perhaps closest to the earliest conceptions of what bureaucrats do, management deals with the myriad of activities that actually implement the decisions made by the leader on the basis of the information he or she obtained. In most cases, bureaucratic leaders actually do very little of the management themselves. For example, the commissioner of the Social Security Administration does not actually write checks or put them in envelopes, just as it is highly unusual for the secretary of state to personally vet visa applications. Nonetheless, each of these leaders is concerned with how these tasks are carried out, in terms of both clientele/service delivery and policy motivations. In addition to maintaining the image of their organizations, these day-to-day activities represent the principal means by which the policy decisions are actually put into practical effect. To make the point clear, changing the eligibility requirements for Social Security benefits has real-world impact only to the degree that these changes are actually reflected in the issuance and delivery of these benefits. Similarly, changes of border security policy, both small and large, will take effect only to the degree that they are reflected in how visas are issued.

Instead, bureaucratic leaders exert most of their day-to-day influence on implementation through the management of the internal workings of the organization. The seminal modern representation of management is due to Gulick (1937), who distinguished between two goals of management: the division of work and the coordination of work.[26] In terms of the types of decisions that bureaucratic leaders have to make on a day-to-day basis, this binary distinction can be thought of in organizational terms. Viewing a bureaucratic leader as guiding two or more teams of subordinates, where the members of each team are bound by (say) function, managing the division of work generally deals with the question of "who is on which team?" and "what teams are responsible for each task?" On the other hand, coordination of work involves ensuring a match between the actions of the various teams. Of course, the importance of managing coordination varies across tasks and organizations, but any sequential production process necessarily requires coordination. After all, it's impossible to (at least legitimately) enforce clean air regulations before those regulations are written and promulgated.

A Ternary Division of Bureaucratic Leadership

I now sketch out a ternary structure of bureaucratic leadership. The three parts of the structure correspond to the three components of policy making described above.

Getting Advice

Any practically relevant notion of leadership must begin with the question of how, and from whom, the leader gathers information and advice. There are two dimensions of gathering advice that determine its value. The first of these rests on flexibility: if the leader is able (in both formal and practical terms) to choose his or her own advisers, then standard signaling logic (Connelly et al. 2011; Gailmard and Patty 2013a) suggests that credibility can be endogenously created by the leader, and accordingly information can be conveyed to the leader. In contrast, the second dimension of tactics for getting advice is based on inflexibility: if the leader can commit himself or herself to using truthful advice in a way that is advantageous to the adviser, then this ability can stand in place of flexibility in the leader's ability to choose his or her own advisers.

The first dimension is theoretically dominant over the second, but the stochastic nature of empirical constraints on the set of possible advisers implies that the second dimension is often more relevant, particularly as it is more clearly a product of a priori institutional design. That said, I discuss each of these in turn.

The Importance of Selecting One's Own Advisers. Formal theories of bureaucratic decision making have explored various aspects of the informational problems facing bureaucratic leaders, often in the form of signaling models, which focus attention on the details of policy-making arrangements that render an adviser's policy recommendations credible. Of central importance in all of these theories is the role of preference (or goal) congruence between the leader and his or her adviser in establishing the credibility of communication between them (Gailmard and Patty 2013a). From a practical standpoint, this conclusion immediately suggests an important benefit of allowing leaders to choose their own advisers (Bendor and Meirowitz 2004; Gailmard and Patty 2012).

A related implication of this conclusion—though one that has not to my knowledge received much attention—is that, given transactions costs for both principals and agents, effective leadership is bolstered by granting leaders the freedom to *not* solicit advice. That is, when the preferences of the leader are sufficiently divergent from those of a given subordinate, there may be little reason to require the two actors to invest any time in attempting to communicate with each other. Relatedly, there is potential value to allowing the leader to pick the audience of his or her advisers. Especially when multiple actors possess unilateral authority, a leader's ability to extract reliable advice from an adviser may depend on which other decision makers observe the adviser's recommendation to the leader (Groseclose and McCarty 2001; Stasavage 2007; Gailmard 2009b).

However, this kind of control by audience is nuanced (Patty 2015; Gailmard and Patty 2017). In some cases, credibility of an adviser's message—i.e., the adviser's incentive to be truthful in his or her recommendation to the leader—is amplified by allowing other decision makers, or other leaders, to observe the adviser's recommendation. For example, when the leader has more liberal-leaning preferences than the adviser, the leader can induce truthfulness by this adviser by providing a more conservative-leaning decision maker access to the adviser's report. At the same time, this inducement relies on the ability of the leader to preclude private communications (sidebars) between the adviser and the other decision maker, a point that further highlights the adage that (control of) information is power.

Finally, these theories indicate that allowing too many individuals to observe an adviser's recommendation can undermine the adviser's credibility (Galeotti, Ghiglino, and Squintani 2009; Patty and Penn 2014a; Dewan et al. 2014; Dewan and Squintani 2015). In particular, allowing too many other decision makers who share the leader's ideological goals relative to those of the adviser can provide too much temptation to the adviser to slant or bias his or her recommendation. Furthermore, this same effect can flow from the leader holding too much power. In a practical sense, and leveraging a model common to several new theories of organization and information aggregation, Patty's (2015) model suggests that when pursuing policy advice, leaders have an incentive to retain a moderate amount of power and/ or place the adviser among an audience of decision makers whose ideological preferences lie on both sides of those of the adviser. These approaches suggest a more general role of institutions in aiding an adviser in obtaining information from his or her subordinates, a matter to which I now turn.

Making Advice Credible through Institutions. The value of allowing leaders to handpick their own advisers is particularly compelling when the advice that the adviser can offer is composed of what is referred to as cheap talk (Crawford and Sobel 1982). For example, when the adviser's advice is unverifiable,[27] the foundation of the advice's credibility is the similarity between the goals of the leader and adviser. Of course, advice can be made more credible by mechanisms other than simple goal similarity. For example, the adviser may have looming concerns about his or her reputation either with the leader (i.e., the two expect to interact regularly in the future) or with external audiences (e.g., the adviser's advice is observable by other actors). Similarly, the ability of the leader to condition future rewards (e.g., promotion or increased authority, as in Gailmard and Patty 2007) on the adviser acquiring and providing valuable information can generate appropriate incentives for the acquisition and reliable conveyance of information to the leader.[28]

Each of these mechanisms for establishing credibility between an adviser and leader with conflicting goals is practically relevant. Specifically, both are partially determined by manipulable features of institutions: repeated interactions emerge naturally from civil service protections such as tenure in office combined with clear policy jurisdictions, and the availability of external audiences obviously depends on the transparency of the internal workings of the leader's decision-making process.

Some of the most high profile of these levers (e.g., civil service statutes, open meeting requirements, sunshine laws) are typically controlled by political principals in the legislative and executive branches (though, of course, the details of how they are interpreted and enforced often depends on the judiciary as well). But it would be too simple to say that such institutional details are beyond the control of bureaucratic leaders. In particular, federal agencies generally promulgate and curate their own internal procedures, and agencies and bureaus always retain some positive amount of discretion with respect to these procedures, usually jointly composed of deliberately delegated (see, e.g., the Administrative Procedure Act[29]) and residual/ traditional forms of discretion.

Much of the literature on information transmission in hierarchical settings has focused on dyadic relationships between a leader and an adviser. Once one moves to larger groups, the structure, or sequencing, of decisions quickly emerges as an important element of procuring credible advice from one's subordinates. For example, Patty and Penn (2014a) consider situations in which two subordinates make decisions sequentially, on the basis of their own private information and aware that their decisions will be observed by the leader (and possibly another subordinate). Patty and Penn's model illustrates that the sequencing of the subordinates' decisions—and their observability to each other—can have important effects on the subordinates' incentives to reveal their private information to the leader. That is, holding the policy goals and biases of the subordinates fixed, changing the hierarchy in the sense of (say) assigning Subordinate A a position in which his or her decision is observable by Subordinate B might provide each subordinate with an incentive to reveal his or her private information, but this incentive would be destroyed if Subordinate B was assigned the responsibility of making his or her decision before Subordinate A.

Making Decisions

As discussed earlier in this chapter, a foundational normative question about bureaucratic leadership is the amount of discretion bureaucratic leaders should have when making important policy decisions. Of course, "importance" is not a binary distinction: various decisions can typically be arrayed on a continuum of increasing importance.[30] Regardless, it is clear that some decisions must be left to bureaucratic leaders, and I set aside the question of what decisions are properly left to the bureaucratic leader and focus here on the structure of making decisions where the leader has presumptive discretionary authority.[31]

Prioritization: Choosing Which Jobs to Tackle. The information that is presented to leaders often has some implications for which the organization's optimal allocation of effort between the various tasks is responsible. A simpler way of thinking of this problem is choosing which job to do first. This is a deceptively easy problem, and one that has attracted little attention in the political science literature.

At least within political science, most theories of bureaucratic decision making suppose that the jurisdiction of the agency and the task with which it is charged are clear and fixed once the agency is allowed to make policy.[32] Of course, in reality, modern bureaucracies are often implicitly charged with prioritizing a variety of de jure responsibilities. Furthermore, because tasks differ with respect to the time, resources, risks, and rewards they offer, then even if one is willing to accept that an agency can be described as a unilateral actor describable by a single payoff function (Shepsle 1992), the optimal prioritization of a set of tasks can be far from simple to compute, even in theory (Ullman 1975).

Even though we currently do not have a complete understanding of best practices for leaders charged with managing prioritization/scheduling problems, we do know that prioritization matters and, more interestingly, that the power to prioritize can have broad impacts on performance through its effect on the strategic incentives of subordinates within the organization.[33] Accordingly, it follows that effective bureaucratic leadership involves a perhaps implicit understanding of how to prioritize varying tasks, often in a real-time setting.

Transparency: Knowing What to Tell Your Subordinates. It is nearly a truism that effective leadership involves making good decisions. More interesting is the question of when, whether, and how much a leader should make transparent to his or her subordinates what decisions the leader will ultimately make.[34] This point is related to the theory presented in Gailmard and Patty (2017), which demonstrates that the transparency of the leader's information—and hence his or her predisposition with respect to his or her ultimate policy choice—can have significant implications for the incentives of the leader's subordinates. In particular, Gailmard and Patty show that greater transparency about the leader's information generally reduces the costs that a subordinate must incur to manipulate the leader's ultimate decision. Accordingly, subordinates whose goals diverge from those of the leader are more likely to find it profitable to choose policy inaccurately in an attempt to alter the leader's ultimate decisions. In this respect, making upper-level information more transparent within an organization can ironically lead to less informed decision making at the lower levels.[35]

Of course, making higher-level information transparent is not necessarily a bad idea. In particular, whenever the goals of the leader and a subordinate are similar enough, making the goals of, and information held by, the leader transparent to the subordinates is performance enhancing. In addition, as discussed above, an ex ante commitment to making subordinates' advice and/or decisions transparent to policy makers other than the leader can also promote efficient decision making by the subordinate in question.

This juxtaposition highlights the practical and strategic importance of leaders knowing, and being responsive to, goal divergence within their organization. Simply put, the question "who should know what, and when?" has no easy answer. Furthermore, and most intriguingly from the standpoint of organizations with many agents, is the fact that the optimal transparency arrangement between any subordinate and the leader depends not only on the congruence of their goals but also the relationship between their own goals and the other subordinates whose decisions will be observed by either or both of them.

Giving Directions

Given the information and choices of the leader, the final stage of leadership involves giving effect to the choices. In line with Gulick's (1937) distinction between division and coordination of tasks, the various acts that compose "giving directions" can be usefully divided into two categories: assignment of individuals to tasks and coordination of those individuals' actions. I examine these in turn.

Assignment. Theory suggests two principal determinants of optimal assignment of individuals from a leader's perspective. The first of these focuses on the abilities or expertise of the various individuals. The second determinant is a function of the alignment of preferences and goals between the leader and each individual on each task. If the set of available agents is unconstrained, then the optimal assignment problem is unsurprisingly trivial: the leader should assign to each task a perfectly expert agent who shares the leader's goals. The management problem becomes complicated once the leader faces constraints on the set of agents from whom he or she must choose. There are two types of constraints, both of which generally bind in various ways in the real world. The first of these types of constraint is exogenous and generally boils down to the fact that the set of agents the leader may choose between is fixed and finite at the time the leader must make assignments.[36] Bendor and Meirowitz (2004) present an admirably comprehensive consideration of the simplest case of this problem in which the leader must choose exactly one agent to make decisions on his or her behalf.[37] They show that in a broad (but not exhaustive) array of cases, the leader's optimal choice is determined entirely by the similarity between the goals of the leader and the potential subordinates: the leader should assign the task to the agent whose preferences are most similar to the leader's own. This conclusion, known as the ally principle, is intuitive, and, setting aside the question of how one ferrets out agents' true policy goals, it is simple to implement.

The second type of constraint encompasses endogenous limitations on the agents. While there are many possible instantiations of such limitations, the two that have received the most theoretical attention revolve around the fact that the appointed agents have some inherent discretion over not only policy decisions but also how hard to work. Examples of factors that theory indicates can be important in this regard include team production, which highlights the importance of considering how subordinates' own career concerns and motivations interact in forming the subordinates' strategic incentives to exert effort, and the incentive compatibility concerns, which highlight the importance of both credibility and goal congruence between the leader and his or her subordinates. The practical distinction between assignment as I am considering it here and the question of picking one's advisers is that the assignment problem occurs much more often in real time than the problem of picking one's advisers. In other words, management through assignment is a recurring problem, where any one assignment decision typically has low risk and low rewards for the leader, but the choice of an optimal strategy, once amplified by the number of times that strategy is used during the leader's tenure, may greatly affect organizational performance.

Coordination. Peters (1998) points out an apparent disconnect between political principals and the bureaucrats they oversee in terms of the expectations of coordinating actions. As discussed throughout this chapter, most of the modern theoretical understanding of bureaucratic decision making is based on two-player models. Such an approach necessarily sets aside most, if not all, concerns about coordination, particularly between and among agents other than the leader.

To the degree that the issue has been addressed in modern theories of bureaucratic decision making, considerations of multiagent bureaucracies have generally focused on team production.[38] In general, the theories that have addressed coordination have extended the seminal analysis of Holmstrom and Milgrom (1991), which considers the question of how best to assign (potentially overlapping) tasks across agents (Ting 2002; Tommasi and Weinschelbaum 2007). A key predictor of successful coordination in team production settings is clarification of responsibility and reduction of uncertainty among the team members regarding their colleagues' effort levels. Particularly in public bureaucracies, individual bureaucrats necessarily at least partially ensure the downside risk of team production in the sense that their wages are generally not tied to individual effort decisions. Instead, a primary motivation for bureaucrats is necessarily policy/outcome driven and based on their own intrinsic (career and/or policy-based) motivations. To the degree that these motivations are intertwined with the efforts of other bureaucrats, a key role for leaders is organizing and shepherding subordinates so as to maximize interpersonal clarity of those subordinates' motivations and efforts.

Bureaucratic Leadership: Why It Should Be Studied, and How

As alluded to in the beginning of the chapter, and at least as a phenomenon distinct from other forms of leadership, it is not entirely clear at first blush that bureaucratic leadership is all that important. Indeed, before writing this, I was unsure whether bureaucratic leadership was that important. Writing this chapter caused me to alter my opinion somewhat. Ironically, the classical division of politics versus administration and the separation of powers arguments that suggest that good bureaucratic leadership consists of faithful implementation of the elected principals' directions also jointly suggest that bureaucratic leadership needs to be studied both empirically and theoretically. Partly this is due to the well-known and inevitable commingling of politics and administration: regardless of its desirability, achieving a neat and clear distinction between the legitimate roles of elected and appointed officials is impossible from a practical standpoint. Accordingly, what bureaucratic leaders do, and how their actions and predispositions affect governance in different situations and settings, is of interest even if one does accept that the ideal role of a bureaucratic leader is that of a faithful implementer of the wishes of the people and their elected representatives.

In terms of how to study bureaucratic leadership, a key first step is to get closer to the action. The preliminary ternary division of leadership offered in this chapter is intended to separate the act of bureaucratic leadership into its constituent actions. While the layers of leadership that I describe overlap and interact in multiple and varied ways, each of them represents an identifiable, and intelligible, part of the average bureaucratic leader's work flow. In addition, as I have attempted to illustrate here, each of these parts has significant overlap both with existing theories and other, complementary aspects of governance. Leveraging the analogies between leadership in bureaucracies and decision making in other organizations and settings will not only make the work more efficient but also bolster the linkages between the fields of political science and public administration.

Acknowledgments

I thank Sean Gailmard, William Howell, Jeff Jenkins, Maggie Penn, Jeff Staton, Craig Volden, audience members at Emory University and the University of Virginia, and an anonymous reviewer for helpful conversations about, and comments on, this project. All errors are mine.

References

Adams, Guy B., and Danny L. Balfour. 2009. *Unmasking Administrative Evil.* Armonk, NY: M. E. Sharpe.

Ahlquist, John S., and Margaret Levi. 2011. "Leadership: What It Means, What It Does, and What We Want to Know about It." *Annual Review of Political Science* 14:1–24.

Allison, Graham T. 1986. "Public and Private Administrative Leadership: Are They Fundamentally Alike in All Unimportant Respects?" In *Leadership and Organizational Culture: New Perspectives on Administrative Theory and Practice,* edited by T. J. Sergiovanni and J. F. Corbally, 214–239. Urbana-Champaign: University of Illinois Press.

Ariely, Gal. 2011. "Why People (Dis)like the Public Service: Citizen Perception of the Public Service and the NPM Doctrine." *Politics and Policy* 39 (6): 997–1019.

Arrow, Kenneth J. 1963. *Social Choice and Individual Values.* 2nd ed. New York: Wiley.

Bass, Bernard M. 1985. *Leadership and Performance Beyond Expectations.* New York: Collier Macmillan.

Bass, Bernard M., and Ronald E. Riggio. 2012. *Transformational Leadership.* New York: Psychology Press.

Bawn, Kathleen. 1995. "Political Control versus Expertise: Congressional Choices about Administrative Procedures." *American Political Science Review* 89 (1): 62–73.

Bendor, Jonathan, and Adam Meirowitz. 2004. "Spatial Models of Delegation." *American Political Science Review* 98 (2): 293–310.

Bendor, Jonathan, Serge Taylor, and Roland van Gaalen. 1987. "Stacking the Deck: Bureaucratic Missions and Policy Design." *American Political Science Review* 81 (3): 873–896.

Besley, Timothy. 2011. *Principled Agents? The Political Economy of Good Government.* New York: Oxford University Press.

Biber, Eric. 2009. "Too Many Things to Do: How to Deal with the Dysfunctions of Multiple-goal Agencies." *Harvard Environmental Law Review* 33:1–63.

Blake, Robert R., and Jane S. Mouton. 1984. "Overcoming Group Warfare." *Harvard Business Review* 62:98–108.

Blanchard, Kenneth H., Drea Zigarmi, and Robert B. Nelson. 1993. "Situational Leadership after 25 Years: A Retrospective." *Journal of Leadership and Organizational Studies* 1 (1): 21–36.

Blau, Peter Michael. 1955. *The Dynamics of Bureaucracy.* Chicago: Chicago University Press.

Boehmke, Frederick, Sean Gailmard, and John Patty. 2006. "Whose Ear to Bend? Information Sources and Venue Choice in Policy Making." *Quarterly Journal of Political Science* 1 (2): 139–169.

Bouckaert, Geert, Steven van de Walle, and Jarl K. Kampen. 2005. "Potential for Comparative Public Opinion Research in Public Administration." *International Review of Administrative Sciences* 71 (2): 229–240.

Bueno de Mesquita, Ethan. 2010. "Regime Change and Revolutionary Entrepreneurs." *American Political Science Review* 104 (3): 446–466.

Bueno de Mesquita, Ethan, and Matthew Stephenson. 2007. "Regulatory Quality under Imperfect Oversight." *American Political Science Review* 101 (3): 605–620.

Burns, James MacGregor. 1978. *Leadership.* New York: Harper & Row.

———. 2003. *Transforming Leadership: A New Pursuit of Happiness.* New York: Grove Press.

Calvert, Randall L. 1985. "The Value of Biased Information: A Rational Choice Model of Political Advice." *Journal of Politics* 47 (2): 530–555.

Christensen, Tom, and Per Lægreid. 2005. "Trust in Government: The Relative Importance of Service Satisfaction, Political Factors, and Demography." *Public Performance and Management Review* 28 (4): 487–511.

Chwe, Michael Suk-Young. 2001. *Rational Ritual: Culture, Coordination, and Common Knowledge.* Princeton, NJ: Princeton University Press.

Connelly, Brian L., S. Trevis Certo, R. Duane Ireland, and Christopher R. Reutzel. 2011. "Signaling Theory: A Review and Assessment." *Journal of Management* 37 (1): 39–67.

Cox, Gary W. 1997. *Making Votes Count.* Cambridge: Cambridge University Press.

Crawford, Vincent P., and Joel Sobel. 1982. "Strategic Information Transmission." *Econometrica* 50 (6): 1431–1451.

Denhardt, Janet V., and Robert B. Denhardt. 2011. *The New Public Service: Serving, Not Steering.* Armonk, NY: M. E. Sharpe.

Dessein, Wouter. 2002. "Authority and Communication in Organizations." *Review of Economic Studies* 69 (4): 811–838.

Dewan, Torun, Andrea Galeotti, Christian Ghiglino, and Francesco Squintani. 2014. "Information Aggregation and Optimal Structure of the Executive." *American Journal of Political Science* 59:475–494.

Dewan, Torun, and David P. Myatt. 2007. "Leading the Party: Coordination, Direction, and Communication." *American Political Science Review* 101 (4): 827–845.

———. 2008. "The Qualities of Leadership: Direction, Communication, and Obfuscation." *American Political Science Review* 102 (3): 351–368.

Dewan, Torun, and Francesco Squintani. 2015. "In Defense of Factions." *American Journal of Political Science* 60:860–881.

Epstein, David, and Sharyn O'Halloran. 1999. *Delegating Powers: A Transaction Cost Politics Approach to Policy Making under Separate Powers.* New York: Cambridge University Press.

Federal Register. 2010. "Prevention of Significant Deterioration and Title V Greenhouse Gas Tailoring Rule." *Federal Register* 75 (106): 31513–31608.

———. 2012. "Prevention of Significant Deterioration and Title V Greenhouse Gas Tailoring

Rule Step 3 and GHG Plantwide Applicability Limits." *Federal Register* 77 (134): 14225–14264.

Fiedler, Fred E. 1964. "A Contingency Model of Leadership Effectiveness." In *Advances in Experimental Social Psychology*, edited by Leonard Berkowitz, 1:149–190. New York: Elsevier.

——. 1967. *A Theory of Leadership Effectiveness*. New York: McGraw-Hill.

Filley, Alan C., Robert J. House, and Steven Kerr. 1976. *Managerial Process and Organizational Behavior*. Glenview, IL: Scott, Foresman.

Fleishman, Edwin A. 1953. "The Description of Supervisory Behavior." *Journal of Applied Psychology* 37 (1): 1.

Fleishman, Edwin A., and David R. Peters. 1962. "Interpersonal Values, Leadership Attitudes, and Managerial 'Success.'" *Personnel Psychology* 15 (2): 127–143.

Fox, Justin. 2007. "Government Transparency and Policymaking." *Public Choice* 131 (1): 23–44.

Frug, G. E. 1984. "The Ideology of Bureaucracy in American Law." *Harvard Law Review* 97:1276–1388.

Gailmard, Sean. 2002. "Expertise, Subversion, and Bureaucratic Discretion." *Journal of Law, Economics, and Organization* 18 (2): 536–555.

——. 2009a. "Discretion Rather Than Rules: Choice of Instruments to Constrain Bureaucratic Policy-Making." *Political Analysis* 17 (1): 25–44.

——. 2009b. "Multiple Principals and Oversight of Bureaucratic Policy-Making." *Journal of Theoretical Politics* 21 (2): 161–186.

——. 2009c. "Oversight and Agency Problems in Legislative–Bureaucratic Interaction." *Journal of Theoretical Politics* 121 (2): 161–186.

Gailmard, Sean, and John W. Patty. 2007. "Slackers and Zealots: Civil Service, Policy Discretion, and Bureaucratic Expertise." *American Journal of Political Science* 51 (4): 873–889.

——. 2012. *Learning While Governing: Information, Accountability, and Executive Branch Institutions*. Chicago: University of Chicago Press.

——. 2013a. "Formal Models of Bureaucracy." *Annual Review of Political Science* 15:353–377.

——. 2013b. "Stovepiping." *Journal of Theoretical Politics* 25 (3): 388–411.

——. 2017. "Giving Advice vs. Making Decisions: Transparency, Information, and Delegation." Working paper, University of Chicago. https://www.dropbox.com/s/0zxbhhuf4b jff5c/GailmardPatty-TransparencyInformationDelegation-Latest.pdf.

Galeotti, Andrea, Christian Ghiglino, and Francesco Squintani. 2009. "Strategic Information Transmission in Networks." Department of Economics Discussion Paper No. 668. University of Essex.

Graeff, Claude L. 1997. "Evolution of Situational Leadership Theory: A Critical Review." *Leadership Quarterly* 8 (2): 153–170.

Groseclose, Tim, and Nolan McCarty. 2001. "The Politics of Blame: Bargaining Before an Audience." *American Journal of Political Science* 45 (1): 100–119.

Gulick, Luther. 1937. "Notes on the Theory of Organization." In *Papers on the Science of Administration*, edited by L. Gulick and L. Urwick, 1–49. New York: Institute of Public Administration.

Hersey, Paul, and Kenneth H. Blanchard. 1969. *Management of Organizational Behavior.* Englewood Cliffs, NJ: Prentice-Hall.

Hollyer, James R., B. Peter Rosendorff, and James Raymond Vreeland. 2011. "Democracy and Transparency." *Journal of Politics* 73 (4): 1191–1205.

Holmstrom, Bengt, and Paul Milgrom. 1991. "Multitask Principal–Agent Analyses: Incentive Contracts, Asset Ownership, and Job Design." *Journal of Law, Economics, and Organization* 7:24–52.

Hood, Christopher. 1991. "A Public Management for All Seasons?" *Public Administration* 69 (1): 3–19.

House, Robert J. 1971. "A Path Goal Theory of Leader Effectiveness." *Administrative Science Quarterly* pp. 321–339.

———. 1996. "Path–Goal Theory of Leadership: Lessons, Legacy, and a Reformulated Theory." *Leadership Quarterly* 7 (3): 323–352.

House, Robert J., and Terence R. Mitchell. 1974. "Path–Goal Theory of Leadership." *Journal of Contemporary Business* 3 (4): 81–97.

Hyneman, Charles S. 1950. *Bureaucracy in a Democracy.* New York: Harper & Brothers.

Kirkpatick, Shelley A., and Edwin A. Locke. 1991. "Leadership: Do Traits Matter?" *Executive* 5 (2): 48–60.

Laitin, David D. 1994. "The Tower of Babel as a Coordination Game: Political Linguistics in Ghana." *American Political Science Review* 88 (3): 622–634.

Levy, Gilat. 2007. "Decision Making in Committees: Transparency, Reputation, and Voting Rules." *American Economic Review* 97 (1): 150–168.

Magill, Elizabeth. 2008. "Agency Self-Regulation." *George Washington Law Review* 77:859–903.

McCubbins, Mathew, and Tom Schwartz. 1984. "Congressional Oversight Overlooked: Police Patrols versus Fire Alarms." *American Journal of Political Science* 28:165–179.

Miller, David. 1992. "Deliberative Democracy and Social Choice." *Political Studies* 40 (5): 54–67.

Mintzberg, Henry. 1973. *The Nature of Managerial Work.* New York: Harper & Row.

———. 1979. *The Structuring of Organizations: A Synthesis of the Research.* Upper Saddle River, NJ: Prentice-Hall.

Morris, Stephen, and Hyun Song Shin. 2002. "Social Value of Public Information." *American Economic Review* 92 (5): 1521–1534.

Osborne, Stephen P. 2006. "The New Public Governance?" *Public Management Review* 8 (3): 377–387.

Patty, John W. 2009. "The Politics of Biased Information." *Journal of Politics* 71 (2): 385–397.

———. 2015. "A Theory of Cabinet-Making: The Politics of Inclusion, Exclusion, and Information." Working paper, University of Chicago.

Patty, John W., and Elizabeth Maggie Penn. 2014a. "Sequential Decision-Making and Information Aggregation in Small Networks." *Political Science Research and Methods* 2 (2): 249–271.

———. 2014b. *Social Choice and Legitimacy: The Possibilities of Impossibility.* New York: Cambridge University Press.

Peters, B. Guy. 1998. "Managing Horizontal Government: The Politics of Co-ordination." *Public Administration* 76 (2): 295–311.

Prat, Andrea. 2005. "The Wrong Kind of Transparency." *American Economic Review* 95 (2): 862–877.

Rainey, Hal G. 2014. *Understanding and Managing Public Organizations.* 5th ed. San Francisco, CA: John Wiley & Sons.

Rosenbloom, David H. 1983. "Public Administrative Theory and the Separation of Powers." *Public Administration Review* 43:219–227.

———. 2000. *Building a Legislative-Centered Public Administration.* Tuscaloosa: University of Alabama Press.

Ryan, James E. 2004. "The Perverse Incentives of the No Child Left Behind Act." *New York University Law Review* 79:932–989.

Scharpf, Fritz W. 1994. "Games Real Actors Could Play: Positive and Negative Coordination in Embedded Negotiations." *Journal of Theoretical Politics* 6 (1): 27–53.

Shepsle, Kenneth A. 1992. "Congress Is a 'They,' Not an 'It': Legislative Intent as Oxymoron." *International Review of Law and Economics* 12 (2): 239–256.

Simon, Herbert Alexander. 1947. *Administrative Behavior.* New York: Macmillan.

Stasavage, David. 2003. "Transparency, Democratic Accountability, and the Economic Consequences of Monetary Institutions." *American Journal of Political Science* 47 (3): 389–402.

———. 2007. "Polarization and Publicity: Rethinking the Benefits of Deliberative Democracy." *Journal of Politics* 69 (1): 59–72.

Strauss, Peter L. 1984. "The Place of Agencies in Government: Separation of Powers and the Fourth Branch." *Columbia Law Review* 84:573–669.

———. 1996. "From Expertise to Politics: The Transformation of American Rulemaking." *Wake Forest Law Review* 31:745–777.

Taylor, Frederick Winslow. 1947. *Scientific Management.* New York: Harper & Row.

Terry, Larry D. 2003. *Leadership of Public Bureaucracies: The Administrator as Conservator.* 2nd ed. Armonk, NY: M. E. Sharpe.

Ting, Michael M. 2002. "A Theory of Jurisdictional Assignments in Bureaucracies." *American Journal of Political Science* 46 (2): 364–378.

Tommasi, Mariano, and Federico Weinschelbaum. 2007. "Centralization vs. Decentralization: A Principal–Agent Analysis." *Journal of Public Economic Theory* 9 (2): 369–389.

Ullman, Jeffrey D. 1975. "NP-Complete Scheduling Problems." *Journal of Computer and System Sciences* 10 (3): 384–393.

Vroom, Victor H., and Arthur G. Jago. 1974. "Decision Making as a Social Process: Normative and Descriptive Models of Leader Behavior." *Decision Sciences* 5 (4): 743–769.

———. 1978. "On the Validity of the Vroom–Yetton Model." *Journal of Applied Psychology* 63 (2): 151–162.

Vroom, Victor H., and Philip W. Yetton. 1973. *Leadership and Decision-Making.* Pittsburgh, PA: University of Pittsburgh Press.

Walle, Steven van de, Steven van Roosbroek, and Geert Bouckaert. 2008. "Trust in the

Public Sector: Is There Any Evidence for a Long-Term Decline?" *International Review of Administrative Sciences* 74 (1): 47–64.

Wart, Montgomery van. 2003. "Public-Sector Leadership Theory: An Assessment." *Public Administration Review* 63 (2): 214–228.

Weber, Max. 1968. *Economy and Society.* Berkeley: University of California Press.

Weingast, Barry R. 1997. "The Political Foundations of Democracy and the Rule of Law." *American Political Science Review* 91 (2): 245–263.

West, William F. 2004. "Formal Procedures, Informal Processes, Accountability, and Responsiveness in Bureaucratic Policy Making: An Institutional Policy Analysis." *Public Administration Review* 64 (1): 66–80.

Wilson, James Q. 2000. *Bureaucracy.* 2nd ed. New York: Basic Books.

Notes

1. Indeed, the phrase "bureaucratic leadership" is itself formally ambiguous, depending on whether one is using bureaucracy to describe a style of administration (Weber 1968) or "a body of nonelective government officials" (Merriam-Webster, https://www.merriam-webster.com/). Noting, without comment, that this ambiguity might indicate how little anyone cares about defining the concept in a clear way, I will adopt the second usage in this chapter.

2. Frug (1984) also provides a comprehensive review of the theories of bureaucratic legitimacy.

3. Though this is a caricature, it is telling. Perhaps good bureaucratic leadership is akin to good firefighting: it is important only after something has caught on fire. Such a conclusion also suggests why what one might call bureaucratic leadership is more often described as (public) management or administration.

4. For a recent discussion of the theoretical difficulties inherent in defining "the public interest" in administrative policy making, see Patty and Penn (2014b).

5. A less directly related but still relevant vein of research considers the interaction of government service provision and public opinion (Christensen and Lægreid 2005).

6. For example, while representation within and by the bureaucracy has attracted significant attention within the scholarly and policy communities, the measurement of such representation is not typically done in terms of the decisions of individual bureaucrats. Rather, the unit of analysis is either macro-level policy or the descriptive characteristics of bureaucrats, viewed as a group.

7. See, as one example, Ariely (2011) and literature therein. A contrarian take on the question of how broad and sustained this decline has been and continues to be is offered by van de Walle, van Roosbroek, and Bouckaert (2008).

8. Broadly associated with Hood (1991), new public management is generally used to describe proposals for administrative reform that lead to bureaucratic institutions, incentives, and decision making more closely mimicking their private sector analogues.

9. My thinking on this has been shaped indelibly by Wilson's (2000, chap. 9) typology of

agencies. However, while I am using some of the same language ("outputs" and "outcomes") as he does, my meaning is slightly different, as some of what I call inputs he would include as outputs. The principal distinction is that I think outputs are best thought of as being produced by the organization, while the actions of individuals within the organization are more usefully distinguished. This distinction is less important to Wilson, who is considering how and why agencies operate as they do, whereas I am more interested in considering how a leader within an agency operates.

10. Here "things" include tangible objects, intangibles such as information, and individual actions.

11. More precisely, outcomes are things actually, potentially, or intended to be affected by the agency.

12. At least one such standard argument is based on Arrow's (1963) impossibility theorem. For more on the generality of the dilemma raised by Arrow's theorem for the construction of sensible measures of performance, see Patty and Penn (2014b).

13. In particular, one might argue that it is precisely those policy realms in which performance evaluation is contested and/or highly ambiguous (but in which no organization is widely thought to be inferior) that active government involvement is sustained.

14. If they weren't, the agency would probably be tasked with directly outputting the outcomes themselves.

15. Contrast this with measuring the effectiveness of military deterrence, policies intended to prevent the spread of unsafe sexual behaviors, or measures to deter tax fraud.

16. The most obvious example of this is the matter of how to finance and manage administration of the evaluation instrument itself.

17. A cogent and concise review of this voluminous literature is provided in Rainey (2014, chap. 11). Much of this brief discussion is drawn from there.

18. Allison (1986), arguing along these lines, famously asserted that there is little difference between public and private bureaucratic leadership.

19. Wilson (2000, 159) cites Mintzberg (1979) as the inspiration for his typology.

20. For example, Calvert (1985) and Patty (2009) each demonstrate how the leader having a bias in the decision stage can influence the optimal strategies for information collection.

21. Any pollutant designated a criteria air pollutant is subjected to an EPA-imposed cap, known as the National Ambient Air Quality Standards. Until 2009, there were six criteria for determining air pollutants: carbon monoxide, lead, nitrogen oxide, ozone, particle pollution, and sulfur dioxide.

22. In addition to the direct cost, the efficiency of a police patrol strategy is often reduced by the other transaction costs of decision making. Specifically, achieving maximal precision from the information gleaned from continuous monitoring requires that the leader can both make decisions and manage his or her implementation instantaneously. Obviously, this is not the case with most policies of any significance.

23. Space prohibits consideration of how and when bureaucrats can faithfully reconcile conflicting goals when making decisions. Patty and Penn (2014b) consider the practical realities of criteria-based decisions and discuss the implications of conflicting goals within

the context of social choice theory. For the purposes of this chapter, their conclusion that there will generally be more than one legitimate decision further bolsters the importance of bureaucratic leadership in both theoretical and empirical terms.

24. Specifically, the threshold is either 100 or 250 tons per year.

25. *Chevron U.S.A. Inc. v. NRDC*, 467 U.S. 837 (1984).

26. Gulick (1937) also laid out a set of seven types of activities that compose administrative management. Widely known as POSDCORB, the seven categories are planning, organizing, staffing, directing, coordinating, reporting, and budgeting.

27. Specifically, preference alignment is required for advice to be credible if the advice is unverifiable before the leader must make his or her decisions.

28. A side note, especially with respect to Gailmard and Patty (2007) (see also Boehmke, Gailmard, and Patty 2006), is that information acquisition can sometimes be most effectively incentivized by delegating authority directly to the putative adviser, thereby obviating the need for the adviser to message his or her procured information to the leader of ultimate disposition of policy.

29. 60 Stat. 237, enacted June 11, 1946.

30. More subtly, the fact that bureaucrats serve multiple principals immediately implies that the importance of any given decision might be best thought of as multidimensional.

31. While it is beyond the scope of this chapter, it would be interesting to consider the relationship between leadership and the vexing problem of deciding whether one properly has the authority to make a decision. In particular, this question is intimately related to the central issues of *Chevron* and the related theory of agency self-limitation, as discussed in *Whitman v. American Trucking Associations*, 531 U.S. 457 (2001). See also Magill (2008) and Patty and Penn (2014a).

32. See, among others, Bawn (1995), Epstein and O'Halloran (1999), and Gailmard (2009a). Slight extensions of this basic framework are considered by Gailmard (2002, 2009c), Bueno de Mesquita and Stephenson (2007), and Patty (2009).

33. This is implied in a variety of related settings by Dessein (2002), Patty (2009), Gailmard and Patty (2013a), and Patty and Penn (2014a).

34. For reasons of space, I leave aside a large theoretical literature on transparency as it relates to accountability and oversight (Bendor, Taylor, and van Gaalen 1987; Stasavage 2003; Prat 2005; Fox 2007; Levy 2007; Besley 2011; Hollyer, Rosendorff, and Vreeland 2011). This distinction can be thought of as representing the practical and theoretical differences between ex post transparency for the purposes of oversight or auditing by a third party and transparency within and between the different components of a policy-making organization.

35. This point also follows, in a different informational framework, from the bottom-up dynamics considered by Gailmard and Patty (2013b), where providing greater transparency of a subordinate's information to the leader can distort the incentives of the subordinate to produce and/or retain high-quality information.

36. Of course, as civil service procedures, licensing requirements, and partisan/separation of powers considerations attest, these exogenous constraints may themselves be endogenous to the larger political and economic processes within which the organization operates.

37. The more general question of how to pick several agents from a fixed set to perform several tasks is analogous to the prioritization problem I described above and accordingly is quite difficult to solve even if one makes very strong simplifying assumptions. Nonetheless, it represents a ubiquitous part of leadership and management and deserves more theoretical and empirical attention.

38. Of course, coordination problems have received theoretical attention from various scholars, including Laitin (1994), Scharpf (1994), Cox (1997), Weingast (1997), Chwe (2001), Morris and Shin (2002), Dewan and Myatt (2007, 2008), and Bueno de Mesquita (2010).

CHAPTER NINE

Leadership in the States

James Coleman Battista

Leadership in the states is a broad set of topics, questions, and occasionally even answers. Leadership in the state context does not differ at the raw conceptual level from its counterparts at the federal level. Leaders still use the authority granted to them and their powers of persuasion to shift other actors toward outcomes they might otherwise not have arrived at. Governors face the same problems of getting a large executive branch to adhere to their own policy goals as do presidents, and contend with legislatures over policy and budgetary priority. State legislative leaders face the same core problems of control and accountability that Representative Paul Ryan (R-WI) and Senator Mitch McConnell (R-KY) do in Congress. Here I offer what is primarily a review essay, focusing on recent scholarship, that details some of the ways in which looking to the states can help us generate and assess theories about leadership more generally and especially what conduces to effective or strong leadership.

Substantively, studies of leadership at the state level can be divided into two groups of subjects: leadership between institutions and leadership within institutions.[1] Studies of leadership between institutions are strongly clustered in the ability of governors to get their legislative agenda enacted, though of course there are other examples. Studies of leadership within institutions are concentrated in legislative leadership.

In each of these areas, the variation among states means that generalizations are difficult. Do governors exercise effective leadership when dealing with the legislature? Yes, except when they do not. Do legislative leaders keep a firm hand on the legislative process and thereby promote structured and efficient debate, or do they limit the collective action and social choice problems faced by the majority? Yes, when they do, but not otherwise. Because the set of topics is wide, the fundamental processes similar to those at the federal level, and the ability to deliver clear overall answers limited, I will focus less on the substantive questions and answers that studies relevant to leadership in the states have arrived at and more on how look-ing to the states helps us to understand leadership in ways that would be difficult, impractical, or impossible when examining only the federal government. This is not to dismiss the substantive importance of leadership in the states; leadership in any political office or setting can be as important as the policies that are set there, and state governments control much of the policy that is most directly relevant to ordinary peoples' lives, such as the provision and regulation of education.

Operationalizing Leadership

An obvious first question is, what is leadership? While this question lends itself to baroque complications, much like the question "what is power?" I will offer a simple concept of leadership that I think contains most of the denotations and connotations of the term "leadership." Leadership is directing outcomes away from those that might be chosen in the absence of leadership, but in such a way that those being led consent ex post. In the terms of spatial modeling, leadership is shifting outcomes away from those that are likely to be chosen but still within the feasible set. That is, if the observed outcome would have been realized even without the leader's action, their leadership can hardly have been effective. But at the same time, one difference between being led and being simply dominated is that even though the outcome is not one that that would have been chosen, the combination of the realized outcome and the processes used to get there are, ex post, acceptable to (enough of) those being led. Many of the classic studies of federal institutions at least approach an understanding of leadership, or at least power, along these lines. Most obviously, Neustadt's (1960) classic view of presidential leadership as persua-sion takes a similar perspective. Ferguson's (2003, 159) definition of gubernatorial leadership as "determining what the public wants and what is legislatively and po-litically feasible, and then advocating for policies to achieve these goals" contains these same elements but adds the constraint that the leader is not pushing solely for his or her own personal preferences. In a similar way, we can think of the lit-erature on bargaining between the president and Congress (Cameron 2000; Poole and McCarty 1995) as dancing around this idea of leadership. And, especially after Krehbiel's (1998) critiques and the responses to it, we can see an understanding of legislative leadership as both controlling or constraining the majority while also respecting and being responsive to it (Ansolabehere, Snyder, and Stewart 2001; Cox and McCubbins 2005).

Operationally and empirically, studies of governors and gubernatorial–legislative relations generally define leadership (or the related concepts of power, strength, and effectiveness) with the degree of success the governor has in getting his or her polit-ical goals enacted, which usually means working with the legislature. Typically this degree of success means generating a measure of gubernatorial goals either from statements such as the state of the state speech or from his or her initial budget proposal, and then examining their success rate or the success of individual bills promoted by the governor (Ferguson 2003; Kousser and Phillips 2012). However, another approach has been to go more straightforwardly after gubernatorial strength by surveying knowledgeable informants such as legislators (Carey, Niemi, and Powell 1998; Carey et al. 2006) or administrators (Dometrius and Wright 2010) and asking them directly how influential various actors are in determining policy and budgetary outcomes. That is, studies of gubernatorial leadership typically either ask informants to rate it or look for objective results of effective leadership.

This pattern is true in state legislatures as well, with one addition. While the formal authority held by governors is generally constitutional or statutory, and thus does not change very much or very often, the formal authority held by legislative leaders is more heavily vested in sets of rules that, at least notionally, must be adopted at the beginning of every session and so are, at least theoretically, more frequent objects of choice. State legislative leadership is then typically operationalized in three ways. First, it assesses the formal authority held by the leader. Clucas (2001) analyzed parts of the constitutions and legislative rules of all forty-nine state lower chambers in 1995 to create an index of Speakers' formal authority. Miller, Nicholson-Crotty, and Nicholson-Crotty (2011) later extended the index to upper chambers and broadened it to include the powers of the full leadership team, and Mooney (2013a) compiled a similar index by chamber year for the years 1981 to 2010. A second way researchers have operationalized legislative leadership is by querying knowledgeable informants, usually legislators themselves (Carey, Niemi, and Powell 1998; Carey et al. 2006; Clucas 2007). Finally, researchers have generated objective indicators of the results of effective leadership, such as observable leadership influence on roll-call votes (Battista and Richman 2011), defending existing outcomes against potential threats from the minority party (Cox, Kousser, and Mc-Cubbins 2010), or preventing votes where a majority of the majority party would be on the losing side (Anzia and Jackman 2013; Jackman 2014). As will be seen, one complication in that state legislative world is that these operationalizations of leadership or power do not themselves hang together very neatly.

States and the Study of Leadership

While the substantive findings rising from studies of leadership and power in the states are at least as important as the policy decisions that flow from state governments, the strongest benefit of looking to the states for the larger communities of Americanists and those interested in leadership lies in understanding the exercise of leadership in a more general way and exploiting the wide variation between states to generate firmer inferences about leadership. This claim is far from unique; indeed, almost any prominent work on comparative state politics will at some point note the broader utility of studying state politics in much these terms. The common point of them is that comparative work on state politics allows researchers to better ask and answer their questions, even if those questions relate to federal-level politics. There is a central question for studies of leadership that emerges repeatedly from the literature and from the essays in this volume: what conduces to effective leadership? What traits or skills of the leader are associated with firmer leadership? Conversely, are there identifiable traits of followers or negotiating partners that make them easier or more difficult to lead? What effects do the various institutional or institutionalized tools available to leaders, such as appointment powers, the veto, or the ability to control a legislature's agenda, have on their ability to lead?

What the states offer to students of leadership is new ways to test the implications of theories about effective leadership and its covariates, new venues for the development of theory, and new empirical puzzles to serve as the initial prod toward theory. While generalization is important, I should be clear that I do not mean only the generalization of existing federal-level results to the states. Rather, a core benefit of state-level work is that variation among the states provides sufficient leverage to empirically test or assess observable implications that had previously been either not examinable or were so obviously not examinable that they were never even proposed. Further, these new or newly assessable implications can be drawn directly from a theory's core rather than being secondary concerns that happen to be observable. For example, consider a researcher arguing that the president's veto power is an important tool the president uses to shift policy outcomes in his or her direction while bargaining with Congress,[2] resulting in some set of observable implications at the federal level. However, the most obvious implication of the theory—if the president did not have the veto, then the president would be less able to secure favored outcomes—is obviously untestable with federal data. Looking to the states, however, shows clear potential to confront that implication with data and so directly address the core of the theory. Most obviously, until 1997 the governor of North Carolina had no veto, and one could study the effect of its introduction on the bargaining power of the governor.[3] Or one could look at variation in governors' veto powers to see if they affect bargaining success; stronger vetoes seem to have at most limited and conditional effects.

There are (at least) two ways in which comparative state analysis can further the study of leadership by allowing better and more direct assessment of the observable implications drawn from a theory. First, states have wide variation in their formal institutions, considered in the usual broad neoinstitutionalist sense (Riker 1986; Coase 1937; North 1990). These can exist at the level of state constitutions, statute law, or formalized rules in a legislature or bureaucracy. While all governors now have a veto, six governors do not have a line-item veto, and the vote requirements for veto overrides vary. Some states impose term limits on their governors, legislators, or both, while others do not. Some state constitutions directly regulate aspects of the legislative process, such as Colorado's prohibition against binding caucus votes, while others leave the chambers to mostly govern themselves as they choose. These institutions vary widely. While there has been no variation in the president's veto power apart from the brief flirtation with a statutory line-item veto, until 1997 governors of Wisconsin had effectively used the veto authority granted them to delete individual letters from bills, while the governor of North Carolina had no veto authority whatsoever. While Congress scholars made use of small changes in the votes required to support a discharge petition, state legislatures range between granting the leader the authority to assign every member to committee, including members of other parties, and formally entrenching a seniority rule. Further, while it would be stretching to say that these institutions change frequently, there is at least a notably higher level of institutional change across the states than we observe in federal politics, and thus more natural experiments to exploit.

Second, contexts—by which I mean all relevant aspects of political life other than institutions—also vary. A context might be precisely who populates the legislature a governor is dealing with, or it might be the political circumstances of a given state in a given year, or it might be the set of personal skills held by a particular governor. Even among states with highly similar institutional structures, some might have divided government while others have unified government, allowing the effects of both institutions and contexts to be more clearly resolved with appropriate studies. Similarly, institutionally similar states might have different estimates of overall policy liberalism (Erikson, Wright, and McIver 1993; Berry et al. 2010; Carsey and Harden 2010), or one legislature might have a less unified majority party than does a state with an otherwise similarly arranged legislature. As with institutions, these contexts can vary widely. For example, while tied chambers have been rare in Congress, they occur with some regularity (if still not frequently) among the states. In any given year, some governors will enjoy far greater public support than do others when they begin negotiating with their legislatures, and legislatures will run the range from overwhelming Republican majorities through tied or nearly tied chambers to overwhelming Democratic majorities.

Finally, in addition to allowing better, deeper, and more direct assessment of a theory's observable implications, comparative state analysis can aid in the development of theory. The variation in institutions and contexts provides an obvious spur to think about what the effects of those institutions and contexts might be when they might have been ignored at the federal level. Similarly, the comparative study of the states can expose new empirical puzzles that demand theoretically oriented study.

All of the ways in which states vary, both in cross section and across time, can aid in the understanding of leadership, as with so many other aspects of American political life. The next sections describe how the existing literature exploits variation in institutions and contexts to better understand each of these forms of leadership, and offer an extended example of how an empirical puzzle revealed by the states can potentially lead to theoretical development that is relevant both to the states and to federal-level politics.

Variation in Institutions

Institutional variation have an obvious potential role in interactions between governors and legislatures. At the most abstract level, researchers have assembled indices of governors' formal powers, such as Beyle's (see Krupnikov and Shipan 2012). However, results for these indices are mixed. Ferguson (2003) and Dometrius and Wright (2010) found little evidence that governors' formal powers affected gubernatorial success. However, Dilger, Krause, and Moffett (1995) found at least conditional effects using a different index, and Barrilleaux and Berkman (2003) found that governors with more formal tools to control the budget were more likely to focus on statewide rather than locally parochial issues.

Moving to specific institutions, federal work (Cameron 2000) gives us good reason to think that the veto matters in presidential interactions with Congress. The power of the governor's veto varies strongly, usually but not always including some sort of line-item veto, and we would naturally expect stronger veto powers to be associated with more effective leadership by the governor. Override requirements in the states cluster at a majority of members, two-thirds of those present, and two-thirds of members. The obvious inference would thus be that governors enjoying stronger veto powers should have an enhanced ability to take a leadership role in negotiations with the legislature. However, researchers have found that as an empirical matter the strength of the veto is at most only conditionally relevant. Ferguson (2003) found no discernible effect for strong veto powers, while Kousser and Phillips (2012), using matching methods to focus more strongly on causal effects, found that line-item vetoes only had an effect when the governor preferred less overall spending than did the legislature and the legislature could not be expected to override a veto. These results echo a long-standing series of results showing that the line-item veto should not in theory, and does not empirically, substantially reduce state spending.

However, the null results for veto strength do not mean that the veto itself is irrelevant. Kousser and Phillips (2012) argued that gubernatorial veto threats can be effective when the legislature is impatient and the reversion point—the outcome when no bill becomes law—is unacceptable to the legislature. Kousser and Phillips extended their argument, noting that the legislature is more likely to be impatient about budgetary and spending issues, where the reversion point could be politically disastrous, than they are about policy bills, where the reversion point is simply the status quo. Because gubernatorial success in the budget is more driven by veto threats, they argued, successful leadership should vary with factors that increase legislator impatience, such as shorter sessions, while policy success is driven largely by the governor's ability to give side payments to legislators.[4] Spinning comparative statics out of formal models, they found support for this difference, indirectly supporting the veto as an important but limited leadership tool for governors.

A second obvious institution that could affect gubernatorial–legislative interaction is term limits for legislators.[5] Supporting results from some existing models (Grofman and Sutherland 1996), Carey, Niemi, and Powell (1998) and Carey et al. (2006) both surveyed legislators and found that term limits increased perceived gubernatorial influence over legislation while decreasing the influence of their own leadership. Focusing on term limits from the legislative side, Miller, Nicholson-Crotty, and Nicholson-Crotty (2011) extended this work by controlling for the formal authority held by legislative leadership. They found that in states that had adopted term limits, Speakers with low formal authority saw their perceived power fall, but there was no effect on formally strong Speakers. In states where term limits had actually begun to eject legislators, Speakers with low formal authority saw an increase in perceived power, while formally powerful Speakers saw a decrease. Overall, these changes suggest that term limits were again associated with an overall reduction of Speakers' perceived power. Clark (2012) found that legislators who had been termed out and who had no plans for future political work did not change their voting patterns on final passage votes but were less likely to go along with the party's position in procedural votes, implying that their leadership had less leverage over their voting patterns than they had previously held. Finally, Apollonio and La Raja (2006) reasoned that if interest groups make contributions to influence important legislative actors, then for an actor to see a drop in contributions implies a drop in power. Using this unique measure of leadership power, they found that term limits reduced the power of party leaders.

Variation in institutions can also be used to help understand leadership within legislatures. One of the core concepts in state legislative research is professionalization. Conceptually, professionalization captures aspects of the institutional structure of the legislature and the orientation of legislators toward their service, placing it between institutions and context. However, the most common operationalization, Squire's (1992) index, essentially assesses how Congresslike a state legislature is in terms of its pay, session length, and staff support, placing it firmly among institutions. While researchers would typically argue that professionalization should reduce legislators' willingness to be led and more firmly insist on their own priorities, and so reduce the authority they would willingly hand to their leadership (Jewell and Whicker 1994), the empirical results have been mixed. Clucas (2001) found that professionalization was uncorrelated with Speakers' formal authority, but that it was associated with higher levels of leadership strength as perceived by legislators (Clucas 2007). Richman (2010) found that professionalization was associated with formally weaker Speakers, though this effect was not apparent in the

Speaker's procedural authority. Battista and Richman (2011) found that career legislatures were associated with a greater party effect on roll-call votes. Mooney (2013b), however, found that professionalization was associated with leaders perceived to be more powerful holding their formal authority constant. On the gubernatorial side, Dilger, Krause, and Moffett (1995) found that professionalized chambers were associated with greater gubernatorial success, as did Ferguson (2003). Kousser and Phillips (2012), however, found that longer sessions were associated with governors having less success in the budgetary arena.

Another variable that has had unclear and mixed effects, when it has been considered as an independent variable, is the formal powers held by the leader. This is most commonly operationalized either with Clucas's (2001) index for 1995 or updates of the index for additional sessions; it is sometimes used as a dependent variable for leadership authority. Battista (2011) found that this index of formal authority was only barely related to how powerful legislators perceived their leader to be. That is, much as with governors, the formal authority held by the leadership seemed to have little impact on how effectively or firmly they were able to lead. Mooney (2013b) expanded on this analysis by considering legislators' perceptions of leadership power explicitly as a survey response rather than a simple measure of leadership. What, he posited, would prompt a legislator to state that a leader was influential? Minority party respondents might rate the Speaker as more influential to rationalize their policy losses, and women might systematically view Speakers as more influential, both of which turn out to be the case. Mooney found that apparent influence is best understood as a response to potential organizational problems in the chamber, but more importantly he found that even with the additional controls and in a fuller model, the formal powers held by the leader still do not offer any explanatory leverage over how influential the leader is seen to be.

Other ways in which internal legislative institutions vary have clearer effects, however. One of the clearest examples involves a natural experiment in which the electorate of Colorado used the initiative process to strip legislative leaders of almost all control over the legislative agenda, imposing the so-called GAVEL (Give a Vote to Every Legislator) amendment on them. Cox, Kousser, and McCubbins (2010) found that this initiative reduced the leader's negative agenda control (Cox and McCubbins 2005) or ability to defend existing outcomes against bills preferred primarily by minority party members. Likewise, Anzia and Jackman (2013) and Jackman (2014) found that stronger leadership control over committees, especially when committees had substantial power to keep bills from receiving a vote, was associated with a lower rate of majority "rolls," which take place when a majority of the majority party is on the losing side of a vote. And as noted earlier, Carey and colleagues found that term limits reduced leaders' perceived influence over legislative outcomes.

Overall, a key takeaway point from studies using institutional variation to help understand gubernatorial and legislative leadership is that institutional factors affect the leadership capacity of legislative leaders more strongly than they do gubernatorial leadership. In general, this should not be particularly surprising. Gubernatorial leadership, when it entails working with and negotiating with the legislature, as it does in these studies, involves relatively intimate negotiations with a small set of actors, while legislative leadership involves the management of a substantial organization where most legislators might have no position of authority but are still not the leader's actual subordinates. It should be little surprise that organizational management of multiple systems with many moving parts, and people in many roles, is more responsive to changes in how those organizations are set up than are governorships. A secondary point is that many institutional variables, and especially the grander and more overarching variables such as formal power indices or professionalization, are dogs that don't bark, or at least don't bark consistently. Instead, the institutional variables whose effects seem clear and consistent are those smaller-scale institutions that have clear and immediate links to control of the agenda or other procedural power. Finally, these studies include work that would be impossible or infeasible at the federal level. Developing an empirically grounded prediction for what might happen if the president were granted a line-item veto, or if term limits were imposed on Congress, is impossible without access to the variation in these institutions present at the state level, and such predictions would be important to the debate over any realistic proposals to enact those changes. Similarly, Anzia and Jackman's (2013) analysis, as well as Jackman's (2014) related solo work, would be impossible to examine at the federal level because there has simply not been enough variation in party and committee structures in the modern era, even though their analyses speak strongly to the origins of effective leadership in the modern Congress.

Variation in Contexts

The Personal Context

Variation in the personal, political, and economic contexts is also an important tool in learning what conduces to effective leadership, especially because some of these factors can at least theoretically be manipulated by voters through elections or by constructing institutions designed to foster desired traits of political life. Perhaps the most obvious context is the personal context: leadership inheres in individuals, and who those individuals are and what skills they have can make a difference in how effective they are as leaders. Personal skills and traits have been studied most intensely for executives, with classic studies like Barber's (1985) psychological study of presidents. In the states, perhaps the closest recent analogue to Barber's typology is Ferguson and Barth's (2002) analysis of governors. By analyzing the texts of their inaugural addresses, Ferguson and Barth generated estimates of the relative strength of governors' achievement motive (a drive toward excellence), affiliation motive (a drive toward closer relations with people), and power motive (a drive toward prestige and influence), finding that gubernatorial success rates with the legislature are associated with an interactive variable tapping both the achievement and power motives. More recently, Crew and Lewis (2011) analyzed state of the state speeches in Florida to assess the governor's verbal style using preestablished methods. They found that governors whose speeches more frequently used words or phrases that connote enthusiasm or activity had greater success rates in their dealings with the legislature. In the legislative setting, there has been little systematic and comparative work on leaders' psychological traits or skills. The only relatively recent example is Jewell and Whicker's (1994) book using interviews in twenty-two states. However, they generally limit themselves to developing typologies of the various factors they consider, including personality and style, and when they do make causal or associational arguments, they are not backed up by any formalized empirical analysis.

The Political Context

Another obvious context is the political context of the state—which parties control which chambers, how large the legislative majority is in each state, and so on. To be clear, some of these findings appear as control variables rather than the central focus of the works in question, and some of the findings are unsurprising. For example, Ferguson (2003) found that governors were less successful with legislatures at least partially controlled by the opposite party. Kousser and Phillips (2012) added nuance by finding that the legislature's seat share held by the governor's party enhanced gubernatorial success in policy proposals but not with budgetary proposals (which, again, they found were driven primarily by impatience, because budgetary items are more likely to have unacceptable reversion points).

In legislatures, the most frequently examined element of the political context is the arrangement of the legislators' ideal points, especially the homogeneity of the majority party and the distance between parties. These are the core elements of conditional party government, originally developed for the US House of Representatives (Rohde 1991; Aldrich and Rohde 2000). The underlying argument is essentially that distance between the parties gives the minority a greater incentive to prevent legislation from passing, and thereby gives the majority a greater incentive to give the chamber leadership more institutional tools to control the agenda. At the same time, ideological homogeneity within the majority party reduces the principal–agency problem for backbench members and allows rank-and-file majority members to more easily trust that these agenda-control tools will not be deployed against them, but only against the minority. At the state level, there has been relatively little support for predictions derived from conditional party government.

Jenkins (2008) found that party ideological heterogeneity, measured using survey responses, was actually positively associated with consistent voting with the party, directly contradicting the predictions of conditional party government, but she examined majority and minority parties simultaneously. She also found, however, that more ideologically heterogeneous majority parties did give their Speakers less power over committee assignments and referrals. Richman (2010) refined conditional party government theory by arguing that a further condition should be relevant—the degree to which policy making is complicated by large and diverse populations, a thriving interest group ecosystem, preexisting government interventions in the economy, and a large number of legislators. Richman (2010, 213) found that "well-aligned" preferences were associated with more formally powerful Speakers only in states that faced substantial policy-making challenges. This finding was reinforced by Battista and Richman (2011), who operationalized Speaker power by effect of party on voting. They found that in chambers facing few challenges polarization reduced the effect of leadership, at average challenge levels polarization had no effect, and at high levels it had an effect consistent with conditional party government. Mooney (2013b), however, found no evidence to support conditional party government in his analysis of Speakers' perceived power, controlling for formal authority (or "tools"). Finally, Anzia and Jackman (2013) found that partisan polarization did not generally affect majority roll rates, which should be reduced by effective and firm majority leadership.

Several studies have also explored the related idea that the size of the majority might be a predictor of legislative leadership strength (or its complement, minority rights). This topic has also been a source of lively discussion in the congressional literature (Dion 1997; Schickler and Rich 1997; Cox and McCubbins 1997; Binder 1996; Schickler 2000). In the congressional setting, Dion (1997) argued that large majorities might be more generous to the minority because leadership and discipline become important when there are no votes to spare, while Binder (1996) argued that smaller or shrinking majorities might be more generous to the minority in the expectation of future generosity should they become the minority. Accordingly, there are plausible theoretical mechanisms by which majority size either increases or decreases Speaker strength. In practice, the empirical results in the states are mixed. Explicitly testing the effect of majority size on minority rights, Martorano (2004) found that majority size was associated with fewer minority rights in her sample of twenty-three states from 1955 to 1995. Similarly, Anzia and Jackman (2013) found that larger majorities experienced lower roll rates, which is consistent with large majorities, leading to strong Speakers. Mooney (2013b), on the other hand, found no effect of majority size. McGrath and Ryan (2014) examined state legislative chambers that were in a partisan tie and so had no majority party; their results were consistent with partisan deadlocks reducing the possibilities for effective leadership. Finally, Battista and Richman (2011) found that smaller majorities exerted a stronger effect on voting, consistent with large majorities leading to weaker Speakers.

Another element of the political context frequently examined in analyses of state legislative leadership is collective action problems or similar obstacles. If leadership offers a way out of collective action problems and social choice problems, then we ought to expect legislatures facing stronger problems to grant their leaders more power to constrain them. For example, we might expect higher diversity in most any relevant metric among the majority party to increase the frequency with which majority members have at least partially opposed goals. Jenkins (2008) found that high constituency diversity was associated with lower levels of party support in voting, indicative of reduced strength, but only for Democrats. Overcoming collective action problems and other challenges to the policy-making process was central to Richman's (2010) study, where he found that government intervention in the economy, the state's population, the number of lobbyists, and the number of legislators were all associated with more formally powerful Speakers, as was an index built from these variables. Battista and Richman (2011) used Richman's challenges index interacted with ideal point polarization and found that leaders (or at least parties) exert more force over voting when there are strong challenges and high polarization, but not otherwise. Mooney (2013b) refined Richman's argument and distinguished between state-level policy problems, such as diversity and unemployment, and organizational problems internal to the legislature, such as chamber size, turnover, and term limits. Mooney found that state-level policy problems generally were not associated with perceived power when controlling for formal authority, but that internal organizational problems were, with the exception of majority size, firmly associated with stronger Speakers.

The Temporal Context

Finally, another relevant context is the nature of the times. In general, analysis using time has been much more common for governors or gubernatorial–legislative relations than for internal legislative leadership. This difference presumably reflects the simple fact that the deep bill data, vote data, and related data such as estimated ideal points are only now coming online for extended periods; the literature on legislative leadership has been overwhelmingly cross-sectional. One element of time is what might be called political time—where in their terms the relevant actors are, especially when they are term limited, or when during a legislative session some action is taking place. Political time is clearly central to Kousser and Phillips's (2012) work because their theory posits that interactions around the budget are driven by impatience. Kousser and Phillips argued that governors should be at their most patient about budgetary matters when in their last year in office, at least if term limits render them ineligible to run again, because they can face no realistic political consequences even if no budget passes, and found substantial empirical support. In contrast, however, Ferguson (2003) found that governors were less successful overall in their last year. There are of course other elements of the temporal context that can be relevant to gubernatorial–legislative relations. Perhaps most obvious is the state of the economy and/or the fiscal situation of the state, which we would expect to be related. The overall findings here are consistent and unsurprising. Governors get more of what they ask for when economic times are good and/or when the state is doing well financially (Dilger, Krause, and Moffett 1995; Kousser and Phillips 2012; Ferguson 2003). On the purely legislative front, Clark's (2012) finding that termed-out legislators seem less willing to vote the party line on procedural matters, referenced earlier, can also be understood as a temporal effect.

The overall findings with respect to context mirror those for institutions. Here there are clear effects for governors, and indeed models whose emphasis is on time and patience as a context for leadership (Kousser and Phillips 2012). Except as the necessary other side of the coin—if governors are better able to get what they ask for, at least in budgetary matters, in their last terms, it follows that the legislature must be less able to drive a hard bargain then—time seems to play less of a role with legislative leadership. Similarly, several studies have found important effects for the personal skills and traits of governors, while this topic has not, in the recent past, received any firmly grounded empirical analysis for legislative leaders. As with institutions, looking to the states allows inferences that would be impossible or difficult with purely federal-level analysis and exposes new nuance that should be amenable to examination. For example, in their study of party/leadership pressure in the House, Ansolabehere, Snyder, and Stewart (2001) found that party pressure was more common in close votes, which they interpreted as strategic use of party pressure. That is, why keep exerting pressure over representatives when the leaders know that the results are already safely in the bag? In contrast, Battista and Richman (2011) found that while there were statistical effects on close votes, party or leadership pressure was strongest on votes that were party-line votes or close to the party line. This is obvious after the fact: if leaders have manipulated the legislative process or the content of bills to help ensure desired outcomes, rather than offering side payments to individual legislators, the resulting final passage votes should be close to party-line votes. However, the distinction between close votes and party-line votes had never been made in the congressional literature for the obvious reason that in the recent past party-line votes were also close votes. In contrast, in state legislatures party-line votes might have margins near zero or of fifty points. This distinction also leads to further work that has yet to be performed. We might expect leaders to expend the most effort on passage on those bills that are both significant and expected, absent leadership effort, to result in a close vote. That is, we should see party or leadership effects on those votes that would have been close. While examining counterfactuals is always difficult, this could in principle be approached at the federal level using Evans's (2012) data on whip counts, though (to my knowledge) whip count data do not yet exist for state legislatures.

Problems, Questions, and the Potential for Theoretical Development

A final way in which looking to the states can help us better understand leadership is that the problems or questions raised from examination of the states can, at least in potential, lead to further theoretical development. I should be clear that this remains mostly in potential and that scholars of leadership in the states at present remain closely bound to the theoretical literatures from their federal analogs. Kousser and Phillips (2012), for example, share much of their base with Cameron's (2000) work. In the legislative subfield, many of the works on state legislatures speak more to the congressional literature than to the other works on state legislatures, and my own work both individually and jointly is no exception.[6] Battista and Richman (2011), for example, straightforwardly addressed Krehbiel's (1998) critique of work on congressional party leadership with data from the states, and did so using the methods Ansolabehere, Snyder, and Stewart (2011) used for Congress. Anzia and Jackman (2013) directly address Cox and McCubbins's (2005) legislative cartel theory, as does Clark (2012), and Martorano (2004) is in a stronger dialogue with the work on minority rights in the House than with arguments about state legislatures per se.

Here I will describe a problem or question revealed by the states and describe how it could potentially lead to theoretical development that will help us better understand leadership. I will not, however, offer a fully developed model. The underlying problem or question is that revealed by my own work and amplified by Mooney (2013b): legislative leaders' formal powers seem largely unrelated to the influence they wield over the chamber. When the South is excluded for data reliability concerns, formal authority and the majority leadership's average perceived power are correlated only at 0.186, and formal authority is correlated with power as perceived by legislators only at 0.086, and neither is statistically significant (Battista 2011). Likewise, in regression models, formal authority is not a statistically significant predictor of perceived power. These findings should be disturbing given the face validity of both measures. While no measure is immune to measurement error, Clucas's (2001) formal powers index was constructed using publicly available sources of high quality—either legislative clerks and leaders themselves or the Council of State Government's *Book of the States*. We should thus fully expect that it accurately captures which grants of formal authority a Speaker has received and which he or she has not. Similarly, it is hard to find a survey measure more simple and direct than simply asking legislators, "What do you think is the relative influence of the following actors in determining legislative outcomes in your chamber?"

Further, the problem here differs from the ways scholars of federal politics might deal with differences between formal authority and effective capacity to lead. At the federal level, scholars usually consider how actors can use tools or skills outside their formal powers to enhance their ability to lead; how presidents can influence Congress even though they only possess the formal authority to accept or reject bills after Congress passes them; or how Senate leaders can move beyond the relatively meager grant of formal authority given to them by that highly collegial chamber. In contrast, in state legislatures, we are forced to confront chambers where the rank and file have given their leader a far-reaching formal authority over most aspects of the legislative process, but nonetheless the leader is not seen as particularly influential. Squire and Hamm (2005) placed then-Speaker Dennis Hastert (R-IL) and early twentieth-century Speaker Joe Cannon (R-IL) on the same index of Speaker power as that used by Clucas (2001). Joe Cannon is widely regarded as the strongest Speaker in the history of the chamber, while Hastert is one of the moderately strong Speakers to hold office following the ideological sorting of the House and the Republican takeover in 1995. Only six Speakers had less formal authority than Hastert, while eleven had more formal authority than even Cannon.[7] It is quite common for state legislative leaders to have the formal authority to personally assign every member of the chamber, including minority party members, to committee, to have the personal authority to create and abolish committees, or to assign any bill to any committee irrespective of its formal jurisdiction.

What the states show us are leaders with wide grants of authority who are nonetheless perceived as less than influential, or leaders who are formally powerful but informally constrained. The question this raises—and this is one that should be amenable to theoretical development—is how and why informal constraints limit the actions of leaders—or, rather, how this constraint is shaped by institutional and contextual factors. The raw form that informal constraint of legislative leaders takes is relatively obvious: leaders who act in ways that their own copartisans find unacceptable are likely to cease to be leaders. Further, this is not an idle threat in the states. Lawrence Denney was removed as Speaker of the Idaho House in 2012, Tom Craddick was removed as Speaker of the Texas House in 2009, and in a related move, the minority Democrats successfully rolled the majority Republicans on the vote for the leadership of the Tennessee House.

For example, consider the basic outline of a simple model. Suppose a small legislature with an additional leader who does not vote but has an extreme ideal point, voting on a stream of randomly generated bills, with full and complete information. On any bill, the leader can do nothing, allowing a vote to proceed according to legislators' preferences; can use agenda-control tools to prevent the bill from coming to a vote, which imposes disutility on legislators who would have voted for it; or can use procedural tools and pressure to induce the bill to pass with a minimum winning coalition, which imposes disutility on those whose voting was insincere. Individual legislators might compare, after every bill, their expected utility with the current leader, their expected utility from a lottery over new leaders from the majority party, and their expected utility from a lottery over new leaders from the minority party, and act accordingly if their interests favor a new leader. Here I do not offer a proof, but it seems obvious that unless the leader has a very short time horizon, there will be some equilibria in which the leader restrains himself or herself enough such that the members of the majority party retain the leader, though we would expect the leader to extract most of the utility gains from this process.

A model along these lines might function as a model of leadership restraint in the US House. Even without adding details from the states, such a model might have something useful to add to current discussions of party leadership in the House. A concept of informal constraint appears in Rohde's (1991) discussion of conditional party government, in which leaders are expected to deploy their procedural tools only when there is substantial agreement within the party to do so. Similar concerns have only become more important as former Speaker John Boehner (R-OH) and current Speaker Ryan have struggled with the Tea Party contingent of their own party, but have generally been unwilling to use institutional tools to bypass them. For example, comparative statics derived from a fully explicated model might show how the distribution of preferences affects the ability of leaders to actually exert control over the legislative process, or equivalently how the distribution of preferences affects the ability of the majority's median voter to pull outcomes toward their ideal point. However, thinking about the basic outline of a model of constraint that was generated in the states adds more possibilities. In the states, for example, we might add an additional option to rank-and-file legislators: they might compare his or her current expected utility, the expected utility from a new majority party leader, the expected utility from a new leader from the minority, and the utility of simply leaving the chamber and regaining whatever utility stream they enjoyed before taking office. In the states, this additional option would be important, given the sometimes high levels of voluntary turnover in state legislatures. It also raises a new possibility for leaders: to treat some legislators so badly that they prefer to return to life as a private citizen. While such a choice would probably not be a realistic option for recent federal Speakers, it might be relevant to earlier Congresses when US House service was far from the pinnacle of most politicians' opportunity structures. Along similar lines, we would expect term-limited legislative leaders to have short time horizons, along with their legislators, and could build models that illustrate how changes in the time horizon or discount rate affect the ability of leaders to effectively use the tools at their disposal.

All of which is to say that the informal constraint of leaders with strong formal authority is a topic that, while not totally ignored at the federal level, has not been modeled with any rigor. However, the constraint or self-constraint of leaders is an important part of leadership. Again, if we think of leadership as opposed to simple domination, then a true leader maintains some form of collective consent from those he or she is leading. This is especially true in the legislative or gubernatorial–legislative arenas, where leadership is over others who are formal equals rather than being actual subordinates. Looking to the states reveals data that force scholars of legislative leadership to directly confront the problem of leadership constraint, and do so in ways that lead to parts of theoretical models that might not be used in a purely congressional model.

Conclusions

In sum, scholars of leadership should consider looking at the states. Many of the aspects of leadership at the federal level are present in the states as well, except with a much larger number of cases. Governors and legislatures interact in, at base, a way similar to the president and Congress, and legislative leaders face the same underlying challenges and opportunities as do congressional leaders. Being spread across the fifty states, however, adds the opportunity to assess the generalizability of theories that do (or do not) seem to hold at the federal level. Looking to the states adds more than simple generalization tests. Variation in the relevant institutions allows the assessment of theories in ways that would be impossible at the federal level, and differences in data availability may result in even more improvement. Theories based on veto power, claims about a federal line-item veto or federal term limitation, and theories about party leadership in legislatures can all benefit from reexamination at the state level. In addition to variation in institutions, the relevant contexts in which institutions are emplaced also vary, allowing new empirical assessment of theories of leadership. Studies of leaders' personalities expand from already well-explored time series to cross sections, and in principle to time-series cross-sectional work, though the data requirements for such work remain daunting. Similarly, variation in political circumstances such as legislative majority size, divided government, or the current state of the economy allows researchers to better home in on the separate effects of both contexts and institutions. And finally, opening one's research to the states can reveal new data or other opportunities that can, at least in potential, lead to the development of new data.

Where and how should the study of state leadership develop? Here I concentrate on state legislatures, being reluctant to speak outside of my own research subfield. Scholars of legislative leadership should better understand the core concept of leadership as a complex object rather than as a single simple dimension where different operationalizations are more or less interchangeable with some noise, something already practiced by researchers on the executive branch. At least in the states, formal authority and perceived power do not seem to be just noisy versions of the same underlying dimension, and in the states we see nontrivial numbers of Speakers who are given wide, sweeping grants of authority that they are then expected not to use.

Here we need both theory and empirical analysis directed at understanding how Speakers with strong formal powers—again, sometimes stronger than Cannon—are restrained by less formal mechanisms, and what factors influence this constraint.

Empirically, a greater focus on operationalizing leadership strength ex post, by observing the effects of leadership, might be helpful. Note that this is again an area where executive branch scholars already act in this way, especially when studying executive–legislative relations. If we want to single out a single dimension of leadership, a good candidate is the ability to deflect outcomes toward your preferred positions, or away from the median voter and toward the median of the majority. Majority roll rates, as Anzia and Jackman (2013) examined, are an obvious way to examine this. One candidate for an empirical model is an interactive model where preference configurations and other elements of the political environment interact with the formal authority granted to the Speaker, similar to the approach taken by Mooney (2013b); another might be a multiequation system where these various forces act directly on outcomes and also through the Speakers' formal authority. Here Jackman's (2014) work is a clear step in the right direction.

References

Aldrich, John H., and David W. Rohde. 2000. "The Republican Revolution and the House Appropriations Committee." *Journal of Politics* 62:1–33.

Ansolabehere, Stephen, James M. Snyder Jr., and Charles Stewart III. 2001. "The Effects of Party and Preferences on Congressional Roll-Call Voting." *Legislative Studies Quarterly* 26:533–572.

Anzia, Sarah F., and Molly C. Jackman. 2013. "Legislative Organization and the Second Face of Power: Evidence from US State Legislatures." *Journal of Politics* 75:210–224.

Apollonio, D. E., and Raymond J. La Raja. 2006. "Term Limits, Campaign Contributions, and the Distribution of Power in State Legislatures." *Legislative Studies Quarterly* 31:259–281.

Barber, James David. 1985. *The Presidential Character: Predicting Performance in the White House.* Englewood Cliffs, NJ: Prentice-Hall.

Barrilleaux, Charles, and Michael Berkman. 2003. "Do Governors Matter? Budgeting Rules and the Politics of State Policymaking." *Political Research Quarterly* 56 (4): 409–417.

Battista, James Coleman. 2011. "Formal and Perceived Leadership Power in US State Legislatures." *State Politics and Policy Quarterly* 11:1–17.

Battista, James Coleman, and Jesse T. Richman. 2011. "Party Pressure in the US State Legislatures." *Legislative Studies Quarterly* 36:397–422.

Berry, William D., Richard C. Fording, Evan J. Ringquist, Russell L. Hanson, and Carl E. Klarner. 2010. "Measuring Citizen and Government Ideology in the US States: A Reappraisal." *State Politics and Policy Quarterly* 10:117–135.

Binder, Sarah A. 1996. "The Partisan Basis of Procedural Choice: Allocating Parliamentary Rights in the House, 1789–1990." *American Political Science Review* 90:8–20.

Cameron, Charles. 2000. *Veto Bargaining.* Cambridge: Cambridge University Press.

Carey, John M., Richard G. Niemi, and Lynda W. Powell. 1998. "The Effects of Term Limits on State Legislatures." *Legislative Studies Quarterly* 23 (2): 271–300.

Carey, John M., Richard G. Niemi, Lynda W. Powell, and Gary Moncrief. 2006. "The Effects of Term Limits on State Legislatures: A New Survey of the 50 States." *Legislative Studies Quarterly* 31 (1): 105–134.

Carsey, Thomas M., and Jeffrey J. Harden. 2010. "New Measures of Partisanship, Ideology, and Public Mood in the American States." *State Politics and Policy Quarterly* 10:136–156.

Clark, Jennifer Hayes. 2012. "Examining Parties as Legislative Cartels: Evidence from the US States." *Legislative Studies Quarterly* 37:491–507.

Clucas, Richard A. 2001. "Principal–Agent Theory and the Power of State House Speakers." *Legislative Studies Quarterly* 26:319–338.

———. 2007. "Legislative Professionalism and the Power of State House Leaders." *State Politics and Policy Quarterly* 7 (1): 1–19.

Coase, Ronald H. 1937. "The Nature of the Firm." *Economica* 4:386–405.

Cox, Gary W., Thad Kousser, and Mathew D. McCubbins. 2010. "Party Power or Preferences? Quasi-Experimental Evidence from American State Legislatures." *Journal of Politics* 72:799–811.

Cox, Gary W., and Mathew McCubbins. 1997. "Toward a Theory of Legislative Rules Changes: Assessing Schickler and Rich's Evidence." *American Journal of Political Science* 41:1376–1386.

———. 2005. *Setting the Agenda: Responsible Party Government in the US House of Representatives.* Cambridge: Cambridge University Press.

Crew, Robert E., and Christopher Lewis. 2011. "Verbal Style, Gubernatorial Strategies, and Legislative Success." *Political Psychology* 32:623–642.

Dilger, Robert Jay, George A. Krause, and Randolph R. Moffett. 1995. "State Legislative Professionalism and Gubernatorial Effectiveness." *Legislative Studies Quarterly* 20:553–571.

Dion, Douglas. 1997. *Turning the Legislative Thumbscrews: Minority Rights and Procedural Change in Legislative Politics.* Ann Arbor: University of Michigan Press.

Dometrius, Nelson C., and Deil S. Wright. 2010. "Governors, Legislatures, and State Budgets across Time." *Political Research Quarterly* 63:783–795.

Erikson, Robert S., Gerald C. Wright, and John P. McIver. 1993. *Statehouse Democracy: Public Opinion and Policy in the American States.* Cambridge: Cambridge University Press.

Evans, C. Lawrence. 2012. *Congressional Whip Count Database.* College of William and Mary, January 2012.

Ferguson, Margaret Robertson. 2003. "Chief Executive Success in the Legislative Arena." *State Politics and Policy Quarterly* 3:158–182.

Ferguson, Margaret R., and Jay Barth. 2002. "Governors in the Legislative Arena: The Importance of Personality in Shaping Success." *Political Psychology* 23:787–808.

Grofman, Bernard, and Neil Sutherland. 1996. "The Effect of Term Limits When Competition Is Completely Endogenized." In *Legislative Term Limits: Public Choice Perspectives,* edited by Bernard Grofman, 175–182. Boston: Kluwer.

Jackman, Molly C. 2014. "Parties, Median Legislators, and Agenda Setting: How Legislative Institutions Matter." *Journal of Politics* 76:259-272.

Jenkins, Shannon. 2008. "Party Influence on Roll-Call Voting: A View from the US States." *State Politics and Policy Quarterly* 8 (3): 239-262.

Jewell, Malcolm E., and Marcia Lynn Whicker. 1994. *Legislative Leadership in the American States.* Ann Arbor: University of Michigan Press.

Kousser, Thad, and Justin Phillips. 2012. *The Power of American Governors.* Cambridge: Cambridge University Press.

Krehbiel, Keith. 1998. *Pivotal Politics.* Chicago: University of Chicago Press.

Krupnikov, Yanna, and Charles Shipan. 2012. "Measuring Gubernatorial Budgetary Power: A New Approach." *State Politics and Policy Quarterly* 12:438-455.

Martorano, Nancy. 2004. "Cohesion or Reciprocity? Majority Party Strength and Minority Party Procedural Rights in the Legislative Process." *State Politics and Policy Quarterly* 4:55-73.

McGrath, Robert J., Jon C. Rogowski, and Josh M. Ryan. 2015. "Gubernatorial Veto Powers and the Size of Legislative Coalitions." *Legislative Studies Quarterly* 40:571-598.

McGrath, Robert J., and Josh M. Ryan. 2014. "Even Money: Tied Chambers, Power Sharing, and Party Effects in Legislatures." Paper presented at the annual State Politics and Policy Conference, Bloomington, IN.

Miller, Susan M., Jill Nicholson-Crotty, and Sean Nicholson-Crotty. 2011. "Reexamining the Institutional Effects of Term Limits in US State Legislatures." *Legislative Studies Quarterly* 36:71-98.

Mooney, Christopher Z. 2013a. "Explaining Legislative Leadership Influence: Simple Collective Action or Conditional Explanations?" *Political Research Quarterly* 66:559-571.

——. 2013b. "Measuring State House Speakers' Formal Powers, 1980-2010." *State Politics and Policy Quarterly* 13:262-273.

Neustadt, Richard. 1960. *Presidential Power.* New York: Free Press.

North, Douglass C. 1990. *Institutions, Institutional Change, and Economic Performance.* Cambridge: Cambridge University Press.

Poole, Keith, and Nolan McCarty. 1995. "Veto Power and Legislation." *Journal of Law, Economics, and Organization* 11:282-312.

Richman, Jesse T. 2010. "The Logic of Legislative Leadership." *Legislative Studies Quarterly* 35:211-233.

Riker, William H. 1986. *The Art of Political Manipulation.* New Haven, CT: Yale University Press.

Rohde, David W. 1991. *Parties and Leaders in the Postreform House.* Chicago: University of Chicago Press.

Schickler, Eric. 2000. "Institutional Change in the House of Representatives, 1867-1998: A Test of Partisan and Ideological Power Balance Models." *American Political Science Review* 94:269-288.

Schickler, Eric, and Andrew Rich. 1997. "Controlling the Floor: Parties as Procedural Coalitions in the House." *American Journal of Political Science* 41:1340-1375.

Squire, Peverill. 1992. "Legislative Professionalism and Membership Diversity in State Legis-latures." *Legislative Studies Quarterly* 17 (1): 69–79.

Squire, Peverill, and Keith E. Hamm. 2005. *101 Chambers: Congress, State Legislatures, and the Future of Legislative Studies.* Columbus: Ohio State University Press.

Walker, Jack L. 1969. "The Diffusion of Innovations in the American States." *American Political Science Review* 63:880–899.

Notes

1. We might also consider leadership between states. That is, some states tend to innovate or lead in policy, while others follow or never adopt the policy. Following Walker's (1969) study of innovation and diffusion, this literature has blossomed into a large and rich field of study in its own right. Because I lack room to consider both innovation and diffusion, and intrastate leadership, and because every policy adoption contains within it a story of state-level leadership (or its absence), I will not further discuss the diffusion literature.

2. There are many of these, such as Cameron's (2000) prominent analysis, but I do not refer to any specific existing theory.

3. To my knowledge, this specifically has not yet been done, though McGrath, Rogowski, and Ryan (2015) showed that the introduction of the veto was associated with larger winning coalitions in the legislature.

4. Which can include not vetoing their pet bills.

5. Term limits for governors are not universal and are usually incorporated into measures of the governor's institutional powers, as in Beyle (1968).

6. Consider the many pieces subtitled "Evidence from the States" or similar.

7. In fairness to Cannon's memory, he falls short primarily because he did not control a campaign committee, which would have been less relevant in the early 1900s. Apart from that, he would rank among the most powerful state legislative Speakers.

PART THREE

Assessing Leadership in American Politics

CHAPTER TEN

Leadership

A Definition

William G. Howell and Stephane Wolton

A leader, like an institution or culture, is typically understood in its instantiated rather than its essential form. We are reasonably confident that Congress, marriage, and the stock market are institutions, even though we are not especially sure what exactly defines an institution. Hip-hop, Coco Chanel, and Dada all express aspects of culture, while culture itself remains elusive. And so it is with leaders. We are confident that Adolf Hitler, Martin Luther King Jr., and Mao Tse-tung count in the category. Though we may not admire them all, we recognize that each indisputably was a leader. Still, as a purely conceptual matter, we know very little about what distinguishes these three men from other agents of social change.

There exists, of course, a massive body of work on leadership. The vast preponderance of such scholarship, however, focuses on what leaders do, what traits they exhibit, and what modes of persuasion they use. We see them in motion, fully formed, exercising influence and attracting plaudits. The expressed purpose of this sort of scholarship is to unearth the personal qualities and styles of leadership (Greenstein 2004; George and George 1998); assess the capacity of leaders to refashion the environments in which they work (Burns 2004; Edwards 2009; Hargrove 1989); fit leaders within broader theories of democratic representation by distinguishing, for instance, delegates from trustees (Jacobs and Shapiro 2000); catalog the biographies of individuals we all would consider leaders (highlights include Robert Caro's magisterial works on Lyndon Johnson and Edmund Morris's on Theodore Roosevelt); and identify the structural conditions under which leaders exercise more or less influence (Skowronek 1997).

Rarely, though, does this research pause and define its terms. It speaks elliptically about leadership, making the class of individuals it wishes to call leaders opaque and undifferentiated. As Morris Fiorina and Kenneth Shepsle (1989, 17) recognized a quarter century ago, most studies of leadership are, from a theoretical standpoint, "neither precise nor reliable," and the overall literature on the topic is sufficiently fragmented that "few formal deductive treatments of the subject have emerged." Or as John Alquist and Margaret Levi (2011, 3) argue in a literature review, "The theoretical understanding of the causal importance of leadership is still fairly impoverished," in no small part because the concept of leadership itself is "vague" and "contested." Our definitions of leaders are akin to definitions of dogs as animals with four legs. They are accurate as far as they go, but they do not go nearly far enough.

This volume constitutes an important corrective to this state of affairs. The chapters herein help us understand when leaders succeed, when they fail, and the various contextual environments—bureaucratic, legislative, judicial, and executive— in which they work. We see the particular challenges that congressional leaders, agency leaders, and executive leaders face, as well as the strategies that they must use to overcome them.

Still, we often are left to wonder what makes these women and men leaders rather than, say, managers, organizers, statesmen, or everyday politicians. Thus in this chapter we try to add some conceptual clarity to the discussion. We do so in two steps. First, we characterize, rather axiomatically, basic criteria that any definition of leadership must satisfy. Then, after illustrating some of the deficiencies of existing definitions, we present our own. In it, we suggest that a leader distinguishes herself by the objectives that she extols; the followers who not only revere her but who also willingly take actions that advance these objectives; and the ways in which she comes to personify these objectives. To be a leader, all of these conditions must be met. Should any one of these criteria not be satisfied, an individual, no matter how influential, relinquishes her status as leader.

From the outset, we want to be clear about our own objectives for this chapter. We do not seek to explain how one can reliably identify leaders in the material world. We have little to say about the very real challenges of detection, except insofar as we distill a minimal understanding of what one ought to look for.[1] We also do not evaluate the impacts of leaders on the real world. We do not argue that leadership is indispensable for the realization of social order; nor do we require that the actions of leaders and their followers are in any sense "good." Our objectives are more circumscribed than all of this.

We hope to provide some conceptual clarity about the meaning of leadership, and to do so, we offer a definition of leadership. We make no pretense that ours is the only definition worthy of its name. But we do think that ours, more than most, satisfies the prerequisites of leadership, and for that reason alone may do some good.

Definitional Criteria

Given the pervasive lack of conceptual clarity about leadership, along with the pervasive sense, which we share, that leaders constitute vital, though not unique, agents of social change, it is worth pausing for a moment before offering a formal definition. We now distill some basic criteria that any definition—including our own—must satisfy. We offer five (Table 10.1), three of which are conceptual in nature and two of which concern their empirical regularities. These criteria are deliberately cast in general terms to allow for the possibility that leaders, like those considered in this volume, work in diverse professions and contexts.

We begin with the conceptual criteria (Table 10.1, left column). The first requires that leadership be understood in relational terms. As Eric Beerbohm (2015, 639) observes, leadership is a "relational property between one agent and a set of agents." Leaders are not leaders for the traits that they exhibit or the authority—formal or otherwise—that they possess. People are not born leaders. Nor do they become leaders through some training regimen or by studying the habits of past leaders. Nor do they acquire the status of leader simply by virtue of their election or assignment to some post. Rather, leaders become leaders because of the relationships that they foster and maintain with followers. It is through the relationships with followers that they cultivate, and the unique opportunities of influence that subsequently arise, that leadership presents itself. Any definition of leadership as such must recognize and then characterize the relationships between leaders and followers.

Second, a definition of leader makes at least one normative distinction about the publicly expressed ends that leaders seek. Rather than accepting any and all ends and focusing exclusively on means, a definition of leadership must have something to say about the purposes to which it is put. It need not distinguish good from bad ends (though it may). Nor need it require that leaders pursue moral objectives rather than immoral ones (though it might). All that we require is that the definition eschew agnosticism and embrace partiality. Intrinsic to the definition itself must be some bounds on the variable goals that intermittently motivate leaders and that find their translation into action through the actions of followers.

Table 10.1. Definitional Criteria

Conceptual Criteria	Empirical Criteria
Relationality	Exceptionality
Normative distinction	Publicity
Exclusivity	

Third, a definition of leadership must distinguish leaders from other agents of change, such as statesmen, martyrs, tyrants, or organizers. Too often, leaders represent anyone who advances social change. As a consequence, leadership—the essential task of leaders—becomes synonymous with power, influence, or office holding. But to meet this criterion, a definition of leadership cannot be so capacious as to apply to anyone who exercises influence, captures public attention, sits in a position of authority, or has the word "leader" in her job title, as many of the individuals surveyed in this volume do. Rather, the definition must identify a bounded subset of people operating in a clear subset of contexts and times.[2] Conceptually, the definition must isolate those individuals nurturing those relationships that uniquely apply to leaders and that manifest as leadership. In so doing, it must cede conceptual space to other definitions that characterize other agents of social change.

The final two criteria reference empirical regularities about leadership (Table 10.1, second column). The first follows from the third conceptual criterion and concerns the exceptional nature of leadership. Leaders are rare, just as leadership is precarious. Few individuals ever become leaders, and even among those who do, the status of leader is never assured. Definitions that seek to democratize the incidence of leadership—insisting that we all have the potential to be leaders, or that we all, in one domain of life or another, exercise leadership—invariably miss what sets Lincoln, King, and Mao apart not only from the rest of humanity but from the subset of individuals who expressly seek to change the world we inhabit. Similarly, definitions that cast individuals as perennial leaders overlook leadership's fleeting nature. If leadership can be won, it also can be lost. As we shall see, the conditions that support its exercise are sufficiently tenuous that leadership all too often eludes those who seek it.

Finally, leaders are known. Rather than skulking in the shadows or organizing behind closed doors, leaders, whether anointed or ordained, stand before their public. Leaders do not merely facilitate change. They come to embody change, and they do so for all to see. Followers, as followers, may gain recognition for their sacrifices; but leaders, as leaders, cannot escape recognition. There are no hidden leaders. Leadership is not exercised behind the scenes. Rather, leaders perform in the light of day. For their part, followers beckon and laud not just the chosen ends of leadership but the leaders themselves. Leaders not only speak to a public, they themselves are public.

These five criteria establish what we expect of any definition of leadership. To be sure, an insistence that leaders be understood in relational terms, accommodate specific kinds of ends, differ conceptually from other agents of change, and, as an empirical matter, be rare and public leaves ample room for competing definitions. But fail any one, as plenty do, and a definition of leadership runs aground.[3]

Existing Definitions

Without pausing to clarify what they mean by leadership, scholars too often proceed straight to delineating the qualities that individual leaders supposedly exhibit. Still, the literature is not entirely bereft of definitions. Broadly speaking, such definitions tend to fall into one of three categories: consequentialist, functionalist, and essentialist. While definitions within all categories have their strengths, most, though not all, violate at least one of our evaluative criteria.

Consequentialist Definitions

Scholars often define leaders by the extraordinary actions that they take. Leaders see a higher purpose or possibility that is lost on others, and they then take action, often at great risk and sacrifice, in the service of that purpose. Consequences, then, function as a sort of litmus test for leadership, separating true from faux leaders. While plenty of people claim to be leaders, and plenty more resemble leaders, genuine leaders brandish their credentials by taking—or perhaps more accurately, instigating the taking of—extraordinary actions.[4]

James Read and Ian Shapiro (2014) provide a recent example. They celebrate the work of leaders who see conflicts as positive sum, where others see only zero-sum outcomes, then take the rather extraordinary step of strengthening the bargaining position of their adversary in order to demonstrate "hope for a positive future," albeit at great personal risk. Leaders distinguish themselves by realizing outcomes that, under standard norms and protocols of political engagement, would seem impossible. By defying normal principles of bargaining arrangements, Read and Shapiro's leaders break through impasses and realize mutually beneficial outcomes. Leadership, by this definition, clearly satisfies both of the empirical criteria: exceptionality and publicity. The empathy and self-sacrifice required of Read and Shapiro's leaders certainly make them exceptional, and the "performative ingredient" of their labors puts them squarely in the public spotlight. Moreover, to the extent that it focuses on the mutual gains to be realized between warring states, their definition also satisfies the second conceptual criterion: the distinction between objectives.

It is on the first and third conceptual criteria that this definition founders. Leaders are not intrinsically defined by the relations that they hold with followers. Rather, successful leaders are ones who cultivate certain kinds of relations with their adversaries. Moreover, leaders under this definition are not obviously different from other individuals—statesmen, for instance—who also settle conflict. The word "leader" functions as a generic type of ruler. To qualify as a leader, one must overcome a specific kind of impasse, and it does not matter so much what relationship one holds (if any) with followers or whether the achievement is realized by edict or suasion.

Functionalist Definitions

Whereas consequentialist definitions emphasize the accomplishments of leaders, functionalist definitions focus on their actions. The two are obviously linked, for it is through actions that consequences arise. The distinction thus concerns matters of emphasis. Whereas consequentialist definitions establish standards for what leaders must accomplish, functionalist definitions focus primarily on the specific role performed by leaders and the actions that they take within a political or social ecosystem.

In this regard, several recent papers in formal theory are particularly instructive (Dewan and Myatt 2008, 2012; Bolton, Veldkamp, and Brunnermeier 2010). Leaders, within this literature, perform the task of orienting and coordinating the actions of followers in view of a common goal. The great advance of this literature is to take seriously how a leader induces followers to act. Followers want to take correct actions, but they also want to act in common purpose. As such, tensions may arise between direction and coordination. Followers prefer a leader who indicates clearly the direction to follow (either because she speaks clearly or because she believes strongly in a cause) to a leader who exhibits good judgment. Contrary to the intuition of many scholars (Keohane 2010), good judgment is not the most essential quality for leaders. The definition advanced in this literature, however, applies as much to individuals we recognize as leaders as to any person in charge of a team.[5]

In no small part because of its analytic clarity, the definition of leadership that emerges from this literature clearly satisfies the first and third conceptual criteria, the first by denoting a clear relationship between leaders and would-be followers and the third by identifying the precise functions that leaders, and only leaders, perform. In a purely technical sense, the definition also satisfies the second empirical criterion. In all of the models, the identity of leaders and the possible actions that they can take are known to the other players. Nothing about this definition, however, requires that leaders be rare, the first empirical criterion. Furthermore, this definition does not distinguish among the many objectives that a leader may pursue. The cause advanced by a leader can be anything from a mundane objective such as winning an election (a leading example in Dewan and Myatt 2008) to the most grandiose goal (such as coordinating a march on Washington, DC, for racial justice). This definition thus fails our second conceptual criterion.

Essentialist Definitions

Rather than characterize what leaders accomplish or do, essentialist definitions try to make sense of what leaders are. A considerable body of scholarship—not to mention piles of self-help books—seeks to discern the core values that leaders hold, the skills that they use, and the postures that they assume. In so doing, some of these studies are intended to counsel us, their audience, on how we too might become leaders.

The paradigmatic essentialist definition of leadership comes from Weber (1947), according to whom a "charismatic" leader exhibits a "certain quality of an individual personality, by virtue of which he is set apart from ordinary men and treated as endowed with supernatural, superhuman, or at least specifically exceptional powers or qualities. These are such as are not accessible to the ordinary person, but are regarded as of divine origin or as exemplary, and on the basis of them the individual concerned is treated as a leader." It is the qualities that charismatic leaders have, much more than the specific acts they perform or the accomplishments they achieve, that make them leaders. Endowed with "supernatural" and "superhuman" powers, charismatic leaders plainly are exceptional.[6] Moreover, Weber recognizes, the retention of charisma can be fleeting, making charismatic leadership itself not only precarious but, as he puts it, "unstable."[7] Weber's definition thus plainly satisfies our first empirical criterion of leadership. It satisfies the second in insisting that leaders cultivate and retain a followership that recognizes the unique qualities of a charismatic leader. Recognition, in Weber's formulation, requires publicity, for the leader's "charismatic claim breaks down if his mission is not recognized by those to whom he feels he has been sent" ([1946] 1948, 20). The simple fact that charismatic leaders, by definition, have followers also satisfies the relational criterion, while the attention paid to the unique skills and qualities of leadership distinguish charismatic leaders from Weber's legal and traditional authorities.

Least developed, though not entirely missing, in Weber's definition is any recognition of the various ends of leadership. Treatment of the subject, to the extent that it exists, appears in the larger corpus of Weber's work. For Weber, charisma is a great deal more than just style or panache. Leaders are "regarded as of divine origin or as exemplary" because they themselves communicate "divine" and "exemplary" ends. To establish their status as charismatic leaders, therefore, they must perform "miracles" and "heroic deeds." Such acts, then, must support ends that will evoke the requisite awe and inspiration among followers. The qualities that leaders exhibit are in this sense linked to the ends they serve. Charismatic leaders, according to this reading of Weber, distinguish themselves by their unique capacity to translate distinctly charismatic ends.

Reading Weber more narrowly, however, it is possible to come to the opposite conclusion. Formally, Weber does not require charismatic leaders to pursue certain kinds of objectives and eschew others. Indeed, for the purposes of definition, Weber expresses general indifference toward the objectives that charismatic leaders pursue. Again, all that is required is a shared evocation of awe. It is precisely for this reason that Weber casts his attention nearly exclusively on the attributes of charismatic leaders, the spell that they cast on their followers, and the devotion that follows. The main purpose of followers, in Weber's sociology, is to legitimate charismatic leaders and the formal authority that they exercise. Followers, in this construction, are largely passive, and the relationship between followers and the leader is limited and nearly always one-sided, a point to which we return below.

Depending on which reading one finds more persuasive—and scholars of Weber differ on this account—one draws very different conclusions about whether his definition satisfies the normative distinction criterion of leadership. The consequences of this judgment, as we discuss at greater length below, relate to the population of definitions that speak to the essential meanings of leadership.

Hybrid Definitions

Distinctions among consequentialist, functionalist, and essentialist definition are usually ones of emphasis rather than omission. In any one, we often find elements of the others. What sets a definition apart is typically what its author chooses to place at its center. Even so, not all definitions permit such categorization. Consider, for instance, Nannerl Keohane's (2010, 19) observation that leaders "provid[e] solutions to common problems or offer[] ideas about to how accomplish collective purposes, and mobiliz[e] the energies of others to follow these courses of action."[8] In this definition, we understand leaders by reference to both the things that they accomplish (collective purposes) and the functions that they serve (mobilize energies of others). Moreover, Keohane goes on to emphasize the particular qualities that leaders, both on the basis of her study as a political theorist and her experience as a university president, tend to exhibit, above all judgment.

Keohane's (2010) definition clearly satisfies the relational criteria, as leaders are understood by reference to their relationship with followers. While she does not explicitly carve out a well-defined subset of possible objectives that leaders might serve, in her examples, Keohane also has in mind purposes that are, in some sense, worthy of public emulation. As a definition of leadership, however, Keohane's plainly fails on both empirical criteria and the third conceptual criterion. Under her definition, nearly anyone can be a leader. Thus, in her treatment of the subject, she intermittently recognizes the leadership qualities of everyone—presidents, friends, university administrators—as being leaders. Moreover, her definition does not require that her leaders be publicly recognized. Midlevel managers and community organizers both find their place under this definition. Finally, and relatedly, the definition is so capacious that it does not permit distinctions between leaders from the many other agents of change. In her efforts to recognize the pervasive need for leadership, Keohane misses what is conspicuous, exceptional, and distinctive about leaders.

A New Definition

Having briefly surveyed some existing definitions of leadership, we now offer our own:

> *A Leader publicly defines, extols, and eventually personifies higher objectives, thereby orienting and coordinating the efforts of followers who seek to advance such objectives.*

The definition, you'll notice, is cast in general terms. It makes no mention of the specific feats that Leaders must accomplish and hence does not join company with other consequentialist definitions. Nor does it stipulate the specific traits that Leaders have and thus forgoes essentialist understandings. In identifying things that Leaders and their followers do, the definition most closely resembles functionalist arguments. But even so, it offers no mention of the exact acts that Leaders take, the precise appeals they make, the powers they exercise, or the styles they adopt.

Still, the definition has real content. A Leader, thus stipulated, is revealed in four parts. The first identifies the class of objectives that a Leader defines, the second characterizes the Leader's dependence on followers to advance those objectives, the third recognizes the Leader's personification of those objectives, and the fourth distinguishes the mere "leader" from "Leader." Each warrants some elaboration.

Objectives

As pure types, we consider two classes of objectives that agents of change may pursue. The first, which we call lower ends, concerns an individual's immediate and often material self-interests—personal enrichment, fame, political survival, and the like. The second type, which we call higher ends, concerns larger objectives that stand apart from any individual—justice, nationalism, country, and the like. These are ends that persist, even flourish, in the absence of any single individual. Such ends, as Weber ([1917] 2004, 30) puts it, contribute "something of enduring value to a suprapersonal realm." Whereas lower ends are person specific, higher ends are impersonal. It is higher ends that Leaders define, extol, and personify.

Higher and lower ends should not be confused with John Stuart Mill's (1969) distinction between higher and lower pleasure. Mill sought to distinguish activities that, by virtue of their intrinsic qualities, evoked qualitatively different types of pleasure. For him, those that entertained higher faculties (e.g., the intellect, imagination, and moral sensibilities) were of greater value than those that engaged one's lower (i.e., purely physical) senses. The distinction we wish to draw, by contrast, principally concerns the relationship between an objective and the person who advocates it; and, more specifically, the integrity of an objective apart from any individual who speaks on its behalf. No matter what faculties it entertains, no matter what pleasures it renders, an objective cannot be considered higher if it exclusively relates to the personal welfare of a would-be Leader.

Higher ends may satisfy what G. A. Cohen (1991, 280) calls the "impersonal test," but they need not. Such a test is expressly intended to evaluate the robustness of an argument on behalf of a particular policy by different combinations of speakers and audiences. If the perceived merits of the policy depend on the identity of either the speaker or audience, then, says Cohen, it fails the impersonal test. To be sure, arguments about lower ends necessarily fail such a test, for the very meaning of such ends depends on the identity of its sponsor. One can imagine ends, though, that fail the impersonal test but that nonetheless count among higher ends. Arguments about the greatness of country, of course, assume different hues depending on the country discussed and the citizenship of the sponsor and her audience. Such arguments plainly fail the impersonal test. The fact that such arguments have meaning and integrity apart from the sponsor is all that is required in order for them to count among higher ends.

Likewise, higher ends may count among the charismatic qualities that Weber says leaders exhibit. Such qualities, for Weber, are largely irreducible in form, and as Edward Shils (1965, 199) notes, they reveal "some *very central* feature of man's existence and the cosmos in which he lives." But as with Cohen's impersonal test, Shils's interpretation of Weber may set too high a benchmark for leadership qualities, excluding more distant and material objectives that nonetheless count among higher ends—the elimination of malaria or the practice of female genital mutilation, for instance. Higher ends may reveal something essential about the human condition or its principled aspirations, but they need not. All that matters is that the ends reside, and hence can be understood, outside of the Leader who espouses them.

Weber's ([1946] 1948, 24) own insistence that charismatic leaders renounce "rationalist deductions from abstract principles" may rule out other sorts of higher ends. Leaders, under our definition, may channel the divine, but they need not. In the service of higher ends, Leaders may espouse and extol distinctly rational principles that bear no resemblance to Weber's charismatic qualities.

A Leader also may derive personal pleasure and fulfillment in the pursuit of higher ends. A Leader's commitment to higher ends need not be selfless. Leaders, like all of us, have egos, and their egos surely influence both their selection and understanding of objectives. Further, Leaders may materially benefit from the realization of higher ends. The Leader's wealth, status, or power may be enhanced through the work of followers who work steadily on behalf of higher ends. Once again, though, the distinction that matters is that higher ends can be understood on their own terms, apart from the person who advocates them, whereas lower ends necessarily and unavoidably implicate their sponsor. Our definition merely requires that a Leader's enrichment is incidental to the work of followers, rather than the central objective.

To illustrate the point, consider Martin Luther King Jr.'s professed commitment to racial justice and the welfare of African Americans and other minorities. To be sure, King's notoriety and personal wealth were enhanced by the work of his followers. These, however, were not the higher ends that King defined, extolled, and eventually personified. King spoke on behalf of a promised land of racial and economic justice; that promised land shone just as brightly whether he himself made it there. Indeed, as he presciently told his followers, he expected not to do so. It is precisely for this reason that King's objectives counted among higher ends. King's higher ends could be understood apart from himself. In his absence, they nonetheless had integrity and meaning.

In no way is the distinction between higher and lower ends, however, meant to connote any sort of normative endorsement. It is perfectly possible that an individual's lower ends warrant plaudits when a Leader's higher ends elicit justified abhorrence. The dominance of the Aryan race or the glory of nation qualify as higher objectives, just as a family's efforts to pull themselves out of poverty or a wife's interest in fleeing an abusive husband count among lower ends. What matters instead is the relationship between the objective and its sponsor. Objectives that can be understood without reference to the needs, wants, or egoistic aspirations of the sponsor constitute higher ends. Lower ends, by contrast, cannot be understood except by reference to the individual who holds them.

Our characterization of higher ends, as such, is capacious. While ruling out strictly personal—read, egoistic and self-serving—objectives, it keeps in play many objectives that would not satisfy normative standards, including consciously impersonal ones, such as John Rawls's difference principle.

Followers

People cannot be Leaders unless they have followers. While there exists a large class of rulers, including statesmen, who may exercise power to directly translate objectives into outcomes,[9] Leaders belong to the adjacent class of entrepreneurs who depend on followers to do their bidding. The Leader cannot simply assert her will, exercise her power, issue a command, and expect the world to change. Rather, she must look to her followers to take actions that realize outcomes corresponding with her higher ends.

What is it that followers do? They do not merely applaud, celebrate, or worship their Leader. The entertainer who returns to the stage for a third standing ovation is not exercising Leadership. Nor is the celebrity whose every move is meticulously tracked and documented by a roving paparazzi. Nor is the public figure whose Twitter feed has millions of followers. That others are interested in what you say or do does not in itself establish a basis for Leadership.

Followers do not merely track their Leader. Though they may monitor their

Leader, draw insight and inspiration from her, and come to understand their purposes through her, followers subsequently must pivot and take actions of their own that accord with their Leader's directives. Having sat before their Leader, they then must stand and do something that advances a Leader's expressed objectives. Fans become followers when they commit private resources—time, energy, money, and the like—that are consonant with their Leader's directions. To follow a Leader is to give of one's resources in order to advance higher objectives that are expressly understood through the Leader.

Followers, as a consequence, stand between a Leader and her goals. It is through the collective activities of followers that a Leader makes a difference in the world. It is through followers that a Leader's objective is advanced. Without followers, nothing is accomplished that can be meaningfully attributed to Leadership.[10]

In this regard, our definition differs dramatically from Weber's. Weber, to be sure, recognizes a role for followers, seeing their existence as a prerequisite for the exercise of leadership. But that is about as far as he goes. For Weber, the relationship between charismatic Leaders and followers is decidedly one-sided. The bulk of Weber's sociology, after all, is devoted to examining how charismatic leadership becomes routinized into an organizational apparatus—how essentialist qualities of an individual leader become essentialist qualities of a state. Ours, by contrast, recognizes both the dependency and agency of followers. Followers depend on a Leader to define and extol higher ends. When such a Leader vanishes, the relationship between followers and these higher ends is deeply disrupted. However, by our definition, followers are not passive. Rather, they retain the capacity to act on their own. Followers, by our definition, are responsible for anointing a Leader, who in turn depends on followers in order to accomplish anything of consequence.

In their work to advance higher ends, however, followers must follow. They must abide their Leader's instructions. We would not call someone a Leader if her followers disregard her, even if they subsequently act in ways that do in fact advance her higher ends. Such a person amounts to a mere head. A Leader, by contrast, has followers who recognize and abide the content of her appeals, and who subsequently behave in ways that are consistent with her directions, no matter how misguided or harmful. Followers must "bow to the greater man," to paraphrase Joseph Goebbels's yearning soon after meeting Hitler in 1926 (Toland 1976, 217). When enough followers break ranks, openly disobey their Leader's commands, and commit themselves to new pathways to realize the very same higher ends that initially brought them together, the Leader's status as Leader is imperiled. When her followers cease to listen to her instructions, she ceases to be a Leader at all.

A Leader's instructions and a follower's actions need not be identical. What we must insist upon, however, is that the Leader holds the attention of her followers, and that these followers take their guidance from their Leader. An impartial observer ought to be able to see some fidelity between a Leader's instructions and a follower's action. Such an observer may be appalled by the actions, just as she may be convinced that the Leader is a fraud. The key test, though, is whether this observer witnesses followers who take actions that broadly comport with the Leader's instructions. The individual who captivates and directs her followers has the making of Leadership. The one who loses all control over her followers, meanwhile, ceases to exercise Leadership.

In this way, followers retain agency of their own. As Benjamin Hermalin (2012, 435) puts it, a "defining feature of Leadership is that a Leader is someone with *voluntary* followers." Leadership is revealed through the demonstrated willingness of followers to abide instructions from someone who does not exercise formal control over them. The class of followers must include individuals who freely and independently devote their own resources in the service of a Leader's objectives. The manager who dictates orders about how employees are to spend their time during work hours is not exercising Leadership. Nor is the tyrant who threatens his subjects, on pain of death, to obey his commands. Nor is the slave master whose slaves, as his property, are formally bound to his indiscriminate intentions.[11]

Leadership, as expressed through the communications between a Leader and followers, can be manipulative, minacious, and ugly—just so long as followers retain some free will and the actions they take on behalf of their Leader are based on that free will. This freedom distinguishes the rule of a Leader from that of a manager, and likewise the available options of subjects and followers.[12]

Leadership, in this way, does not preclude the existence of formal authority. It is possible for someone to be a Leader who is also endowed with clear power that can be formally exercised over her followers. Leadership, however, finds its clearest expression beyond authority. When an individual convinces a follower to take an action that she cannot command, or to exert a level of effort she cannot require, then her Leadership qualities come into view. In the extreme, when an individual can attract the attention and direct the energies of followers over whom they exercise no formal control whatsoever, her position as Leader appears in full bloom.

Of course, a Leader's relationship with her followers may have more to do with emotion than rationality. When in her presence, followers may become spellbound. But when they turn to act, followers must recover their senses, and with them the commitment to exercise their own free will. Followers are neither dupes nor stooges. They work consciously and deliberately on behalf of their Leader and the higher ends she embodies. When doing so, followers enjoy a certain measure of freedom. Followers are not merely the arm or instrument of a Leader. Rather, they have agency and autonomy, and thus the capacity to abandon their Leader—or even to work against her—without formal sanction.[13]

What keeps followers from exercising such options? It is here that higher ends come into play. Again to cite Goebbels (Toland 1976, 233), higher ends instill in followers a sense of purpose and place in the universe. Higher ends fulfill the existential needs of followers. If followers freely abide a Leader's instructions, they do so primarily out of commitment to the higher ends that a Leader publicly defines, extols, and personifies.

A Leader's higher ends must therefore resonate with her followers. It will not suffice for followers to follow instructions without regard for the higher ends involved. Nor will it suffice for a Leader to declare higher ends with a wink and a nod, while her followers embark on a project that all recognize as serving low objectives. The Leader's public expression of higher ends must be accompanied by the follower's belief in higher ends. The Leader may be engaging in a charade, but for followers, the commitment—no matter how misguided—must be genuine.[14]

Personification

While Leaders depend on followers for their higher objectives to be realized, so too do followers depend on their Leader to understand these objectives. As followers stand between a Leader and the actualization of her goals, so does the Leader stand between followers and the expression of a higher goal. It is through a Leader that followers identify with and come to understand their purpose.

Leaders, however, do more than just instruct and orchestrate about higher objectives. Leaders, at the peak of their influence, come to embody these higher objectives. In King, followers see racial justice, just as in Jesus followers see God's Word. Hitler became "the personalization of flag, freedom, and racial purity" (Toland 1976, 203). Mao was the "Red Sun in Our Hearts" (Short 2000, 543). By personifying higher ends, all Leaders imbue in their followers a sense of meaning, purpose, and common regard for the stakes involved in their shared work.

We are agnostic about the particular ways in which this personification comes about. For some Leaders, charisma may be the key. For others, it may be fear, carefully calibrated and selectively used. Fervor, inspiration, or treachery all may play a part. Still others may come to personify higher aims through tireless work, self-sacrifice, wisdom, or enlightenment. What matters is not how the Leader comes to personify higher ends, but that she does.

By personifying higher ends, however she comes to do so, the Leader distinguishes herself from the organizer. While the organizer also depends on followers, the organizer remains anonymous, working discreetly behind the scenes, offering guidance and support without attracting the public spotlight. While some organizers may be especially adept, all organizers are interchangeable. Although the work that organizers perform may be indispensable, the individuals who serve as organizers are not. What organizers do, in essence, is coordinate the actions of others who independently understand their higher ends. They facilitate change without themselves representing change. Followers do not cede judgment to organizers, nor do they see organizers as the living embodiment of higher ends. There are no monuments to organizers. The image of organizers does not emblazon the national conscious.

Not so with Leaders. Leaders do not merely speak of higher ends. Leaders personify higher ends. In Leaders, followers not only understand what action they should take but they also draw existential meaning and sustenance. They work on behalf of a higher objective because they come to believe in the Leader who personifies it. When this Leader dies and no one stands to replace her, followers do not merely mourn. They appear lost, reeling, unsure of what to do and (crucially) what to believe.

In this sense, we reject those definitions of Leadership that see Leaders and followers in a common community with shared understandings of values and objectives (Gardiner 1990). Leaders depend on followers, just as followers depend on Leaders. However, this reciprocity does not make Leaders and followers of a piece when it comes to larger objectives. For Leaders, the connection to objectives is immediate. For followers, understandings of objectives are channeled through Leaders.

In this sense, exactly what makes Leaders loom so large is also what makes followers so dependent. Anointed by their followers, Leaders articulate and defend grand tasks. In their biography, their imagery, their voice, Leaders also come to represent these tasks and the higher purposes to which they are put. Prospective followers may choose their Leader with cause, selecting an individual worthy of their adulation and doing so for clear, instrumental reasons. But once chosen, prospective followers become actual followers, and as a consequence their independent judgment, their critical faculties, their capacity to not only see what is right but also to determine what is required to make right, begin to deteriorate.[15]

It is for precisely this reason that Leaders are best evaluated one at a time. Each Leader is understood on her own terms, through her own relationships, via her own objectives and followers. Individuals who on their own would not qualify as Leaders cannot bind together and collectively assume the status of Leader. An individual is recognized as a Leader singularly or not at all, for it is only a single individual who can come to personify a higher objective.

"Leader" versus "leader"

By requiring that a leader personify objectives, our definition rules out many of the kinds of activities and relationships discussed in this volume. While a party leader in Congress or an agency head assuredly directs followers toward certain higher objectives, she does not obviously personify these ends. Rank-and-file members of Congress do not see in their leaders the living embodiment of higher ends. In precisely this way, party leaders of the sort we are accustomed to electing (and then bemoaning) work in the shadows of Leaders such as Mao, King, Hitler, or Jesus.

With the requirement of personification, we have set a high bar for the criterion of exceptionality. Were one interested in lowering it, a distinction may be useful: whereas a Leader personifies higher ends, a leader merely defines and extols them. A leader, thus understood, assuredly performs vital functions. She transmits information about the world, makes the case for the primacy of certain objectives, and dispenses directions on how best to achieve them. Unlike the anonymous organizers, moreover, a leader curries the attention of followers. She works in the public realm, and she directs the efforts not of coequals but of followers.

A leader, however, does not come to symbolize higher objectives. In her image, followers do not see, understand, and derive meaning from higher ends. Portraits of leaders do not rest on mantelpieces. Statutes of them are not erected in public squares. Followers do not weep in their presence. All of this is reserved for Leaders, who are known for more than just what they do, but for what they are, and what they represent. Capital-L Leaders are far more than celestial guides. They are celestial beings.

Qualifiers

As we have seen, a Leader is not the same as a leader, statesman, manager, or organizer. But to say that someone is a Leader, under our definition, may not say enough. For this reason, a variety of qualifiers can be productively invoked.[16]

Good

The first qualifiers, and perhaps the most urgently needed, are "good" and "bad." These particular qualifiers relate to the higher ends that a Leader commends to her followers. A good Leader pursues higher ends that are not only recognizable apart from the individual who espouses them but that also have clear moral content. A bad Leader, by contrast, pursues objectives that are depraved, unethical, or immoral. Good and bad, as such, relate to the normative distinctions we make about different higher ends. With these qualifiers, we can most easily distinguish Adolf Hitler from Martin Luther King Jr. Both, irrefutably, were Leaders. Only one would we call good.

Notice that the qualifiers "good" and "bad" do not relate to the Leader herself. It is possible, even likely, that a good Leader is not good herself. As long as she extols higher ends that are moral and just, a Leader is free to wantonly abuse her partner, her children, and her dog and still remain good. The fact that King was a philanderer or that Hitler remained faithful to Eva Braun does not in any way force us to reconsider our evaluations of these Leaders as good and bad, respectively.

Authentic

While deliberately allowing Leaders to pursue a wide range of higher objectives, our definition also establishes rather lax standards regarding authenticity. To qualify as a Leader, an individual must commit herself to one or more higher ends. However, there may be instances when Leaders express higher objectives when, at heart, they are more truly dedicated to lower ends. The pastor who calls on his flock to follow God's Word may in truth merely want to increase his coffers. The politician who rhapsodizes about the glory of country or the imperatives of equality may mask a baser interest in his individual hold on power. Our definition of Leadership, however, does not demand any fidelity between expressed and true objectives. Leadership can accommodate insincerity, even duplicity. All that matters is that the Leader publicly define, extol, and personify higher ends.

To be an authentic Leader, however, the higher aims that an individual professes must be the true source of her motivation, the true content of her beliefs. For the authentic Leader, higher aims do not stand in for lower aims. The authentic Leader preaches the Word of God because she believes it, not because she sees its instrumental value. Higher aims are not delivery mechanisms for personal enrichment. When an authentic Leader speaks of higher aims, she is being candid and true.

Both King and Hitler, most would agree, were authentic. Though their higher aims could not differ more from one another, King and Hitler each held his own dearly. For each of these authentic Leaders, what they said was a fair representation of what they believed. As a result, though their followers might subsequently complain about their lack of effectiveness, they could not reasonably argue that they were ever duped. These were not charlatans.

Not so with Mao Tse-tung, perhaps the quintessential inauthentic Leader. While extolling collectivism, workers' welfare, and the birth of a proletarian culture, Mao, historians nearly universally recognize (Short 2000), was principally concerned about his own hold on power and his own glory. For Mao, higher ends were important only insofar as they were useful, allowing him to conduct a carefully orchestrated ruse. Unable to carry out a campaign of terror against his political opponents, Mao launched a cultural revolution, one that in expression held forth higher ends but that in execution yielded a "stultifying shallowness" (Short 2000, 583), the direct product of Mao's lower ends. Mao may have been great and effective, but he was neither good nor authentic.

Democratic

Under our formulation, the only restriction on a leader's chosen objective is that it be counted among all possible higher ends. Whether good or bad, the specific higher end a Leader defines and extols need not correspond with either the prior or latent moral commitments of followers. For the democratic Leader, however, such a correspondence exists, while for the undemocratic Leader it does not, even though followers freely take actions on behalf of the leader's chosen higher ends.

A great deal of scholarship on democratic theory is devoted to the particular mechanisms that intermittently encourage and impel Leaders to pursue objectives that represent, in any meaningful sense, their constituents.[17] Many of these democratic theorists seek criteria that Leaders must satisfy not only in their selection of chosen objectives but also in how they communicate with their followers about such objectives and the inherent rights that followers retain in their pursuit. The details of these debates are beyond the scope of this chapter. For here, we need only recognize the stakes of such debates, which center on the appropriateness of the "democratic" qualifier and not the status of "Leader" itself.

Great

A great Leader distinguishes herself by the followers she keeps. A great Leader attracts many followers who wholly commit themselves, often at considerable sacrifice to themselves, to her chosen cause. The more followers a Leader has and the harder these followers work on behalf of a leader's higher ends, the greater she becomes. The modest Leader, by contrast, garners merely respect and admiration. Her followers, however, are not especially plentiful, and their devotion to her objectives, as measured by the actions that they take, generally underwhelm. They may speak fondly of their Leader and dutifully purchase overpriced and overcooked cupcakes at her fund-raisers, but that is about all. Modest Leaders do not have followers who fervently seek out opportunities to take actions on behalf of the leader's ends—actions that disrupt their daily routines, invite personal risk, and even lead to their death.

The greatness of Martin Luther King Jr., as such, is not to be seen in King himself, in the soaring rhetoric he delivered, or in the brilliance of his mind. Rather, King's greatness is seen in the devoted actions of his followers—marchers being attacked by police dogs in Selma, protesters at segregated lunch counters being hauled off to jail in Nashville, freedom riders being ambushed by a white mob in Montgomery, lawyers abandoning their Northern practices in order to fight prejudice in the South, strikers who would rather lose their jobs than perpetrate perceived injustice. These actions, taken by so many people at such great personal sacrifice, constitute the true testimony to King's greatness.

To be great, meanwhile, is not to be good. So too can we find greatness in Hitler's Leadership. Indeed, it is precisely the great lengths to which so many under his rule went in order to perpetrate what we now recognize as radical evil that we know that Hitler was great. The steadfast commitment of so many Germans to fight the Allied powers while committing genocide at home speaks to Hitler's greatness. Indeed, Hitler could not have left so much carnage in his wake had he not been great.

Effective

The effectiveness of a Leader is determined by the actions that followers take. To be a Leader, an individual's followers must take actions that accord with her instructions. But to be an effective Leader, these actions must meaningfully promote the higher ends that she extols. Followers must do things that are not merely consistent with a higher end. They must take actions that realize these higher ends. By virtue of these actions, the higher ends must appear less removed, and more entrenched, in the lives that we live.

There is, of course, a temporal dimension to effectiveness. In one moment a Leader may appear effective, while in the next she may not. In his quest to promote the glory of Germany, Hitler appeared extraordinarily effective as he built the National Socialist German Worker's Party and went on to annex Poland in 1939. Six years later, though, with his troops in retreat and his nation in ruin, our judgment of Hitler's effectiveness takes a dramatic turn for the worse.

Our judgments of a Leader's effectiveness also depend on the standards we use. Insofar as his follower's actions paved the way for the 1964 and 1965 Civil Rights Acts, altered the racial attitudes of millions of Americans, and brought the racial and class injustices into the full light of day, Martin Luther King Jr. was undoubtedly effective. But his followers' actions—extraordinary though they were—did not realize outcomes that met King's own aspirations. Racism, class disparities, segregation, and a great deal more all persist. Depending on the stringency of our standards, we might argue that King was a distinctly ineffective Leader.

Summary

In this chapter, we offer a new definition of Leadership and, more generally, a vocabulary for talking about the larger class of rulers (whose influence is realized by the direct application of power) and entrepreneurs (who instead require the voluntary support of followers). Leaders, we argue, distinguish themselves by the objectives they extol, the followers whose actions they orient and coordinate, and the ways in which they personify higher aims. Only when specific conditions are met is Leadership possible. Relax any one and Leadership promptly dissipates, just as Leaders become something else entirely.

Ours is not the only definition of Leadership. But unlike many other prominent definitions, ours satisfies each of the criteria we laid out at the beginning of this chapter. For starters, it recognizes the relational nature of Leadership. Leadership is not realized through the mere execution of power. It is not about status, employment, or the collection of personality traits that constitute an individual. Rather, Leadership is defined through the mutual dependencies of Leaders and followers. It is through followers that Leaders can effect change, just as it is through Leaders that followers come to understand higher aims.

Built into our definition is a distinction between higher and lower ends. What distinguishes the two is neither their moral content nor their normative appeal. Rather, the distinction hinges on the relationship between an objective and the individual who espouses it. When Leaders espouse higher aims, they point toward principles and imagined states of the world that are larger than themselves and that in no way depend on the leader's participation or support. Lower ends, by contrast, cannot be understood except by reference to personal wealth, glory, or fame and attain meaning only through the life of the individual who pursues them.

Higher ends have integrity and meaning quite apart from Leaders. It would be a mistake, though, to conclude that the Leaders who extol them are dispensable. They are not. Indeed, it is precisely because Leaders come to personify higher ends that actions in the service of such higher ends so crucially depend on Leadership. Take away the Leader and the intrinsic meanings of higher ends remain undisturbed. But take away the Leader and the meanings of higher ends for followers become more remote. The immediate reactions of followers may differ. In some instances they may see fit to honor the legacy of their Leader and work with renewed fervor to fulfill his stated objectives. They tend to do so, though, in highly disorganized fashion, as various factions of followers vie with one another as the true spokespersons of a leader's heritage.[18] Alternatively, with the loss of the individual who connected them to their higher ends, followers may become alienated from the very objectives that once kept them in common purpose. The tragedy of Leadership is found in its personification.

Crucially, our definition also establishes a template for distinguishing Leaders from organizers, statesmen, and everyday politicians. The constellation of relationships and commitments of Leaders and organizers is the same save one: the personification of higher ends. Whereas organizers coordinate and orient followers toward higher objectives, they do not come to personify these objectives; as a result, organizers are anonymous and interchangeable, whereas Leaders are public and indispensable.[19] The differences between Leaders and statesmen and everyday politicians, meanwhile, are more pronounced. These latter two groups, after all, do not depend on followers to do their bidding. Rather, both are capable of exercising powers of their own in order to advance either higher ends (in the case of the statesman) or lower ends (in the case of the everyday politician).

As an empirical matter, of course, individuals intermittently behave as all sorts of agents of social change. In one moment, they may take independent actions that directly advance their cause; in the next, they rely on followers to do so. With some, they commend higher ends; with others, they admit their interest in lower ends. No person is a Leader all of the time. The notion of the born Leader, as such, is utterly nonsensical. However, depending on the ends they pursue and the relationships they cultivate, all persons have the capacity to exercise Leadership.

Our definition also comports with our empirical criteria for Leadership, the first of which concerns its exceptionality. Leadership under our definition is exceptional because it is rare. Individuals may extol higher aims, other individuals may act in the service of these aims, and other individuals may come to personify these higher aims. The joint probability that these individuals will be found together as Leader and followers, each fulfilling their prescribed roles and all connected with one another, is, if nothing else, uncommon. But Leadership is also exceptional because it is precarious. Should Leaders abandon their higher aims, should followers refuse to act, and should neither recognize the personification of higher aims, then the preconditions of Leadership—no matter how robust they once might have seemed—promptly disappear.

Finally, our definition not only recognizes the fact of Leaders' publicity but also identifies the mechanism by which this publicity is sustained: the personification of higher ends. We keep images of our Leaders not out of reverence to the persons themselves but because of what such images signify. In their image, we see the higher ends to which we devote our energies and resources. As a result, in their image, we find existential meaning and sustenance in our daily lives. We know our Leaders not merely for the instructions and guidance that they offer but for the relevance they impart.

References

Alquist, John, and Margaret Levi. 2011. "Leadership: What It Means, What It Does, and What We Want to Know About It." *Annual Review of Political Science* 14:1–24.

Beerbohm, Eric. 2015. "Is Democratic Leadership Possible?" *American Political Science Review* 109 (4): 639–652.

Bolton, Patrick, Laura Veldkamp, and Markus Brunnermeier. 2010. "Economists' Perspectives on Leadership." In *Handbook of Leadership Theory and Practice*, edited by Nitin Nohria and Rakesh Khurana. Cambridge, MA: Harvard Business School Publishing Corporation.

Burns, James MacGregor. 2004. *Transforming Leadership*. New York: Grove Press.

Clinton, Bill. 2014. "World's Best Leaders: Clinton" (interview). *Fortune*, March 20.

Cohen, G. A. 1991. "Incentives, Inequality, and Community." Tanner Lectures on Human Values. Stanford University.

Dewan, Torun, and David Myatt. 2008. "The Qualities of Leadership: Direction, Communication, and Obfuscation." *American Political Science Review* 102 (3): 351–368.

——. 2012. "The Rhetorical Strategies of Leaders: Speaking Clearly, Standing Back, and Stepping Down." *Journal of Theoretical Politics* 24 (4): 431–460.

Edwards, George. 2009. *The Strategic President: Persuasion and Opportunity in Presidential Leadership.* Princeton, NJ: Princeton University Press.

Fiorina, Morris, and Kenneth Shepsle. 1989. "Formal Theories of Leadership: Agents, Agenda-Setters, and Entrepreneurs." In *Leadership and Politics*, edited by Bryon D. Jones. Lawrence: University Press of Kansas.

Gardiner, John. 1990. *On Leadership.* New York: Free Press.

George, Alexander, and Juliette George. 1998. *Presidential Personality and Performance.* Boulder, CO: Westview Press.

Greenstein, Fred. 2004. *The Presidential Difference: Leadership Style from FDR to George W. Bush.* 2nd ed. Princeton, NJ: Princeton University Press.

Hargrove, Erwin C. 1989. "Two Conceptions of Institutional Leadership." In *Leadership and Politics*, edited by Bryan D. Jones, 57–86. Lawrence: University Press of Kansas.

Hermalin, Benjamin. 2012. "Leadership and Corporate Culture." In *Handbook of Organizational Economics*, edited by Robert Gibbons and John Roberts. Princeton, NJ: Princeton University Press.

Jacobs, Lawrence, and Robert Shapiro. 2000. *Politicians Don't Pander: Political Manipulation and the Loss of Democratic Responsiveness.* Chicago: University of Chicago Press.

Keohane, Nannerrl. 2010. *Thinking about Leadership.* Princeton, NJ: Princeton University Press.

Landa, Dimitri, and Scott Tyson. 2016. "Coercive Leadership." New York University Working Paper. http://politics.as.nyu.edu/docs/IO/2790/LeaderC_FinSD.pdf.

Levi, Margaret. 1988. *Of Rule and Revenue.* Berkeley: University of California Press.

Mill, John Stuart. 1969. *Collected Works.* Toronto: University of Toronto Press.

Read, James, and Ian Shapiro. 2014. "Transforming Power Relationships: Leadership, Risk, and Hope." *American Political Science Review* 108 (1): 40–53.

Shils, Edward. 1965. "Charisma, Order, and Status." *American Sociological Review* 30 (2): 199–213.

Short, Philip. 2000. *Mao: A Life.* New York: Henry Holt.

Skowronek, Stephen. 1997. *The Politics Presidents Make: Leadership from John Adams to Bill Clinton.* Rev. ed. New York: Belknap Press.

Toland, Johen. 1976. *Adolf Hitler.* Garden City, NY: Doubleday.

Weber, Max. (1917) 2004. "Science as a Vocation." In *The Vocation Lectures*, translated by Rodney Livingstone, edited by David Owen and Tracy Strong, 1–31. Indianapolis, IN: Hackett Books.

———. (1946) 1968. "The Sociology of Charismatic Authority." In *On Charisma and Institution Building*, edited by S. N. Eisenstadt, 18–27. Chicago: University of Chicago Press.

———. 1947. *Theory of Social and Economic Organization.* New York: Oxford University Press.

Notes

1. The well-meaning empiricist who is equipped with a conceptual definition may fail to identify the true leaders who live among us. Corroborating evidence of leadership simply

may not exist, while leaders and followers deliberately misrepresent their true intentions and relationships, making it impossible, as an observational matter, to sort leadership from the many other forces that order our social, economic, and political lives.

2. Conceptually, designations of different types of social entrepreneurs (and rules) are mutually exclusive. As a practical matter, though, these designations may apply to the same person. It is quite possible that an individual may appear in one instance or domain as a leader and in the next as a statesman.

3. Other chapters in this volume implicitly adopt easier standards for identifying leaders and leadership. As a consequence, our criteria rule out some of the individuals and activities presented in this volume as leaders and leadership. From our vantage point, this is fine and well. The point of this exercise is not to affirm the pervasiveness of leadership. Rather, it is to be clear about what constitutes leadership and, just as importantly, what does not. Others are free to offer limiting criteria of their own—and we hope they do. As the conversation matures, studies may recover a language to speak clearly about the perquisites for and characteristic traits of leadership.

4. Of course, empiricists who use this formulation regularly fall into the trap of sampling on the dependent variable. Who is a leader? Answer: one who accomplishes great things. How do we identify leaders? Answer: by spotting the individual responsible for great things.

5. Landa and Tyson (2016) underscore the importance of trust between candidates to leadership and followers. When followers are uncertain about the preferences of their potential leaders, leadership, as we define it, can never emerge. The agent in charge, therefore, must resort to coercion to coordinate the actions of other agents.

6. On this score, Weber's definition differs from many other essentialist definitions of leadership, which often insist that rather pedestrian qualities—for example, keeping an open mind or listening with care and attention—are the tickets to leadership.

7. It is precisely for this reason that Weber is so interested in how rational bureaucracies come to replace charismatic leaders. According to Weber, mature states depend less on the personal qualities of individual leaders and more on new organizational forms characterized by divisions of labor and rational hierarchies.

8. Keohane's (2010) definition has more than a passing resemblance to Bill Clinton's (2014), which stipulates that "leadership means bringing people together in pursuit of a common cause, developing a plan to achieve it, and staying with it until the goal is achieved."

9. Statesmen therefore distinguish themselves from Leaders in at least two ways. Because they do not require followers, statesmen, unlike Leaders, need not personify their objectives.

10. As an empirical matter, Leaders often take actions that translate directly into the realization of objectives, for as an empirical matter, Leaders often hold power that enables them to intervene into and reshape the material world as they see fit. When they do so, however, they are not acting as Leaders. Being a Leader does not preclude the opportunity to take direct action. It simply means that when Leaders take such actions, they are not behaving as Leaders per se. In their capacity as Leaders, subjects depend on followers to advance—in any meaningful capacity—their stated higher objectives.

11. Leaders differ from managers, tyrants, and slaveholders in other ways as well. To be-

gin, they need not direct the energies of followers in the service of higher objectives, which in turn they themselves need not personify.

12. Insofar as the concept allows for a modicum of agency among followers, Margaret Levi's (1988) notion of quasi-voluntary compliance might establish a lower bound on the necessary freedoms available to followers in order for Leadership to function. Levi, of course, recognizes the coercive capabilities of the Leadership and the state. But in insisting that citizens (read, potential followers) draw on normative considerations when deciding whether to comply with government taxes, Levi also carves out a space for independent action among followers.

13. Here again we see differences between our definition of Leadership and Weber's. Weber does not take nearly as hard a line as we do on with respect to the free will of followers. Indeed, as Weber traces the institutionalization of charisma into the state, he not only allows for the possibility that Leaders exercise formal authority over their followers but also demands as much. In their efforts to prove their worthiness to followers, as Weber insists they must do, charismatic Leaders also can wield the various forms of formal authority that, by our schema, are available to the larger class of rulers but not entrepreneurs, of which Leaders are a part.

14. Roving bandits and marauding armies whose sole purpose is self-enrichment do not establish the basis for Leadership, even if their commanders regularly and devoutly pay homage to higher ends. Nonetheless, followers may behave in ways that, to an impartial outsider, appear to be entirely self-serving as long as the followers themselves believe that they are advancing a higher end. If bandits and armies act out of their commitment to tribe or country, which their commander, their Leader, defines and extols, then the first principle of Leadership is satisfied, even if the actions that followers take are abhorrent, and even if the Leader's commitment to the higher end is not true.

15. This dependence might itself be rational. For example, it might help coordinate followers' actions toward the objectives personified by the Leader.

16. Though we focus on Leaders, these qualifiers might also apply to other agents of social changes, including mere leaders.

17. To be sure, the literature on democratic theory focuses on more than just this specific correspondence. According to some definitions, such as Beerbohm's (2015), a democratic leader must do more than just advance objectives shared by a larger public. Her expressed objectives must also correspond with her true objectives, which in our parlance signifies authenticity.

18. For illustration, one need not look any further than the persistent infighting among the familial heirs to Mahatma Gandhi and Martin Luther King Jr.

19. The difference between organizers and leaders is more subtle, for both are counted, along with Leaders, among the larger class of entrepreneurs. Neither the organizer nor the leader personifies higher ends, but only the latter satisfies the criterion of publicity. Whereas an organizer works behind the scenes, a leader stands in full view before her followers.

CHAPTER ELEVEN

Filters and Pegs in Holes

How Selection Mechanisms and Institutional Positions Shape (Perceptions of) Political Leadership

Alan E. Wiseman

Across a wide range of institutions and political forums, the authors who contributed to this volume collectively wrestle with several questions that are central to understanding the process and efficacy of leadership in American politics. What does it mean to be a leader in a particular political institution? Why are some leaders successful while others fail? Where do leaders come from? In answering these and many other questions, the authors draw on a collection of large-sample empirical findings, case studies, and stylized facts, that could, and I hope will, serve as the foundation for theory building around the roles and impacts of leaders and leadership in political environments.

Building on these and other insights about leadership, I argue that efforts to study and explain the relative efficacy of particular leaders must engage two variables that are pervasive across political environments: selection mechanisms and institutional contexts. More specifically, the criteria that are used to choose any particular leader vary by office and position. These varying criteria can facilitate what I call filter-induced leadership, wherein the relative efficacy of any given leader follows, at least in part, directly from the qualities of the filter that she was subjected to during the selection process. Second, upon assuming a position of leadership, individuals are influenced or constrained by the particular contexts into which they are placed. Hence, the performance of any given leader is, at least in part, an artifact of what I call pegs-in-holes leadership, wherein leadership efficacy follows directly from the opportunities and constraints that are presented to leaders, independent of their personal qualities.

Thinking about the implications of filter-induced leadership and pegs-in-holes leadership requires scholars to engage arguments about leadership in a new way. Rather than attributing policy outcomes to the competence (or lack thereof) of any given leader, scholars (and practitioners) need to first articulate how policy outcomes were more favorable than what would be expected to be obtained, given the selection mechanisms that were used to choose the leader, and the institutional constraints and opportunities that she encountered in her position. This is not to say that leaders completely lack agency. Rather, I would argue that before we can make substantively meaningful claims about the efficacy of any particular leader (and how to improve leader performance, broadly defined), we need to understand the impacts of these selection effects and institutional constraints on our perceptions of leadership performance.

What Is a Leader?

In an effort to answer many of the questions articulated above, it is constructive (indeed, one might argue, necessary) to begin with a working definition of the terms "leadership" and "leader." While many of us use these terms on a day-to-day basis, it is truthfully quite rare for most of us to articulate what precisely we mean when we refer to a person as a leader, or to say that someone displays leadership.

Beyond a few obvious cases in American politics, such as when the word "leader" is part of a person's formal title (e.g., "majority party leader" or "minority party leader"), it can often be the case that those individuals who are formally at the top of an organizational hierarchy, whether it be a legislature, a bureaucracy, an interest group, or a chief executive, such as a president or governor, might not always be viewed as the true leader of the organization. Likewise, even if one believes that formal hierarchical positions correspond to leadership roles, it is not always the case that leaders display, for a lack of a better word, leadership. The exploration of such concepts can quickly become messy without clarification; on this point, a wide range of works that broadly construe leadership studies have articulated various definitions for leaders and leadership.[1]

In her recent scholarly treatment of leadership, for example, Keohane (2010, 23), an accomplished scholar of political theory and past president of Wellesley College and Duke University, states, "Leaders determine or clarify goals for a group of individuals and bring together the energies of members of that group to accomplish a goal." Does Keohane's definition of leadership seem reasonable and appropriate in the context of American politics and political institutions? Is there an alternative definition that should be used when thinking about political institutions compared to other formal organizations or collections of individuals in society?

On this point, the authors in this volume have much to say. Howell and Wolton, for example, devote an entire chapter to how scholars and practitioners might conceptualize leadership, in which they describe "basic criteria that any definition of leadership must satisfy." They then identify how a wide range of definitions of leadership that are invoked in the extant scholarly literatures violate at least one of these criteria. They ultimately provide an explicit definition of a leader as an individual who "publicly defines, extols, and eventually personifies higher objectives, thereby orienting and coordinating the efforts of followers who seek to advance such objectives," and they explore how their definition of leadership comports with scholarly and practitioner-based analyses of leadership in contemporary political settings.

Moving beyond an explicit general definition of leadership, several other authors in this volume articulate how leadership is relevant to their particular areas of expertise. Battista, in his chapter on leadership in state politics, defines leadership as "directing outcomes away from those that might be chosen in the absence of leadership, but in such a way that those being led consent ex post." Patty, in his discussion of leadership in the bureaucracy, draws on Terry's (2003, 4) definition of "bureaucratic leadership as an active process that 'entails the exercise of power, authority, and strategic discretion in pursuit of the public interest.'" Cameron and Shadmehr, in their analysis of leadership on the Court, use Hermalin's (2013) definition of leadership to say that "leadership is defined by voluntary followership." Potter begins his chapter on presidential influence over foreign policy by noting that "in the public's mind, foreign policy leadership means presidential initiatives that are assertive, decisive, and successful." While not providing an explicit definition of leadership in the US House, Sinclair and Koger state that congressional leaders, in most cases, are expected to "use delegated power to serve the interests of party members." Smith, in his chapter on leadership in the Senate, identifies various qualities that contribute to senators being good leaders and notes how Harry Reid (D-NV) came to be recognized for "being a good listener, for carefully observing, recording, and accounting for his colleagues' interests and requests, and for being ideologically flexible."

In all of these cases, the authors have articulated definitions of leadership, either implicitly or explicitly, that seem particularly salient for the institutions that they study, and the qualities that political actors who operate in these environments must have if they are to become effective leaders. Likewise, though not stating it explicitly, the authors in this volume also point to many aspects of the process of leadership, and the selection of leaders, that comport with my arguments about filter-induced leadership and pegs-in-holes leadership.

Pegs-in-Holes Leadership

Putting aside questions about how people become leaders for a moment, in reading through the chapters, a common theme that is raised by many of the authors is how opportunities for leadership, and the possibility of effective leadership, are greatly influenced by context. Leaders' prospects for advancing their agendas are profoundly related to the political and institutional constraints that they face at the time that they are making decisions. Sinclair and Koger, for example, write in one of the opening passages of their chapter that "congressional scholars agree that the political and institutional contexts are crucial to understanding congressional leadership." In this volume, Smith argues that "the political competition between the parties, the ideological polarization of the parties, and the institutional context of the Senate—its rules and practices—[shape] their colleagues' expectations and the strategic challenges faced as party leaders." Hence, to understand leadership in the Senate, one must appreciate "important features of party politics that have changed that drive the strategies of Senate floor leaders and important features of the Senate that exacerbate partisanship even further." Among these factors, Smith argues, are interparty competition, the distribution of policy preferences in the chamber, and the Senate's rules and practices. All of these factors influence the scope of opportunities that are available to potential leaders.

Turning to the states, Battista identifies a range of studies that explore how variations in political institutions, as well as how variations in personal, political, and temporal contexts correlate with the scope of state political leaders' successes. Patty argues that "there are more and less effective forms of bureaucratic leadership, and the relative effectiveness of these leadership styles varies across management situations." The prospects for judicial leadership, in Cameron and Shadmehr's model in this volume, hinge on the (exogenous) probability that a judge may receive a "public signal" regarding whether a new doctrine should be established by the Court.[2] Potter notes that presidents face relatively fewer constraints in engaging foreign policy matters, in contrast to domestic policy matters, which provides them with more substantial opportunities for "clear and assertive" leadership in foreign policy. In a similar vein, Beckmann notes how much of the extant "presidency-centered" scholarship embraces the approaches of scholars such as Cameron (2000) and Canes-Wrone (2009), who argue that "the context of presidential–congressional bargaining means institutional designs and political incentives leave less room for presidents' individual discretion and impact." Beckmann also demonstrates that presidential success on "key votes" is related to the partisan composition of each chamber of Congress. In other words, context matters.

What are we to make of such statements in our efforts to study leaders and/or evaluate the leadership efforts of particular political actors? One possibility is to argue that the scope and potential influence of any leader in the American political system is so greatly constrained by various institutional factors that a leadership position is essentially a hole in an organization, and any potential leader is basically a peg who fills the hole and performs various functions that come with the office. This pegs-in-holes view of leadership would suggest that any variance in leadership success isn't necessarily attributable to the person who holds the office. Indeed, it is entirely plausible that, holding institutions and political circumstances constant, leaders (or at least those who hold formal leadership positions) should be essentially interchangeable with regard to the scope of potential influence over any given policy agenda.

Of course, as noted by Keohane (2010, 25), "leaders make decisions." Hence, in the real world, one would expect that there should be some differences in the discrete policy choices that are made by particular leaders, even if one embraces the pegs-in-holes perspective. Consistent with this argument, Beckmann points to President Obama's nominations of Sonia Sotomayor and Elena Kagan, his decision to send in SEAL Team Six to capture or kill Osama bin Laden, and his changing American national policy toward Cuba as examples of several decisions that likely would have not been obtained by other presidents. Likewise, Beckmann and Keohane (2010) both point to President George W. Bush's decision to invade Iraq as an example of how "individual leaders matter also" (Keohane 2010, 12–13) as they both explicate the likely foreign policy consequences of Gore, rather than Bush, being elected, given that he would have inherited an identical institutional environment and (nearly) identical political environment to that of Bush. Rather, an implication of pegs-in-holes leadership is that the scope of leader-induced substantive policy changes (which cannot be obtained solely by her undertaking unilateral actions) is heavily influenced by a range of factors that she has essentially no control over. Hence, one could conceivably swap out one leader for another without any meaningful changes being obtained for much of the policy-making and policy-execution activities that come with the office.

While the concept of pegs-in-holes leadership might seem unusual to many observers of American politics,[3] it is consistent with several of the perspectives that are advanced in this volume. Patty, for example, concludes his chapter by stating, "it is not entirely clear at first blush that bureaucratic leadership is all that important," given the range of tasks that are essentially intrinsic to the various positions that bureaucratic leaders might occupy. Sinclair and Koger (essentially) argue that Boehner was ineffective as a Speaker of the House because of the intraparty tensions that he had to navigate. Hence (they intimate), one would expect that any other lawmaker in his position, being placed in a situation where "the character of the Republican membership made effective leadership uncommonly difficult," would have fared just as well as Boehner did in trying to navigate the debates surrounding budgetary politics (and other policy matters) in the 112th and 113th Congresses. While Smith, in this volume, points to personality-specific features of Harry Reid and Mitch McConnell that influenced their respective successes as leaders, he argues that their behaviors and tactics were heavily, if not entirely, influenced by the political environments in which they operated. While Reid was not "a widely recognized liberal leader" and McConnell had been "known as a deal maker . . . rather than as a leading conservative," the partisan composition and institutional rules of the Senate channeled their energies so that they emerged as staunch partisans who were willing to use highly combative and one-sided legislative tactics that benefited their respective parties.

If it is indeed the case that most leaders' actions are heavily influenced and/or constrained by the environments in which they operate, then it might not be entirely constructive to try to evaluate the relative efficacy of one leader compared to another in isolation. Rather, it would be more appropriate (and constructive) to evaluate leaders against each other when accounting for the relevant institutional considerations that either leader or both leaders faced during their times in positions of authority. To provide a simple example from legislative politics, consider Figure 11.1, which presents the legislative effectiveness scores (LESs) for those representatives who have served as chairs of the House Administration Committee and the House Transportation and Infrastructure Committee from 1973 to 2014.

As described in Volden and Wiseman (2014), a representative's LES is a summary metric that is drawn from publicly available data from the Library of Congress's website to capture how successful an individual member of the US House of Representatives is at moving his or her sponsored legislative agenda items through five stages of the legislative process in every two-year Congress, and where each bill is weighted to account for its substantive significance. Within each two-year Congress, LESs are normalized to take an average value of 1. Hence, any representative who has an LES above 1 is more effective than the average representative in the Congress in which she served; and any representative who has an LES below 1 is below average (Figure 11.1).

At first glance, it is obvious that the representatives who have served as chair of the House Transportation and Infrastructure Committee have (almost) always had a higher LES than the representative who has served as the chair of the House Administration Committee. Drawing inferences beyond this basic comparison of scores, however, is somewhat complicated. It might not be appropriate, for example, to argue that the representative who chaired the Transportation and Infrastructure Committee was a more effective leader than the chair of the Administration Committee solely on the basis of the differences in their scores in any particular Congress. The committees handle different policy portfolios, as dictated by House rules and precedents. Hence, the person who chairs the Transportation and Infrastructure Committee will generally have natural opportunities to be engaged in more, and more high-profile, legislation than if she were chair of the Administration Committee. While the chair of Transportation and Infrastructure appears to be generally more effective than the chair of Administration, it's important to remember that the differences in scores are greatly influenced by the range of policy tasks that each of these chairs must navigate, by design, given the offices that she holds.

Perhaps, then, it might be more constructive to draw lessons about leadership effectiveness by comparing the relative effectiveness of chairs of the same commit-

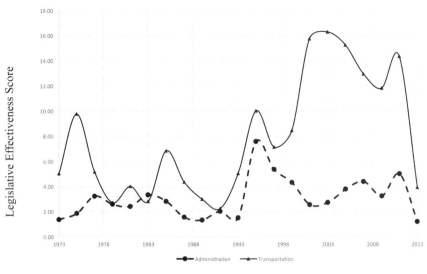

First Year of Congress

Figure 11.1. LESs of Chairs of House Administration and Transportation Committees. *Note:* The dots (House Administration Committee) or triangles (House Transportation and Infrastructure Committee) represent the LES of a given representative in a two-year Congress; the dot (triangle) is placed in the first year of the two-year Congress in which she served as chair. The LES of the chair of the House Transportation and Infrastructure Committee is almost always substantially higher than the LES of the chair of the House Administration Committee. LES = legislative effectiveness score.

tee over time. For example, Don Young (R-AK) was the chair of Transportation in 2001–2006 (107th to 109th Congresses), which corresponds to the high-water marks of the LESs of that committee's chair for the entire time period in Figure 11.1. Are there tactics that Don Young used when he was chair that allowed him to appear to be such an effective leader, especially compared to someone such as James Howard (D-NJ), who served as chair of the committee from 1981 to 1986 (97th to 99th Congresses)? Engaging in such comparisons, whereby we hold the institutional arrangements (relatively) constant, can be fruitful if we seek to assess the relative efficacy of one leader compared to another; but here too we need to be careful, as political context can still influence the prospects for leadership success, even holding institutions constant.

To illustrate this point with a simple theoretical model, consider Figure 11.2, which provides spatial representations of two hypothetical leadership regimes for the majority party—in this case, the Democratic Party. In Figure 11.2, D represents the ideal point of the Democratic Party leader, and M (or M') represents the ideal

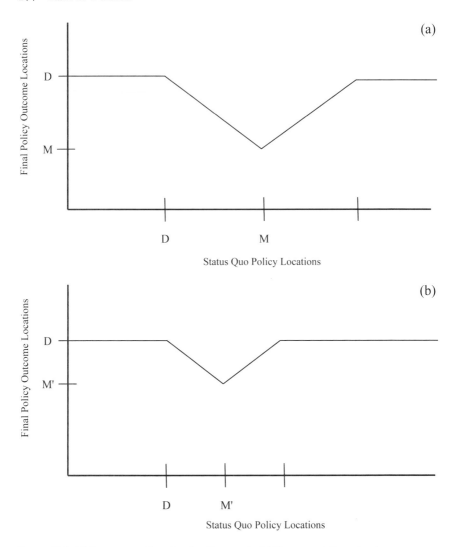

Figure 11.2. (a) Democratic Party Leader, Regime A. (b) Democratic Party Leader, Regime B.

point of the legislative median. Suppose that much of legislative policy making is analogous to a Romer and Rosenthal (1978) agenda-setting game, where the majority party leader is the agenda setter, who makes policy proposals subject to a closed amendment rule, and bills require a simple majority for passage. Then we can identify the final policy outcomes from such a game on the *y*-axes for all status quo policy locations on the *x*-axes, given the ideal point configurations in Figure 11.2.

As can be seen, given the underlying modeling assumptions, the Democratic Party leader is able to induce a notable increase in policy change under Regime B compared to what might be obtained by the party leader under Regime A. More specifically, the party leader is able to obtain a final policy located at his ideal point for a larger range of status quo locations under Regime B than Regime A. Likewise, a smaller range of status quo policies remain gridlocked under Regime B than under Regime A (whereby the party leader is able to propose a policy that is amenable to the preferences of the legislative median while still being located away from the leader's ideal point).[4] Hence, if one simply considered the final policy outcomes under both of these regimes, it might be reasonable to argue that the Democratic Party leader in Regime B was notably stronger and/or more effective than the Democratic Party leader in Regime A. Such a conclusion, however, would fail to account for differences in their strategic environments. More specifically, the Democratic Party leader in Regime A faces a more right-leaning chamber median (M) than the Democratic Party leader in Regime B (M' < M), which greatly constrains the extent to which she was able to move policy outcomes in a manner that favors Democratic Party interests.

The examples in Figures 11.1 and 11.2 illustrate that in evaluating the relative efficacy of any leader, it is important to identify how much of her perceived policy influence is a function of institutional and political circumstances and how much is directly attributable to her own efforts. In the context of legislative politics, for example, there are several well-articulated theories that describe how party leaders, acting as coalition builders, can engage in strategic vote buying (Snyder 1991; Groseclose and Snyder 1996; Krehbiel, Meirowitz, and Wiseman 2015), and how they have the ability to make particular bills generally more attractive to all legislators, independent of spatial ideological position (Hitt, Volden, and Wiseman, 2017; Volden and Wiseman 2016; Hirsch and Shotts 2011, 2015). The ability to deploy such tactics and resources essentially allows leaders to transcend whatever institutional circumstances they might face as a result of the ideological preference configuration and/or the particular parliamentary rules of the legislative chamber. If, however, leaders lack such tools and abilities, and if policy outcomes are almost entirely a function of institutional considerations, then any statements about leadership efficacy are really statements about institutional constraints and opportunities. Hence, scholars who seek to study leaders and leadership in a systematic way should really be studying (and making statements about) constraints (or lack thereof) on leaders and opportunities for leadership.

Filter-Induced Leadership

In describing the various demands and constraints placed on leaders, Keohane (2010, 28) states, "All leaders face limits on the scope of their power, including the capacities of the leader and the institutional context in which she operates, as well as the inclinations and preferences of other actors. In many cases a leader's power is limited by a superior authority in a hierarchy; the actions of colleagues, competitors, or subordinates; or the interests of constituencies whose support is important if the leader is to retain power." The first sentence of this passage speaks directly to the points raised above, which was a dominant theme in many of the chapters in this volume: context matters, and leaders are greatly influenced and/or constrained by the particular contexts in which they operate. The second sentence of the passage relates to a theme that was less clearly articulated by many of the authors in this volume, but one that I believe is important to consider if we seek to understand the impacts of leaders on policy outcomes: the relationships between leaders and their positions in various hierarchies, how their opportunities for advancement are influenced by their colleagues and subordinates, and the interests and preferences of their constituents (and constituencies). All of these matters relate, to varying degrees, to the ways in which leaders are selected and to the filters that potential leaders must pass through in order to assume positions of leadership.

In the American political system, leaders of many political institutions and organizations are selected by some sort of electoral mechanism. Presidents, governors, and legislators at both the state and national level are selected on the basis of the outcome of an electoral process. Likewise, many of the types of leaders who are considered in this book are also selected via some sort of electoral mechanism, even if the electorate is not composed of rank-and-file citizens per se. The Speaker of the US House of Representatives is formally elected by the entire membership of the House. Party leaders in both the House and Senate are selected by their parties' members by an electoral mechanism. National party leaders who do not hold elected office are nonetheless elected by their membership. Some interest groups formally elect their leaders as well. For those situations where leaders of political organizations or institutions are not elected, they are often appointed, sometimes subject to the acquiescence of external actors, such as the requirement of Senate confirmation for certain presidential appointees to the federal bureaucracy. For each specific selection mechanism that is used, different criteria, or filters, are used to identify likely candidates for leadership and to select and promote potential leaders into positions of authority. How does the design of these filter mechanisms relate to the efficacy of the leaders who survive the selection process?

While none of the contributors to this volume frame their arguments explicitly around this question, a consideration of the relationships between leadership selection mechanisms and leaders' influence tacitly emerges in many of their chapters. Smith, for example, cites Truman's (1959) "middleman thesis" when he states, "As a general rule, leaders could not function if their own policy positions did not fit the central tendencies of their parties." A natural implication of this claim is that those legislators who have policy preferences that correspond to the central tendencies of their parties should be more likely to be elevated to leadership roles. In a similar vein, Battista notes in this volume that "leaders who act in ways that their own co-partisans find unacceptable are likely to cease to be leaders." He likewise points to several examples wherein leaders engaged in behaviors that were inconsistent with the will of their parties, and they were subsequently stripped of their leadership positions. In contrast to these perspectives, Sinclair and Koger suggest that Boehner was supported by his fellow Republicans to become Speaker in the 111th Congress in large part because of "his legislative acumen and ability to work with his liberal ranking member" to produce substantively important legislation (such as the No Child Left Behind bill).[5]

Turning to a different institution, LaPira's discussion of the career trajectories of Vin Weber and Sandi Stuart compared to that of Allison McKay and Sarah Alexander is instructive, in that it points to a variety of steps that these pairs of individuals had to undertake to become go-to power broker lobbyists (Weber and Stuart) or leaders of more targeted interest group associations (McKay and Alexander). Likewise, while Karol states that "there is no truly paramount leader even of the formal party structure" and that "parties are best understood as coalitions that seek to gain control of the government via elections," much of his narrative lays out the ways in which different individuals came to be particularly influential in their respective party organizations. He also provides a nuanced view on how the Republicans and Democrats differ from each other in regard to how their party members have historically moved up the formal hierarchy within Congress to become committee chairs, party leaders, or both.

These examples collectively help to motivate the following claim: leaders in all contexts, but in political contexts in particular, are selected according to varying criteria, depending on the particular position that they will potentially obtain. As a result, individuals who might be generally well suited to be leaders in a wide range of contexts will only obtain leadership roles if they are able to survive whatever filter they are subjected to during the selection process. Moreover, the considerations that those who select leaders bring to bear on the decision vary substantially by institution and political environment. Unlike many private sector environments, it is not (typically) the case that political leaders are selected because of their actual or perceived ability to generate and maximize profit. Indeed, it is often the case that for any given organization or institution in the American political system, goals are multifaceted; they might involve seeking to produce good public policy (in the broadest sense), or increasing economic welfare, or securing and expanding civil liberties and civil rights, or maximizing substantive representation (i.e., voting with one's constituents, regardless of policy consequences), or maximizing descriptive representation, or something else altogether. Depending on which goal, or goals, is viewed as most salient at the time that a leader is being chosen, the filter that is used

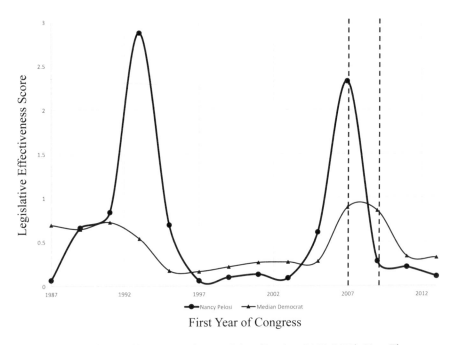

First Year of Congress

Figure 11.3. Legislative Effectiveness of Nancy Pelosi (Speaker, 2007–2011). *Note:* The dashed lines identify the first years of the first (110th) and last (111th) Congresses during which Pelosi (D-CA) held the position of Speaker. Pelosi's legislative effectiveness score was below the median member of the Democratic Party in the House for four of the five Congresses before her becoming Speaker.

for selecting a leader might vary significantly across organizations and institutions, and even across time within the same organization or institution.

For example, one type of political candidate might be more likely to be elected to Congress than to become a congressional party leader because the criteria that her constituency value when choosing between candidates might significantly deviate from the criteria that her party value when selecting its leaders inside the chamber. The same arguments would apply when thinking about the kinds of individuals who might likely pass muster with a state-level electorate so as to become governor but might be insufficiently appealing to command a majority of the Electoral College so as to become president. (We can, of course, engage in similar thought exercises for a wide range of political offices and positions.) Hence, when evaluating the performance of leaders in the relative or absolute sense, it is important for us to be cognizant of the process through which they attained their positions of leadership and how that process might facilitate filter-induced leadership. That is, the characteristics of the filter that is used to select leaders might ensure that particular types of individuals obtain leadership roles who are well or ill equipped to handle the tasks that they face in their new positions.

To illustrate these considerations in the context of congressional leadership, consider Figure 11.3, which plots the LES of Representative Nancy Pelosi (D-CA) and the LES of the median member of the Democratic Party from the time that Pelosi first took office in the 100th Congress (in the beginning of 1987) until the 113th Congress (2013–2014).

As discussed in Volden and Wiseman (2014), a consideration of Pelosi's LESs across her years in the House provides an interesting lens with which to analyze the legislative strategies that she used as her congressional career evolved.[6] While Pelosi began her congressional career well below the median Democrat in the House in regard to legislative effectiveness (she was actually below the median member in her freshman Democratic cohort), she quickly rose through the ranks until she was in the top quartile of majority-party members in the 103rd Congress (which began in 1993). While her LES declined significantly in the 104th Congress (which began in 1995), to correspond with the Republican takeover in the House, she continued to outperform her Democratic peers. After the 104th Congress, however, she dropped steeply in regard to her LESs, and she was consistently below the median member of the Democratic Party for the next four Congresses. While not engaging in much lawmaking activity (at least as measured by the LES), as followers of congressional politics are well aware, Pelosi was quite busy during these Congresses, as she ramped up her fund-raising and campaign contribution activities for the party, which also corresponded with her moving into the leadership ranks of the Democrats. She became minority whip in 2001 and minority leader in 2003, and she became the first female Speaker of the House in 2007.

Though her term as Speaker was relatively short (only two Congresses), most observers of congressional politics would agree that Pelosi was an effective leader, both in regard to managing the Democratic Party and advancing substantively important legislation (such as the Affordable Care Act) through the House. In considering her legislative policy-making activities (as captured by her LES), one wonders how representative her pattern of behavior is for other legislators who are elected Speaker. Do all Speakers tend to downplay advancing their own legislative agenda items in the Congress before they are elevated to the speakership to focus on other, more party-centric matters? If so, such a finding would suggest that parties tend to seek out and promote leaders who do not focus their efforts and energies primarily on lawmaking.

While there has not been a Democratic Speaker of the House other than Pelosi for more than twenty years, which limits our ability to engage in intraparty comparisons of leadership trajectories among Democrats, some insights can still be gleaned by considering the paths that have been followed by the past Republican Speakers. More specifically, Figures 11.4, 11.5, and 11.6 plot the LESs of Newt Gingrich

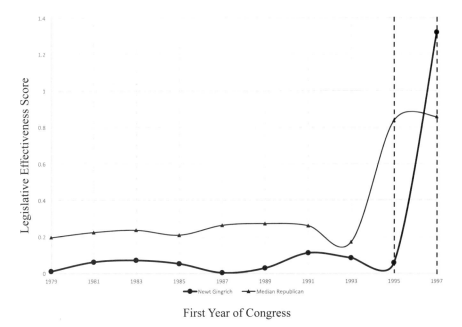

First Year of Congress

Figure 11.4. Legislative Effectiveness of Newt Gingrich (Speaker, 1995–1999). *Note:* The dashed lines identify the first years of the first (104th) and last (105th) Congresses during which Gingrich (R-GA) held the position of Speaker. Gingrich's legislative effectiveness score was below the median member of the Republican Party in the House for every Congress in which he served before becoming Speaker.

(R-GA), Dennis Hastert (R-IL), and John Boehner (R-OH) (and the LES of the median members of the Republican Party), who served as Speaker from 1995 to 1997, 1997 to 2007, and 2011 to 2015, respectively.

One point that emerges from Figures 11.4, 11.5, and 11.6 is how two of the Speakers, Gingrich and Hastert, seemed to have charted a pattern of legislative engagement that was quite similar to that of Pelosi in the Congresses before their becoming Speaker. Neither Gingrich nor Hastert was particularly focused on (or effective at) moving their own bills through the legislative process (compared to the median Republican) in the five Congresses before becoming Speaker. In fact, neither Gingrich nor Hastert was ever more effective than the median House Republican for any Congress in which they served before becoming Speaker. Boehner, however, seems to be the exception that proves the rule about leaders being chosen who do not engage in substantial lawmaking activity. For three of the five Congresses before becoming Speaker, his LES was greater than that of the median House Republican. Of course, as noted by Sinclair and Koger, Boehner also distinguished himself from his Republican predecessors in that he was generally unable

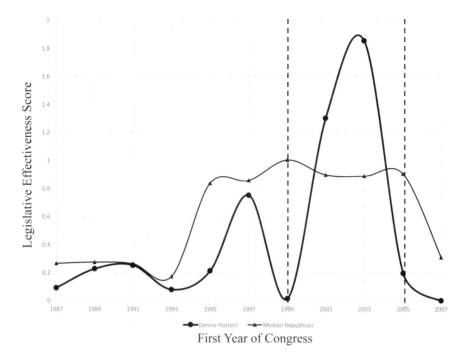

First Year of Congress

Figure 11.5. Legislative Effectiveness of Dennis Hastert (Speaker, 1999–2007). *Note:* The dashed lines identify the first years of the first (106th) and last (109th) Congresses during which Hastert (R-IL) held the position of Speaker. Hastert's legislative effectiveness score was below the median member of the Republican Party in the House for every Congress in which he served before becoming Speaker.

to manage his caucus, which led to a series of leadership challenges and his ultimate resignation from office in October 2015. Sinclair and Koger essentially argue that Boehner found himself in a particular political context in regard to the preferences of the Republican membership, which made him unable to successfully navigate the legislative landscape as Speaker while still appeasing the demands of his fellow partisans. In other words, it was the context that doomed Boehner.

While Sinclair and Koger's arguments are quite reasonable, their analysis fails to appreciate another possibility that emerges from Figure 11.6: Boehner was a different type of lawmaker than his Republican predecessors. For whatever reason, it appears that a different filter was being applied by the Republican membership to potential leadership candidates when Boehner was first elected Speaker than what had likely been applied when Hastert and/or Gingrich were elected. Hence, it should be unsurprising that the Republicans (and the House, more generally considered) ended up with a different type of Speaker. Unfortunately, the lawmaking

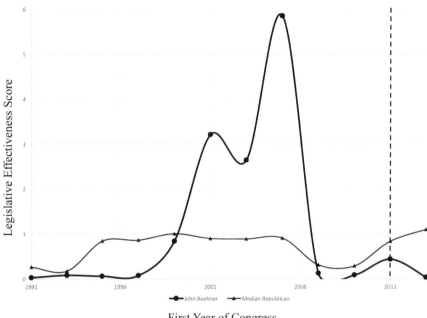

First Year of Congress

Figure 11.6. Legislative Effectiveness of John Boehner (Speaker, 2011–2015). *Note:* The dashed lines identify the first years of the first (112th) and last (114th) Congresses during which Boehner (R-OH) held the position of Speaker. Boehner's legislative effectiveness score was above the median member of the Republican Party in the House for three of the five Congresses in which he served before becoming Speaker.

skills that Boehner had cultivated before becoming Speaker appear to have been of less use to him once he assumed the role of leadership. By using a different filter for selecting their leader, the Republicans ended up with a different type of Speaker, but he wasn't the type of Speaker that they ultimately wanted.

As a bookend to this discussion, it is useful to note how the current Speaker of the House, Paul Ryan (R-WI), compares to his Republican predecessors. As illustrated in Figure 11.7, Speaker Ryan seems to have followed a pattern of legislative engagement that is more consistent with Speakers Gingrich and Hastert than Boehner. For the five Congresses before being elected Speaker, Ryan's LES was above the median Republican of the House only once (the 112th Congress, which began in 2011). In fact, with the exception of the 112th Congress and the 108th Congress (which began in 2003), Ryan's LES was never higher than that of the median House Republican. A casual observer might infer that in choosing Ryan, the Republican caucus used a filter that was more similar to the one that it used when choosing Gingrich and Hastert for Speaker compared to how it evalu-

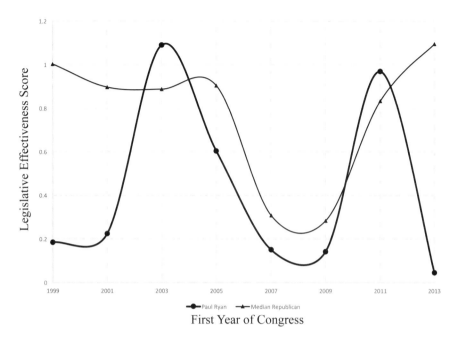

First Year of Congress

Figure 11.7. Legislative Effectiveness of Paul Ryan (Speaker, 2015–present). *Note:* Ryan's (R-WI) legislative effectiveness score was below the median member of the Republican Party in the House in nearly every Congress during which he served before becoming Speaker. He began serving as Speaker in the 114th Congress.

ated Boehner's candidacy for the office. The question is still open as to whether the Republican membership will ultimately decide that they made the choice that served them best.

Finally, it is worth pointing out that, as illustrated in Figures 11.4, 11.5, 11.6, and 11.7, none of the past four Republican Speakers (current Speaker Ryan included) ever had an LES that was greater than the score of the median Republican representative when the Republicans were the minority party. As Volden and Wiseman (2014), and Volden, Wiseman, and Wittmer (2013) note, it is essential for minority party members to be able to reach across the aisle, so to speak, in order to get their bills through the legislative process, as they do not have a built-in majority coalition to help them advance their legislative agenda items. Given that none of these four representatives ever cultivated a practice of bipartisan lawmaking activities when they were in the minority, it should perhaps be unsurprising that none of them would naturally use bipartisan tactics when they were in the majority. Hence, one should likely not have expected any of them to advance bipartisan legislative solutions to pressing policy problems when they led the House as Speaker.

Concluding Thoughts: Pegs in Holes, Filters, or Both?

What makes for a good or bad leader? Who becomes leaders? How might one evaluate a leader? These are some of the many questions that are engaged by the authors in this volume; and in writing their contributions, they have provided a great service to those of us who think about the role and impact of leaders in the American political system. At the very least, several of the contributions in this volume, such as Patty's chapter on bureaucracy, Battista's chapter on state politics, and LaPira's chapter on interest groups, provide outstanding reviews of extant literatures that will be of interest to scholars and students of leadership in each of these political environments. Moreover, as noted above, these and many other chapters in this volume provide various kinds of data, through anecdote, case study, and large-sample empirical analysis, which can serve as the building blocks of new theoretical and empirical scholarship on leadership in American politics.

For those of us who are interested in trying to understand where leaders come from and what makes some leaders more effective than others, I would conclude with the following thought exercise. Consider a situation in which for any particular leadership position (e.g., president, governor, party leader, interest group leader) there is a range of possible candidates who could plausibly fill the position. For any given position, these candidates will each be evaluated according to a set of specific criteria (subjected to a filter), such that only one of them ultimately becomes a leader of the organization. Upon assuming the mantle of leadership, the leader will find herself faced with a variety of institutional and political considerations, which will influence and (perhaps) constrain her behavior and choices. Finally, the leader will make particular choices, and policy outcomes will ensue.

Given the dynamic that I describe, one wonders what will occur if the leader (call her Leader A) of our hypothetical institution is replaced with a new leader (call him Leader B)? Suppose we observe essentially no changes in policy outcomes following the replacement of Leader A with Leader B. Why might that be? One possibility is that both Leader A and Leader B had to survive the same selection filter in order to become a leader. Hence, both of them possessed essentially the same characteristics that made them plausible choices for leadership; they are, personal characteristics aside, functionally interchangeable. Alternatively, perhaps it is the case that Leaders A and B were subjected to different selection filters, but upon assuming office, they faced identical institutional and political constraints, which channeled their choices in the same manner, yielding essentially identical policy outcomes. Finally, perhaps both possibilities are true: all leaders of the organization were subjected to the same selection filter, and upon assuming office, they all faced identical (binding) institutional constraints.

Alternatively, suppose that there are notable changes in policy outcomes when Leader B replaces Leader A. What could explain such variations in outcomes? Consistent with the discussion above, the variations in outcomes could follow from the leaders being subjected to different selection filters, from them inheriting different institutional environments, or both. (Of course, while not explored much in this chapter, it is also possible that leaders can exercise agency, such that they can influence policy outcomes in meaningful ways, independent of selection mechanisms and institutional constraints.)

To put a bit more flesh on the bones of this thought exercise, consider the following specific, and timely, question: are women more effective political leaders then men? After the attention that was drawn to a collection of female senators who worked behind the scenes to try to avoid the fiscal cliff in winter 2012, and several other high-profile incidents of similar legislative maneuvers being undertaken by female members of Congress in recent years, many observers of politics have suggested that female legislators are more effective lawmakers than their male peers. This claim likewise comports with recent scholarship on the lawmaking effectiveness of women (Anzia and Berry 2011; Volden, Wiseman, Wittmer 2013; Volden and Wiseman 2014).

In explicating their findings, Anzia and Berry (2011) argue that female members of Congress have to overcome numerous hurdles in order to be elected, which their male counterparts are not subjected to. Hence, any female candidates who are ultimately elected are essentially higher-quality politicians than the average male member of Congress.[7] In other words, women look like stronger leaders because they are subjected to a different (more stringent) filter than men. While conceding that female candidates are subjected to more challenging electoral environments than men, Volden, Wiseman, and Wittmer (2013) argue that their findings suggest that female legislators engage in more consensus-oriented lawmaking activities that allow them to outperform their male counterparts (in the minority party in particular), in regard to their abilities to advance their legislative agenda items. In other words, even if they are subjected to a more stringent filter than men in order to be elected, it is still the case that women engage in different strategies than men, which allow them to experience greater levels of legislative success and to transcend their institutional constraints. In contrast to either of these perspectives, however, Ferreira and Gyourko's (2014) analysis of US municipalities reveals that there are essentially no differences in policy outcomes across municipalities attributable to the gender of a city's mayor.

How might Ferreira and Gyourko's (2014) findings comport with the analyses of Anzia and Berry (2011), and Volden, Wiseman, and Wittmer (2013)? Perhaps it's the case that the filter that is applied for electing someone to executive office (e.g., mayor) is different than that which is applied for electing someone to Congress. Hence, women who engage in whatever gender-correlated differences in legislative strategy that are suggested by Volden, Wiseman, and Wittmer (2013) are not usually elected to executive offices. Alternatively, perhaps it is the case, as Keohane (2010,

154) argues, drawing on her own leadership experiences, that "the effects of organizational culture and the demands of institutional leadership outweigh any effects of gender." In other words, institutional and political constraints are so significant for some executive offices that leaders who occupy executive offices are essentially pegs in holes, regardless of their descriptive characteristics.

Scholars who seek to identify the drivers of effective leaders and leadership, and educational institutions (such as public policy schools) that seek to train the next generation of political leaders, need to be cognizant of these considerations when they undertake their analyses and develop their curricular materials. Failing to account for the likely consequences of filter-induced leadership and pegs-in-holes leadership, which are pervasive across virtually all political environments and institutions, can lead to scholars and practitioners drawing inappropriate inferences about the factors that facilitate and enhance leadership efficacy. While leaders can almost always exercise some degree of agency in their own right, the burden is on the scholar (and/or the practitioner) to identify how much of any given policy outcome is attributable to a leader's actions, independent of the institutional constraints she faces and/or the selection mechanisms that brought her into power. Undertaking a research agenda to engage these two separate yet complementary drivers of leadership outcomes can be challenging in that it requires one to appreciate the profound connections between two often disconnected fields in political science: mass political behavior (which often influences the designs of the filters that are used for selecting leaders) and elite political institutions (which often influence the constraints that leaders face after obtaining their positions). The potential for making meaningful contributions in leadership studies so conceived, however, is substantial, and ambitious scholars who explore these topics will find much in this volume to help guide their endeavors.

Acknowledgments

This chapter benefited from several constructive conversations with attendees at the Leadership in American Politics conference, University of Virginia, June 2–3, 2014, and feedback from seminar participants at the Center for Democratic Institutions at Vanderbilt University. I also thank Craig Volden for helpful comments on an early draft and the Madison Initiative of the William and Flora Hewlett Foundation for its ongoing financial support of the Legislative Effectiveness Project.

References

Ahlquist, John S., and Margaret Levi. 2011. "Leadership: What It Means, What It Does, and What We Want to Know About It." *Annual Review of Political Science* 14:1–24.

Anzia, Sarah, and Christopher R. Berry. 2011. "The Jackie (and Jill) Robinson Effect: Why

Do Congresswomen Outperform Congressmen?" *American Journal of Political Science* 55 (3): 478–493.

Cameron, Charles M. 2000. *Veto Bargaining: Presidents and the Politics of Negative Power.* New York: Cambridge University Press.

Canes-Wrone, Brandice. 2009. "Game Theory and Studying the Presidency." In *The Oxford Handbook of the American Presidency,* edited by William G. Howell and George C. Edwards III, 30–50. New York: Oxford University Press.

Ferreira, Fernando, and Joseph Gyourko. 2014. "Does Gender Matter for Political Leadership? The Case of US Mayors." *Journal of Public Economics* 112 (1): 24–39.

Greenstein, Fred I. 2009. *The Presidential Difference: Leadership Style from FDR to Barack Obama.* 3rd ed. Princeton, NJ: Princeton University Press.

Groseclose, Tim, and James M. Snyder Jr. 1996. "Buying Supermajorities." *American Political Science Review* 90 (2): 303–315.

Hermalin, Benjamin E. 2013. "Leadership and Corporate Culture." In *The Handbook of Organizational Economics,* edited by Robert Gibbons and John Roberts, 432–478. Princeton, NJ: Princeton University Press.

Hirsch, Alexander V., and Kenneth W. Shotts. 2011. "Competitive Policy Entrepreneurship in Legislatures." Paper presented at the annual meeting of the American Political Science Association.

———. 2015. "Competitive Policy Entrepreneurship." *American Economic Review* 105 (4): 1646–1664.

Hitt, Matthew P., Craig Volden, and Alan E. Wiseman. 2017. "Spatial Models of Legislative Effectiveness." *American Journal of Political Science.* 61 (3): 575–590.

Jenkins, Shannon. 2007. "A Women's Work Is Never Done? Fund-raising Perception and Effort among Female State Legislative Candidates." *Political Research Quarterly* 60 (2): 230–239.

Keohane, Nannerl O. 2010. *Thinking About Leadership.* Princeton, NJ: Princeton University Press.

Krehbiel, Keith, Adam Meirowitz, and Alan E. Wiseman. 2015. "A Theory of Competitive Partisan Lawmaking." *Political Science Research and Methods* 3 (3): 423–448.

Lawless, Jennifer L., and Kathryn Pearson. 2008. "The Primary Reason for Women's Underrepresentation? Reevaluating the Conventional Wisdom." *Journal of Politics* 70 (1): 67–82.

Romer, Thomas, and Howard Rosenthal. 1978. "Political Resources, Allocation, Controlled Agendas, and the Status Quo." *Public Choice* 33 (4): 27–43.

Sanbonmatsu, Kira. 2006. *Where Women Run: Gender and Party in the American States.* Ann Arbor: University of Michigan Press.

Snyder, James. 1991. "On Buying Legislatures." *Economics and Politics* 3 (2): 93–109.

Terry, Larry D. 2003. *Leadership of Public Bureaucracies: The Administrator as Conservator.* 2nd ed. Armonk, NY: M. E. Sharpe.

Truman, David B. 1959. *The Congressional Party: A Case Study.* New York: Wiley.

Volden, Craig, and Alan E. Wiseman. 2014. *Legislative Effectiveness in the United States Congress: The Lawmakers.* New York: Cambridge University Press.

———. 2016. "Incorporating Legislative Effectiveness into Nonmarket Strategy: The Case of

Financial Services Reform and the Great Recession." *Advances in Strategic Management* 34:67–118.

Volden, Craig, Alan E. Wiseman, and Dana E. Wittmer. 2013. "When Are Women More Effective Lawmakers Than Men?" *American Journal of Political Science* 57 (2): 326–341.

Notes

1. Ahlquist and Levi (2011) provide an extensive review of the extant literature of leadership studies and its ties to various subfields in political science.

2. Cameron and Shadmehr do, however, suggest that a judge might be able to exert some degree of agency over the doctrine-making process, and that she might be able to influence the probability that other judges receive her signal regarding the appropriateness of a given legal doctrine.

3. Indeed, the pegs-in-holes perspective completely flies in the face of president-centered theories of executive policy (Greenstein 2009), as articulated by Beckmann.

4. Formally, for any status location q, the location of the new policy p will be: $p = 2M - q$.

5. Sinclair and Koger note that all 241 House Republicans voted for Boehner for Speaker at the beginning of the 112th Congress.

6. Volden and Wiseman's (2014) analyses stop at 2003, whereas I extend the time series until 2013 (the 113th Congress), drawing on data from The Lawmakers (http://www.thelaw makers.org/).

7. As documented by a wide range of scholars (Lawless and Pearson 2008; Sanbonmatsu 2006; Jenkins 2007), female candidates tend to receive less support from their party organizations, face more vibrant competition in their elections, and have to work harder for campaign contributions than male candidates.

CHAPTER TWELVE

What Do Political Leaders Do?

Eric M. Patashnik

Leaders make a difference in politics. They shape the authoritative allocation of values, mediate between group preferences and policy outcomes, and can even bend the arc of history. Yet if leaders clearly matter, political leadership is nonetheless a challenging topic to study. This is so for three reasons.

First, leadership manifests itself in diverse ways in politics. Leaders may or may not possess formal authority, may or may not be charismatic, and may or may not have managerial responsibilities for an organization. Some political leaders conform to the Great Man model of leadership, striding boldly across the public stage, but others exercise quiet influence, helping groups to achieve shared goals in less conspicuous ways. Some political leaders stride noisily across the public stage, drawing attention to their own actions, but other leaders exercise quiet influence, helping their groups to achieve shared goals in less conspicuous ways. But if leadership personalities, attributes, traits and styles vary enormously, what is the fundamental essence that all political leaders share? How do we distinguish leaders from other influential actors, such as strongmen, statesmen, and rulers? Leadership is also challenging to study because it is deeply contextual. To lead a congressional party is one thing; to lead an army, bureaucracy, or social movement is quite another. If contextual factors mediate what leaders do, how do we formulate a theory of political leadership that transcends the rules, cultures, and norms of particular institutions? Finally, political leadership involves the exercise of power, and power is itself a notoriously difficult concept to operationalize and measure. In sum, leadership is an elusive topic because it is both domain specific and general. Little wonder that the political science literature on leadership has long been regarded as theoretically underdeveloped, poorly integrated, and empirically disappointing.

Yet in recent years a promising literature on leadership in politics has begun to emerge. This literature is forging tighter connections between leadership studies and mainstream political science research on agency, institutions and civic engagement (for an excellent critical review essay, see Ahlquist and Levi 2011). Building on this intellectual momentum, Jeffery A. Jenkins and Craig Volden have assembled compelling essays that add materially to our knowledge about the causes and consequences of leadership behavior across political settings. In my reflections, I will highlight a few themes that emerge from this illuminating volume and suggest avenues for future research suggested by the chapters and by the emerging leadership challenges of the twenty-first century.

Understanding What Leadership Means

The political science literature on leadership has been bedeviled by the failure of many scholars to articulate a clear definition of leadership. This failure is understandable. Any definition of leadership that has analytic bite must exclude something; if leadership is everything, it becomes nothing. Research on leadership cannot progress without bounding the scope of inquiry.

In their insightful essay, William G. Howell and Stephane Wolton offer a potent definition of leadership: "A Leader publicly defines, extols, and eventually personifies higher objectives, thereby orienting and coordinating the efforts of followers who seek to advance such objectives." Howell and Wolton's signal contribution in their chapter is not the particular definition of leadership they nominate—although I find it compelling—but rather their provocative claim that scholarship on leadership cannot move forward unless scholars are much more precise about their terms. In my view, Howell and Wolton are right to insist that leadership be understood in relational terms. The sine qua non of leadership is the mutually constitutive association that leaders foster and maintain with their followers. There are many agents of social change—many actors who get things done—but change agents are not leaders if they lack followers. While Howell and Wolton's definition of leadership is incisive, it covers a wide terrain. The definition permits leaders to be effective or ineffective, disruptive or calming, moral or immoral. Martin Luther King Jr. and Adolph Hitler were thus both leaders because they both (obviously in different ways and for different ends) mobilized followers and personified higher-order goals. Leaders' goodness or badness, as well as the magnitude, durability, style, and character of their influence, remain crucial normative and empirical dimensions for evaluation, but they are distinct from an actor's status as a leader itself. This is a clarifying move. Too often scholars fail to distinguish leadership from ethical behavior as well as from other governance tasks, such as management. The key managerial charge is to cope with complexity (Kotter 2001); the burden of leadership is to get followers to give their resources (e.g., time, energy, support) to promote shared goals. Leaders may exercise power and authority over followers; they needn't be democrats or egalitarians. But followers must retain free will to follow or not follow a leader's lead, else they become merely subjects. As James Coleman Battista observes in his chapter on leadership in the American states, the constraint or self-constraint of leadership is an important part of leadership, for "if we think of leadership as opposed to simple domination, then a true leader maintains some form of collective consent from those he or she is leading." As the other essays in this volume demonstrate, not every scholar of leadership behavior will wish to use an exclusive definition of leadership. Some researchers will find it useful for their purposes to define leadership more inclusively, focusing on various things that leaders (and other actors) do, such as resolving conflicts or negotiating deals. However, more scholarship is clearly needed, in my view, which treats leadership as a holistic phenomenon.

Moving from What Leadership Is to What Leaders Do

A second theme of the volume shifts from what leadership is to what leaders do. A social science of leadership requires scholars to move beyond proper nouns in order to gain a systematic understanding of leadership behavior and identify empirical regularities. The chapters in this volume show that leaders perform five critical functions or roles in politics (Fiorina and Shepsle 1989). I address them in turn.

Leaders as Coordinators

In any polity, but especially in modern, pluralistic democratic societies, actors will possess imperfect information about what to do and how to translate their preferences into collective outcomes. There is also uncertainty about how much others will contribute to group efforts. How can the behavior of complex, multiactor organizations be synchronized in the absence of any simple coordinating mechanism like the price system? One thing leaders do is provide signals to facilitate team behavior. For example, John W. Patty suggests that a key role of bureaucratic leaders it to organize and shepherd subordinates in order to maximize the group's efforts. As Wilson (1989) has argued, avoiding shirking is a serious challenge in public bureaucracies because the outputs of an agency may be not only unobservable but unknowable. (Consider an agency with a vague goal such as the State Department.) Yet most bureaucrats do not actually take every opportunity to shirk. Doubtless there are many reasons why shirking is rare, including professional norms and the desire to do a good job, situational imperatives, and material incentives. (As Wilson notes, while bureaucrats are hard to fire, they can be given miserable job assignments.) Yet leaders clearly play a key role in motivating and coordinating followers. More research on how leaders perform this vital coordinating function in different organizational settings would be useful. There are insights to be gleaned not only from the traditional public administration literature on organizational culture but also from psychology research on social norms and self-reinforcing processes (Kelman 2005).

Leaders as Agents

Leaders use their delegated authority to promote the collective goals of group members. Elected officials, for example, are often viewed as agents of their constituents. Viewing leaders as agents (rather than as principals) is logical when members of a group enjoy equal status on key dimensions and are not dependent on the leader for their standing. For example, all members of the US House of Representatives are duly elected by voters, enjoy many of the same prerequisites of office, and can shape their reelection chances through their own actions. Yet members of a party caucus in Congress also have linked fates because their party's reputation influences their respective electoral prospects, power, and opportunity to shape public policy. As a result of this mutual dependence, lawmakers who share a party label are willing to grant some powers and resources to their leaders when the benefits from such delegation exceed the costs. Leadership in a principal–agent (P-A) framework is typically viewed as transactional rather than transformational. Followers/principals want their leaders/agents to help them achieve preexisting collective goals, such as reelection; followers are not necessarily empowering leaders to elevate or redefine group objectives.

Barbara Sinclair and Gregory Koger use P-A theory to guide their informative analysis of the troubled speakership of John Boehner. P-A theory predicts that the level of formal power delegated to party leaders hinges on the costs and benefits of such delegation to principals; all else being equal, the payoff from delegation increases with both the level of preference homogeneity of a party caucus and the competitive threat posed by the other party. Consistent with this expectation, House Republicans granted Speaker Boehner the ability to set the legislative agenda. Yet despite enjoying a relatively unified caucus to work with, Boehner found himself in an untenable position, unable to achieve the radical conservative policy objectives of his members without damaging the electoral reputation of the party. To avoid a voter backlash that would tarnish the GOP brand, Boehner had little choice but to violate the so-called Hastert rule of bringing to the floor only bills that a majority of his membership supported. Congressional leadership is never easy, but Sinclair and Koger show that it becomes virtually impossible when members hold unrealistic expectations about what is politically feasible, when they do not trust their leader, and when the leader lacks an intuitive sense of what actions his followers will accept. An interesting question is why followers would develop or hold unrealistic expectations about what leaders can achieve. Do these misguided expectations reflect imperfect or biased information, poor communication between the leader and party members, conflicting attitudes toward risk, or other reasons? Also, under what conditions can leaders' mold their followers' beliefs about what is achievable? Did Boehner attempt to persuade fellow Republicans that they would need to scale back their ambitions? If so, why did his appeals fall on deaf ears? More generally, we need to better understand why gaps emerge between the perceptions, beliefs, and worldviews of leaders and followers, and whether and how leaders can use their influence to bring followers' beliefs into alignment with the true state of the world. The authors argue that the unrealistic goals of rank-and-file House Republicans were more important than Boehner's style or personality traits in explaining his leadership dilemma. Still, while Boehner was clearly dealt a bad hand, he might have played it better. Leadership skill, not just external conditions, clearly matters in legislative politics (Bardach 1972). Scholars have long struggled to measure the skill of different leaders. However, Volden and Wiseman (2014) have recently developed innovative quantitative measures of the legislative effectiveness of individual lawmakers, advancing systematic understanding of why some legislators are better at moving bills than others.

Leaders as Agenda Setters

The capacity to set the agenda—to shape the menu of policy choices and thereby determine what politics is about—is a crucial leadership power. Matthew N. Beckmann cites research that shows that US presidents gain influence on Capitol Hill by constructing and credibly signaling their legislative priorities, drafting legislative initiatives, and building winning coalitions for their agenda. Related to the discussion above about leadership skill, Beckmann persuasively argues that the scholars should avoid straw man empirical tests to evaluate leaders' impact. To advance understanding, scholars should use a variety of research methodologies to assess how much difference leaders really make. In particular, thought experiments, elite interviews, and in-depth case studies (Greenstein 2004) can supplement statistical methods to shed light on what other plausible leaders would have done facing the same situation and institutional context. It seems obvious, for example, that President Donald Trump's first-year agenda differs not only from the agenda that Hillary Clinton would have brought with her to the Oval Office had she won election, but also from at least some of the priorities of Trump's GOP rivals in the 2016 primary campaign. By posing more nuanced questions about the scope and limits of leadership influence, scholars will gain new insights into what leaders actually do and how much they really matter.

Leaders as Problem Solvers

Politics is not only about distributing power; it is also about solving problems that individuals, communities, and markets cannot mitigate on their own, including providing for national defense, mitigating poverty, and generating the information needed to rationalize health care delivery (Gerber and Patashnk 2007). Often market failures (e.g., public goods or externalities), breakdowns of civil society (e.g., conflicts over scarce resources), or failures of self-mastery (e.g., excessive alcohol use) are addressed institutionally—through the establishment of an expert agency, the allocation of property rights, or the prohibition of certain behaviors. But leaders also play a vital role in the problem-solving process. Leaders can be institutional framers, situational designers, and decision architects who set the context in which actors make decisions (Converse 2011). In the case of emergent problems, there may be no extant institutional solution for society to fall back on. Leadership energy and initiative then becomes essential to designing and mobilizing support for novel solutions. For example, Patty describes how bureaucratic leaders at the Environmental Protection Agency took the lead on climate change policy using their administrative discretion to subject power plants and other greenhouse gas emitters to permitting rules. Different environmental policy leaders in the same context might not have acted. The political science literature has tended to view institutional factors mainly as constraints on leadership behavior—think of Neustadt's (1960) argument that the limits on presidents' formal authority compels them to lead through persuasion—but leaders and institutions can also be viewed as complements (and even substitutes) in government's problem-solving function.

To the extent leaders are construed as problem solvers, it becomes important to distinguish among the full variety of problems that societies face. Leadership scholar Ronald Heifetz (1994) makes a crisp distinction between technical problems and adaptive challenges. The former are easy to identify, often can be solved by an expert relying on existing knowledge, and entail change that can be carried out within existing organizational boundaries, whereas the latter challenges are difficult to identify (and hence easy for people to deny), require changes in values, beliefs, roles, and relationships, entail solutions that cross organizational boundaries, and may require experiments and new discoveries. To appraise the effectiveness of particular leaders as problem solvers, it is critical to hold roughly constant not only the institutional and political context in which leaders are situated but also the nature of the problems they tried to solve.

Leaders as Political Entrepreneurs

Political entrepreneurs are creative actors who invest their own time, energy, resources, and political reputation to advocate for an idea or proposal in order to capture a political reward (Kingdon 2003). They frame issues, create new public demands, build coalitions, and expand the set of issues it is considered legitimate and expected for government to address (Sheingate 2003). To use an economics analogy, political entrepreneurs are sellers of problem definitions and proposed solutions who seek to satisfy an unmet social need—for a price. In a sense, they are creative leaders who are in the market for followers. Leaders cum entrepreneurs need to find people who will embrace their ideas—but the ideas come first. As legal theorist and federal judge Richard Posner (2003, 194) observes, leaders cum entrepreneurs can have a large influence on public policy: "The voting public did not know that it wanted social security, conscription, public education, an interstate highway system, a Presidency opened to a divorced or Catholic person, the North Atlantic Treaty Organization, or the auctioning of rights to the use of the electromagnetic spectrum before these things were proposed by political entrepreneurs, as distinct from run-of-the-mill politicians."

Political entrepreneurship can be risky for officeholders; there is no guarantee that the creation of a new policy product will generate a positive return. Stakeholders will not want to see existing arrangements disrupted, and novel policy ideas may be greeted with skepticism by relevant publics (Gerber, Patashnik, and Dowling 2017).

It would be interesting to appraise the incentives and rewards that different political actors face to engage in entrepreneurial leadership on different issues. Philip B. K. Potter observes that foreign policy leadership tends to create lower electoral and political rewards for presidents than does domestic policy leadership, despite the greater constitutional and institutional leeway that presidents enjoy in foreign policy. Even when foreign policy decisions are salient, most voters vote on the basis of the economy and domestic issues. This incentivizes presidents to focus on bread-and-butter issues, such as promoting economic growth. But of course presidents sometimes do choose to exercise energetic foreign policy leadership, proposing wars, interventions, and other kinds of foreign policy products for which there may have been little existing political demand. As Potter observes, presidents may invest in foreign policy making for institutional reasons. The president's leadership in foreign policy, when compared to domestic policy, is less constrained by Congress and clientele groups. But another reason why presidents may behave entrepreneurially in the foreign policy area is arguably because they believe that the future political and policy gains from taking robust actions are worth the potential losses, even at the expense of focusing their (finite) leadership resources on issues with lower rewards and downside risk.

Philip B. K. Potter suggests that powerful presidents have an incentive to favor domestic initiatives. This seems plausible, but the distinction between the relative payoffs of presidential leadership of foreign and domestic policy may cut too deeply. While the domestic policy arena does offer plenty of safe bets, such as supporting tax breaks favored by well-organized constituencies, it is notable that presidents sometimes undertake extremely risky initiatives in domestic affairs, aiming to deliver benefits to marginalized groups or to withdraw benefits from powerful clienteles. For example, President Obama chose to prioritize subsidizing health care coverage for less affluent Americans even though most upper- and middle-class voters (who already had insurance) were not clamoring for reform and feared changes that would disrupt their own coverage. Further, several of Obama's key advisers warned him against pursuing health reform in a weak economy (Suskind 2011). Obama gambled that the Affordable Care Act would win adoption and gain enormous popularity over time. Similarly, President George W. Bush's proposal to partly privatize Social Security was another risky entrepreneurial venture—and one that failed to gain traction. While there are clearly important differences between presidential leadership of foreign and domestic policy that result from differences in institutional and political constraints, presidents and other actors make gambles in all policy domains. More research is needed that explores the incentives and disincentives for entrepreneurial leadership (by presidents and other actors) on issues across the domestic–foreign policy divide.

Separating the Act of Leadership into Its Constituent Actions

John Patty discusses three steps of bureaucratic leadership: getting advice, making decisions, and giving directions. This is a perfectly sensible typology, although it is certainly not the only way to conceptualize the sequence of leadership activities. But Patty's broader point is that research on leadership does not always need to be comprehensive; disaggregating the act of leadership into its constituent actions may render research questions more tractable. To the extent this is the case, leadership studies would become a more "normal" political science. Deeper but partial analysis has advanced empirical understanding of complex phenomena in many areas. For example, scholars of political behavior have generated literatures on public opinion formation, voter participation, and the influence of economic factors on election outcomes. We have learned a great deal about these individual topics, even as we have profited from synthetic research that poses integrative questions about how political systems work as a whole. Similarly, research on political leadership can make tangible progress in formulating hypotheses and testing claims by examining discrete questions, such as how bureaucratic leaders make decisions, provided scholars maintain contact with fundamental issues.

Contextual Factors and Leadership

The study of how interests, institutions, and ideas shape political outcomes is the bread and butter of political science, far more so than the study of individual leaders, yet the essays in this volume suggest that scholars could be much more systematic in investigating how contextual factors shape leadership opportunities and constraints. David Karol's chapter raises a fascinating question: How does the context of congressional leadership differ between the Republican and Democratic parties? While the similarities between America's two mainstream parties appear significant in a cross-national perspective—the behavior of both parties is driven by the incentives embedded in the constitutional framework and the electoral system—there are nonetheless notable differences in the two parties' respective leadership practices. In particular, Karol notes that "congressional Republicans are more likely to force out their leaders, less likely to replace them with the next in line, and much less respectful of seniority than Democrats." This antileadership behavior is not consistent with the conventional wisdom that the Republicans are a hierarchical, deferential party or composed of members with authoritarian personality traits. Karol intriguingly suggests that the greater ideological homogeneity of the Republicans "may make it is easier for consensus to form against leaders and lead GOP legislators to place less stock in norms that keep the peace, such as the seniority system." More generally, political scientists should devote more attention to how partisanship mediates leader–follower relations. The nomination of Donald Trump as the GOP's standard-bearer in 2016 (despite concerns among many Republican stalwarts about Trump's Republican credentials and commitment to conservatism) raises timely questions not only about the changing policy stance of the GOP on issues like trade but also about the evolving leadership roles of elites, interest groups, and rank-and-file voters in the Republican party network.

More broadly still, scholars could explore how changes in the macropolitical context of politics—such as intensifying partisan polarization, the growing scope of government, and the increasing complexity of policy making—are changing leadership selection, incentives, and behavior. Timothy M. LaPira makes a fascinating argument that this changing context is having far-reaching consequences for interest group politics, increasing the demand among constituencies for leaders, lobbyists, and agents who possess generalized political process knowledge, rather than the specialized policy knowledge and substantive expertise that was said to be the coin of the realm back in the 1970s, when the interest group environment was thought to be organized around issue networks (Heclo 1978; see also Pierson 2014). The skills and capacities that make an actor an effective political leader in one setting clearly may be less valuable in another context.

Back to Relations between Leaders and Followers

At the heart of leadership is a leader's relations with his or her followers, as Howell and Wolton emphasize. Several of the essays shed new light on these relations. For example, Steven S. Smith shows how Senate Democratic leader Harry Reid of Nevada moved with his caucus in order to personify Senate liberalism. When he was first elected to the Senate in 1988, Reid was known as a probusiness social conservative who was "somewhat out of step with most of his Senate Democratic colleagues." But Reid adapted successfully to the expectations of his followers. Smith shows that Reid's voting record shifted from the conservative to the liberal side of the Democratic caucus in his first Congress (1999–2000) as party whip. During

Reid's tenure as Senate leader, he also deferred to committee chairs and let other Senate Democrats take the lead in writing legislation. In sum, Reid led by following his caucus. A key question to be asked about any leader is whether he or she is leading from the front or from behind. It is often possible to gain empirical leverage on this question through roll-call vote analysis (for leaders in legislative settings), process tracing, and interviews. Mapping the convergence and divergence of the positions, rhetoric, and actions of leaders and followers over time can reveal a great deal about leader–follower relations and the mechanisms of group influence.

Leadership Studies and the Future of American Politics

Leadership is integral to the study of political science today because the institutional norms of American politics have been unsettled as a result of the emergence of the new populism, raising fresh questions about the scope and mechanisms of contemporary leadership influence. Few predicted Donald Trump's victory over Hillary Clinton in the 2016 election, but the current political moment has been many decades in the making. The most obvious causes of the rise of the new populism are economic (e.g., the Great Recession and its aftermath, wage stagnation and rising inequality) and cultural (anxiety among rural white Americans about immigration, demographic change, and the redefinition of the American community). But arguably as important have been shifts in the dynamics of the American political system itself resulting from the decline of the institutions that traditionally connected citizens to government, such as party organizations, families, and geographically based and occupational interest groups. More than thirty years ago, political scientist Nelson W. Polsby (1983) presciently wrote about shifts in what he called the intermediation processes as a result of political reform (the displacement of party elders by primary electorates) and the increasing reliance on mass marketing rather than face-to-face democratic persuasion. While Polsby was concerned then with the rise of television (he did not anticipate Twitter or Facebook), and he did not use the terms "fake news" or "alternative facts," many of the political developments he anticipated have come to pass. These include the increasing importance of crazes and manias, the resuscitation of ideology, and a new electoral politics in which there is a premium on celebrity and name recognition. Perhaps Polsby's most potent insight was that governing elites—leaders—do not disappear under a mass persuasion system. They do, however, become "less accountable to one another and more subject to the constraints of poplar fashion" (148).

Since the 1960s, the low level of public trust in government has created a challenging environment for leadership, but until recently, the paucity of public information about politics and policy making gave leaders a modicum of space (out of the public's view) to bargain, negotiate, and make decisions on behalf of their followers. Today, the ease with which voters can obtain information (whether fact based or not) has increased the tension between representation (doing what followers want) and governance (making decisions consistent with followers' interests). Contemporary leaders, whether inside or outside government, know that citizens are monitoring everything they do far more closely than in the past. How can leaders serve as effective agents who exercise judgment and discretion to promote a group's goals in a fluid and highly complex political environment when they are (and know they are) being constantly watched? Hyperaccountability can undermine leadership effectiveness, at least sometimes.

Similarly, the rise of fake news and the tendency for citizens to trust information only from ideologically certified, celebrity, or trusted partisan sources creates new barriers to the problem-solving and entrepreneurial functions of leadership. Analyzing the use, nonuse, and misuse of facts in various cases—such as the response to global warming and beliefs about Barack Obama's birthplace—Hochschild and Einstein (2015) argue there are three key asymmetries that emerge as one views the role of facts in politics from the vantage point of leaders who might try to educate the public. First, inertia is more likely than change as a general inclination in public opinion. Second, given this inertia, it is a much easier task for leaders to encourage uninformed people to remain uninformed than it is for leaders to get uninformed people to become informed. Finally, "politicians' incentives to keep people misinformed but active [in politics] tend to be much more powerful than (other) politicians' incentives to try to move people away from using falsehoods into using facts" (585). All this encourages demagogic behavior at the expense of the exercise of democratic leadership.

A final concern raised by contemporary developments is the intergenerational durability of leadership influence. Historically, current political leaders have honored past leaders of their organizations or groups (such as ex-presidents or former party leaders) in various ways, such as by reciting the accomplishments of previous leaders at conventions or other important group events, or by giving former leaders a visible role in the current policy-making apparatus, such as an appointment to a blue-ribbon commission. The motivation for current leaders to show respect to their predecessors is not simply to tap the institutional knowledge and networks of political veterans, but to help ensure that a group such as a political party remains faithful to its core principles over time. As politics becomes more populist and plebiscitary, however, current leaders are pressured to be attentive to their followers' current demands, no matter how unrealistic they are or how detrimental these desires may be to the group's future prospects.

Yet former leaders of a group who have something to contribute do not have to wait to be summoned; they can act on their own to help the current leaders of the group pivot toward more effective governing options. For example, three former Republican party elders concerned about the policy drift of the GOP—former secretary of state James Baker III, former secretary of state George P. Shultz, and former

300 Eric M. Patashnik

secretary of the treasury Henry M. Paulson Jr.—endorsed taxing carbon pollution as "a conservative climate solution" based on free-market principles (Schwartz 2017). A key question for research is thus not only how current leaders can motivate their followers and mobilize them into action in the contemporary era but also whether and under what conditions former leaders can influence, goad, protect, and inspire subsequent leaders, their successors, to act in ways consistent with a group's long-term interests.

References

Ahlquist, John S., and Margaret Levi. 2011. "Leadership: What It Means, What It Does, and What We Want to Know About It." *Annual Review of Political Science* 14:1–24.

Bardach, Eugene. 1972. *The Skill Factor in Politics: Repealing the Mental Commitment Laws in California.* Berkeley: University of California Press.

Converse, B. A. 2011. "How Social Psychology Is Liberating Leadership from the Great-Person Mold." *Virginia Policy Review* 5 (2): 12–17.

Fiorina, Morris P., and Kenneth A. Shepsle. 1989. "Formal Theories of Leadership: Agents, Agenda Setters, and Entrepreneurs." In *Leadership and Politics: New Perspectives in Political Science*, edited by B. D. Jones, 17–40. Lawrence: University Press of Kansas.

Gerber, Alan S., and Eric M. Patashnik, eds. 2007. *Promoting the General Welfare: New Perspectives on Government Performance.* Washington, DC: Brookings Institution Press.

Greenstein, Fred I. 2004. *The Presidential Difference: Leadership Style from FDR to George W. Bush.* Princeton, NJ: Princeton University Press.

Heclo, Hugh. 1978. "Issue Networks and the Executive Establishment." *Public Administration: Concepts and Cases* 413:46–57.

Heifetz, Ronald A. 1994. *Leadership without Easy Answers.* Cambridge, MA: Harvard University Press.

Hochschild, Jennifer L., and Katherine Levine Einstein. 2015. "Do Facts Matter? Information and Misinformation in American Politics." *Political Science Quarterly* 130 (4): 585–624.

Kelman, Steven. 2005. *Unleashing Change: A Study of Organizational Renewal in Government.* Washington, DC: Brookings Institution Press.

Kingdon, John W. 2003. *Agendas, Alternatives, and Public Policies.* 2nd ed. New York: Longman.

Kotter, John P. 2001. *What Leaders Really Do.* Cambridge, MA: Harvard Business School.

Neustadt, Richard E. 1960. *Presidential Power.* New York: New American Library.

Patashnik, Eric M., Alan S. Gerber, and Conor M. Dowling. 2017. *Unhealthy Politics: The Battle over Evidence-Based Medicine.* Princeton, NJ: Princeton University Press.

Pierson, Paul. 2014. "Madison Upside Down: The Policy Roots of Our Polarized Politics." In *The Politics of Major Policy Reform in Postwar America*, edited by Jeffrey A. Jenkins and Sidney M. Milkis, 282–381. Cambridge: Cambridge University Press.

Polsby, Nelson W. 1983. *Consequences of Party Reform.* Berkeley, CA: Institute of Governmental Studies Press.

Posner, Richard A. 2005. *Law, Pragmatism, and Democracy.* Cambridge, MA: Harvard University Press.

Schwartz, John. 2017. "A Conservative Climate Solution: Republican Group Calls for a Carbon Tax." *New York Times,* February 8. https://www.nytimes.com/.

Sheingate, Adam D. 2003. "Political Entrepreneurship, Institutional Change, and American Political Development." *Studies in American Political Development* 17 (2): 185–203.

Suskind, Ron. 2011. *Confidence Men: Wall Street, Washington, and the Education of a President.* New York: HarperCollins.

Volden, Craig, and Alan E. Wiseman. 2014. *Legislative Effectiveness in the United States Congress: The Lawmakers.* New York: Cambridge University Press.

Wilson, James Q. 1989. *Bureaucracy: What Government Agencies Do and Why They Do It.* New York: Basic Books.

Notes on Contributors

James Coleman Battista is associate professor of political science at the University at Buffalo, SUNY. His work focuses on internal governance in state legislatures, such as committee systems or party leadership power, and has appeared in such journals as *State Politics & Policy Quarterly* and *Legislative Studies Quarterly*.

Matthew N. Beckmann is associate professor of political science at the University of California, Irvine. His research and teaching explores politics in the United States, especially those related to the modern presidency. He is the author of *Pushing the Agenda: Presidential Leadership in US Lawmaking, 1953–2004* (2010).

Charles M. Cameron is jointly appointed in the Department of Politics and the Woodrow Wilson School of Public and International Affairs at Princeton University. He specializes in the analysis of political institutions, particularly courts and law, the American presidency, and legislatures. The author of many articles in leading journals of political science, he is also the author of *Veto Bargaining: Presidents and the Politics of Negative Power* (2000) and winner of the American Political Science Association's Fenno Prize, for best book in legislative studies, and the William Riker Award, for best book in political economy. He was elected a member of the American Academy of Arts and Sciences in 2014.

William G. Howell is Sydney Stein Professor in American Politics at the University of Chicago, where he holds appointments in the Department of Political Science and the Harris School of Public Policy. He has written widely on separation-of-powers issues and American political institutions, especially the presidency. Most recently he is the coauthor (with Terry Moe) of *Relic: How Our Constitution Undermines Effective Government–And Why We Need a More Powerful Presidency* (2016). He is currently working on research projects on Obama's education initiatives, authority acquisition, and the normative foundations of executive power.

Jeffery A. Jenkins is Provost Professor of Public Policy, Political Science, and Law, director of the Bedrosian Center, and Judith and John Bedrosian Chair in Governance and the Public Enterprise at the Sol Price School of Public Policy, University of Southern California. His work focuses on congressional lawmaking and organization. He is coauthor (with Charles Stewart III) of *Fighting for the Speakership: The House and the Rise of Party Government* (2013).

David Karol is associate professor of government and politics at the University of Maryland. He is the author of *Party Position Change in American Politics: Coalition Management* (2009) and coauthor (with Marty Cohen, Hans Noel, and John Zaller) of *The Party Decides: Presidential Nominations Before and After Reform* (2008).

Gregory Koger is associate professor of political science at the University of Miami. He specializes in legislative politics and political parties. He is the author of *Filibustering* (2010) and coauthor (with Matthew Lebo) of *Strategic Party Government* (2017).

Timothy M. LaPira is associate professor of political science at James Madison University. He is coauthor (with Herschel F. Thomas) of *Revolving Door Lobbying: Public Service, Private Influence, and the Unequal Representation of Interests* (University Press of Kansas, 2017). LaPira's academic expertise is on Congress, legislative staff, interest groups, and lobbying.

Eric M. Patashnik is Julis-Rabinowitz Professor of Public Policy and Political Science at the Watson Institute for International and Public Affairs at Brown University. He is the director of the Brown Public Policy Program and the editor of the *Journal of Health Politics, Policy and Law*. His latest book (with Alan S. Gerber and Conor M. Dowling) is *Unhealthy Politics: The Battle over Evidence-Based Medicine* (2017).

John W. Patty is professor of political science at the University of Chicago and coeditor of the *Journal of Theoretical Politics*. His recent publications include *Social Choice and Legitimacy* (with Elizabeth Maggie Penn, 2014) and *Learning While Governing* (with Sean Gailmard, 2012).

Philip B. K. Potter is associate professor in the Department of Politics and director of the National Security Policy Center in the Frank Batten School of Leadership and Public Policy at the University of Virginia. His recent book, *War and Democratic Constraint* (with Matthew Baum, 2015), was a CHOICE outstanding academic title.

Mehdi Shadmehr is associate professor in the Department of Economics at the University of Calgary. He specializes in microeconomics, political economy, and comparative politics. He has published articles in the *American Political Science Review*, *Journal of Politics*, and *Games and Economic Behavior*.

Barbara Sinclair was professor emerita at UCLA. She specialized in American politics, particularly the US Congress. She was the author of several important books, including *Party Wars* (2006) and *Unorthodox Lawmaking* (5th ed., 2016).

Steven S. Smith is the director of the Weidenbaum Center, the Kate M. Gregg Professor of Social Science, and professor of political science at Washington University in St. Louis. He is also the director of The American Panel Survey (TAPS), which provides one of the best survey research platforms in the social sciences. He is coauthor (with Hong Min Park and Ryan J. Vander Wielen) of *Politics Over Process: Partisan Conflict and Post-Passage Processes in the US Congress* (2018).

Craig Volden is associate dean for academic affairs and professor of public policy and politics, with appointments in the Frank Batten School of Leadership and Public Policy and the Woodrow Wilson Department of Politics at the University of Virginia. He studies legislative politics and the interaction among political institutions, including within American federalism. He is coauthor (with Alan E. Wiseman) of *Legislative Effectiveness in the United States Congress: The Lawmakers* (2014). His current projects include studies of innovation and policy diffusion across states and localities, as well as an analysis of the legislative effectiveness of individual members of Congress. He is codirector of the Legislative Effectiveness Project (http://www .thelawmakers.org/).

Alan E. Wiseman is Cornelius Vanderbilt Professor of Political Economy and professor of political science and law (by courtesy) at Vanderbilt University. He has research and teaching interests in American political institutions and positive political economy, focusing on legislative and electoral politics, regulation, bureaucratic policy making, and business–government relations. He is coauthor (with Craig Volden) of *Legislative Effectiveness in the United States Congress: The Lawmakers* (2014). His research has been published in the *American Political Science Review*, *American Journal of Political Science*, *Journal of Politics*, and *Legislative Studies Quarterly*. He is codirector of the Legislative Effectiveness Project (http://www.thelawmakers.org/).

Stephane Wolton is assistant professor at the London School of Economics and Political Science. He studies problems of accountability in democracy as well as autocracy. He is currently working on research projects on authority acquisition and the role of special interest groups in American politics.

Index